Imoinda's Shade

Free West Indian Dominicans,
ca. 1770, Agostino Brunias (1728–96)

Imoinda's Shade

*Marriage and the African Woman in
Eighteenth-Century British Literature, 1759–1808*

Lyndon J. Dominique

The Ohio State University Press
Columbus

Copyright © 2012 by The Ohio State University.
All rights reserved.

Library of Congress Cataloging-in-Publication Data
Dominique, Lyndon Janson, 1972–
 Imoinda's shade : marriage and the African woman in eighteenth-century British literature, 1759–1808 / Lyndon J. Dominique.
     p. cm.
 Includes bibliographical references and index.
  ISBN 978-0-8142-1185-4 (cloth : alk. paper) — ISBN 0-8142-1185-2 (cloth : alk. paper) — ISBN 978-0-8142-9286-0 (cd-rom)
 1. English literature—18th century—History and criticism. 2. Race in literature. 3. Women, Black, in literature. 4. Marriage in literature. I. Title.
 PR448.R33D66 2012
 820.9'3552—dc23
                              2011049519
Paper (ISBN: 978-0-8142-5625-1)
Cover design by Mia Risberg
Type set in Adobe Garamond Pro

∞

*For my mother and father,
Rita and Victor Dominique*

CONTENTS

Illustrations — ix
Acknowledgments — xi

Introduction Imoinda, Marriage, Slavery — 1

Part One.
Imoinda's Original Shades: African Women in British Antislavery Literature

Chapter 1   Altering *Oroonoko* and Imoinda in Mid-Eighteenth-Century British Drama — 27

Chapter 2   Amelioration, African Women, and The Soft, Strategic Voice of Paternal Tyranny in *The Grateful Negro* — 70

Chapter 3   "Between the saints and the rebels": Imoinda and the Resurrection of the Black African Heroine — 104

Part Two.
Imoinda's Shade Extends: Abolition and Interracial Marriage in England

Chapter 4   Creoles, Closure, and Cubba's Comedy of Pain: Abolition and the Politics of Homecoming in Eighteenth-Century British Farce — 143

Chapter 5   "'What!' cried the delighted mulatto, 'are we going to prosecu massa?'": *Adeline Mowbray*'s Distinguished Complexion of Abolition — 185

Chapter 6   "An unportioned girl of *my* complexion can . . . be a dangerous object." Abolition and the Mulatto Heiress in England — 223

Afterword	260
Bibliography	269
Index	281

ILLUSTRATIONS

Figure 1	Title page, *Oroonoko,* 1759, John Hawkesworth (1715–73)	42
Figure 2	Title page, *Oroonoko,* 1760, Francis Gentleman (1728–84)	43
Figure 3	Title page, *Oroonoko,* 1760, Anonymous	44
Figure 4	Mrs. S. Kemble as Imoinda, 1791. Elizabeth Kemble (1763?-1841)	48
Figure 5	Harriet Litchfield (1777–1854) as Imoinda, 1807	49
Figure 6	Mrs. Hartley in the character of Imoinda, 1777. Elizabeth Hartley (1750?-1824)	50
Figure 7	Miss Smith as Imoinda, 1806. Sarah Smith (1783–1850)	51
Figure 8	Title page, *The Benevolent Planters,* 1789, Thomas Bellamy (1745–1800)	53
Figure 9	Title page, *The Negro Slaves,* 1796, August Von Kotzebue (1761–1819)	114
Figure 10	"Am I Not a Man and A Brother?" Cameo marketed and popularized by Josiah Wedgwood (1730–95)	117
Figure 11	Title page, *High Life Below Stairs*, 1759, James Townley (1714–78)	149
Figure 12	Title page, *Love in the City,* 1767, Isaac Bickerstaff (1735–1812)	150
Figure 13	Title page, *The Irishman in London; or, The Happy African,* 1792, William Macready (d. 1829)	151
Figure 14	A Female Negro Slave, with a Weight chained to her Ancle, John Gabriel Stedman (1744–97) in his *Narrative of a Five Years Expedition against the Revolted Negroes of Surinam* (1796)	153
Figure 15	A Negro Hung alive by the Ribs to a Gallows, John Gabriel Stedman (1744–97) in his *Narrative of a Five Years Expedition against the Revolted Negroes of Surinam* (1796)	154

Figure 16	"Noon," 1736, from *The Four Times of Day*, William Hogarth (1697–1764)	156
Figure 17	Plate 1 of *A Harlot's Progress*, 1732, William Hogarth (1697–1764)	191
Figure 18	"Washing the Blackamoor White," 1807, William Mulready (1786–1863) (illustrated in William Godwin's *Fables, Ancient and Modern*)	230
Figure 19	"Washing the Blackamoor," 1795, Isaac Cruikshank (1756–1811)	233

ACKNOWLEDGMENTS

Mere thanks hardly seem adequate for all the help and support that I have received while bringing this book to completion. But I extend them sincerely and heartily to the mentors, colleagues, friends, family and students without whom Imoinda would have remained in the shade.

This project began under the tutelage of Claudia L. Johnson and Jonathan Lamb and was helped along with the good will and support of my former colleagues at Georgetown, especially Dennis Todd, Gay Gibson Cima, Duncan Wu, Joy Younge, Mark McMorris, Patrick O'Malley Paul Betz, John Hirsh, Sarah MacNamer, Lori Merish, David Gewanter, Angelyn Mitchell, Libbie Rifkin, Norma Tilden, Maureen Corrigan, Steve Wurtzler, M. Lindsay Kaplan, Christine So, Leona Fisher, Patricia O'Connor, Samantha Pinto, Jennifer Fink, Andrew Rubin and Kelly Wickham-Crowley. Deep thanks to all of them. Danny O'Quinn, and Jessica Richard provided immense support when I needed it, as did Tim Watson, who I must thank twice. Without you, Tim, *The Woman of Colour* would have never seen the light of day. Many sincere thanks for supporting me at all stages of my career. To my esteemed friend and colleague R. Scott Heath, the gin and tonics are on you this time, brother! To my new colleagues at Lehigh University: Scott Paul Gordon, Bob Watts, Stephanie Powell-Watts, Dawn Keetley, Elizabeth Fifer, Elizabeth Dolan, Michael Kramp, Ed Whitley, Jenna Lay and Amardeep Singh—you welcomed me into our department with warmth and graciousness, and your comments and questions during my talk helped me refine my argument in Chapter One. Thank you. To Nicole Aljoe, the S.E.A. roundtable rocked thanks to you and Thaddious Davis, and it helped me complete Chapter Six. To Sandra Strachan-Vieira, Nolana Yip, Rebecca Boylan, and Joseph Fruscione, for so many kind words and deeds, thank you. To Elizabeth Velez, Dennis Williams and all the students under the C.M.E.A. banner, thanks for helping me grow as a person and a teacher, as did my wonderful former English mentees Meaghan Fritz, Meaghan Orie, Bridget Macfarland, Katie Sagal, Pamela Nwaoko and Susan Weeber.

A number of people deserve thanks for making the writing process bearable for me even when I wasn't: Leroy Dominique, Alonzo Brown, Roderick McGuire, Tawanna Bradley, Gladys Hamilton, Scott Bibbins. Jabella Hinton, Sadie Boone, Irving "Skinner" Hutchinson, Jim Haynes, Jean and Vernon Nembhard, Julian, Julien and Jan Pierre, Andrina Dominique, Terry Carter, Anthony Udu-Gama, Corey Daniels, Maurice Smith, Tammy Brown, Danielle Elliot, Craig Johnson, Larry Bruce, Marcus Sharpless, Rolf Barber, Corwin Jay Mathews, Chester, Sandra Pierre, Sinead Pierre, Louise, Valdora and Enord Leatham, Jeff, Jeffi and Brad Mathieu, Royden, Sandra and Kelley Dominique, Simon Regis, Catherine Legrande, Barry Talley and Jaunita Beau-Pierre.

A very gracious thank you to Sandy Crooms for keeping me on schedule with such good humor, and also to the readers and editorial staff at The Ohio State University Press, especially Kristen Ebert-Wagner, Eugene O'Connor, Malcolm Litchfield, and Kathy Edwards, whose wonderful comments and suggestions pushed me to sharpen my arguments, structure and prose to produce a better book.

The Agostino Brunias prints are used with the kind permission of the Yale Center for British Art. The Imoinda prints are used with the permission of the University of Illinois at Urbana-Champaign. The Isaac Cruikshank print is used with the permission of Heritage Images.

This book is also dedicated to Michael Ragussis who inspired me to seek out these fictional African women, and to my uncles, Emanuel Fevrier and Patrick Dominique. Wherever you are, I hope you all will read it with a smile.

INTRODUCTION

Imoinda, Marriage, Slavery

IN 1707, the year that the Act of Union between Scotland and England officially established the United Kingdom of Great Britain, two extremely contradictory illustrations of the literary heroine Imoinda appear in genres that are, themselves, extreme exercises in the art of contradiction. In the first, a paradox titled "*That* a Black-a-moor Woman is the *greatest* Beauty; *in a Letter* to a *Lady exceeding Fair*," a male speaker, clearly influenced by the black African heroine from Aphra Behn's novella, *Oroonoko* (1688), apostrophizes,

Oh *Imoinda!* how can they look upon you, for

I.

Those Heavenly Attracts of yours, your Eyes
And Face, that all the World surprize,
Do dazle all that look upon ye,
And Scorch all other Ladies tawny.[1]

In the second, "A Satyr . . . Against the Luxury of the Town in Eating and Drinking," another poet explains in a footnote: "Imoinda is a Name us'd by Mr. *Southern* in the Tragedy of *Oroonoko*. The Part was very often acted by Mrs. *B.*"[2] This knowledge is an important precursor to the warning delivered by the satire's male speaker:

---

1. *Athenian Sport* (London: Bragg, 1707), 103. Although originally published anonymously, John Dunton has been subsequently identified as the author.

2. Anonymous, *Reflections, Moral, Comical, Satyrical, &c. on the Vices and Folies of the Age* (London, 1707), 7, note n.

> Soft Imoinda's tender Air despise;
> Beware the force of her designing Eyes:
> She sells her Vertue, and complexion buys.
> Who thinks her chaste, perchance may be mistook,
> Her innocence is only in her look.³

The tone of apprehension used to refer to the unnamed, though suggestively inferred, actress who "very often" played the role of the virtuous white heroine that Thomas Southerne premiered in 1695 contrasts explicitly with the tone of admiration leveled at the black Imoinda in the previous poem, and offers a clear indication that attitudes toward this fictional character were extremely contradictory in 1707. The basis for this contradiction in tone as well as a possible reason why these Imoindas appear in 1707 lie in each poet's skillful use of Imoinda's skin color.

Both passages make much of the extreme racial contradictions that Imoinda's black and white bodies had commonly come to engender within the twenty-year period of her inception and influence as a fictional character. In John Dunton's paradox, the black Imoinda's "Heavenly . . . Eyes / And Face" eclipse all "other [presumably white] ladies" by overshadowing them, not with the darkness that her black complexion would lead one to expect, but with light; her features emit a dazzling glow of beauty so intensely bright that they resemble a cross between the sun and the Greek gorgon, Medusa, in the way that they render white women "tawny" (rather than stony), and hence, just as scorched and unattractive as contemporaries decried the celestial orb did to white women in the world at large. Dunton was not completely original in using this paradoxical conceit to vindicate a black lady's beauty to a non-black lady. In a 1701 translation of a letter "To Mademoiselle Paulet: from Barbary," the "very amorously inclined"⁴ French traveler and writer Vincent Voiture celebrates African women's beauty using language similar to Dunton's when he expresses joy at the idea that he "shall have the satisfaction in some days, to see . . . African Ladies, who have nothing Barbarous about 'em, but the name, and altho' they are burnt by the sun, are yet fairer, and cast a greater brightness then he."⁵ But Dunton's specific use of Imoinda is entirely original. It is surely the first, and probably the only, time in the entire century when this fictional black African woman's character is employed outside of Behn's novella to deliberately undermine traditional standards of Caucasian beauty.

---

3. Ibid., 7–8.
4. *Biographia Gallica*, vol. 1 (London: Griffiths, 1752), 89.
5. *Familiar and Courtly Letters, To Persons of Honour and Quality*, vol. 2 (London: Briscoe, 1701), 47.

At the same historical moment that a fictional black Imoinda and her actual African counterparts are employed to change the way European women think about the darkening effects of eclipsing and sunburning, however, the anonymous satire presents a white woman's performance of Imoinda in a manner that suggests that she deliberately employs whiteness as a duplicitous disguise rather than a "Heavenly" and attractive quality. Since "Vertue" is stereotypically associated with purity and whiteness, the speaker's insinuation that Imoinda "sells her Vertue, and complexion buys" implies that the actress playing the role is known for exchanging one form of licit whiteness ("Vertue") for an illicit, deceptive one ("complexion"). In short, the speaker accuses this actress of deliberately assuming the popular role of Southerne's white African in order to present herself in the "innocence," "tender air," and "chaste" demeanor associated with this role, thereby cosmetically masking her alarming offstage reputation for sexual profligacy.

The oblique footnote's reference to "Mrs. B." suggests that the author might be referring to Elizabeth Barry or Anne Bracegirdle, both of whom were famous at the time and known for playing "young girl" parts that signified "a virginal and virtuous young heroine."[6] Of these two possibilities, Barry is the most likely choice since, as Elizabeth Howe points out, "her combination of toughness and success made her the target for some of the most vicious and vituperative satire of the whole period. In lurid language, Barry was pictured as a mercenary prostitute, unbounded in her lust for money, prepared to do anything for profit."[7] Whether it was true or not, the life that Barry led as a Restoration actress left her open to the charge of being a woman who "sells her Vertue" at the same time that she is well known for playing the part of the extremely virtuous ingénue.[8] This is the contradiction about which the speaker exhorts the reader and theatrical spectator to "Beware."

Ultimately, whereas the satire aims to make readers question the motives, character, and "designing Eyes" of the white actress playing Imoinda, the paradox wants readers to succumb to the "Heavenly . . . Eyes" of the fictional black Imoinda and acknowledge her as a dazzling and virtuous beauty. As different as these attempts are at challenging prevailing stereotypes about black ugliness and white virtue, they are employed for similar purposes. Both the satire and the paradox present Imoinda's eyes as scrutinizing and influencing her actual and fictional audiences; "Heavenly" and "designing" eyes have power enough to demean as well as dupe members of English

---

6. Elizabeth Howe, *The First English Actresses* (Cambridge: Cambridge University Press, 1992), 178.

7. Ibid., 30.

8. Ibid., 32–36, for more on "The Actress as Prostitute."

society. Additionally, the fact that both passages refer to the same literary character, Imoinda, offers a clear illustration of the way in which white British poets have, from the beginning of her inception, consciously evoked this eighteenth-century character plucked from the *Oroonoko* novel and popular drama, and used her as an effective literary touchstone to provide direct social commentary and criticism. The titles of each text leave no doubt that both of these Imoindas have been devised and utilized exactly for this end: speakers have employed them not merely to expose, but also to begin to correct, something egregious about the vulgar excesses of consumption and vanity that are prevalent in the lives of contemporary English men and women.

In addition to having this power to scrutinize, criticize, and seek to improve Britons' behavior, these fictional Imoindas can also be seen to cast a critical eye over Britain's contemporary political situation if we consider the racial and physical depictions of Imoinda's fictional body in relation to the prevailing political climate in 1707. As I have already mentioned, this year saw the establishment of the United Kingdom of Great Britain. By achieving this feat, the Act of Union also ostensibly put to rest one of the longstanding political problems in the history of English–Scottish relations when it attempted to resolve a contradiction that had been established over one hundred years earlier.[9] Following Queen Elizabeth I's death in 1603, the Scottish King, James VI, became James I of England without renouncing his Scottish throne. Under this Union of Crowns, James ruled over both states separately and simultaneously; however, each state had its own individual parliament that could, in theory, diverge on certain issues of joint concern. After the Scottish parliament declared that the 1701 Act of Settlement did not apply to Scotland, this theory became a reality. Frank O'Gorman recounts that the Act of Settlement had been designed primarily to provide for a Protestant successor to the throne following "the death of Princess Anne's one surviving child, William Duke of Gloucester, on 30 July 1700 [which] had thrown the political world into uncertainty."[10] With the Scottish parliament declaring that they were not bound by this act, O'Gorman states that this opened up "the possibility that on Anne's death, Scotland might determine its own dynastic succession. The prospect of Scotland pursuing an independent foreign policy horrified the English."[11] The 1707 Act sought to resolve these problems by merging the dialogic power that these two separate yet simultaneous political bodies represented and dissolving them into one body located

---

9. For more on the Act of Union, see Frank O'Gorman's *The Long Eighteenth Century: British Political and Social History 1688–1832* (London: Arnold Press, 1997), 29–64.

10. Ibid., 37.

11. Ibid., 56.

under the authority of the same monarch. Under one parliament located in London, Scotland joined England and Wales to become one united kingdom bereft of the potential for political contradiction that had existed for over one hundred years.

On the surface, the only similarity between these political acts of unification and consolidation and the black and white depictions of Imoinda appears to be the year in which they both occur. Yet, when the depictions of Imoinda's bodily power in the satire and the paradox are considered allegorically and dialogically, and viewed in relation to the 1707 political landscape, these two seemingly dissimilar yet coterminous bodily events can actually be seen and interpreted in a manner that speaks to English and Scottish contemporaries' adversarial responses toward the Act of Union. For although this Act claimed to have resolved the longstanding contradiction of parliamentary power by uniting the Scottish and English political bodies, all groups of people influenced by it were not happy. Much of the dissent against it came from ordinary Scottish people, many of whom did not even have the power to vote. As a body of people opposed to the idea of unification, they burned copies of the treaty, threw stones at parliament, and even rioted and held the city of Glasgow under siege for a month. In *Britons* (1992), Linda Colley has indicated that many eighteenth-century Englishmen were bitterly opposed to the union as well because it "seemed a blatant affront to older identities . . . 'English' and 'England' giving way to 'British' and 'Great Britain.'"[12] Such anger and aggression toward the act reveals that distinct bodies of people in England and Scotland were more for the separation than the unification of that state's parliamentary power, and, by extension, the maintenance of each nation's unique homogeneous identity.

The 1707 appearance of Imoinda's black and white bodies, each with its own racial contradictions, can be seen as bolstering the implicit case made by those riotous Scots and angry Englishmen about the necessity of preserving the separation of two distinct bodies of power rather than uniting them as one unified whole. Because her evocations in the satire and the paradox only gain power through the ways in which the authors exploit the oxymorons and stereotypes associated with each individually colored body, Imoinda's black and white incarnations in 1707 resist unification into one cohesive and powerful African female character despite the fact that they refer to the same woman. As such, these two closely related yet powerfully distinct and contradictory bodies of the same woman can stand as a potent allegorical contrast to the recently united states of England and Scotland, and the Act of Union's claims to having resolved political contradiction by joining the

---

12. (New Haven: Yale University Press, 1992), 13.

two parliamentary bodies, each with its own internal contradictions, to form a new, powerful, and ostensibly cohesive United Kingdom of Great Britain.

On the other hand, British writers such as Daniel Defoe had already identified England and Englishmen as "het'rogeneous" things in his popular political poem *The True Born Englishman* (1701), so the idea of English cultural difference was not unheard of at the time. It was even encouraged. As Leith Davis points out, "Defoe, as an English tradesman," and avid supporter of the Act of Union, "realized that . . . national images stood in the way of the economic expansion of England and Britain; for Defoe, prosperity necessarily entailed roping conflicting interests together."[13] With Defoe's support for "conflicting interests" and his recognition of the nation's heterogeneity as a backdrop, the contradictory black and white bodies that refer to the same woman could also be employed to stand in for the messy contradictions of a new nation trying to pull its extreme differences together to form a new state of being.

To be clear, I am not implying that Imoinda's differing depictions in the satire and the paradox were *expressly* created to challenge or support the Act of Union's move toward unification; I am, however, suggesting that when we consider the contradictory evocations of Imoinda, dialogically, the social power and influence they each individually display in 1707 can be employed to align with arguments made for either resisting or accepting the establishment of a unified body of power. As powerful, separate yet dialogic entities, Imoinda's black and white bodies create skepticism about acts that claim to resolve two contradictory and powerful bodies into one cohesive whole in a year in which an Act of Union claimed to have done just that, at the same time in which they also convey a powerful inclination to unite two distinct yet contradictory bodies to form one whole one in 1707.

The idea that a fictional African woman can be employed to reflect on the political situation of the English nation-state in a pivotal year of national refashioning gains even more traction when we understand that 1707 was not the first time that Imoinda's name and body had been evoked in this manner. As is commonly known, the precedent was set in 1688 when Imoinda made her debut in Behn's *Oroonoko,* the same year that the Glorious Revolution saw England bloodlessly reaffirming its Protestant identity. Critics have drawn parallels between Oroonoko and James II, a comparison that, if drawn out, presents Imoinda and the baby she carries but never gives birth to as the stand-ins for James's second wife, Mary of Modena, and their son, James Francis Edward, who never officially assumed the throne of England.[14]

---

13. *Acts of Union* (Stanford, CA: Stanford University Press, 1998), 20.
14. Behn's Royalist and Catholic sensibilities are detected in the "Epistle Dedicatory" dedicated

I begin with these illustrations of ways in which Imoinda was employed to scrutinize, criticize, and seek to improve the mores of English subjects as well as the ways she could be, and has been, employed to reflect on pivotal events in English political life as the nation was actively refashioning itself in order to call attention to one of the major themes of this book: at crucial, originating moments from the very beginning of the long eighteenth century, representations of this fictional African woman have been connected to, are a significant literal presence in, and can be read as having a direct impact on, English culture well outside the confines of the *Oroonoko* texts that initially established her as an important literary presence. Within twenty years of her first appearance as a black woman in Behn's *Oroonoko,* and a little over a decade from her first appearance as a white woman in Thomas Southerne's play of the same name, the two 1707 evocations confirm that Imoindas of both complexions were on their way to becoming popular-cultural references as well as factual symbols that British writers think their readers should know about. As such, the influence wielded by this fictionally constructed yet socially deployed African woman cannot be understated and must be further investigated. Literary critics such as Lynda Boose and Kim Hall have associated Early Modern African women in general with this kind of threatening power and ability to dominate the British psyche,[15] but no subsequent work has been done on fictional Imoindas constructed independently of the *Oroonoko* text after the Restoration period, or explorations of the ways that these specific constructions are crucial factors in the scrutiny and critique of English mores and customs. This book begins to address this absence.

THE CONTRADICTIONS and political tensions surrounding the literary character Imoinda are merely starting points for this book, which argues that this fictional female figure from the late Restoration is actually a crucial, constructed presence in late-eighteenth-century British literature—one that is evoked sometimes obliquely, and at others overtly, by British writers from that period. In *Imoinda's Shade: Marriage and the African Woman in Eighteenth-Century British Literature, 1759–1808,* I attempt to do two

---

to Lord Maitland, a known supporter of James's claim to the throne. See note 1 in *Oroonoko,* ed. Joanna Lipking (New York: Norton, 1997), 5. Also see Anthony S. Jarrells's *Britain's Bloodless Revolutions: 1688 and the Romantic Reform of Literature* (Hampshire, UK: Palgrave, 2005), 163–64, for a brief discussion of Behn's continued support of James II in one of her poems.

15. See "'The Getting of a Lawful Race': Racial Discourse in Early Modern England and the Unrepresentable Black Woman," in *Women, "Race," and Writing in the Early Modern Period* (London: Routledge, 1994); and "Reading What Isn't There: 'Black' Studies in Early Modern England," *Stanford Humanities Review* 3 (1993): 23–33.

things: examine the extent of Imoinda's impact in late-eighteenth-century British literature, and use this as a vehicle by which to explore the ways that other fictional African women created in Imoinda's image are employed to make interventions into marriage plots as well as antislavery and abolitionist discourse during this particularly tumultuous time in Britain's history.

I draw my main title and take as my keynote for this book a couplet from a poem that deliberately evokes the name of this dominant and idealized African heroine within the context of marriage. Due largely to the popularity of Thomas Southerne's *Oroonoko,* "Imoinda" would have been a very familiar name to eighteenth-century Britons,[16] especially by the time the presumably male speaker in Capel Lofft's[17] *The Praises of Poetry* (1775) remarks, "The genius of connubial love / Points me to Imoinda's shade." The couplet clearly presents the speaker as a human compass who "Points" out that a particular facet of the popular African woman's characterization—her "shade"—is the true marker for the recognition of ideal "connubial love." Yet, despite the speaker's great confidence that the reader will not only recognize Imoinda but also accept her as the ideal embodiment of "connubial love," he is extremely vague about the facet of her identity that he expects readers to idealize. What exactly *is* "Imoinda's shade"? Is he pointing out her literal complexion? If he is, what particular "shade" of Imoinda—that of Aphra Behn's "beautiful *Black Venus*"[18] in *Oroonoko* or the white-skinned Imoinda from Southerne's adaptation of Behn's novella—best represents "The genius of connubial love"? Or is the speaker using "Imoinda's shade" to literally refer to her as a disembodied spirit—a ghost who best represents "The genius of connubial love" because she willingly makes the ultimate sacrifice and ends her life in order to preserve, inviolate, her union with Oroonoko? Or is "Imoinda's shade" a metaphorical reference to the spectral shadow that her combined appearances have cast over the idea of "connubial love" in the almost one hundred years of *Oroonoko* dramas that had featured her prior to the publication of Lofft's poem? Or is it an actual symbolic space—a protective bower of influence—wherein we find an ideal essence of "connubial love" that is capable of shielding all women from the glare of extramarital infamy? And, moreover, why does this presumably English speaker direct his audience to look for "The genius of connubial love" in an African-based woman's "shade"?

---

16. *The London Stage* shows that *Oroonoko* and its many adaptations were performed every year throughout the entire eighteenth century.

17. Capel Lofft (1751–1824) was an English lawyer and politician well known for his liberal views on a variety of topics (notably the French Revolution) and a prolific writer on a many issues legal, political, critical, and literary.

18. Behn, *Oroonoko,* 14.

Because Behn's novella and Southerne's tragicomedy are the first to dramatize and popularize Imoinda's connubial experiences both as a black woman in Africa and as a white woman in British colonial Surinam, it is logical to go back to these texts as starting points for a focused investigation of "Imoinda's shade" and what its connection to "connubial love" might have meant to Lofft's speaker. But throughout the century, there are numerous other examples of racialized and nationalized Imoindas who are neither black nor African nor even referred to within the scope of the *Oroonoko* texts, and these examples are important sources for understanding the influence of this fictional character and her connection to the theme of love.

One instance can be found in the anonymous four-stanza poem "An Indian Love Song" (1783).[19] In the first three stanzas, a male speaker adorns the woman he refers to as "Love" with random beauties taken from Nature, decking her "with a wreath / Pluck'd from the spreading plantain-tree" and a "pearly oyster from beneath / The Dashing wave." She is not merely made to wear these naturally occurring, exotic garments, however; the speaker states: "My Love is like yon golden ball / Her voice is like the waterfall." Physically, this woman resembles nature's elements fire and water. Yet the speaker also believes that, in comparison to his "Love," "the hillock green" "nor shews so fair," / "Nor scuds the flying Elk so fleet, / Nor bounds so light the mountain Roe" (27), references that all connect the female muse to Nature's elements air and earth, and suggest that her grace and features outdo some of the natural world's most dynamic landscapes and gravity-defying creatures. Thus, adorned by, living with, looking like, and even exceeding Nature itself, these first three stanzas present the still-unnamed woman referred to as "Love" in the guise of an idealized pastoral Indian. As a living expression of this peoples' most fruitful commune with Nature, she *is* the "Indian Love Song" that the male speaker sings.

It is the last line of the last stanza, however, that explicitly confirms this woman's association with a specific type of Indian-ness:

Sweet is the breath of opening flow'rs,
Sweetly the Birds disport in air,
But sweeter far are evening bowers,
When Imoinda meets me there.

For the speaker, Nature's essence—its "sweet" sights and sounds—are enhanced only when the woman he identifies as "Love" in the very first line of the poem finally makes her appearance as "Imoinda." The anonymous

---

19. *Mele Ephemeria* (Oxford, 1783), 27–28.

poet has consciously resisted naming her until the very end in order to establish Imoinda's idealized connection to Nature; but in so doing, he builds her up as a depiction of idealized "Love" very different from Behn, who refers to her Imoinda as a "beautiful Black" version of Venus, the Greek goddess of Love. In Behn's *Oroonoko* it is the Indians who are depicted as living and loving according to nature,[20] while the Africans are consigned to living and loving in the more structured and stylized arenas of the idealized court and the less-than-idealized plantation. Therefore, rather than an African source, this anonymous poet must have taken to heart William Congreve's reference to Southerne's white Imoinda as a woman who expresses an "Indian's fondness of her spouse,"[21] and inspired by this reference, used it to construct his Imoinda as a tactile embodiment of love in the pastoral Indian tradition conceived by white writers.[22]

In comparison to these depictions of Indian Imoindas as traditional examples of connubial love, and love embodied in Nature, *The Life of John Buncle* (1756) contains a rather unusual representation of Imoinda. As John Buncle, the novel's Irish hero, stands in a room, he remarks that,

> a door was opened, and a lady entred, who was vastly pretty, and richly drest beyond what I have ever seen. She had diamonds enough for a queen. I was amazed at the sight of her . . . she asked me in *Irish,* how I did. . . . My surprize was so great I could not speak, and upon this, she said, in the same language, I see, Sir, you have no remembrance of me. You cannot recollect the least idea of me. You have quite forgot young *Imoinda* of the county of *Gallway* in *Ireland* who was your partner in country dances, when you passed the Christmas of the year 1715, at her father's house. What (I said) Miss *Wolf* of *Balineskay? O my Imoinda!* And snatching her to my arms, I almost stifled her with kisses.[23]

Clearly, the appearance of a "vastly pretty," "richly drest," Irish lady, bejeweled "enough for a queen," is sufficient to render the hero completely enamored. Yet, Buncle is also completely immobilized by her dazzling appearance and her Irish language: when he sees her, he is awestruck ("I was amazed"); when she speaks to him, he is mute ("I could not speak"). Miss Wolf's

---

20. Behn, *Oroonoko,* 9–10.

21. Thomas Southerne, *Oroonoko* (Glasgow: Foulis, 1753), 88. See Srinivas Aravamudan's *Tropicopolitans* (Durham: Duke University Press, 2000), 57–59, for more about the significance of Imoinda's Indian-ness.

22. See Roxann Wheeler's reference to the Noble Savage tradition in *The Complexion of Race* (Philadelphia: University of Pennsylvania Press, 2000), 69.

23. Thomas Amory, The Life of John Buncle, Esq., vol. 2 (London: Johnson and Davenport, 1766), 182–83.

unique qualities neither identify her nor animate him. It is only when she refers to herself as "young Imoinda" that he finally becomes physically, mentally and emotionally inspired; he immediately recognizes her as "Miss Wolf of *Balineskay*," claims her as "my Imoinda," "And snatching her to [his] arms . . . almost stifled her with kisses." This clear difference between the hero immobilized by the appearance of Miss Wolf yet inspired by the memory of "young Imoinda" implies that the dazzling, Irish-speaking lady's dominance is certainly not the most affecting. Rather, in the role of a youthful innocent who lightheartedly scrutinizes Buncle and accuses him of having forgotten her, "young Imoinda" inspires the spontaneous action of love where Miss Wolf inspires the controlled inaction of awe. Thus, the activity that this young Irish Imoinda's influence evokes in Buncle reveals that his outward love is primarily for the dramatic role that this woman had formerly embodied and not the actual woman herself.

In a 1725 letter addressed to "Hibernicus" and taken from James Arbuckle's edited *Collection of Letters and Essays on Several Subjects, lately Publish'd in The Dublin Journal* (1729), an imagined Imoinda adopts a scrutinizing and accusatory role similar to, but more aggressive than, Miss Wolf's, this time using it to enter the psyche of a white Irishman and inspire in him another outward expression of love. In this letter, the writer identifies himself as "N.N.," a "free Batchelor" (287)[24] who has always had a "concern for the decency and dignity of the theatre" (283). He recounts a vivid dream that he has after an evening's dramatic entertainment. In this dream, "several things [he] had observed to be faulty" about the Irish stage "blended themselves in such a manner in [his] head" (283). He imagines himself in a rarified setting—the underworld of "Pluto's Dominions . . . standing near his tribunal, when . . . a great croud [approached] in a very tumultuous manner" and they reveal to N.N. that "they were bringing some complaints, occasioned by . . . indignities offered them upon the stage in the upper world" (283). From amongst this group, "Imoinda . . . advanc'd" and "represented to Pluto,"

> that [the subject of circle petticoats] was no Subject of Merriment to any of those who were daily killed at the Theatre; and that for her part, the aforesaid machine had such an ill effect once, when her representative fell dead on a certain stage, that if her Oroonoko had not had the presence of Mind to tread on the Circle of her petticoat, she should have been in such confusion, that ten to one she would never have been able to get up again. (285)

---

24. Vol. 1 (London: Darby and Browne, 1729).

Amidst the presumed seriousness of N.N.'s "concern for the decency and dignity of the theatre" and his solemn references to the underworld, Pluto, and his tribunal, Imoinda's complaint is bathetic, trivial, and completely humorous. The "Ill effect" that she mentions involves her own underworld being exposed to her audience because the shape of her circle petticoat allows viewers to gawp directly up it as she "fell dead" during a scene from *Oroonoko*. Because this wardrobe malfunction occurs during one of the play's most dramatic moments, N.N.'s Imoinda reduces the poignancy of Southerne's suicide scene to a joke. For Imoinda's hilarious depiction of her own death from the embarrassment of exposure ("she would never have been able to get up again") takes precedence over her involvement in the actual death scene, thereby making both Oroonoko's and her own acting within the scene appear more like the romp of a low farce than the poignancy of a high tragedy. Far from a serious meditation on theatrical decorum, then, N.N.'s dream depicts Imoinda's appeal for decency as absurd given the ways she debases the acting of the play she appears in, overscrutinizes stage fashions, and elevates the cause of a petticoat (she calls it a "machine"). By using her to probe this hidden, comic side of the serious acting world, N.N.'s Imoinda reveals this Irishman's love of wit and stage farce.

The impression of a scrutinizing and accusatory Imoinda who inspires white men's passions is detected, once again, in another depiction that is fictionalized, very briefly, in *The Lounger* (1788). At the very beginning of "Lounger no. 85,"[25] as a prelude to a short disputation "On the decreased power of love in modern times" (iv), a male critic named "Z"[26] identifies the source for this subject as "one of my correspondents," a woman "who writes in a fair Italian hand . . . subscribes herself *Imoinda,*" and asks, "why have you so little of Love in the Lounger?" (154). In this example, Imoinda's connection to "Love" is evoked not only by her name and inquiry, but also by the "fair Italian hand" in which she writes her romantic correspondence. Her question identifies her as a mildly accusatory critic of "Z" and a scrutinizing reader of his periodical. Both lack a critical examination of "Love." Once again, this example shows that a fictional construction of, in this instance, an Italianized Imoinda inspires the white male critic to outwardly express his own passion: a philosophical treatise on the absence of love in contemporary life.

---

25. Vol. 3 (London: Strahan and Cadell, 1788), 146.

26. "Z" is explicitly identified as male in other areas of *The Lounger*. For instance, in "Lounger No.87" he remarks: "I have long cultivated a talent very fortunate for a man of my disposition . . . " (ibid., 163). This identity is further complicated by Marcus Wood's assertion that "Z" was Hannah More's "normal way of indicating her authorship within the multi-authored Cheap Repository Tracts." *The Poetry of Slavery* (Oxford: Oxford University Press, 2004), 100.

Last, in two anonymous poems, both titled "To the Bee,"[27] an English Imoinda forms the inspiration for yet another outward expression of love by a white male lover. In the narrative of the first poem, the male speaker, Henry, enlists a bee to bestow "on Imoinda's lip the gift" of a "tear." This "tear" is an emblem of Henry's suffering brought on by "the idle god of jealous Love." Unnerved by his inability to see her, Henry imagines that "the blush he lov'd to view" on Imoinda's face becomes "faithless" toward him when she is out in public, "'midst the gay," fashionable society, responding to the attentions of any male "Rival's eye." Here, the attractive "blush" not only identifies Imoinda as the epitome of English health and beauty, it also becomes the marker of her inconstancy toward Henry, its bloom of imagined faithlessness causing him to "sicken." The second "To the Bee" poem presents a defensive Imoinda, completely incensed by Henry's accusations. She twice dismisses the bee with barely concealed anger: "Go idle bee . . . Go tell thy jealous master truth like mine / Rejects the doubts his cautious fears betray." Moreover, she encourages this bee to scrutinize her own behavior "when mix'd in fashions gay" and "Mark, if the flattering circle gives delight / When in my listening ear their praises sound . . . / Or if the timid blush of soft surprise / With chasten'd rapture, mantles o'er my cheek." Where Henry only imagines Imoinda's blush as a mark of inconstancy, Imoinda invites its public scrutiny as an actual testament to, and vindication of, her constancy as well as a marker of her anger at having that constancy questioned. Public attentions from rivals do not change her feelings for her lover, but his doubts about her do have this effect. So she commands the bee to deliver one final message: "Tell him in death, the only balm is found, / When with unerring skill, the hand we love / By cold suspicion dares inflict the wound." In what is, apparently, a pointed reference to the suicide scene from Southerne's *Oroonoko* where the hero holds a dagger to Imoinda's breast but is reluctant to kill her, a white English Imoinda rewrites this scene and depicts her own lover's "cold suspicion" of her constancy as the devastating emotion that mortally wounds her. In this poem, Imoinda's self-scrutiny counters her lover's accusations of inconstancy in an attempt to inspire in him a less suspicious and more constant appreciation of her love.

So far, my discussions of these non-black, non-African Imoindas create the impression that this fictional character's influence outside of the

---

27. *The Poetry of the World*, vol. 6 (London: Gosnell, 1791): "To the Bee" (101–2, n.d.) and "To the Bee" (178–79, August 9, 1790). This collection contains another poem titled "To a Bee" (176–77, August 5, 1790) that is also addressed to Imoinda and signed by "Oroonoko" rather than "Henry." Since Oroonoko and Henry express the same sentiments about Imoinda in both poems, I assume that the same man wrote them and Imoinda is responding to the aspersions that both of his poems cast on her character.

Oroonoko text is restricted to inspiring the numerous loves of white men; yet, as a critic in *The Mirror* points out, references to Imoinda that are grounded in, but separate from, *Oroonoko,* also have the power to affect and inspire English women. This unnamed speaker remarks: "Every one must have observed the utility of a proper selection of names to a play or a novel. The bare sounds of Monimia or Imoinda set a tender-hearted young lady a-crying."[28] Apparently, these fictional characters' names are well known as sparking the imaginations of impressionable young ladies; "bare sounds" alone have the ability to create sentimental tear floods. Sir Walter Scott was well aware of the influence commanded by the bare sound of Monimia, the orphan-heroine from Thomas Otway's *The Orphan* (1680). He writes, "More tears have been shed, probably for the sorrows of . . . Monimia, than for those of Juliet and Desdemona."[29] "Sorrows," then, form the basis of the emotion attached to the Monimia name. But what of Imoinda? What emotion is attached to the bare sound of this name? Although this eighteenth-century speaker does not provide an answer to this question, one possible answer might be "sorrows," as it is with Monimia. Yet another might be love: the delicate nerves of tender-hearted young ladies are, perhaps, sentimentally affected by the scrutinizing and accusatory glare that the name inspires in them for never being able to measure up to the idealized illustration of love that the fictional Imoinda embodies in the novel and drama that display her.

This last reference to an African Imoinda drawn from either the "play or . . . novel" joins the rich assortment of Irish, Italian, Indian, and English constructions of this fictional character that I have discussed in this section. Each of them refers to her in ways that are grounded in, yet distinct from, the *Oroonoko* texts that created her. Together they reveal that British writers continually employ this fictional character as a scrutinizing, accusatory, and critical source capable of inspiring white men and women to reflect outwardly on ideals of love in guises as diffuse as Nature, the stage, characters from the stage, wit, farce, dreams, pain, philosophy, poetry, and sentimentality. Moreover, the very fact that this collection of Imoindas is primarily non-black-, non-African-, and non-*Oroonoko*-based offers an important counterpoint to 'imoindaism,' the term coined by Srinivas Aravamudan in *Tropicopolitans* (1999), which draws attention to the growing body of work that focuses on Behn's black heroine to combat what Aravamudan perceives as a critical hole in contemporary discussions of Behn and the *Oroonoko* text. Imoindaism seeks to reorient and challenge "a veritable oroonokoism" (29) that, Aravamudan believes, accepts and promotes "narratives of Behn's

---

28. *The Mirror, A Periodical Paper,* vol. 1 (London: Strahan and Cadell, 1786), 41.
29. *The Miscellaneous Prose Works of Sir Walter Scott, Bart,* vol. 6 (Edinburgh: Caddell and Co., 1827), 424.

progressive ideology, Feminism, and empathy for slaves" (31). For critics who ascribe to these views, "imoindaism is the stumbling block, revealing unrecognized complicities" (31–32), and the critical productions of numerous imoindaists have done much to expose these "complicities" by presenting this fictional woman at the center of new discussions about rape, "new hystericism," "gynecological rebellion," and interracial desire that problematize easy, modern understandings of Behn, her text, and her African hero.[30] However, although "critiques of oroonokoism have taken the route of reclaiming imoindaism" in order to expose "a number of interpretive blind spots," Aravamudan warns that a balanced critical approach to *Oroonoko* "should not just end there" (59). I agree.

In this book, I seek to make my own contribution to imoindaism by reclaiming the African Imoinda, but not merely the one found within Behn's *Oroonoko,* nor even the ones depicted in the *Oroonoko* dramas that were popular throughout the century; rather, because my assortment of non-black, non-African Imoindas imply a gap in the contemporary critical understanding of Imoinda by revealing the wealth of fictional references about this character that portray her acting as an influential inspiration for love independent of her spouse, Oroonoko, and that refer to her in ways that may be grounded in, but are completely separate from, the *Oroonoko* texts that created her, I want to examine some other ways in which British writers have taken this fictional African woman and employed her as a scrutinizing, accusatory, and critical source outside the confines of the *Oroonoko* text and the Oroonoko love story. This approach provides a solution to the critical problem that Aravamudan identifies when he asserts, "The politics of representing Imoinda appears to be a dialectical counter to that of representing Oroonoko" (58). Identifying and analyzing the representations of the African Imoindas that are not wholly reliant on Behn, Southerne, their *Oroonoko*s, and Oroonoko undermine this dialectic as well as its politics; as I will show, this approach still allows for examinations of, and discussions about, all of the same issues that imoindaists are concerned with—rape, "new hystericism," "gynecological rebellion," and interracial desire—all, however, without being driven by the reactionary critical response to either Behn, Southerne, or Oroonoko that Aravamudan believes is a defining and, perhaps, confining mark of contemporary imoindaism. Far from being "an analogue of liberal desires for affirmative action" (59), my approach to imoindaism also has the effect of transforming what Aravamudan calls the "negative theology" of imoindaism "that mourns the absences created by colonialist representation" (58).

---

30. In *Tropicopolitans,* Aravamudan identifies Ros Ballaster as "perhaps the first imoindaist" (31), and lists others: Margaret Ferguson, Stephanie Athey, Daniel Cooper Alarcon, Charlotte Sussman, and Susan Andrade.

By recreating and reclaiming the many instances where factual and imaginative aspects of the fictional African Imoinda appear outside the confines of the *Oroonoko* texts, this book marks the numerous *presences* created by this particular colonialist representation, which collectively form a narrative about the British nation's largely conservative, yet at times quite progressive, attempt to redeem itself. My approach to imoindaism will show that the fictional African woman, grounded in, but distinct from, Behn's and Southerne's texts, is employed to provide the "renewed purchase on agency" that Aravamudan critiques readers for seeking "far too earnestly, in [the] ironic text" (33) that he believes *Oroonoko* to be. The nonironic constructions of African Imoindas that I read and discuss throughout this book have been employed with influence and agency in texts that are designed to inspire Britons to scrutinize and critically assess one of their most notorious behaviors as well as reflect outwardly on one of their very specific forms of love.

In the previous section, I made reference to the "Heavenly" and "designing" eyes of the black and white Imoindas in the satire and the paradox, which are designed to scrutinize the behaviors as well as critique and improve the actions of British men and women. In this current section, I have shown that the scrutiny of many non-black, non-African Imoindas has this same power to inspire Britons to consider, pursue, or display their various individual conceptions of love. However, none of the Imoindas that I have discussed heretofore explicitly take up the one issue that this fictional character is most connected to—the issue of slavery.

Imoinda's Shade proposes that there are many fictional representations of African women who are created in the image of Imoinda and are employed to scrutinize slavery in the British Empire. Together, these accusatory depictions that are grounded in, but distinct from, the *Oroonoko* novella and drama offer opportunities to observe and critique how British writers are inspired to reflect on the nation's love of freedom as well as the concerns of the black slave woman at various times in British history. Both of these preoccupations are found when we examine the images of "connubial love" initially witnessed in Behn's and Southerne's depictions of the African Imoinda, but they are developed further in a series of eighteenth-century texts published well after the Restoration. Within these texts, the African Imoinda is evoked as an imaginative and critical figure whose experience of "connubial love" inspires British writers to reflect on the issue of slavery and the nation's love of freedom in their own unique representations of African women involved in marriage plots.

Thus, within this book, "Imoinda's shade" is, essentially, two separate yet closely related things. It is, first, a motif about the ideal African woman's experience of slavery and marriage, the issues and concerns of which we begin to understand when we examine Imoinda's connubial predicaments in Behn's and Southerne's texts and the ideal qualities she displays as an African woman who struggles under the adversities of slavery; thereafter, "Imoinda's shade" is a motif about the imaginative aspects of Imoinda's experience that white British writers use to cast an influential shadow over the characterizations of other fictional heroines of African descent who find themselves similarly enslaved and intimately involved in British and colonial marriage plots. Together, these understandings of "Imoinda's shade" will attempt to reclaim the African Imoinda and allow for a critical examination of how the fictional African woman is constructed and employed to not only test the successes and failures of Britain's preoccupation with the issue of slavery and the extent of the nation's love of freedom; in the absence of British texts authored by black women of the period, they also provide what may prove to be one of only a few ways to construct a comprehensive historical narrative about black women's concerns under the slavery of the long eighteenth century.

IN MY WORK elsewhere I have pointed out the usefulness of the terms "unrepresentable," unnoticed, "disappearing," and "spectral" used respectively by Lynda Boose, Kim Hall, Joyce Green Macdonald, and Felicity Nussbaum to discuss the African woman in British literature.[31] But these terms seem inadequate when applied to the black and white Imoindas depicted in the paradox and satire at the beginning of this introduction, because they all rely on understanding the fictional African woman as an invisible presence in British literature rather than the active, literal presence in British culture that the satire and paradox present.

Therefore, to account for the impact of these literal references and begin the work of reclaiming the African Imoinda, *Imoinda's Shade* reads literal and imaginative references to Imoindas throughout the eighteenth century as indications that the idea of this fictional African woman made a collective impact, especially in late-eighteenth-century British literature. I contend that British writers were very familiar with the symbolic resonance surrounding Behn's and Southerne's heroines and used these fictional constructions of African women as sources for their own creative attempts to illustrate issues and concerns relating to race, gender, and slavery in ways that readers would immediately recognize. Their attempts were not always successful or completely progressive, but they are there in significant numbers, and as such, they provide opportunities to, in Toni Morrison's words, "contemplate

---

31. See my introduction to *The Woman of Colour* (Peterborough: Broadview, 2007), 11–18.

limitation, suffering, rebellion, and to speculate on . . . ethics, social and universal codes of behavior, and assertions about the definitions of civilization and reason,"[32] all within the British imagination.

To this end, *Imoinda's Shade* is not a chronological attempt to trace the representations of either African women or marriage in eighteenth-century British literature.[33] Neither does it present these literary illustrations of Imoinda as stand-ins for realistic representations of black women and marriage since it restricts itself (with one possible exception)[34] to white writers in British literature. Rather, *Imoinda's Shade* offers itself up as a counterpart to Jenny Sharpe's *Ghosts of Slavery: A Literary Archaeology of Black Women's Lives* (2003) since it mines fictional rather than biographical constructions of only one well-known, yet still elusive, African woman to establish what Morrison calls an "investigation into the ways in which [an] Africanlike (or Africanist) presence or persona was constructed . . . and the imaginative uses this fabricated presence served"[35] in British literature. This approach to British Africanism answers Morrison's call for "studies that analyze the strategic use of black characters to define the goals and enhance the qualities of white characters,"[36] but in doing so, it also reveals another critical quandary about authorial intent.

Apart from what is commonly known about Amelia Opie's later life as a Quaker and member of the British Antislavery Society, not much is known about the particular stances on slavery held by many of the authors that I discuss. Either they left no extensive documented record of their opinions or their identities are completely anonymous. However, each of them did leave behind texts that feature fictional female African characters. I demonstrate that because the appearances of these fictional African women are sometimes deliberate, at other times imaginative, but always strategic, manifestations of the African heroine from the popular text about slavery that was used to mobilize antislavery thought and feeling in eighteenth-century England, reading Imoinda as the known strategic touchstone for the constructions of these later fictional African women offers a legitimate method of making as informed as assessment as possible of each author's stance on slavery in the absence of more direct forms of evidence. This methodology uncovers the kinds of positive and negative pro- and antislavery messages each author's

---

32. *Playing in the Dark* (New York: Vintage, 1992), 53.
33. For a chronology of eighteenth-century black women in literature see my edition of *The Woman of Colour* (Peterborough: Broadview, 2007).
34. The authorship of *The Woman of Colour* is anonymous. I suspect that it was written by or about a person of color named Ann Maitland. See my edition of *The Woman of Colour*.
35. Morrison, *Playing in the Dark*, 6.
36. Ibid., 52–53.

text is capable of conveying about a slave problem that dominated the national discourse at the end of the century.

To be clear, Imoinda is not the only strategic African woman that could be used to explore the connection between British Africanism, marriage, and antislavery, for there are numerous other references to African women in British poetry and prose that could be threaded together to make additional assessments of Britons' dedication to freedom and interest in the African woman. Philippa from Henry Neville's *Isle of Pines* (1668) could have been used as the ideological basis for this critical discussion about British responses to the fictionalized representations of the black woman, marriage, and empire. From this foundation, the black women Zelma from Mary Robinson's poem "The Negro Girl" (1806) and Yamba from Hannah More's poem *The Sorrows of Yamba; or, the Negro Woman's Lamentation* (1795) could have been discussed as Philippa's fictional descendents since they wrest the conversation about the black woman and marriage from dystopic allegory about the fall of man to a more deliberate focus on slavery and the psyche of the black slave wife and mother separated from her male lover because of it. These antislavery poems are part of "a brand of abolition verse" that Marcus Wood identifies as "written almost exclusively by white women . . . exploring the suffering of black women."[37] But male poets are also concerned with Africans, slavery, and marriage. Henry Chatterton's poem *Heccar and Gaira: An African Ecologue* (written 1770, published 1778) could also have been added to this framework and used to explore the African warrior Gaira's separation from his wife Cawna as an extreme example of what Wood calls "the abused African's right to perpetual 'Vengeance' as a result of the enormities of the slave trade."[38] Collectively, these texts, and others like them, might well have made for an equally interesting and informative focus on fictional constructions of black African women, marriage, and slavery by white writers.

However, as the satire, paradox, and Imoindas at the beginning of this Introduction show, Restoration and eighteenth-century readers and audiences were confronted with a racially and nationally diverse Imoinda who transcends boundaries in a way other fictional African women do not. Although the wider social significance of this fictional character's national diversity is not within the purview of this book, a critical focus on, and discussion about, the African Imoinda does allow for an expansive exploration of what African-ness meant and how it was seen, not only at the beginning of the century, where Imoinda's whiteness appears to imply that African-

---

37. Wood, *The Poetry of Slavery*, 49.
38. Ibid., 73.

ness was not exclusively tethered to blackness (a point I address more thoroughly in Chapter One), but also at the century's end when African-ness becomes further complicated by black Creole and black British constructions of identity.

In addition, the force of those other historically scattered, fictional references to African women evoked throughout the century pales when compared with the historical consistency and combined influence of the *Oroonoko* legend that Behn and Southerne create. The Oroonoko story was, quite simply, the most popular, and arguably the most probable, source for all Britons of any rank and age to experience the concerns and interests of African men and women purely on the basis of its long reign in the nation's theatre history and performances at county fairs as well as its presence in collections of literature throughout the century.[39] British writers were surely aware of the extent of its reach, and as my readings of eighteenth-century texts will show, many of them always considered *Oroonoko* a source in their own research on Africa and Africans in addition to, or despite the appearance of, any other African references. They had good reason to think of it in this way. The combination of popularity, historical consistency, reputations for social and factual realism, as well as the racial fluidity they provide when exploring the eighteenth-century idea of Africa and African-ness altogether make Behn's novella and Southerne's drama better fictional barometers for effectively articulating the concerns of the African slave woman than other forms of poetry and prose about African women in general.

However, I approach these connections between Imoinda, marriage, and slavery that Behn and Southerne establish with care because of the way in which discussions of gender, marriage, and slavery have been, literally, rooted in eighteenth-century social discourse from its very beginning. Mary Astell's popular polemic, *Some Reflections upon Marriage* (1700), is a classic instance of a British woman's ability to appropriate the discourse of slavery in a way that only sheds light on British women's oppression within marriage without any consideration for actual black slaves in the British colonies. As contemporaries of Astell, Behn and Southerne might also be guilty of her bias. Behn's *Oroonoko* might be more concerned with allegorizing the Glorious Revolution than with presenting Imoinda's petition against paternalism and slavery, and, like Astell, Southerne might be interested more in elevating the concerns of white women in the marriage market than those relating to a white African heroine's enslavement.

My skepticism about Behn's and Southerne's motivations is tempered, however, when I consider that their textual interest in Africans, slavery, and marriage brings their works directly in line with the critical perspective

---

39. See note 16 above.

that Ann duCille identifies and traces in her book *The Coupling Convention* (1993). In her examination of African American novels, duCille shows "how these . . . texts—and others like them—inscribe, replot, subvert, exploit, and explode the middle-class wedlock ideal" (17). In the absence of African British texts that do this work, Behn's and Southerne's *Oroonoko*s offer a suitable (if incomplete) substitute for an analysis of the concerns of blacks and marriage since they both underscore two of duCille's major points: the marriage plot is an important device for understanding African people and their connection to freedom, and they both have idealized characters whose expressions of "connubial love" challenge middle-class British assumptions about marriage in many of the ways duCille lays out. Therefore, despite the risk that Imoinda's Africanism may reflect more on white British xenophobia, inhumanity, and enslavement and end up being what Emily Bartels has called reading "race through racism,"[40] a focus on Imoinda, marriage, and slavery in white-authored texts still provides an important introduction and crucial first step in understanding how the fictional African woman became critically involved in these British preoccupations as well as intimately involved in the antislavery movement's attempts to address them. This focus on Imoinda, marriage, and slavery also serves as a literary response to the question that Cecilia Green raises in her lucid examination of the slave marriage debate in 1823. She argues

> that the question of "slave marriage" was central to the question of "slave status" and that the question of the status of the enslaved depended on three sets of interlinked relations and their mediated outcomes: (a) the relation between colony and metropole . . . (b) the relation between (European) Master and (African) slave . . . and (c) relations of patriarchy, both familial and extra-familial, private and public, religious and secular. These relations ultimately determined the answer to the following question: what kind of "other" was the enslaved and/or colonized African going to be—an incorporated but differently subjectified other or an excluded and objectified other?[41]

Imoinda and the fictional African women who fall under her imaginative influence all fit squarely within each of the three "interlinked relations" Green lays out, and thus, the literature that features them presents an opportunity to witness British writers engaging with "the question of 'slave

---

40. Emily Bartels, "*Othello* and Africa: Postcolonialism Reconsidered," *William and Mary Quarterly* 54 (1997): 47.
41. "'A Civil Inconvenience'? The Vexed Question of Slave Marriage in the British West Indies," *Law and History Review* 25 (2007): 7.

marriage'" and, in the process, struggling to understand the "status" of the fictional African woman as she oscillates between inclusion and exclusion, subjectification and objectification.

AS A WHOLE, this book examines a number of texts in which Imoinda's literal and imaginative presence can be felt at crucial moments throughout the eighteenth century; however, I restrict my analysis to the period 1759–1808—a period that roughly corresponds with the timeline that Marcus Wood identifies as most fruitful for the emergence and development of antislavery poetry in his anthology, *The Poetry of Slavery, 1764–1865* (2003). I identify novelists and dramatists who are, at this same time, actively presenting to their reading and viewing publics African women in marriage plots informed by, but independent of, Behn's and Southerne's texts and, in doing so, sometimes producing and promoting complicated antislavery and abolitionist messages.

This fifty-year span of time is one of great instability, change, fear, violence, and terror in the antislavery movement, marked by events at home and abroad such as the Sierra Leone colonial experiment, the Zong Case, the Mansfield Judgment, the abolition of the slave trade in the British Colonies, the American, French, and Haitian revolutions, Tacky's Rebellion, and numerous other slave revolts. Each of these incidents has bearing on the tone of the time and the literature that was produced within it. To illustrate this tone, I read mid-century adaptations of *Oroonoko* as well as texts such as *High Life Below Stairs* (1759), *Love in the City* (1767), *The Irishman in London; or, The Happy African* (1793), *The Negro Slaves* (1796), *Obi; or, The History of Three Fingered Jack* (1800), *The Grateful Negro* (1804), *Adeline Mowbray* (1805), and *The Woman of Colour* (1808) as indications that the writers, John Hawkesworth, Francis Gentleman, James Townley, Isaac Bickerstaff, William Macready, August von Kotzebue, William Earle, Maria Edgeworth, Amelia Opie, and two anonymous authors, are part of an increasingly more sophisticated and less sentimentalized attempt to reiterate the interrelated discourses of slavery and marriage in serious terms for a contemporary society that is already accustomed to the blending of these discourses in Southerne's play and Behn's novella, and at the same time becoming increasingly interested in Britain's progressive antislavery and even abolitionist positions.

Part One of *Imoinda's Shade* consists of three chapters that chart the manner in which Imoinda, as a fictional character, influenced the antislavery stances taken in an assortment of British colonial texts written or published between 1759 and 1802. Beginning with the adaptations of *Oroonoko* that, together, mark the first-stage interventions that *Oroonoko* makes into the amelioration debate, and concluding with the alternative possibilities of emancipation depicted in a late-eighteenth-century drama and novel, Part One accounts for the political significance of Behn's and Southerne's fictional African woman and her ability to inspire a progressive reaction to the issue of slavery. But a certain degree of skepticism pervades the progressivism of the chapters in this part. Although they each clearly employ Imoinda and use her literal influence as a basis for articulating concerns about the black woman's experience of slavery, none of the texts in Part One go so far as to completely imagine and depict an African heroine's freedom outside of colonial slavery. Ultimately, they are either too conservative (Chapter One), too biased (Chapter Two) or too schizophrenic and incendiary (Chapter Three) on the issue of African freedom. This fact is a reminder that the British nation's love of freedom may not be as progressive as its literary rhetoric about African women and marriage implies, since the colonial African heroines who are constructed in "Imoinda's shade" point to freedom's glass ceiling as much as or even more than they do its achievement.

By moving to England and discussing African women and their connections to abolition in the years leading up to and immediately after the bill that abolished the British colonial slave trade, Part Two builds from this skepticism, and argues that, in order to detect real progress on the issue of slavery and Britons' dedication to freedom, critics must look at the fictional women of "Imoinda's shade" who are constructed in ways that show them actually *living* that freedom that Behn's and Southerne's texts create a desire for. The three chapters in this part present women of African descent whose experiences of slavery and marriage extend the scope and influence of "Imoinda's shade" by showing fictional black women on British shores striking out aggressively, on behalf of not only antislavery issues, but post-slavery ones too. In doing this, these fictional women present challenges to white male paternalism on its own terra firma and also show how fictional African women break out from the confines of the *Oroonoko* legend while retaining many of the concerns that Imoinda had come to embody and introducing some new ones of their own related to marriage, Englishness, and British citizenship. The texts in this section show how far Britons' love of, and dedication to, freedom can, and should, actually go.

In its insistence on seeing and representing Imoinda as a sustained, literal, and imaginative presence in British literature, *Imoinda's Shade* proposes that the fictional African woman and her interventions into British marriage plots cast a wider and more influential shadow over the white cultural imagination than three hundred years of criticism have led us to acknowledge. In addition, since it traces the idea of a black woman from her African roots to her Caribbean enslavement and ends with her involvement with the theme of abolition in England, *Imoinda's Shade* demonstrates that the imaginative idea of the fictional African woman is a diasporic phenomenon that provides an alternative way to understand Britain's antislavery and abolitionist movements.

PART ONE

Imoinda's Original Shades

African Women in British Antislavery Literature

Allow me, therefore, to contribute a few hints, against this evening; having heard, but yesterday, that you are then to appear, the first time, in the character of *Imoinda*. ... I come to your manner of *looking;* which, in the *usual sense* of the word, it is not possible for you to improve, beyond its present perfection. But, I mean not the *face,* but the *passions* which should appear in it. ... The quite contrary way, of attending to what is answered, as if you really were *Imoinda,* and felt, not acted, her hopes, fears and distresses, will charm and engage an audience the *more,* as it is scarce ever practiced.

—Aaron Hill, *Original Letters* (October 8, 1733). *The Works of the late Aaron Hill, Esq in Four Volumes. Consisting of Letters on Various Subjects, and of Original Poems, Moral and Facetious* (London, 1753), vol. 1: 139-41.

CHAPTER 1

Altering *Oroonoko* and Imoinda in Mid-Eighteenth-Century British Drama

WILLIAM: Have you left a lover behind you in Africa?
ADA: Only a lover? Much more than a lover! A husband.
WILLIAM: It is plain you are not European.
— August Von Kotzebue, *The Negro Slaves*, 34[1]

THIS CURIOUS EXCHANGE between William, a white European abolitionist, and Ada, a black African slave, appears in the English translation of August von Kotzebue's unproduced three-act drama, *The Negro Slaves* (1796). Its peculiarity lies in the unusual way William acknowledges that Ada is "not European." Although his initial question ("Have you left . . . ") clearly reveals his knowledge of Ada's African roots, his subsequent statement ("It is plain . . . ") confirms that her Otherness is most evident when she makes the distinction between a generic "lover" and a cherished "husband." Having been abducted from an African village and sold by white slave traders into the Jamaican society where the play takes place, Ada has left her husband, Zameo, long behind her; but she still insists on acknowledging her marriage to him despite a living separation that is, most likely, permanent. It is this serious display of marital fidelity in the face of complete adversity that forms the basis of William's assertion that Ada is "not European." Yet, his unusual acknowledgment is, itself, perplexing.

Why would William rely on Ada's marital disposition more than her obvious African blackness to distinguish her from Europeans in general?

---

1. Anonymously translated (London: Cadell, 1796). All subsequent references are to this edition.

By 1796, when the play was first published in England, Roxann Wheeler has confirmed that skin color had already emerged "as the most important component of racial identity in Britain"[2]; so the knowledge of an individual's blackness would have been sufficient to distinguish her from a European. William's statement, however, provides a clear, albeit brief, instance from late-eighteenth-century British literature in which skin color was not the most important category of difference used to identify an Other. However, Kotzebue was not the first or only writer to use marital fidelity as a basis on which to distinguish Africans from Europeans. In his own construction of ideal African women in the paradox "*That* a Black-a-moor Woman is the *greatest* Beauty; *in a Letter* to a *Lady exceeding Fair*" (1707), John Dunton exclaims: "What is there that makes a wife *handsomely humor'd*, but *Industry, Fidelity, Humility* and *Obedience?* And where can Europe show us any thing of these, like what we find in the African Ladies?"[3]

Despite these two examples, however, negative depictions of African wives and women in general appear to be far more prevalent than the motif of African marital virtue. In one instance, readers are warned that an unmarried "African girl" is "possessed of all the address of her sex, and all the cunning of her country"[4]—qualities that other novelists saw fit to develop in novels that feature married African women. For example, in a letter describing his observations of Algerian women to his friend Aaron Monceca, Jacob Brito, the narrator of Marquis d'Argens's *The Jewish Spy* (1739), recounts: "An African woman will brave any sort of danger and run any hazard to satiate her passion; and cannot be intimidated even by the fear of death.... Examples of this severe punishment are frequently seen; notwithstanding which the married women and maidens are fired with a most violent passion for the Nazarenes," who are slaves to the Algerians.[5] The African wife's penchant for base infidelity is also depicted in George Lyttleton's *Persian Letters* (1735), a novel that describes Ludovico "tormenting himself for one woman," while "he gave equal uneasiness to another. His master's wife saw him often from her window. The African ladies are utter strangers to delicacy and refinement. She made no scruple to acquaint him with her desires, and sent her favourite slave to introduce him by night into her chambers."[6]

---

2. Roxann Wheeler, *The Complexion of Race*, 9.

3. John Dunton, *Athenian Sport*, 104.

4. "Ovid and Julia: A Fragment," *Town and Country Magazine* 15 (London: Hamilton, 1783), 62.

5. (Dublin: Nelson and Saunders, 1753), 45. Also see the fictionalized account of the African woman Zulima (47–50) as an example of the violence of an African woman's love. Incidentally, d'Argens might be conflating moor with African here.

6. Lord George Lyttleton, *Letters from a Persian in England to his Friend at Ispahan* (London: Harrison & Co., 1785), 10. The aggressive, hypersexual black woman also appears in Henry Neville's

Toward the end of the century, these negative, fictionalized depictions of unfaithful, uncommitted, and immoral married African women appear in documents purportedly describing actual women in Africa and on colonial plantations. In his *History of Jamaica* (1774), Edward Long advises his colonial readers that "To allure [European] men from . . . illicit connexions [with African women] we ought to remove the principal obstacles which deter them from marriage. This will be chiefly effected by rendering women of their own complexion more agreeable companions, more frugal, trusty, and faithful friends than can be met with among the African ladies."[7] In this quote, Long implies that white women should exert themselves more and compete with the "African ladies" by promoting themselves as the indisputable bastions of all the best connubial qualities so that they may counter the white man's easy sexual access to "African ladies" who, as mistresses, display all of these domestic qualities without expecting any commitment of marriage. This, of course, was a battle that white women could not win. As Catherine Hall notes, "A family was an incumbrance: a mistress more convenient."[8] It was Long who also proposed that the "amorous intercourse between [Africans and Orangutans] may be frequent,"[9] a preposterous assertion which caused one critic to make this 1788 statement about the consequences of this most unnatural of couplings: "may it not be fairly conjectured, that the female negroes who live wandering in the wilds of Africa, are, there, frequently surprised and deflowered by the owran-outang [*sic*], or other such brutes; that from thence they become reconciled, as other women who are more civilized easily are, to similar attacks, and continue to cohabit with them?"[10] Grounded as they are in the discourse of factual realism that pervades colonial writings, these depictions of African women and marriage are in direct competition with the ideal impressions of the African marriage and the married African woman that Dunton and Kotzebue create.

If, however, we consider Dunton's paradox and *The Negro Slaves* as forming two ends of a historical frame that stretches from 1707 to 1796, and thus, bookends these negative portrayals of fictional and actual African women, Kotzebue's play can be seen as deliberate in its effort to resurrect the positive portrayal of the African marriage plot *despite* these widely prevailing impressions of extreme and unnatural promiscuity and infidelity that hounded African women. This fictionalized Africanist intervention is, as Toni Morrison points out, not designed to be suggestive of "the larger body

---

Isle of Pines (London, 1668), 11–12.

    7. *History of Jamaica*, vol. 2 (London: Lowndes, 1774), 330.

    8. *Civilising Subjects* (Chicago: University of Chicago Press, 2002), 72.

    9. *History of Jamaica*, vol. 2, 370.

    10. "To the Editor of the European Magazine," *European Magazine* 13 (1788): 75.

of knowledge about Africa . . . nor to suggest the varieties and complexities of African people and their descendants who have inhabited"[11] Britain. Rather, William's acknowledgment of Ada's African marital virtue underscores some anxiety about the European self that the African heroine in Kotzebue's play is designed to identify and perhaps politicize.[12] His employment of the fictional African woman in this manner has an important precursor in the *Oroonoko*s that were altered during the late 1750s.

THIS BOOK traces the interventions that fictional African women make into marriage plots in plays and novels from British literature. In its six chapters, I trace these interventions as they shift from the implicit antislavery roots established in Behn's novella and Southerne's play to a far more pronounced abolitionist tone in texts produced toward the end of the eighteenth and the beginning of the nineteenth centuries. This chapter, however, is devoted exclusively to the Hardwicke Marriage Act of 1753, Southerne's *Oroonoko*, and three *Oroonoko* adaptations that make important interventions into the discourses of marriage and slavery in the late 1750s.

When they are historically paired, the Hardwicke Marriage Act and the three adaptations of Southerne's *Oroonoko* published during the 1759–60 theater season[13] can be read as a collection of markers illustrating the more serious face that British writers and legislators are putting to the nation's approaches to slavery and marriage. By radically altering the clandestine manner in which the marriage institution worked and enforcing a host of marital regulations, Hardwicke's Marriage Act improved the laughable reputation that marriage had prior to 1753. Similarly, John Hawkesworth, Francis Gentleman, and an anonymous author each radically alter Southerne's *Oroonoko* by removing the comedic plot involving Charlotte and Lucy Welldon, thereby focusing exclusive attention on the tragedy befalling the African slaves Oroonoko and Imoinda. These legal and dramatic texts suggest that the 1750s are marked by a deliberate tendency toward seriousness on

---

11. Morrison, *Playing in the Dark*, 6.
12. Wheeler, *The Complexion of Race*, 14.
13. John Hawkesworth, *Oroonoko* (London: Bathhurst, 1759); Francis Gentleman, *Oroonoko, or the Royal Slave* (Glasgow: Foulis, 1760); Anonymous, *Oroonoko A Tragedy* (London: Corbett, 1760). All subsequent references refer to these texts. *The London Stage* (4:I, 378–79) records four performances of a play entitled *The Royal Captive, or A Wife For Ye All* at Southwark Fair (September 18–24, 1753). This could be the earliest attempt to rewrite *Oroonoko* during the 1750s. But *The London Stage* lists no author or playlist, and no manuscript appears to exist. Given the year this play was produced, a double title that establishes a connection between the themes of slavery and marriage, and its performance in the unregulated space of "Southwark Fair," this lost manuscript could have explored an entirely different avenue for examining the Hardwicke Act's relationship to slaves and slavery.

the issues of slavery and marriage, a tendency that the lawyer William Blackstone would refer to as "all the rage of modern improvement" in 1759.[14]

However, far from simply improving the reputations of marriage and slavery, in this chapter I argue that some of the alterations made in these legal and dramatic texts actually serve to strengthen domestic as well as colonial paternalism, and establish a collective threat of paternal tyranny at home in England and abroad in the colonies. In particular, my reading of Hardwicke's eighteenth clause suggests that the threat of paternal tyranny that Hardwicke's act threatened to establish over the marital choices of free minors in England was a reality enjoyed by West Indian masters who ignored the most basic idea of slave unions in order to establish another heinous ideology in its stead. Similarly, although altering Southerne's *Oroonoko* into a complete tragedy that focuses on the enslavement of its African hero and heroine should, theoretically, be a vehicle for making a more profound antislavery statement, the alterations done to the white Imoinda—specifically those made to her religion, dress, and marriage—transform the heroine's confrontation with paternal tyranny in the colonies in ways that do not always aid the antislavery agenda. I read only one of the three *Oroonoko* adaptations as effective in its attempt to transform Southerne's drama into a contemporary response to the social injustice of slavery because it alters Imoinda's characterization in a manner that keeps alive the African spirit of Southerne's heroine, and it identifies the problem of paternal tyranny as a transatlantic issue rather than a purely colonial one. Ultimately, my examination of the Hardwicke Act alongside these altered *Oroonoko*s starts this book's quest to reclaim the African Imoinda by beginning to establish how this fictional woman and her marriage plot become actively involved in antislavery intervention. It also provides a foundational moment for positioning the fictional African woman in British literature, offering an explicit date, text, and occasion from which to see what Felicity Nussbaum has called the "spectral *presence*"[15] of the eighteenth-century black African woman emerging from the shadow of her white African counterpart.

BEFORE 1753 the institution of marriage was a laughable experience in British life. As David Lemmings notes: "the law of marriage that applied in England had degenerated into a confused and contradictory mess by the early eighteenth century."[16] This was because clandestine marriages—irregu-

---

14. *An Analysis of the laws of England* (Oxford: Clarendon Press, 1759), xxvii.
15. *Limits of the Human* (Cambridge: Cambridge University Press, 2003), 188.
16. "Marriage and the Law in the Eighteenth Century: Hardwicke's Marriage Act of 1753," *Historical Journal* 39 (1996): 344.

lar marriages which, most commonly, breached the "church's rules relating to publicity"[17]—were a favored approach for a significant number of Britons of every age and rank, especially in major metropolitan areas. These marriages were cheap, discreet, and readily performed by impoverished clerics who supplemented meager incomes by presiding over as many of these ceremonies as they could. Clandestine marriages were also remarkably quick since clerics usually dispensed with the time-consuming practices of banns and licenses, and took advantage of a loophole in the law that deemed a simple exchange of vows before witnesses enough to ratify a marital union.[18] Such rapidity caused one contemporary commentator to remark, "marriage may be . . . made up in less time than a suit of cloaths."[19] After the Glorious Revolution, many attempts were made to regulate clandestine marriages, but to little avail. Outhwaite notes that "English marriage law experienced . . . remarkably few changes before 1753,"[20] and the clandestine marriage trade continued to thrive as clerics continued marrying Britons in provincial taverns, inns and alehouses, brandy shops and boarding houses. Far from being a solemn act, marriage was, simply, a lucrative business that occupied a wide variety of people of every age, rank, and means.

Ultimately, it was the alarming prospect of wealthy heirs and heiresses being forced or duped into inappropriate marriages that drove Parliament toward a concerted attempt to alter this heretofore laughable institution, force Britons to take it more seriously, and improve the institutional reputation of marriage in general. As its formal title indicates, the 1753 "Act for the better preventing of Clandestine Marriages" was designed to halt the rise of unregulated marriages taking place at alarming rates.[21] Clerics who performed marriage ceremonies without abiding by Hardwicke's strict regu-

---

17. R. B. Outhwaite, *Clandestine Marriage in England, 1500–1800* (London and Rio Grande, OH: Hambledon Press, 1995), 20. Chapter two points out the many different types of clandestine marriages that existed. For an examination of the rise and fall of clandestine marriages and marriage law in England, see Lawrence Stone's *The Family, Sex and Marriage in England, 1500–1800* (New York: Harper & Row, 1977); and Alan Macfarlane's *Marriage and Love in England: Modes of Reproduction, 1300–1840* (Oxford; New York : B. Blackwell, 1986). For contemporary tracts about the Marriage Act, see *The Marriage Act of 1753: Four Tracts,* ed. Randolph Trumbach (New York: Garland, 1984).

18. Outhwaite writes: "the medieval church had taken up the position that wedding vows made in the present tense, freely uttered between two people who were legally at liberty to marry, constituted the very essence of marriage. Once the knot was tied by such verbal exchanges it could not be undone: a valid marriage was technically indissoluble." *Clandestine Marriage,* xiii.

19. *A Letter to the Public* (London: Marsh, 1753), 30–31.

20. Outhwaite, *Clandestine Marriage,* 19.

21. "Wrigley and Schofield have estimated that about 47,500 marriages per annum occurred on average in the years 1750–53. If nearly 6,000 marriages by license were irregular, and there were about an equal number of weddings in the London marriage shops, this would mean that at least a quarter of all weddings taking place were technically clandestine." Ibid., 48–49.

lations concerning banns, licenses, witnesses, age, residence, registration, location, and timing requirements could face serious punishments of fines, transportation, and even death.[22] In this way, the Hardwicke Marriage Act radically transformed the making of marriage in Britain by both regulating and enforcing its contractual terms. Yet for all its presumed interest in promoting the common good of marriage, one political reporter was unsure "whether it would not produce greater mischiefs than it would prevent."[23] His concern was prophetic.

The passage of the Marriage Act in the Commons after its third reading in 1753 and its eventual implementation in 1754 had significant impacts on some very specific segments of English society. For minors under twenty-one, an age restriction gave parents and guardians considerable control over when and to whom their children or wards betrothed themselves. Eve Tavor Bannet has also shown that women became more socially vulnerable under the new terms of the act. For, after 1753, the simple exchange of vows that had previously served as legitimate legal proof of a woman's matrimonial claim to a man became null and void, meaning that if a woman copulated with a man on the expectation of marriage but had not legally married according to Hardwicke's stipulations, the man could refuse to fulfill her matrimonial claim, thereby ruining her reputation and bastardizing her children.[24] Contemporary opponents of the bill, such as Robert Nugent, argued that it "will discourage marriage of the poorer sort . . . by this act they will be prevented from doing it without great deliberation, many will not do it at all,"[25] thereby increasing their perceived propensity for sexual profligacy and the production of bastards. More recently, David Lemmings has even shown that "the Marriage Act was consistently less supportive of the role of *mothers* in marriage decisions."[26] For these groups, Hardwicke's act immediately changed perceptions about a laughable, private act consisting of a simple exchange of vows into a public and legally restrictive one with serious repercussions in terms of losses of power, choice, protection, and access that did not necessarily improve their lives or those of their children.

On the other hand, historians are in complete agreement that one role *was* strengthened and improved under Hardwicke. Misty Anderson's book, *Female Playwrights and Eighteenth-Century Comedy: Negotiating Marriage on*

---

22. Ibid., 84–85 and 125–26.
23. *The Debates and the Proceedings of the British House of Commons during the third fourth and fifth sessions of the third parliament of his late majesty George II*, vol. 5 (London: Almon, 1766), 99.
24. Eve Tavor Bannet, "The Marriage Act of 1753: 'A Most Cruel Act for the Fair Sex,'" *Eighteenth Century Studies* 30, no. 3 (1997): 233–54.
25. *Debates and the Proceedings*, 99.
26. Lemmings, "Marriage and the Law in the Eighteenth Century," 349.

the London Stage, states that "the act favored the interests of parents over the liberty of children,"[27] and Erica Harth is even more precise in defining the exact type of parent whose interest was improved under Hardwicke when she writes that his act "was to close up loopholes in existing legislation on marriage that allowed minors to marry without parental (read, paternal) consent."[28] Lemmings develops Harth's assertion further, claiming that the "rhetoric of M.P.s who promoted the measure and its evolution in parliament provide strong evidence of continuing patriarchal and materialistic instincts. . . . Children and especially daughters . . . remained essential objects of commerce in the accumulation of property that underwrote the power of the male parliamentary elite."[29] Of course, there was a specific economic rationale behind this interest in improving paternalist power. As Harth notes, "for those in power in 1753, considerations of love and marriage were embedded in those of money and property";[30] thus, paternal control over whom heirs would marry meant that property and money could be restricted to families within one social, usually aristocratic, class. This type of paternal control over the economics of marriage was, undoubtedly, an infringement on the free choice of the individual child, and, in particular, it had the potential to greatly affect young marriageable women who could be exposed to the threat of making economic rather than affective unions that suited the wills of their fathers. Thus, while the improvements to the lives of English women, minors, mothers, and the poor were questionable under the new marriage act, the improvement that it gave to its English male proponents is, historically, unquestionable.

LEMMINGS, HARTH, Outhwaite, and others have considered, at length, this unquestionable paternalist bias present in the Hardwicke Marriage Act, yet they devote hardly any consideration as to whether this bias affects groups outside Britain that were still within the purview of British legal control.[31] In this section, I want to consider the serious implications that the Hardwicke Act had on one of the groups deliberately excluded from its field of influence. Many groups were. In its final condition, British Quakers and Jews gained exemption from Hardwicke's tenets, as did Scottish residents and the royal family. But another interesting restriction also lies buried in the eigh-

---

27. (New York: Palgrave, 2002), 48.
28. "The Virtue of Love: Lord Hardwicke's Marriage Act," *Cultural Critique* 9 (1998): 125.
29. Lemmings, "Marriage and the Law in the Eighteenth Century," 344.
30. Harth, "The Virtue of Love," 133.
31. Outhwaite pays attention to the fact that certain sites in Scotland and the Isle of Mann became havens for elopers, but not much else exists on this issue. *Clandestine Marriage*, 95.

teenth clause. It states that this law did not extend to the colonies—"to any marriages solemnized beyond the seas."³² What were the implications of such a statement for individuals who were married in the West Indian colonies?

Given the paucity of information relating to the parliamentary debates, there is no direct evidence available from which to make a positive assertion that this part of the clause was in any way devised with reference to the colonies. What proves striking, however, is the way in which clause xviii allows colonial masters to skillfully bypass the rigorous intent behind the Hardwicke Act. Even though its wording suggests a profound need to make some kind of legal distinction between the rigorously regulated new marriages that were to be performed and celebrated in England post 1753 and those being performed in British territories during the same period, this distinction did not mean that marriages "solemnized beyond the seas" were legally invalid in England. The lawyer Matthew Bacon states, "It has been laid down at the bar, that a marriage in a foreign country must be governed by the law of that country where the marriage was had,"³³ a fact that leads Lord Sandwich to remark that "marriages solemnized beyond sea . . . are valid and binding here, or within the Kingdom of England, notwithstanding the provisions of the marriage act, so that they be legally solemnized according to the municipal laws of the respective countries where the ceremony is performed."³⁴ What clause xviii draws attention to, then, is the liberal underpinnings of Hardwicke's allegedly rigorous legislation: it acknowledges that, post 1754, when the act goes into effect, England will have changed its approach to marriage, while its colonies will be operating under their own, less rigorous, approaches to it. Erica Harth has pointed out that Hardwicke's rigorous regulations were primarily designed to keep the stratification rich and poor intact;³⁵ by controlling marriage, English paternalists could ensure that their rich sons and daughters married within their own rank. Since the Hardwicke Act was designed to accommodate this English paternalist bias, it is worth investigating whether the less rigorous standards pertaining to

---

32. For a complete list of the Marriage Act's clauses as they were finally conceived, see Outhwaite's Appendix 2 in *Clandestine Marriage* (173–80). In Appendix 1 he also includes the bill that preceded the final act. In this bill, the restriction against marriages "solemnized overseas" does not appear to be one of the things legislators were originally concerned with, thereby suggesting that the restriction developed later as Hardwicke imposed his influence over the final drafting of the act. On Hardwicke's influence, Outhwaite writes, "Though the 1753 committee of judges did reveal a determination to bring clandestinity under control by the simple device of annulling irregular marriages, events might well have proceeded as in the past but for the intervention of Lord Chancellor Hardwicke. He took control of the Lords' Bill and refashioned it in his habitual painstaking way" (94).

33. *A New Abridgment of the Law*, vol. 7 (Dublin: White, 1793), 113.

34. *The Kingston Cause* (London: Wheble, 1776), 43.

35. Harth, "The Virtue of Love," 138.

"marriages solemnized beyond the seas" also allowed colonial masters the freedom to control the making of marriage laws and practices in their own way and to their own interest. In short, is the freedom that colonial paternalists had to define and control marriage in the West Indies a bias that is deliberately designed to guarantee the stratification master and slave?

In the West Indian colonies, legal mandates and acts about marriage are remarkably rare. Nothing extensive appears in the acts of assembly passed between 1691 and 1769 in Jamaica or Barbados.[36] In fact, in Jamaica, not one act passed during this period pertained specifically to marriage. Despite this absence, however, marriages between West Indian planter families obviously did take place, presumably in accordance with English law. But masters had no interest in extending slaves legal rights of consent to give and take of each other's hands in marriage. As Cecilia Green shows: "marriage among slaves had not been the subject of law or of the slave codes because, slaves being legal non-entities, the possibility had no conception in law,"[37] an oversight that William Wilberforce would refer to as "the acknowledged neglect of any attempt to introduce regular marriage among [slaves]."[38] But in the 1750s this "acknowledged neglect" was deliberate, willful, and economically motivated. As Green states: "The planters, for their part, were unshaken in their certitude that the slaves were a species of property, *their* property no less, and that the idea of any kind of formal marriage among them was preposterous, a great impertinence, an attack on their authority and rights of property, a threat to public safety, and a dangerous intrusion upon the sacrosanctity of European racial exclusivity and superiority."[39]

Putting aside questions about slaves and the religious practices that could have prevented them from engaging in formal Christian marriages, it may, at first, seem strange that West Indian planters during the 1750s did not even encourage informal coupling to increase a plantation's slave workforce by natural reproduction. Although this practice was successfully used to increase slave populations in American plantations, it made very little economic sense to the minds of West Indian planters. "Before the abolition of the slave trade placed a premium on their reproductive capacity," Green observes, "enslaved African women (like their menfolk) were brought in

---

36. Brief references to marriage appear in passing in *Acts of Assembly, passed in the island of Jamaica, from the year 1681 to the year 1769 inclusive* (Kingston: Aikman, 1787), vol.1: 3, and 25 and vol.2: 5. A reference to marriage appears only once relating to Barbados in *An abridgement of the laws in force and use in Her Majesty's plantations* . . . (London: Nicholson, 1704), 252.

37. "'A Civil Inconvenience'? The Vexed Question of Slave Marriage in the British West Indies," *Law and History Review* 25 (2007): 25.

38. *The Debate on a Motion for the Abolition of the Slave-Trade, in the House of Commons* (London: Woodfall, 1791), 16.

39. Green, "'A Civil Inconvenience'?" 2.

predominantly as estate workhorses or productive laborers,"[40] and rather than rearing new slave hands through a lengthy nurturing period as Richard Beckford attempted on his Jamaican plantation, a far greater majority of Beckford's contemporaries favored what they thought was the most financially expedient method of working existing slave hands to death and replacing them with plentiful supplies coming to the colonies fresh from Africa.[41] This way, planters felt that they avoided the financial costs of maintaining children during the years that they would be all-consuming, nonproducing plantation hands. Slaves were, thus, not required to marry, couple, or procreate to increase a planter's profits; they need only work to death for their masters.

Of course, such a suicidal ideology was not the method used to extort wealth from the British metropolitan work force. Evoking Adam Smith's use of hands as a "synecdoche . . . of Enlightenment Political Economy," Eve Tavor Bannet notes that the 1753 Marriage Act in Britain was essentially a means of forcefully manufacturing British children who would become new working hands for the Empire since Smith and other influential political thinkers had concluded that population increase was essential to a country's economic prosperity. Encouraging marriage was not only a way to force lower-class populations to procreate so as to provide "a continual supply of industrious and laborious poor,"[42] but, as one contemporary supporter of the Hardwicke Act asserts, "marriage produces the greatest number of mature and valuable members of society,"[43] a comment that includes British workers as valued and prized components of metropolitan society both for their longevity as workers and for their material contributions. Thus, while "England was for families," as Catherine Hall has asserted in her book *Civilising Subjects* (2002), "Jamaica was for [African suicide as much as it was about] sex" for colonial whites.[44]

With a political ideology prescribing formal, legal, and Christian marriages as a way to nurture and increase Britain's population and wealth in blatant opposition to the suicidal ideology that did not even encourage informal coupling for slaves in the colonies, the practice of slavery and the ideal of marriage in the 1750s are completely antithetical yet working toward the same ends: the construction of the Great British Empire in a way that

---

40. Ibid., 44.
41. J. R. Ward, *British West Indian Slavery, 1750–1834: The Process of Amelioration* (Oxford: Clarendon Press, 1988), 29–37.
42. Parliamentary History 29, 69, taken from Bannet, "The Marriage Act of 1753," 235.
43. *A Letter to the Public containing the substance of what hath been offered in the late Debates upon the subject of the Act of Parliament for the better preventing of clandestine marriages* (London: Marsh, 1753), 21.
44. Hall, *Civilising Subjects*, 72.

continues the paternalist dominance and control of white men at home and abroad. By legally restricting Britain's newly emerging idea of marriage to British shores, the Hardwicke Act maintained paternal power and control of the making of marriage for individuals at home; but its restrictive clause xviii also had a profound effect on West Indian slaves, not because they were going to be governed by Hardwicke's mandates. Rather, it shows that colonial paternalists have the legal freedom to willfully ignore even the most basic idea of slave coupling out of their own economic self-interest. I am suggesting that the legal latitude to buy slaves rather than breed them through coupling was just as important to the maintenance of paternal power and money as well as the perpetuation of the master–slave dynamic in the colonies as the making of marriage was for the maintenance of aristocratic paternalist power in England. It is the freedom that the Hardwicke Act and its clause xviii gave to paternalists at home and abroad over the making of marriage and the disregard for slave coupling, then, that allows for this rigorous enforcement of a distinction between dying slave hands and living British ones—all working toward the financial improvement of members of the landed classes and the interests of Empire.

To be sure, the economic benefits behind this paternalist freedom to control the making of marriage were not lost on the makers of the Hardwicke Act. But there is also an implicit suggestion that these same lawmakers were also aware of the economic benefits of allowing masters to disregard the idea of slave couplings in the colonies. For it is, certainly, no coincidence that Lord Hardwicke, the magistrate whose name is synonymous with fashioning and influencing the act, was by real name Philip Yorke, the Attorney General who, in 1729 during an after-dinner speech at an inn of court with the Solicitor-General, Charles Talbot, issued the infamous "Yorke–Talbot decision." Their informal decision determined that slaves did not confer freedom on themselves either by becoming Christians or by arriving in England from the colonies.[45] Now, as Lord Chancellor responsible for a bill that Lawrence Stone describes as "a triumph of cunning draftsmanship,"[46] Hardwicke saw that his power and legal influence were greatly enlarged. His Marriage Act and its bias toward paternalists' interests have a direct connection to this earlier Yorke–Talbot decision. With its tacit acknowledgment that the colonial approach to marriage can legally exclude slaves and enforce a working suicide for them, clause xviii of the Hardwicke Marriage Act reinforced the policy that had been informally ratified by the Yorke–Talbot decision:

---

45. *Slavery, Abolition and Emancipation*, ed. Michael Craton, James Walvin, and David Wright (London: Longman, 1976), 165. For more discussion of the Yorke–Talbot decision, see Folarin Shyllon's *Black People in Britain, 1555–1833* (London: Oxford University Press, 1977), 20.

46. See Outhwaite, *Clandestine Marriage*, 95.

masters' property rights and the freedom to safeguard them always superseded slaves' rights to humanity.[47] Lemmings supports this assertion when he identifies this bias at the heart of Hardwicke's marriage act: "For the lord chancellor and for the majority of both houses of parliament in 1753 . . . individual happiness had to take second place when weighted in the scale against the patriarchal family."[48] In other words, minors in England must put their father's family interests before their own matrimonial inclinations. In the colonies, working slaves must do the same for the enslaver.

At its core, then, the Hardwicke Act has a tangibly insidious bias in favor of the paternalist that affects far more than just the white women, minors, wives, and the poor on English shores; its very existence implicates both British law and the lawmakers who sought to standardize metropolitan mores about marriage in the practice of creating conditions that gave paternalists at home and abroad the same economic and social advantage, allowing them the freedom to impose the paternalist ideologies in which the subjection of both enslaved and free individuals in the 1750s festered.[49] Perhaps in anticipation of this potentiality, opponents of the Hardwicke marriage bill discussed the fear of "establishing . . . a tyrannical power in the father."[50] That fear was, certainly, true in the West Indian colonies, and it expressed itself openly in the 1750s adaptations of Southerne's *Oroonoko*.

THIS IS the legal, political, and social landscape in which altered *Oroonokos* make their entrances in the 1759–60 theater season—a landscape in which the making and not-making of marriage is controlled by paternalists at home and abroad, and marriage itself is seen as antithetical to the material interests and progress of slavery, irrelevant in the lives of slaves in the British colonies, yet essential to the economic, social, and moral progress of Britons and Britain itself.

Contemporary events made the 1750s a ripe opportunity for transforming the tragic and comedic marriage plots of Southerne's *Oroonoko* into a more focused political text. Although *Oroonoko* had been an annual staple throughout the early eighteenth century, the *London Stage* reveals that it

---

47. Green acknowledges this connection in her work on Stephen. See "'A Civil Inconvenience'?" 24.

48. Lemmings, "Marriage and the Law in the Eighteenth Century," 349. See also notes 34 and 37 in Lemming's essay.

49. Jamaican slave laws, for example, were not standardized until 1781. Before this, it was generally left up to each planter to mandate his plantation's code of conduct. This desire to publicly regulate the slave codes must be seen as a response to what the planters believed to be an attack on their rights during the 1770s, especially with the 1772 Mansfield Judgment.

50. Lemmings, "Marriage and the Law in the Eighteenth Century," 349. Also see notes 34 and 37 in this chapter.

went through a seasonal drought in one of the patent theaters at the end of the 1740s, when *Oroonoko* "was not acted these last five years."[51] The play's resounding revival at Drury Lane in 1751, with eleven performances that season, seems indirectly influenced by the circulation of well-documented cases involving African princes unjustly abducted into slavery. The 1749 and 1750 editions of the popular periodical the *Gentleman's Magazine* make much of the busts and narratives of two of them—Jon Ben Soloman and William Ansah Sessarakoo—sold into slavery but ultimately rescued.[52] These princes and their narratives obviously coincide with the experience of Southerne's hero except for their more fortunate outcomes. The fact that the same popular periodical mentions another African princely abduction on May 9, 1759,[53] roughly seven months before the first altered *Oroonoko* appears on the Drury Lane stage, suggests that, after a significant lull in the 1740s, the revival of interest in, as well as the subsequent alteration of, Southerne's *Oroonoko* in the 1750s may both be closely tied to the circulation of narratives about the real experiences of enslaved African princes. The recognition that Southerne's play is a theatrical experience that encapsulates, critiques, or, at the very least, comments on the real tyranny befalling African princes in contemporary Britain may have made *Oroonoko* the politically charged expression of social injustice to see during this period.

As a contemporary expression of paternal tyranny and social injustice, however, Southerne's play needed to be updated, and a 1752 *Gentleman's Magazine* article had already suggested how this could be done. In it, an anonymous critic calls for "the first gallant attempt" from a writer "who will first have courage enough to deviate from the beaten track"[54] and institute new scenes in place of the comic ones, thereby transforming Southerne's *Oroonoko* into an "intire tragedy" of five acts associated with all great classical tragedies. Three writers take up this challenge.

---

51. *London Stage* (4:I, 267–68). Notes for the Wednesday 23 performance state that *Oroonoko* "was acted but once these five years." This refers only to the Drury Lane theater, since the play was performed intermittently at Covent Garden during the late 1740s. In the 1750s, performances of *Oroonoko* were chiefly held at Drury Lane under Garrick's management. J. R. Oldfield, in "'The Ties Of soft Humanity': Slavery and Race in British Drama, 1760–1800," states that, "despite the early success of Southerne's *Oroonoko*, by 1750 the play was clearly losing its appeal" (*Huntington Library Quarterly* 56 [1993]: 2). I argue that contemporary references to African princes made interest in the play pick up during the decade.

52. *Gentleman's Magazine* 19 (1749): 89–90 and 20 (1750): 272–73. In the article we are told, "Job Ben Soloman was a person of great distinction in his own country" and William Ansa Sessarakoo has an even more illustrious history as "son of John Bannishee, Corrantee Chinee of Anamaboe and of Euuobab, Daughter of Ansah Sessarakoo, King of Aquamboe and niece to Quishadoe King of Akroan." Also, the *London Stage* (4:I, 95) states that the "mainpiece" *Oroonoko* was presented "for the entertainment of two young Africans" on February 2, 1749, one of whom was Sessarakoo.

53. Ibid., 29 (1759): 240.

54. Ibid., 22 (1752): 163–67.

Significant differences between these writers begin to emerge when we consider how they acknowledge themselves as Southerne's "editors." On his title page (Figure 1), John Hawkesworth appears very circumspect about the extent of his alterations. He does not include his name despite being publicly identified as the editor,[55] and he even gives the impression that his editorial role is minor when he announces that the play is "by Thomas Southerne," "with alterations" in smaller capitals. Gentleman includes his name on his title page (figure 2), but even he does not draw attention to his two major alterations (new characters Massingano and Zinzo) until the dramatis personae. By contrast, the anonymous author's title page boasts of adding "near six hundred lines in place of the comic scenes. Together with the addition of two new characters" (figure 3).

Where Hawkesworth and Gentleman's circumspection about their alterations suggest both modesty and a desire to make sure Southerne's own artistic authenticity live on through his altered text, the anonymous writer deliberately draws attention to the originator's absence, addressing him as "the *late* Thomas Southerne." In boldly advertising and quantifying the alterations while also reminding us of the author's death—all on the first page—the anonymous author seems intent on being recognized as *Oroonoko*'s consummate "editor" in a way that Gentleman and Hawkesworth are not.

A possible reason for these different editorial approaches appears the more closely we examine these title pages. Gentleman's version represents *Oroonoko* "as it was performed at the Theatre in Edinburgh with universal applause," while Hawkesworth's captures *Oroonoko* "as it is now acted at the Theatre at Drury Lane." Publishing their texts after, or during, successful metropolitan runs, these writers are merely recreating, for the reader, performances that they have already viewed or are able to see in each specific locale, a practice of play publication that Peter Holland traces back to the Restoration period.[56] No specific location is mentioned for the anonymous tragedy. It is only randomly "intended for one of the theatres." But the anonymous author directly addresses this text's preface "to the reader," establishing that this tragedy is aimed at a readership irrespective of a viewership. Thus, the anonymous author appears to radically alter *Oroonoko* for a readership that may never see it performed, while Gentleman and Hawkesworth give the appearance that they are resisting altering *Oroonoko* not only out of deference to Southerne, but also because their readers may have already seen it in performance.

---

55. "great alterations in *Oroonoko* by Dr. Hawkesworth—Garr" (Garrick), *London Stage* (4:II, 759).

56. *The Ornament of Action* (Cambridge: Cambridge University Press, 1979), 99.

OROONOKO,

A
TRAGEDY,

As it is now Acted at the

THEATRE-ROYAL

In *DRURY-LANE.*

BY

His MAJESTY's SERVANTS.

By *THOMAS SOUTHERN.*
With ALTERATIONS.

—*Quo fata trahunt, virtus secura sequetur.*
      LUCAN. lib. 2. v. 287.
Virtus, recludens immeritis mori
Cœlum, negatâ tentat iter viâ.   HOR. Od. 2. lib. 3.

LONDON:

Printed for C. BATHURST, at the *Cross-Keys*, in *Fleet-Street*; and the rest of the PROPRIETORS.

MDCCLIX.

Figure 1.
Title page, *Oroonoko*, 1759, John Hawkesworth (1715–73)

OROONOKO:

OR THE
ROYAL SLAVE.

A
TRAGEDY.

ALTERED FROM
SOUTHERNE,

BY
FRANCIS GENTLEMAN.

As it was Performed at the THEATRE in EDINBURGH, with univerſal Applauſe.

GLASGOW:
PRINTED BY ROBERT AND ANDREW FOULIS
M.DCC.LX.

Figure 2.
Title page, *Oroonoko*, 1760, Francis Gentleman (1728–84)

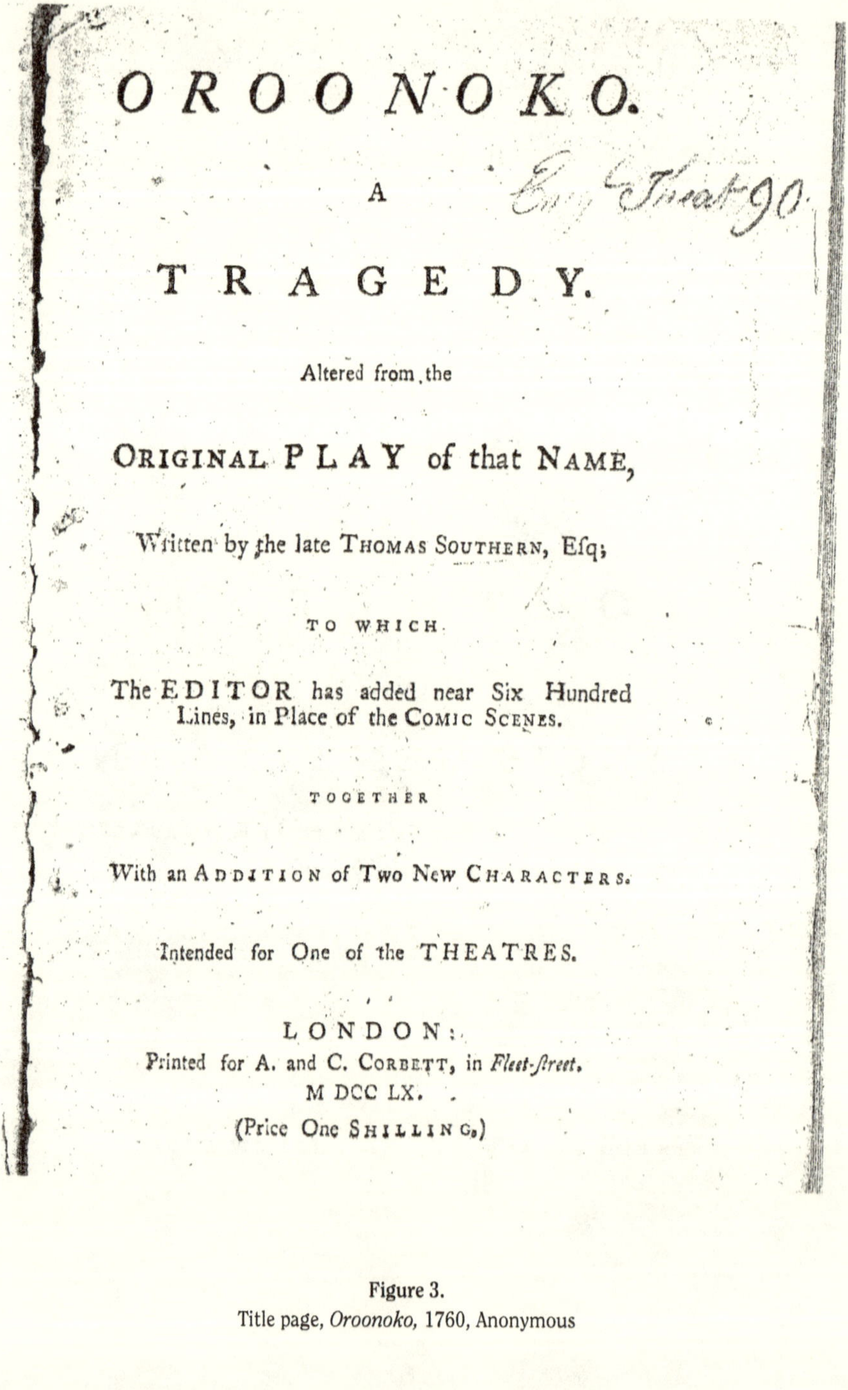

OROONOKO.

A
TRAGEDY.

Altered from the

ORIGINAL PLAY of that NAME,

Written by the late THOMAS SOUTHERN, Efq;

TO WHICH

The EDITOR has added near Six Hundred Lines, in Place of the COMIC SCENES.

TOGETHER

With an ADDITION of Two New CHARACTERS.

Intended for One of the THEATRES.

LONDON:
Printed for A. and C. CORBETT, in *Fleet-street*.
M DCC LX.
(Price One SHILLING.)

Figure 3.
Title page, *Oroonoko*, 1760, Anonymous

In the decade where the *Oroonoko* drama appears to speak to the real contemporary problem of tyranny and social injustice, I point out the extent of each author's desire to be known as an "editor" of Southerne's *Oroonoko* because it leads to a question: what is the best way to update a play that has been in circulation for over sixty years so that it captures the decade's serious mood on tyranny and social injustice? Obviously, Hawkesworth's and Gentleman's tragedies can lay claim to dispersing a far-reaching message. Their tragedies are performed in legitimate theaters with what seem to be minor alterations of Southerne's work that, most importantly, speak to contemporary metropolitan audiences, making the populace more aware of, and open to, the antislavery rhetoric and themes already present in Southerne's text. By contrast, the heavily altered, anonymous *Oroonoko* never gets a viewing. However, the author's address "to the reader" suggests that it wasn't intended to. Perhaps these three *Oroonoko*s, in attempting to reach two different audiences—a viewing one and a reading one—were trying to update *Oroonoko* in two very different ways. J. R. Oldfield, in what is, to my knowledge, the only existing examination of these three *Oroonoko*s simultaneously, suggests that they should be read in a hierarchy of antislavery affect beginning with Hawkesworth's as the least inflammatory and ending with the anonymous author's as the most.[57] While I agree with this general interpretation, I would add that the differences noticed in the title pages and prefaces of these three *Oroonoko*s provide a clear example of what Peter Holland calls "the distinction between reading and seeing, between the two modes of consumption of the text."[58] The effectiveness of each text's response to the contemporary tyranny and social injustice of slavery, therefore, may depend on each author's understanding of whether his "intire tragedy" about African slavery was meant to be seen or to be read during the 1759–60 theatrical season.

THOMAS SOUTHERNE was, in fact, the *first* dramatist to make "the distinction between reading and seeing, between the two modes of consumption of the [*Oroonoko*] text." It was he who changed the genre of the story from Behn's novella and popularized it in a stage drama; it was he who took out the African and middle passage sections of the story and made the action take place solely in Surinam; it was he who also introduced brand new char-

---

57. I extract this idea implicitly from the order in which Oldfield discusses these texts as well as his statement that the anonymous *Oroonoko* "addressed slavery most directly," "'The Ties Of soft Humanity,'" 5. See also the first chapter of his *Popular Politics and British Anti-Slavery* (Manchester, UK: St. Martin's Press, 1994), 7–41.

58. Holland, *The Ornament of Action*, 99.

acters, Aboan and Blandford, as well as the brand new comic plot involving the Welldon sisters. However, one of his alterations had the most profound effect on the difference between seeing and reading *Oroonoko:* he makes his Imoinda white where Behn's is black. Usually, no distinction is made between Southerne's textual and staged white heroine. Critics think of them as the same. However, I want to contend that there are, in fact, two white Imoindas that Southerne creates. One for the stage, the other for the pages of his published text.

Novak and Rhodes indicate that *Oroonoko* was "attractive to the ladies in the audience" and they assume that Southerne's skill at "pathetic tragedy" was the basis of this attraction;[59] yet the hero's tragic demise was not the only thing that made this play "the Favourite of the Ladies."[60] Obviously, by radically altering the skin color of the heroine and presenting a white Imoinda on the stage instead of the black woman that Behn created, Southerne encouraged the women in his audience to visually identify with a white-skinned, virtuous heroine. At least "Mr. Ryan, on the first Time of his playing the part of Oronooko [*sic*]" thought fit to tell them as much: "If Southerne's Imoinda's chaste and beauteous too," he remarks in his prologue, "That Copy, Ladies, he transcrib'd from you."[61] Ryan's soliloquy offers a contemporary explanation for Southerne's radical presentation of a white Imoinda: she is designed to flatter the English female audience who watch her, and much of the criticism about Imoinda's whiteness has been written from this visual perspective. For instance, Joyce Green Macdonald's thoughtful essay, "The Disappearing African Woman: Imoinda in *Oroonoko* after Behn," provides a valid and convincing argument that demonstrates how Southerne's white heroine eclipses black female representations and appropriates a cloak of antislavery, which, surreptitiously, creates more sympathy for oppressed white feminism than African slavery.[62] For Macdonald, Southerne's Imoinda is not seen as an African. But if this is true, then how was she seen?

The frontispieces that appear at the beginnings of some of the published versions of Southerne's play provide a glimpse of how Imoinda was seen onstage. Many of these illustrations are contained in Felicity Nussbaum's *Limits of the Human* (2003),[63] and in the vast majority of these, Imoinda's

---

59. *Oroonoko* (Lincoln: University of Nebraska Press, 1976), xvi.
60. Ibid.
61. Prologue to T. M. Gent, *A Miscellaneous Collection of Poems, Songs and Epigrams* (Dublin: Rhames, 1721).
62. *English Literary History* 66 (1999): 71–86. Also see Macdonald's "Race, Women and the Sentimental in Thomas Southerne's *Oroonoko*," *Criticism* 40, no. 4 (1998) 555–70.
63. Nussbaum, *Limits of the Human*, 180–86.

whiteness is visually and unambiguously self-evident, and, perhaps, underscored even more by the obvious contrast between her white skin color and Oroonoko's blackness. However, Nussbaum includes one frontispiece, "Mrs. S. Kemble as Imoinda" (figure 4), in which the heroine is depicted without Oroonoko, and by a clearly identified living actress. Even though Nussbaum does not include them in her book, there are other frontispieces of this kind from the period featuring Harriet Litchfield (figure 5), Elizabeth Hartley (figure 6), and Sarah Smith (figure 7), each one depicted as standing alone in the character of Imoinda. Altogether, these types of independent illustrations depicting how Imoinda actually appeared onstage offer an opportunity to see how female audiences actually viewed her without the presence of Oroonoko's blackness standing in relief to define her.

Apart from a generalized exoticizing that is sometimes evoked through a well-placed feather as in Kemble's and Litchfield's cases, a bow and arrow as seen in Hartley's portrayal, or the sarilike sash and turban that appear in the majority of these frontispieces, there is nothing about any of these actresses or their costumes that explicitly spells out Imoinda's African origins. The closest attempts to Africanize Imoinda are, perhaps, made in two of the illustrations. In Hartley's, an animal-print pattern overwhelms her elaborate sash and a significant part of her bodice and sleeves, and this exoticizing effect is accompanied by what appear to be feathers and/or other pelts of animals in her hair and on her sleeves, sash, and petticoat. Although this type of costuming creates the visual impression that Hartley is fully adorned in the natural dress of a wild country, these accoutrements do not explicitly Africanize her, nor do they essentially differentiate her elaborate dress from one that a rich, white woman in the audience might wear. In her portrayal of Imoinda, Hartley displays herself as a rich English woman would if she had the economic means to embellish herself with the spoils of empire, and certainly not as a female slave who has spent most of her life in Africa as the play's narrative actually demands. In the second potentially Africanizing depiction, involving Sarah Smith, the actress's skin appears to have been cosmetically darkened. If this is not the case, the alabaster whiteness of Smith's dress and shawl contrast so much with her skin color that it creates the overall impression that she may be a racially indistinct Other, rather than a purely white, Imoinda. But even in this onstage depiction of a dark-skinned Imoinda, nothing specifically ties her cosmetic darkness to Africa, and moreover, Smith's white muslin dress is so completely bereft of any other exotic accoutrements that its plainness forcefully associates the actress with the outfit most recognizable to, and associated with, the everyday English woman. In both of these potentially Africanizing depictions, then, costuming and cosmetic devices do not explicitly convey African-ness in the manner

Figure 4.
Mrs. S. Kemble as Imoinda, 1791. Elizabeth Kemble (1763?–1841)

Figure 5.
Harriet Litchfield (1777–1854) as Imoinda, 1807

Figure 6.
Mrs. Hartley in the character of Imoinda, 1777. Elizabeth Hartley (1750?–1824)

Figure 7.
Miss Smith as Imoinda, 1806. Sarah Smith (1783–1850)

that the frontispiece to Thomas Bellamy's *The Benevolent Planters* (1787) does with its depiction of the black stage-heroine, Selima, who despite having the actress's customary white dress and exotic feather in her hair also has black skin and African hair, as well as what seems to be an actual animal fur rather than an animal-print style fabric draped over her shoulders (Figure 8).[64] Despite whatever exotic accoutrements adorn their white bodies, English actresses are still able to connect and identify with English female audiences of any rank because of their familiarity of dress.

These staged representations of familiar white women in an African role are nothing like the illustration of familiar yet distinct female African-ness in Jane Barker's novel, *Exilius* (1715). The Numidian, Princess Galecia,

> was a Lady of a masculine spirit, and undervalu'd the little delicacies of her sex, making the study of philosophy and the laws of her country, her chief business. . . . Her person was extreamly agreeable; for though she was very tall of stature, and somewhat of an African complexion, nevertheless the exact symmetry of parts, and fine features, render'd her equal to the most compleat European beauty.[65]

In *Limits of the Human*, Nussbaum analyzes a masculinized illustration of Imoinda from 1816 that almost equals this depiction of Galecia, but Nussbaum's illustration is clearly an artist's rendering of a scene from the play produced over 100 years after Barker's novel rather than a staged representation of a living actress in the role.[66] In the frontispieces that I present here, none of the actresses come close to conveying the uncanny impression that Galecia embodies as an African woman who is temperamentally and physically distinct yet equal to her European peers. Instead, the white actresses who play Imoinda onstage are as temperamentally familiar to an English female spectator as their skin color and costumes are. Imoinda's onstage temperament can be detected in the differences between the frontispiece actresses. Kemble, Smith, and Litchfield look well and have fine costumes, but their portrayals of Imoinda are much less gaudy than Hartley's: where they all have turbans, Hartley's wig is swept up in an elaborate bun that cascades down to her shoulders; where they all have relatively flattering petticoats and modestly printed sashes, or a plain white shawl in Smith's case, Hartley's circle petticoat most emphasizes the shapeliness of her figure, giving it the illusion of an extremely narrow waist, and her animal-print pattern dominates most of

---

64. This is, clearly, not an actual depiction of a white woman cosmetically altered. It is, rather, an artist's rendering of the scene.
65. (London: Curll, 1715), 32.
66. Nussbaum, *Limits of the Human*, 182–87.

THE

BENEVOLENT PLANTERS.

A Dramatic Piece,

as performed at the

Theatre Royal, Haymarket.

WRITTEN BY THOMAS BELLAMY.

Sc. 2. For Oran is alas! no more.

LONDON.

printed for J. Debrett opposite Burlington House Piccadilly. 1789.

Figure 8.
Title page, *The Benevolent Planters*, 1789, Thomas Bellamy (1745–1800)

her costume; where the other actresses appear full-frontal with their hands outstretched in a gesture of emotive appeal, Hartley's Imoinda is, defiantly, in profile, her outstretched arms grasping a bow, her intent stare implying that she is taking aim at an intended target (the Deputy Governor, perhaps?). These costume differences capture Hartley and the other actresses who perform the role at different stages in the play and encourage spectators to see Imoinda's onstage temperament as either defiantly rich and awe-inspiring or lovingly simple and sympathetic. But none of them encourage viewers to see her as markedly different in temperament from English women or as far outside the bounds of English femininity as the African princess Galecia is in *Exilius*.

The celebrity of the actresses who perform the Imoinda role also make the female viewer's identification with Imoinda that much stronger. Sarah Kemble, Harriet Litchfield, Sarah Smith, and Elizabeth Hartley were all well known in their own right, and female audiences were drawn to the theater as much to see what these known stars were wearing and how beautiful they looked performing Imoinda than out of a need to see each actress's portrayal of African slavery in Surinam. Despite some exotic visual cues and vague attempts to Otherize her persona, then, Imoinda is not clearly defined as African onstage; she is, in fact, celebrated as remarkably familiar to English women viewers in terms of temperament, appearance, and dress. The act of seeing Imoinda on the eighteenth-century stage is, thus, an experience that English women of any rank could readily identify with. In the final evaluation of her frontispieces, Nussbaum stresses, conclusively, that Oroonoko's presence and Imoinda's appearance had little bearing on the way audiences saw Imoinda. Despite these exoticizing visual cues, "Imoinda remains white."[67] In my examinations of the independent illustrations of actresses in the role of Imoinda, the visual effect is even more specific. Onstage, the supposedly African Imoinda is actually seen as white and familiarly English by female spectators. Macdonald is right. The African woman does disappear on Southerne's stage. An English woman replaces her.[68]

However, in the many published editions of *Oroonoko* that do not contain frontispieces, the female reader's identification and familiarity with Imoinda is not made as easily as it is between female spectators and the actresses who perform the role. In fact, although much is made of Imoinda's beauty throughout the play, whiteness, when it is explicitly mentioned, is not even directly evoked in relation to her character. During the second scene of

---

67. Ibid., 182.
68. Macdonald argues that "an African woman would interfere too greatly with white women's identificatory spectatorship of *Oroonoko*'s racial tragedy." "Race, Women and the Sentimental in Thomas Southerne's *Oroonoko*," 559.

the second act, Oroonoko explains to Blandford, "There was a stranger in my father's court, valu'd and honor'd much: he was a white, the first I ever saw of your complexion" (II.ii.38). Here, it is Imoinda's father's difference that is marked by a unique white complexion and the designation "stranger," not Imoinda's. His original nationality is not even mentioned at this point or elsewhere within the text. Within the same speech, Oroonoko immediately establishes that, whatever his past nationality was, this white man who was "valu'd and honor'd much" while still a "stranger" in the African court had long since established a more important connection to Angolan society that transformed his status within it: he "chang'd his God for ours and so grew great." Whiteness, then, clearly did not preclude this man's ability to be "valu'd and honor'd much" in this African society, but Oroonoko implies that this white man's religious conversion guaranteed his social advancement and complete acceptance in Angolan society. Whiteness is, thus, an important category of difference in the published and read version of *Oroonoko*, but it is not the predominant one defining Imoinda's father's identity as overwhelmingly as it defined Imoinda in the frontispieces and stages that produced *Oroonoko*. Religion is, clearly, far more definitive for understanding the impression that he makes in Africa, and moreover, the way he is understood by the English Christian reader. Roxann Wheeler's *Complexion of Race* (2000) has proved, persuasively, that religion and clothing were more important categories of difference than skin color in the early part of the eighteenth century for understanding how individuals distinguished themselves from each other. So we must read this apparently minor reference to her father's act of religious conversion with the major importance that contemporary readers would have given to it irrespective of the white skin color held by the convert.

    The suggestion that this white man of unknown national origins would give up his presumably Christian religion for a heathen one distinguishes him more as different from the English reader than similar to them merely because "he was a white." Given this white man's complete conversion and identification with African culture, there is every reason to believe that the "only daughter, whom he brought an infant to Angola" followed in her father's footsteps and became even more assimilated to the African culture that their white skin colors indicate they were not born into because this African life is all that she has ever known. In the published text, Imoinda's paganism is suggestively evoked by her father's act of conversion, and like his, it is clearly a mark of her cultural identification with Africa. In addition, the "bow and quiver" (IV.ii) that Southerne's text makes a point of emphasizing as the only identifiable part of her costume offers another reminder both of her African-ness, since it recreates the capacity for the aggressive action that Behn's original black heroine first displayed when she attacked the Governor with her own bow and poisoned arrows,[69] and as a testament to her father's heroism, since he is a war general killed by a bow in battle. Both of these clothing and religious categories of difference suggest that, on the written page, Southerne is deliberately constructing Imoinda with the heathen, savage, martial, and heroic propensities, not out of fear of a fertile black woman, as Lynda Boose believes was common for male writers at this time,[70] but as a specific homage to the temperaments of both the black African heroine depicted in Behn's novella and the white African father evoked but not present in Southerne's own text. Southerne's textual Imoinda is, thus, martially, religiously, temperamentally, and heroically a complete white African.

I am arguing that religion and dress are important signifiers of Imoinda's African disposition in the read versions of Southerne's text. They are far more important categories of difference than skin color because they draw out the full import of Imoinda's identity and underscore how different she is from the Christian English reader, whereas the English temperament, dress, and white skin color seen in the performances of *Oroonoko* allow female spectators to readily identify with Imoinda. To put this distinction plainly, in performances of *Oroonoko*, Imoinda is *seen* as English and familiar; in the read versions of the play, she is *understood* to be African and different.

Given this clear difference between an English Imoinda onstage and an African one on the pages of *Oroonoko*, contemporary critical understandings of Imoinda's effect in Southerne's play demand the ability to make a distinction between seeing her onstage and reading about her on the page, a move that Macdonald does not make when she refers to Imoinda as a "disappearing African"—disappearing itself a practice that, by its very nature, relies more on seeing the African woman than reading about her. Far from disappearing, then, in published versions of Southerne's *Oroonoko* the African presence is marked and fluid enough to incorporate Imoinda's whiteness as much as it does Oroonoko's blackness since they both are shown to have African dispositions. The larger ramifications of this fact are, themselves, very substantial. For, unlike Othello and Desdemona, whose Moorish and Venetian differences form the basis of their marriage and *Othello*'s tension, the read versions of Southerne's play lead to the conclusion that *Oroonoko* is not really an interracial play. It is an intratribal one, since Oroonoko's and Imoinda's dispositions are, undoubtedly, more alike in the published text than their

---

69. See the epigram at the beginning of Chapter Three for a description and analysis of the martial Imoinda.

70. See "'The Getting of a Lawful Race,'" in *Women, "Race," and Writing in the Early Modern Period*, ed. Margo Hendricks and Patricia Parker (London: Routledge, 1994), 35–54.

black and white skin colors immediately suggest onstage. Moreover, the idea of African-ness itself is also revealed to be as fluid a racial concept as Wheeler has indicated phenotype was in the early eighteenth century, but only when the categories of difference identifying Africans are read about and emphasized in a published text and not presented on the stage.

Thus, once we understand the ways in which, and the reasons why, Imoinda's whiteness is emphasized on the stage (to appease English actresses, attract female audiences, and connect with them), and completely deemphasized on the page of the published text (to stay true to the essence of the original African heroine and show how different she is from the English female reader), it becomes clear that while published versions of Southerne's *Oroonoko* have two different white complexions at work—Charlotte's European one as well as Imoinda's African one—Southerne's *Oroonoko*, as it was seen on the stage, presents the two white heroines, Charlotte and Imoinda, as almost identically English and familiar because they have the same ability to completely connect with the female English viewer. Acknowledging this last point, Aravamudan notes that "Restoration spectators may have found an Imoinda standing behind Charlotte as a failed similarity"[71]—failed because her ultimate fate (death) is less appealing that Charlotte's (marriage). Yet, in this section, my discussion has shown that this visual impression of Imoinda's failure would not necessarily be true for Restoration *readers* of Southerne's play who may have recognized Imoinda as not merely a popular manifestation of African-ness, but also as an expression of the marital fidelity that Behn created in *Oroonoko,* and that Dunton and Kotzebue would later reinforce in their own works.

I AM ARGUING that Southerne's text promotes Imoinda as an African woman while his staged play promotes her English female celebrity, and this argument provides a context for distinguishing how Hawkesworth's, Gentleman's, and the anonymous *Oroonoko*s function in addressing contemporary anxieties about tyranny and social injustice in the 1750s.

In his adaptation, Hawkesworth makes what may seem to be small changes to Southerne's text; however, these alterations make his Imoinda markedly different from the one that Southerne created. Even though Southerne's original reference to Imoinda's father's conversion is very brief in the original version, Hawkesworth's draws out its importance in his preface, which states: "Oroonoko, when he mentions the father of Imoinda to Blandford, calls him 'a man of many virtues,' yet says he chang'd Christianity for

---

71. *Tropicopolitans,* 58.

paganism; a sentiment, of which the evil tendency is too manifest to be proved" (ix). Sixty-four years after *Oroonoko* first appeared, Hawkesworth implies that a Christian man's conversion to paganism is an "evil tendency" that puts in doubt the veracity of that man's claim to having "many virtues." Therefore, in order to make Imoinda's father, and, by extension, Imoinda, unproblematically virtuous, he alters Southerne's original intent and completely strikes out the brief but loaded reference to this important act of conversion. With this small alteration, Hawkesworth transforms how contemporary English readers assess Imoinda. Hawkesworth's omission of one of the categories of difference that defined her as African in Southerne's original text transforms Imoinda into a presumed white Christian whose father never converted—a very different textual impression from that which Southerne intended for his heroine and his contemporary reader.

To further de-Africanize her, Hawkesworth also strikes from the published version of his play the stage direction that describes Imoinda costumed and armed with "bow and quiver," thereby removing the other important category of difference that defined her as African in Southerne's original. Add to these clothing and religious alterations of Imoinda's character the fact that all the other English women—Charlotte, Lucy, the Widow Lackitt—and their marital indecencies are expunged from the text so that they are no longer available to appear as foils embellishing Imoinda's ideal African-ness, and the complete effect of Hawkesworth's alteration to Imoinda's characterization becomes apparent. In the absence of the characters and categories of difference that had Africanized the white Imoinda who appeared within the pages of Southerne's text and clearly defined her as different from Southerne's reader, Hawkesworth's Imoinda is transformed into a white woman that an English reader can readily identify with in his altered version of the play.[72]

Hawkesworth's alteration of Imoinda's complexion has even larger repercussions with respect to the African ideal of marriage. I have already indicated that Southerne's African couple are more alike, temperamentally, than their skin colors immediately suggest; however, when he makes Imoinda a white Christian woman distinct from her black heathen husband, Hawkesworth places a greater emphasis on the couple's dissimilarity. Because his published version of the play makes such a point of removing the categories of difference that make Imoinda appear savage, African, and Other to the reader, Imoinda's skin color now becomes the only observable, and therefore predominant, category of difference that enunciates her identity as a European Christian, just as blackness inscribes Oroonoko's African heathenism.

---

72. Her implied Christianity is also the specific means by which oppressed white English women readily identify with her, as Joyce Green Macdonald convincingly argues.

By making this couple's differences so pronounced, the published version of Hawkesworth's *Oroonoko* is exposed as an interracial text in which skin color rigidly inscribes an interracial couple's cultural dissimilarity without the intratribal identity politics that, in Southerne's text, made them both Africans who were culturally more alike than their different complexions outwardly convey. This important point is worth reiterating: with its predominant emphasis on the differences between Oroonoko and Imoinda's skin colors rather than the similarity of their African dispositions, it is Hawkesworth's and not Southerne's *Oroonoko* that actually gives birth to an interracial reading of the play.

Reading Hawkesworth's interracial relationship can potentially do more work instigating British prejudices than promoting a more pronounced antislavery message. For Southerne's drama that was originally about how slavery affected two types of heathen Africans—a black indigenous one as well as an assimilated white one—is transformed into a tragedy about an interracial couple from culturally dissimilar backgrounds whose suicidal deaths can be viewed as dangerous confirmations of Sir George Ellison's idea that interracial relationships are "indelicate and almost unnatural"[73] unions that should not have occurred in the first place.

WITH HIS ostensibly minor alterations to the published text, Hawkesworth's *Oroonoko* has a major effect on Imoinda, essentially de-Africanizing her into a white woman that contemporary readers identify with. And as a consequence, this affects the manner in which his play functions as a visual signifier of tyranny and social injustice onstage. When Hawkesworth removes the comic marriage plot and focuses exclusively on the slave couple whose marriage suffers because of the tyranny of the Deputy Governor, he is not only able to tap into the injustices experienced by captured African princes documented in the *Gentleman's Magazine,* he is also able to show a contemporary British audience exactly how their freedoms to marry in England differ from their slave counterparts in the colonies. He manages to achieve this effect with almost no effort on his part since the elements for Britons to evaluate their freedoms to marry alongside the restrictions imposed on colonial slaves were already present in the comic sections of Southerne's original text. But on December 1, 1759, when Hawkesworth's Europeanized Imoinda makes her debut appearance onstage, a British audience's evaluation of the freedom to marry might have been seen under a new light.

---

73. Sarah Scott, *The History of Sir George Ellison* (Lexington: University Press of Kentucky, 1996), 139.

In a discussion with Blandford, Oroonoko recounts the circumstances of his clandestine marriage to Imoinda—clandestine because the King, Oroonoko's father, has not heard about their wedding when he orders Imoinda brought to court to be one of his own brides. The newly married couple have already consummated their relationship, however, for Imoinda "grew with child," and is "forc'd to own herself [Oroonoko's] wife" (II.i) in front of the King. This chaotic scenario is indicative of the ensuing confusion surrounding clandestine marriages. For having the temerity to choose Oroonoko without his consent and against his self-interest, the supreme African paternalist consigns Imoinda to slavery. In Surinam, Imoinda is, legally, the property of another paternalist figure, the absent Governor; but even when she eventually reunites with Oroonoko, she cannot consolidate her marriage to him without this absent paternalist's consent.

In Africa and Surinam, active and passive paternalism is a palpable and somewhat tyrannical obstacle to minors who demonstrate serious affective commitments to marriage. In Surinam, Imoinda would rather languish over the loss of her African husband than accept the romantic advances of the highest-ranking colonial official. During her marriage to Oroonoko, he declared himself monogamous when he had the cultural license to be polygamous, and after he thinks she is dead, he refuses to marry another woman. They are both committed to the ideal of constancy in marriage even beyond death. Hence, Stanmore is right when he states that Oroonoko "deserves" (II.iii) her as she does him. They are both admired for their abilities to uphold serious ideals of marriage amidst great adversity. Yet, even though they prove their worth, honor, and commitment to each other, they still cannot make any legal claim to own each other even under the most basic idea of marriage without paternal consent.

By focusing the viewer's attention on a tragedy where two young individuals represent serious ideals about marriage but are denied the freedom to marry according to their choice, Hawkesworth's *Oroonoko* produces a message onstage that would resonate offstage. The play exposes the lack of control minors have over the disposal of their own bodies in the marriage market under the Hardwicke Act and points out that a paternalist's interests always outweigh the individual's. These kinds of impressions might have resonated in the late 1750s, especially with English female spectators who, I have already shown, identify with the onstage Imoinda through the devices of dress, skin color, and celebrity. These female spectators might be more easily encouraged to see *Oroonoko* as a commentary on the paternalist bias present in the Hardwicke Act that carefully lays out the circumstances of their own situation under it, thereby providing another unexpected reason why *Oroonoko* was "a favourite of the ladies." It spoke to their situation under the decade's new and serious marriage law. But by encouraging this type of viewing, Hawkesworth's *Oroonoko* visually explores more about English women's problems with Hardwicke than the African woman's problems with slavery.

WHERE HAWKESWORTH'S alterations of Imoinda refocus attention on the English rather than the African woman, the focus of Gentleman's alterations is entirely pro-African. He finds no reason to omit Imoinda's father's conversion to heathenism, especially since this religious practice offers such an exemplary illustration of honorable African behavior. The "Princely Pagan" (V, 87), Oroonoko, may worship, as the "resplendent ruler of the earth," the sun that Christians deem but a "lamp of light" (IV, 61). But his ignorance about the existence of a Christian God does not diminish the exemplary sense of honor that, Gentleman asserts, nature bestows on all African people. His Oroonoko comes from "Those unletter'd shores" of Angola that "claim brighter virtues far than art e'er taught." In this world of the noble savage, "Learning and fraud are equally unknown" (I, 19).

While Gentleman's text in no way advocates a Christian's conversion to heathenism, he does use heathens as moral touchstones whose naturally honorable African exemplarity contrasts with the depiction of Christian colonies where "Christian frauds" (III, 57) are bred, who act with the "Christian lure of fair faced smiles where lurks deceit in friendship's borrow'd guise" (I, 17). Yet, with all these attacks on white colonial Christians it is revealing that Gentleman's Oroonoko levels his most blistering attack of this religion at Massingano, a countryman of his own color whom he deems "worse, if possible, than [a] Christian traitor" (IV, 63). A famed Angolan warrior in his own right, Massingano vows to kill Oroonoko out of revenge because Oroonoko had earlier killed Massingano's brother in battle. But the poisoned dart/javelin that Massingano aims at Oroonoko kills Imoinda's father instead, enabling Oroonoko to go on and defeat Massingano's tribe. After this war ends, Oroonoko spares Massingano's life, only to sell him into slavery in Surinam, where he becomes so physically changed by the experience that one of his fellow countrymen, Zinzo, does not recognize him when he also finds himself a slave newly arrived in the colony. "I must be chang'd indeed when thou forgets'st," Massingano tells Zinzo, "Captivity has grasp'd with iron hand / And thus deform'd the image of thy friend" (I, 21). The lack of physical recognition between Massingano and Zinzo describes these two African men at different stages of enslavement. While Zinzo, fresh from Angola, is still a typical African heathen of Oroonoko's ilk complete with a "fraudless bosom," Massingano's physical deterioration, when coupled with his own admission that he "must become a Christian in [his] scheme" (I, 25) to get revenge on Oroonoko for his brother's death and his own enslavement, highlights the deformation of an honorable African heathen into a seasoned "black Creole"—one of those de-Africanized Africans that Edward Long referred to in his *History of Jamaica* (1774). Christianity, then, is not exclusively a mark of white deviousness; it is used ironically to mark the moral degeneration that generally occurs to people in the colonies.

Massingano, however, is not the only Creole figure Christianized into an unrecognizable manifestation of his former self, and he is certainly not the most powerful. When he works "by stratagem, to gain an end" (I, 25) in which he seeks to overthrow Oroonoko, Massingano is only a less influential black replica of the white Deputy Governor who also works by stratagem to "have the stubborn fair" (IV, 71) Imoinda. In his plan, Imoinda's husband

> shall be taken off—if not
> By bare-faced pow'r, by secret means.
> This Blandford, too, with whom I must keep fair,
> Should he still stand a bar to cross my love,
> Must share the husband's fate. (IV, 71–72)

Clearly, this uncontrolled white Creole advocates the disposal of all Christian and heathen men in order to satiate his lust for Imoinda in the same way that the black Creole, Massingano, wants to satiate his revenge against Oroonoko. Together, these unrestrained examples of Christianized Creole destruction represent the deformations of their former honorable heathen and Christian countries. But because he places a pronounced emphasis on the villainous, colonially deformed Creole figures, Massingano and the Deputy Governor, strategically destroying Oroonoko and Imoinda's marriage, the visual effect that Gentleman's *Oroonoko* generates aligns with Hawkesworth's staged version.

Following Oroonoko's reunion with Imoinda, Hawkesworth's Deputy Governor reveals that he has no intentions of renouncing his amorous pursuit. Stanmore asks him, "Where's your mistress now, Governor?" joking with the colonial administrator about the fact that his long-held passion for Imoinda must now come to an end because of Oroonoko's prior marital claim. The Governor replies, "Why, where most men's mistresses are forced to be sometimes, with her husband it seems. (*Aside.*) But I won't lose her so" (II.iii). His overwhelming desire to violate the sanctity of the slave marriage by deliberate machinations, as his aside foreshadows, is another example of the lack of restraint that was to become one of many definitive characteristics both of the stage and the novelistic West Indian[74]—one that separates him from the level-headed Englishmen, Blandford and Heartfree, who both preach temperance in love, and even the enraged African King, Oroonoko's father, who does not dare to commit "incest" in marrying his son's wife.

Because they focus so assiduously on Creoles' emotional intemperance, Hawkesworth's and Gentleman's *Oroonoko*s blind British spectators to their nation's own legal complicity in creating the paternalist conditions that have allowed slavery and subjection to fester in the first place. Hawkesworth's *Oroonoko* allows female spectators to visualize the problem of paternal tyranny but not identify how close to home its source lies. And one can detect the same political agenda at work in the staged and textual versions of Gentleman's *Oroonoko*, the only difference being that black as well as white Creoles are demonized in ways that exonerate Britons, British Christianity, and British paternalists of all involvement in creating this decidedly unchristian climate of paternal tyranny and social injustice.

THE TEXTUAL and staged versions of Hawkesworth's and Gentleman's *Oroonoko*s are, therefore, at odds with antislavery activism. While they both, ostensibly, focus on the problem of slavery, they do so by altering Imoinda and exaggerating Creole intemperance, actions that refocus the problem of social injustice on the white English woman's experience under Hardwicke and appear to absolve British paternalists of all tyranny despite their legal involvement in legislating tyrannical behavior.

The anonymous *Oroonoko* proves to be very different in all these respects. This exclusively read dramatic text goes about antislavery work with an intertextual awareness that relies most heavily on knowledge of Southerne's original text despite a title page that purports to radically alter *Oroonoko* in Southerne's absence. The anonymous author immediately establishes indebtedness to Southerne, beginning the altered text with "the original preface" and ending it with "the original epilogue, written by Mr. Congreve, and spoken by Mrs. Verbruggen." These editorial decisions would be incidental but for the fact that "Mrs. Verbruggen,"[75] the famous early-eighteenth-century comic actress who excelled in britches parts, had died in 1703, and thus, could not have "spoken" the part in 1760. Moreover, as I have already indicated, the character that she played and originated in the 1695 inaugural

---

74. See Wylie Sypher, *Guinea's Captive Kings* (Chapel Hill: University of North Carolina Press, 1942) and Chapter Four of this book for more discussion of the intemperate Creole.

75. See Novak and Rodes's *Oroonoko* (8–9) for further discussion of Verbruggen and other players in the premier production of Southerne's play.

performance of Southerne's play—Charlotte Welldon—had been expunged from this text altogether. Both the actress's and the epilogue's inclusion in this anonymous *Oroonoko*, then, appear to be glaring editorial errors that Hawkesworth and Gentleman do not make.

But the anonymous author's decision to include her after Hawkesworth and Gentleman had omitted her role also provides an opportunity to see how the anonymous *Oroonoko* makes a deliberate attempt to differentiate Africans from Europeans as Southerne's *Oroonoko* intended. In Congreve's epilogue, Charlotte Welldon, shorn of the britches she has worn for a majority of the drama and suitably attired in women's clothes, soliloquizes directly to an audience of her sexually emancipated peers—those "happy London wives" who "love at large each day / Yet keep [their] lives"—and in a series of bawdy analogies and double entendres she contrasts the freedom these women have to pursue extramarital pleasures with the tragic fate of the African couple, Oroonoko and Imoinda, who so "make a conscience of their vows" that they would rather commit suicide than break them. Indeed, the thought of actually killing oneself, as Imoinda does, to uphold a principle of marital fidelity to an African man so alarms Charlotte that she exclaims on behalf of her peer group, "save us from a spouse of Oroonoko's nations!" Yet even as she belittles Imoinda's poignant fidelity to her African husband and extols the frivolity English women enjoy with theirs, Charlotte's soliloquy conveys a clear satirical message that Congreve has designed to be as reprehensible as it is amusing. Between guffaws, Congreve wants Charlotte's audience to question her flippancy and to recognize that while English sexual freedoms may be more delightful than African marital restraints, they are certainly not more honorable, virtuous, or commendable—a point Srinivas Aravamudan underscores when he writes, "Imoinda's badly done romance against the Welldon successes is one that many spectators may find reprehensible."[76]

When Gentleman and Hawkesworth expunge Charlotte completely from their texts and identify tyranny as a Creole trait rather than a British one, these two acts essentially succeed in absolving England of immorality. However, when the anonymous author resurrects Charlotte's character in the exclusively read version of *Oroonoko*, he or she reinstalls the critique of English immorality that was leveled at her in Southerne's original text. Her reappearance counters Gentleman's and Hawkesworth's tendencies to assign the blame for slavery to the unrestrained passions of Creoles because her soliloquy and its satirical homage to marital infidelity remind Britons that their own free and unrestrained passions are just as immoral as those unrestrained Creole villains when compared with the play's African couple.

---

76. *Tropicopolitans*, 57.

As Southerne does in his textual version, the anonymous author also allows his readers to evaluate two distinct types of white femininity. In this anonymous *Oroonoko,* Imoinda still has her African temperament. The author mentions, verbatim, both her father's conversion and her "bow and quiver," the latter of which even Gentleman avoids in his African version. The anonymous author also accentuates Imoinda's African-ness further when the Englishwoman, Maria, asks her "t'aid my Fancy, in the ornaments befit a Bridal state" (I.i). Imoinda replies, "*my* Fancy long, has lost its force—At best weak—And in the modes which Europe hold, wholly unknowing" (I.i). Her "wholly unknowing" ignorance as to European dress and finery confirms that this author is building upon the category of difference emphasized in the original text and developing it to acknowledge Imoinda as the type of fully assimilated white African that Southerne intended. As such, Imoinda contrasts with the Englishwoman, Maria, who is undergoing her own assimilation to Creole culture, an act that is reflected, initially, by her attachment to her brother, the Deputy Governor of the colony, but more profoundly through her impending marriage to Blandford. Because he is recognized as the temperate colonial authority that replaces the Deputy Governor after his death, Maria's marriage to him and her friendly association with Imoinda represents more of her integration into a new Creole society sympathetic to the injustices of slavery. With this second, influential and futuristic type of Creole whiteness that Maria embodies, the anonymous author develops Southerne's original use of female whiteness in his *Oroonoko.* Where Southerne's text distinguished between Imoinda's exemplary white African virtue and Charlotte's white European vice, the anonymous author also uses the categories of difference relating to dress, marriage, and religion to establish a distinction between Imoinda's African whiteness and Maria's Creole whiteness; however, despite their differences, these women are also united in their oppositions to social injustice and paternal tyranny.

Maria's opposition to social injustice and paternal tyranny is displayed in her relationship with her brother, the Deputy Governor. In this text, the Deputy Governor's uncontrolled passion does not solely interfere with Imoinda and Oroonoko's marriage; his actions also interfere with his sister's marriage to Blandford. At the beginning of the play, Blandford enters rejoicing to Maria that ships have just arrived in port bringing with them "credentials . . . to obviate th' impediment thy brother threw between [his] ardent wishes and Maria's charms" (I.i). The Deputy Governor initially welcomes this news and their impending marriage. But when Blandford interferes with his pursuit of Imoinda, and Maria refuses to aid him in his scheme to "perpetrate / Th' violation of [Oroonoko and Imoinda's] Royal bed" (III.i), the Deputy Governor "pronounc'd his firm immoveable resolve" that Maria

> should be instantly convey'd on board the ship
> Now waiting for a wind, to sail for England
> Anulling [*sic*] thus, the solemn, firm
> Engagement, ratified with Blandford—
> —and sworn before the Throne of Heaven,
> Tho' yet unhallowed by the sacred priest. (III.i)

In this speech, Maria does more than articulate the fraternal villainy impeding her marriage. The Deputy Governor's interference in both Maria's and Imoinda's marriages shows not only his capacity to violate the marriage of royal slaves, but also his refusal to ratify a marital union with the ecclesiastical ceremony that the Hardwicke Act, itself, advocates. It is this all-consuming paternal tyranny that is capable of jeopardizing the marital unions of both African *and* white women in the colony that makes the anonymous *Oroonoko*'s Deputy Governor so much more insidious than his forebears in Gentleman and Hawkesworth, and it makes the anonymous *Oroonoko* so much more effective in its attack on paternal tyranny in general because it shows how all women—slave and free, English and African—are affected by it.

Imoinda expresses her opposition to social injustice and paternal tyranny when she tells her mistress,

> I have heard, Maria, the Isle which gave
> Thee birth,
> Is marked for hospitable Deeds, humane
> Benevolence, Extended charities—
> With ev'ry social virtue—Is't Possible?
> A Nation thus distinguished, by the Ties,
> Of soft Humanity, Should give its Sanction,
> To its dependant States, to exercise,
> This more than savage right, of their
> Disposing, like th' marketable Brute, their
> Fellow creature's blood? (I.i)

In this marked attack on the British metropolis, Imoinda articulates the critique missing from Gentleman's and Hawkesworth's versions of the play. She explicitly blames Britain for sanctioning its "dependent states" to "exercise" savage rights against slaves. Although she does not refer to marriage law directly, Imoinda does so implicitly when she places the blame for the perpetuation of slavery not simply on the colonial practices of Creoles, but on a hypocritical British metropolis that, despite being "marked" for its capacity for all sorts of benevolent and humane action, deliberately and systematically allows the inhumanity of slavery to fester through the unregulated work of insidious colonials who dispose, "like th' marketable Brute, their / Fellow creature's blood." This reference comments not only on the slaves readily disposed by planters in the 1750s suicidal plantation economy, but also on Imoinda's and Maria's disposals under a Deputy Governor who has been given the power to just as easily ship his sister back to England on a whim as he can easily dispose of Oroonoko in order to violate Oroonoko's wife. In this way, the anonymous author creates two distinct types of white femininity—African and Creole—but instead of using them, as Southerne does, to distinguish African virtue from European vice, this anonymous author shows these different white women united in their oppositions to paternal tyrannies of the Deputy Governor and British legislators. For this reason, this exclusively read version of the *Oroonoko* text reveals itself as the most progressive antislavery *Oroonoko* of its day.

ALTHOUGH THE anonymous *Oroonoko* delivers this pronounced antislavery message using its simultaneous African and white Creole marriage plots to implicate and expose Britain's legal "sanction" in allowing paternal tyranny and colonial slavery to fester, its commitment to freedom is tempered once we compare the African marriage with its Creole counterpart—in the end, the appealing Creole underplot threatens to overshadow the African one. The anonymous author attempts to transform the sting of the tragic African marriage plot by including a happy, futuristic Creole one wherein Maria is free to marry Blandford once Oroonoko murders the man who has stood between their union, the Deputy Governor. With his death, the play implies that this Creole couple, who were so actively involved in protecting Oroonoko and Imoinda, will be at the forefront of creating a new colonial society sympathetic to the plight of the remaining slaves entrusted to their care; sympathetic, certainly, but definitely not abolitionist.

Maria and Blandford do not question too rigorously the tenets upon which their authority in the colony is built. Although Maria agrees that Imoinda levels "too just [a] charge" at Britain, she also softens the critique with the statement that she is,

Well perswaded [*sic*]—the justice, Equity,
With Wisdom blended, of the sage rulers
Of my parent country, Cou'd furnish forth
Fit argument, and with humanity
Conjoined, to authorize an Act [that] has much alarm'd [me]. (I.i)[77]

---

77. Mr. Edwards in Maria Edgeworth's *The Grateful Negro* made a similar argument. See Maria Edgeworth's *Tales and Novels*, vol. 2, *Popular Tales* (New York: AMS Press, 1967), 400.

Blandford provides one such "argument":

> There are those who say, this practice carries mercy
> Since in th' wars, they wage, each with the other—
> Were not this channel of commercial intercourse
> Kept open, the prisoners taken would exchange
> This slavery for cruel and tormenting deaths. (IV.i)

With these kinds of arguments, Maria and Blandford countenance prolonging an institution that, as I have already asserted, is, in 1760, primarily interested in working slaves to death. Moreover, they also downplay their own self-interested economic motives for prolonging slavery. Those ambiguous "credentials" that increase Blandford's status, drive his social ascent in the colony, and allow him to marry Maria could be based on the labor of his slaves or the money made from selling them. The anonymous *Oroonoko*, however, does not represent this illustration of Creole advancement negatively; rather, it establishes itself as a literary precursor to the texts that Markman Ellis identifies, whose arena of interest is "humanist but not humanitarian, interested in amelioration but not emancipation or abolition, and concerned, above all, with the hyperbolically asymmetrical power relation of slavery—in other words, sentimentalist."[78] Maria and Blandford "want to transform a social system based on violence into one based on trust."[79] This is the text's contemporary solution to the problem of tyranny and social injustice. But as my next chapter will show, trust in the benevolent paternalist is not always in the African woman's interest.

Of immediate interest in my quest to reclaim the African Imoinda, however, is the fact that the ameliorationist message in the anonymous *Oroonoko* relies heavily on the author's ability to use Southerne's original conception of African-ness in his *Oroonoko* as a touchstone from which to effectively update Imoinda's characterization for a contemporary readership. The anonymous author builds on this spirit of Southerne's white African Imoinda by altering Imoinda's disposition in a completely different manner than Hawkesworth's and Gentleman's versions of *Oroonoko*. Instead of whitening, Christianizing, and civilizing her, the anonymous author maintains and embellishes the categories of difference that originally defined her as African, thereby allowing the focus of the play to remain on Africans despite Imoinda's white skin color; instead of only demonizing Creoles and Creole paternalists, the anonymous author allows Maria to critique her own Creole brother's paternal

---

78. *The Politics of Sensibility* (Cambridge: Cambridge University Press, 1996), 127.
79. Ibid.

tyranny in the colonies and Imoinda to critique English paternalist practices with respect to slavery, thereby providing a more expansive attack of the source as well as the problem of paternal tyranny; instead of focusing on stage performances that allow white female viewers to connect with Imoinda and see *Oroonoko* as an allegory that identifies the potential for paternal tyranny under the Hardwicke Act but misdirects the blame for this problem, the anonymous author's exclusive focus on reading *Oroonoko* creates categories of difference that Africanize Imoinda and distinguish her from the English reader, thereby forcing these readers to confront the issue of African slavery and female oppression under tyrannical paternalists simultaneously. Because it does all of this work, the exclusively read play keeps alive the spirit of the ideal African marriage and the ideal African woman involved in it, and uses these things to effectively attack the prevailing practice of tyranny and social injustice in a progressive, if conservative, manner.

Ultimately, the fact that a white African woman in an exclusively read British drama articulates a direct attack against Britain's involvement in slavery in a way that builds upon the efforts of Behn and Southerne not only provides us with an example of what a progressive antislavery drama begins to be in 1760, it also gives us our first incarnation of what "Imoinda's shade" might have meant to contemporaries when Capel Lofft first used the phrase.[80] By presenting Imoinda as the white African woman Southerne's *Oroonoko* originally intended his readers to recognize, the anonymous Imoinda delivers her antislavery message not only on behalf of contemporary African women, but also on behalf of the black Imoinda whose novella remains in her shadows. In 1760, a black African woman speaks against slavery from the shadows of the white African-nesses who embody her spirit in Southerne's *Oroonoko* and its anonymously altered version. But in 1760, even the most progressive alteration to the *Oroonoko* legend does not change the perception that slaves should be able to live and enjoy both ownership of themselves and ownership of each other in marriage. Such a radical notion won't appear until we consider August von Kotzebue's *The Negro Slaves,* a text in which "Imoinda's shade" is revealed as a space from which the African woman gets to not only critique slavery but also articulate a unique call for freedom. Before we get there, however, we must examine what it means for the fictional African woman to be put in "Imoinda's shade" when the Imoinda towering over her is not white.

---

80. See Introduction, 8.

CHAPTER 2

Amelioration, African Women, and the Soft, Strategic Voice of Paternal Tyranny in *The Grateful Negro*

> Black boy him love Jill Jenkins,
> Tink he'll wed—tink he'll wed.
> His Massa chide him thinking,
> Beat him head—beat him head.
>   —"Possum up a Gum Tree," sung by Tuckey in *Obi; or, Three Finger'd Jack. A Melodrama* (1830), 7.

> *Jackson* is substituted for the husband of Lucy instead of *Juba;* many people having been scandalized at the idea of a black man marrying a white woman. My father says that gentlemen have horrors upon this subject, and would draw conclusions very unfavorable to a female writer who appeared to recommend such unions: as I do not understand the subject, I trust to his better judgment, and end with,—for Juba, read Jackson.
>   —Maria Edgeworth, letter to Mrs. Laetitia Barbauld, Edgeworthstown, January 18, 1810.

> In Montserrat I have seen a negro man staked to the ground, and cut off bit by bit, because he had been connected with a white woman who was a common prostitute: as if it were no crime in the whites to rob an innocent African girl of her virtue; but most heinous in a black man only to gratify a passion of nature, where the temptation was offered by one of a different colour, though the most abandoned woman of her species.
>   —Olaudah Equiano, *Interesting Narrative* (1794), 134.

I LAUNCH this chapter with three epigrams depicting black men and white women in violently thwarted interracial couplings not simply because this is the familiar arena of interracial love echoed in the *Oroonoko* play; these couplings also provide a tangential yet critical context for my explorations of the fictional African women depicted in Maria Edgeworth's short story *The Grateful Negro*, written in 1802 and included in her collection *Popular Tales* (1804). Kathryn Kirkpatrick, Susan Greenfield, Tim Watson, and a host of other contemporary critics have discussed Edgeworth as one of a number of British female writers of the era who demonstrate how a "domestic" novel that "takes place in England . . . centrally concerns the problem of the West Indies."[1] In this chapter, I aim to use *The Grateful Negro* to think more about how Edgeworth presents interracial and African couplings outside of England, and, moreover, how those couplings provide a solution to the problem of slavery that strategically and deliberately minimizes the concerns of common black African women on the colonial plantation.

To contextualize this argument, I want to interrogate what appears to be the least violent of the three epigrams. In the second, taken from a letter written to Mrs. Barbauld concerning the 1810 revisions of *Belinda* (1801), Edgeworth claims that the "subject" of interracial marriage is outside the ken of her understanding. Yet, she must have been aware of the presence of such couplings in eighteenth-century British society, for England at this time was teeming with interracial unions, especially in London. A significant percentage of the couples that sailed to the ill-fated Sierra Leone colony in 1787 were composed of black men and white women.[2] Moreover, the popular black abolitionist writers Olaudah Equiano and Ukawsaw Gronniosaw both had white wives. Whether or not Edgeworth knew about these living examples of interracial unions, the British stage that she was certainly well acquainted with was frequently graced with two of the most popular black male–white female marriages in theatrical history: Oroonoko and Imoinda, and Othello and Desdemona.[3] Even *The Dying Negro* (1773), the Thomas Day poem that Edgeworth refers to in *Belinda*, is based on an actual situation involving one such interracial relationship.[4] So the "subject" is definitely something Edgeworth had some kind of literal or imaginative familiarity with.

---

1. Susan C. Greenfield, "'At Home and Abroad': Sexual Ambiguity, Miscegenation, and Colonial Boundaries in Edgeworth's Belinda," *PMLA* 112 (1997): 215. See also Tim Watson's *Caribbean Culture and British Fiction in the Atlantic World, 1780–1870* (Cambridge: Cambridge University Press, 2008); and Kathryn Kirkpatrick's "'Gentlemen Have Horrors Upon This Subject': West Indian Suitors in Maria Edgeworth's *Belinda*," *Eighteenth Century Fiction* 5 (1993): 331-48.

2. For more on the Sierra Leone colonial project, see Shyllon's *Black People in Britain*, 52–55. A contemporary document states that "400" of the black poor "together with 60 Whites chiefly women of the lowest sort, in ill health, and of bad character . . . were sent out at the charge of government to Sierra Leone." *Substance of the Report of the Court of Directors of the Sierra Leone Company* (London: Philips, 1792), 2.

3. Apart from some isolated instances, *Oroonoko* was performed in the patent theaters throughout the century. The same holds true for *Othello*.

4. See the "Advertisement" to *The Dying Negro*.

Therefore, the lack of understanding she professes to have in her letter to Barbauld seems strategic. I agree with Alison Harvey's suggestion that Edgeworth's "disavowal—'I do not understand the subject'—seems disingenuous . . . and is difficult to read without hearing in it a level of irony."[5] Before 1810 Edgeworth might have had a very progressive understanding of the "subject" of interracial coupling because Juba and Lucy distinctly differ in one important respect from other popular depictions of interracial marriage in literature from the era. Where each of the famous interracial unions involving Oroonoko, Othello, and The Dying Negro routinely end with the tragic death of a black man who is, literally, placed outside of English soil (Surinam, Cyprus, the English Channel, respectively), Juba remains alive and well at the end of the 1801 edition of *Belinda,* free to enjoy married life in the heart of the English countryside with his English bride. Because this interracial coupling has the potential to thrive in British society, Edgeworth might well have been using Juba to recognize and validate freedoms of choice not usually available to black male slaves in the colonies as well as market England's commitment to upholding that freedom for people of all colors within its dominions. If this were the case, she would have been in good company. In a 1788 article written for the London newspaper *Public Advertiser,* Equiano asserts, "Why not establish intermarriages at home, and in our Colonies? And encourage open, free, and generous love, upon Nature's own wide and extensive plan, subservient only to moral rectitude, without distinction of the colour of skin?"[6]

Edgeworth's father strongly objected to such views on "intermarriages at home" as well as his daughter's representation of them. One week before her letter to Barbauld, Edgeworth wrote to her Aunt Ruxton, saying, "Juba the black servant is not allowed to marry the country girl Lucy; because my father has great delicacies and scruples about encouraging such marriages—Therefore one Jackson, a hard-favoured man is Lucy's bridegroom and poor Juba has only the pleasure of the Banjore and dancing at the wedding."[7] Making Lucy's new bridegroom "a hard-favoured man" is, perhaps, Edgeworth's ironic stab at her father's "great delicacies and scruples." She might be making fun of the fact that he'd rather see Lucy with a rough, and presumably violent, white fiancé than a gentle, creative black one.

But a secondhand conversation between two characters in Clara Reeve's

---

5. "West Indian Obeah and English 'Obee': Race, Femininity, and Questions of Colonial Consolidation in Maria Edgeworth's *Belinda,*" in *New Essays on Maria Edgeworth,* ed. Julie Nash (Burlington: Ashgate, 2006), 3.

6. Quoted in Peter Fryer, *Staying Power* (Atlantic Highlands, New Jersey: Humanities Press, 1984), 109.

7. Maria Edgeworth to Mrs. Ruxton, January 9, 1810.

Plans of Education (1792) suggests that Richard Lovell Edgeworth's "great delicacies and scruples" about interracial unions were shared by other English gentlemen. Well before 1810, the fictional Lord A— tells his wife that emancipated Africans "will flock hither [to England] from all parts, mix with the natives, and spoil the breed of the common people. There cannot be greater degradation than this, of which there are too many proofs already in many towns and villages."[8] Clearly, "gentlemen have horrors upon this subject" of interracial coupling because it visually signifies and biologically confirms that uncontrollable freedoms are being extended to black subjects, first in the colonies, and then in England—a "fear of racial amalgamation" that Felicity Nussbaum says "was certainly festering in England from the end of the seventeenth century."[9] In Lord A—'s imagination, extreme "degeneration" is the horrible consequence of such freedoms, and such fears reach the height of hysteria for Richard Edgeworth once the 1807 abolition bill introduced the possibility—however remote—of black men invading Britain and making an indelible biological imprint on the English national identity and culture.[10] If, in the wake of the abolition bill, *Belinda* appears to be legitimizing unions that Sarah Scott had forty years earlier described as "indelicate and almost unnatural,"[11] gentlemen who think like Lord A— may be drawn to the "unfavourable" conclusion that this female writer is, perhaps, endorsing these unnatural unions or even exposing her own latent desires for black men now that one significant step on the road to emancipation has been cleared.[12]

To allay such fears, Edgeworth concedes her implicitly favorable stance on interracial marriages with instructions that Barbauld change a name in the 1810 edition—"for Juba, read Jackson." This act of textual renaming completely erases the interracial union that horrified English gentlemen, appeases their "great delicacies and scruples," and safeguards Edgeworth's reputation as a polite female author. However, the zeal with which the Edgeworths police what, in real terms, amounts to an extremely small episode involving two very minor characters in an especially long three-volume novel, and the significance which they think this small change will have on the characters of the novel, the novelist, and the nation reveal how

---

8. Clara Reeve, *Plans of Education* (London: Hookham and Carpenter, 1792), 90.

9. *Limits of the Human*, 254.

10. Here, I depart from Kathryn Kirkpatrick, who believes interracial marriages were objected to because of anxieties over primogeniture. See "'Gentlemen Have Horrors Upon This Subject,'" 342. I think the primogeniture argument is more effective when it involves the landed and merchant classes as in my discussion of *The Woman of Colour* in Chapter Six of this book. For Juba, the general sense of degeneration is enough to cause alarm.

11. Sarah Scott, *George Ellison*, 139.

12. Alison Harvey comes to a similar conclusion in "West Indian Obeah," 3.

completely out of proportion paternalist fears were concerning both interracial couplings and African freedoms, and also how unified a father and daughter coupling could be in opposing them both.

In the previous chapter, I argued that the staged performances of *Oroonoko* post-1759 provided an opportunity for young English women to visually identify with Imoinda and connect her victimization under paternal tyranny with their own experience of victimization under the Hardwicke Act. My present discussion of Edgeworth's *Belinda* and her letter to Barbauld, however, suggests the opposite—a British woman writer initially promoting and then altering her own progressive stance on a black individual's freedom to marry interracially, and doing so, specifically, to identify with an English paternalism that is first recognized as fearful ("Gentlemen have horrors") and then extremely tyrannical ("For Juba read Jackson") on the "subject." Whether or not Edgeworth personally identified with paternalist fears of national degeneration, her altered *Belinda*, in effect, speaks on behalf of this group by enacting their desire to curtail even a fictional black man's ability to marry freely in England. The textual violence that enables this tyrannical behavior should not be downplayed. By writing Juba's emancipatory story of interracial marriage in England out of existence, Edgeworth's alterations are soft textual weapons, quietly quashing a black man's freedom to love, wed, and reproduce interracially with as much vigor as the "massa" beats out of the black boy's head the "love" he has for "Jill Jenkins" in the first epigram of this chapter, purely because the black boy has articulated his desire to "wed" this white woman. Edgeworth's softer, textual violence speaks to what Tim Watson calls "an instability at the heart of English realism, unable to follow through on its promise of inclusiveness."[13] And it is this "instability" which must be acknowledged in order to understand, and provide a context for, the even more egregious acts of textual violence that underpin Edgeworth's work when she moves out of England to promote fictional interracial couplings in the West Indian colonies—one of which reflects on the amelioration of slavery and markets this as a viable antislavery agenda while minimizing the African woman's horrific experience of slavery that Equiano brings out in the third epigram of this chapter.

I WANT TO explore further examples of Edgeworth's soft textual violence and her interest in interracial couplings by examining how they both influence a text that holds her most pronounced intervention into the political discourse of slavery. In *The Grateful Negro*, Edgeworth pairs the black slave,

---

13. *Caribbean Culture*, 12.

Caesar, with his white master, Mr. Edwards, and she uses this symbolic, nonsexual, interracial coupling to market the appeal of colonial paternalism and to endorse the policy on slavery taken by colonial legislators in the 1798 Amelioration Act. *The Grateful Negro* is a prime illustration of what Tim Watson calls "Creole Realism," that is, "the attempt to narrate the story of the British colonies from the point of view of a planter class defined by their qualities of reasonableness and enterprise."[14]

However, a pointed critique of Edgeworth's "Creole realism" appears when some of *The Grateful Negro*'s intertextual influences are taken into account. The short story was completed within one year of *Belinda*'s initial publication,[15] but four other literary and historical texts have an even greater influence on it. Edgeworth acknowledges two of them—August von Koztebue's *The Negro Slaves* (1796) and Bryan Edwards's *The History, Civil and Commercial, of the British Colonies in the West Indies* (1793)—but elements of the other two—*Oroonoko*, and an anonymously published tale also called "The Grateful Negro" (1800)—appear openly within the text itself but are not explicitly cited by the author. I contend that when Edgeworth chooses to refer to or ignore these literary and historical texts she deliberately undermines the characterization of the African woman, Clara, and her coupling with Caesar because the appeal of their African romance poses the greatest threat to the idealized interracial coupling between Caesar and Mr. Edwards—the coupling that her ameliorative text is designed to privilege. *The Grateful Negro*, then, "operates as an elaborate romance,"[16] as Sharon Murphy has pointed out, but not merely the plantocratic one[17] that Murphy identifies; rather, it is an elaborate competition between the "plantocratic romance" and the African romance—an ideological battle in which Edgeworth commits acts of soft textual violence—acts that I call 'creative defamation'—which deliberately and strategically tip the Romance scales in the plantocrats' favor.

Edgeworth's interest in African and interracial couplings and her acts of creative defamation extend to *The Grateful Negro*'s other black and white female characters—Esther, Hector's wife, and Mrs. Jeffries—who are also designed to bolster the plantocrats' appeal. Collectively, these creatively defamed female representations point out the "instability" at the heart of Edgeworth's Creole Realism: this knowingly skewed promotion of slavery under benevolent paternalism is built upon an extremely dubious ideology if

---

14. Ibid., 17.
15. All subsequent references to this text are parenthetical and are drawn from Maria Edgeworth's *Tales and Novels*, vol. 2, *Popular Tales*.
16. *Maria Edgeworth and Romance* (Dublin: Four Courts Press, 2004), 110.
17. Ibid., 113.

"pro-slavery reformism"[18] can only come about at the expense of the author's deliberate attempts to silence the "horrible instances of cruelty"[19] that she is aware black African women endure under slavery.

My exposure of the infelicity and instability at the heart of *The Grateful Negro* is not simply designed to undermine the ameliorationist tag that George Bouloukos and others have associated with Edgeworth's position on slavery. Having already exposed Edgeworth's willingness to voice and alleviate her father's and other English gentlemen's interracial concerns in her altered *Belinda*, this chapter also foregrounds the concerns of black African women by revealing how *The Grateful Negro* eclipses their interests while voicing those of colonial paternalists. By doing so, *The Grateful Negro* commits a crime that Equiano abhors: it softly and strategically speaks the virtues of benevolent paternalism as "if it were no crime in the whites to rob an innocent African girl of her virtue." As a soft, strategic voice of paternal tyranny, *The Grateful Negro* is not only implicated in maintaining the double standard of violence against African women that Equiano draws attention to, its willful ignorance of the fictional and actual African woman's experience of rape on the plantation—an experience brought out in Behn's *Oroonoko* but magnified in Southerne's—also indicates its involvement in strategically eclipsing Imoinda's force in British literature as a figure capable of articulating this concern.

KATHRYN KIRKPATRICK'S fine job of exploring the intratextual differences between the 1801, 1802, and 1810 editions of *Belinda* have been invaluable in establishing how Edgeworth's position on race changed prior to, and immediately after, the abolition of the British slave trade.[20] And other critics have also made intertextual connections between *The Grateful Negro*, the Edgeworths' Anglo-Irish background, and the history of the 1798 rebellion in Ireland.[21] Along these lines, Edgeworth acknowledges her own debt to intertextuality when she admits to having "adopted—not stolen" (400) ideas from Bryan Edwards's *History of the West Indies* to use in *The Grateful Negro*. Clearly, intertextual readings are useful ways to understand the autho-

---

18. Srinivas Aravamudan describes Edgeworth's position as "within the context of paternalistic and sentimentalist proslavery reformism" in *Obi; or, The History of Three Fingered Jack*, 43.

19. August Von Kotzebue, *The Negro Slaves* (1796), "Dedication."

20. Curiously, Kirkpatrick doesn't actually make this point in "'Gentlemen Have Horrors." In an intertextual move of her own, Kirkpatrick reads *Belinda* using the stock characterization of a Creole garnered from Richard Cumberland's play, *The West Indian* (1771). While this is a perfectly acceptable way of getting at the characterization of Mr. Vincent, it says nothing about Juba. This chapter is, in part, an attempt to excavate the texts that informed both Caesar and Juba.

21. Elizabeth S. Kim's article "Maria Edgeworth's *The Grateful Negro*: A Site for Rewriting Rebellion," *Eighteenth Century Fiction* 16 (2003): 103–26 offers the most recent example of this sort.

rial, political, and racial dynamics at work in *The Grateful Negro*. Because of this, I want to examine more of the immediate yet unheralded intertextual sources that lie within the story itself.[22]

One of them, "The Grateful Negro,"[23] is the first in a collection of short stories titled *Rewards for Attentive Studies; or Stories Moral and Entertaining*, published anonymously in 1800.[24] Appearing two years before Edgeworth's own short story of the same name, the similarity of titles alone suggests that Edgeworth knew it, but its influence on her own text is palpably discerned by the similarities between their plots.[25]

The grateful Negro in the anonymous version begins as a disembodied voice overheard as two English girls, Louisa Dorvile and Charlotte, are walking through an English field on their way to make a social visit to a Miss Benson: "'No money—no friends—no country—no home!' sobbed out a little Negro boy, who was sitting under a hedge by the side of a public road" (5) with "hardly a rag to cover him" (7). "Me *cry* all *day*, me *never laugh*," he tells Louisa, "because me *no friends* here—poor massar dead—and me no get home!" (7). "He absolutely makes me sick" (7), exclaims Charlotte, and she refuses to provide him aid since to do so would be "'to degrade [herself] so much as to think a Negro deserves to be called *my fellow creature*.' 'I cannot help what you *think*,' replied Louisa, 'but I *know* that a Negro is *mine*: and I am persuaded if my mamma knew how unfortunate he was, she would immediately take him under her care'" (8). At this point in the story, the girls reach a symbolic crossroads in their relationship, and while "Charlotte paid a visit of ceremony [to Miss Benson]," "Louisa practiced humanity and benevolence" by returning home and informing her mother of "the African's misfortunes" (9). Mrs. Dorvile

> sent immediately to the captain of the ship in which he had come to England, and finding that his account agreed with the boy's, she engaged him

---

22. Frances R. Botkin's "Questioning the 'Necessary Order of things': Maria Edgeworth's 'The Grateful Negro,' Plantation Slavery and the Abolition of the Slave Trade" briefly discusses many of the intertextual references that I refer to in this chapter but she arrives at a completely different conclusion: "I contend that Edgeworth tells a story that encourages the eradication rather than the preservation of slavery" (206). While I find her recourse to intertextuality extremely apropos for understanding this text, I have found nothing in Edgeworth's intertextual references to support such a strong antislavery position. *Discourses of Slavery and Abolition*, ed. Brycchan Carey, Markman Ellis, and Sara Salih (Hampshire and New York: Palgrave, 2004), 194–208.

23. This appears to be an exciting new find since none of the critics I have read refer to this seminal story. For the sake of clarity, I will refer to this anonymous text as "The Grateful Negro" and to Edgeworth's version as *The Grateful Negro*.

24. (London: Cundee, 1800). All subsequent page numbers are in parentheses.

25. George Boulokos's *The Grateful Slave* (Cambridge: Cambridge University Press, 2008) offers the best and most extensive account of this tradition of grateful Africans.

to wait upon Louisa, and herself. In this situation he behaved with the greatest fidelity, and remained in the family many years; and was as much admired for the rectitude of his principles, as for the grateful feelings of his heart. (9–10)

This grateful Negro has an opportunity to pay his debt of gratitude. "One evening as Louisa was walking in a little paddock that adjoined the house," she is accosted by "a mad dog" (10):

[Louisa's] screams roused the Negro from his work. Like lightning he flew to her assistance, and just as the animal had caught hold of her gown, struck him with a rake he had in his hand, and repeated the blows, until he stretched him dead at her feet. "Oh, my deliverer," said the agitated Louisa, "I owe you more than I can ever pay!" "No, missee, no you owe me not at all; but me owe you for every bliss of life."

"The Grateful Negro" seems, itself, to be a regendered iteration of "the grateful black" (332) episode in Thomas Day's *Sandford and Merton* (1783).[26] The second volume of that novel ends with this "poor half-naked black" (329) humbly imploring the charity of the little gentry with Master Merton:

He had served, he told them, on board an English vessel, and even shewed them the scars of several wounds he had received; but now he was discharged, and without friends, without assistance, he could scarcely find food to support his wretched life, or clothes to cover him from the wintry wind. Some of the young gentry, who from a bad education had been little taught to feel or pity the distress of others, were base enough to attempt to jest upon his dusky colour and foreign accent; but . . . the unfortunate black approached the place where Harry stood, holding out the tattered remains of his hat and imploring charity. Harry had not much to give, but he took six-pence out of his pocket, which was all his riches, and gave it with the kindest look of compassion; saying, Here, poor man, this is all I have; if I had more, it should be at your service. He had no time to add more, for at that instant, three fierce dogs rushed upon [a] bull at once, and by their joint attacks rendered him almost mad. (329–30)

Harry is accosted by the enraged bull:

---

26. *The History of Sandford and Merton*, vol. 2 (Dublin: Byrne, 1787).

But, in that instant, the grateful black rushed on like lightening to assist him, and assailing the bull with a weighty stick which he held in his hand, compelled him to turn his rage upon a new object. The bull indeed attacked him with all the impetuosity of revenge, but the black jumped nimbly aside and eluded his fury. Not contented with this, he wheeled round his fierce antagonist, and seizing him by the tail, began to batter his sides with an unexpected storm of blows. In vain did the enraged animal bellow and writhe himself about in all the convulsions of madness; his intrepid foe, without ever quitting his hold, suffered himself to be dragged about the field, still continuing his discipline, till the creature was almost spent with the fatigue of his own violent agitations. (332)

Since Edgeworth referred to Day's *Dying Negro* in *Belinda* and her father knew him personally, there is every reason to believe that she was aware of this "grateful black" incident in *Sandford and Merton*.[27] Even if she was not, the more than coincidental repetition of "The Grateful Negro" title indicates that she knew the anonymous tale, and was, thus, indirectly channeling Day's episode by evoking it.

These 'grateful Negro' texts appear to impart to young readers the simple precept one good turn deserves another. But they use racialized characters to strategically market and politicize this message for adult readers. The initial meetings between these Negroes and their patrons occur while the latter are engaged in polite and impolite pleasures far removed from pecuniary benevolence (visiting a friend, bull baiting). The black male interrupts these pleasures, offering an instant opportunity to test the white patron's sensibility, morality, and benevolence. The male's black skin color should, itself, be an instant appeal to the white patron's pity because of its connection to slavery; but his tattered clothing and tale of abandonment in England, not to mention the deliberate withholding of his name, are all indications that these stories seek to present representative African males as the collective embodiment of the black poor who were a significant presence in England, particularly on the streets of London. With such an immediately recognizable object of pity before them, the adult reader is expected to partake of, and affirm, the white patron's desire to act immediately in each black man's favor. In turn, the grateful Negroes repay their debts to their benevolent patrons with the same immediacy by putting their lives on the line and averting the patrons' deaths from the random, impetuous violence that

---

27. While not referring to this text specifically, Marilyn Butler does refer to Edgeworth's "many borrowings from Day," a statement that leads me to believe that The Grateful Negro moniker may be another such. "Edgeworth's Stern Father: Escaping Thomas Day, 1795–1801," in *Tradition in Transition* (Oxford: Clarendon, 1996), 87.

occurs in nature. Each story spends time detailing how swiftly ("like lightening") each grateful Negro both offers assistance and completely extirpates the problem of the mad dog and the enraged bull in order to distinguish the black men's well-directed energies toward deserving fellow humans from the unregulated ones of beasts who do indiscriminate harm. The unnamed Negro's capacity to feel so intently for the existence of a fellow creature who also happens to be a kind patron is the quality that is meant to distinguish all blacks from the animalistic stigmas that supporters of the institution of slavery try to impose on them. Here, the Negroes' extreme acts of gratitude are the direct results of the extreme kindnesses that Harry and Louisa dispense, and this dynamic reciprocity is what the texts want to encourage in young and old white readers, bringing them to consider blacks as "fellow creatures" separated from their patrons only by rank not by species.

Thus, for English adults, these stories are making the case that poor black males must be involved in the dynamic reciprocity on which the harmony of the British domestic class system depends. Because they take this stance, these stories are also making a profound intervention into British domestic policy about the black poor in England. When Harry invites his "grateful black" to go home with him, and Louisa acknowledges her "grateful negro" as a "fellow creature" who is employed to wait on the Dorvile women, these texts are attempting to do more than just domesticate Africans. Giving a poor black male a home and employment in England can be read as a political act of nonsexual, interracial coupling that flies in the face of the policy and practice that the English administration took toward the black poor in the period leading up to, and after, the fiasco of the Sierra Leone colonial expedition. As English efforts continued to both establish the colony and get rid of a sight painted by the Sierra Leone report of "the streets of London swarming with a number of Blacks in the most distressed situation, who had no prospect of subsisting in this country but by depredations on the public, or by common charity,"[28] the English government was intent on rounding up the black poor, and cajoling them, by force or bribery, to board the ship bound for the African colony. By finding a domestic home for the black men in *Sandford and Merton* and "The Grateful Negro," the authors of these texts are legitimizing the Africans' right to receive financial assistance to remain on English shores, a move that presents domestic inclusion as an alternative to an English practice and policy of deliberate removal. These 'grateful Negro' stories voice the sentimental hopes and dreams of an enlightened English society following through on its "promise of inclusiveness." More-

---

28. *Substance of the Report of the Court of Directors of the Sierra Leone Company* (London: Philips, 1792), 2.

over, because the 'grateful Negroes' that Harry and Louisa help are male, their legitimized presence offers a tacit reminder of the freedoms that Richard Edgeworth and Lord A— fear black men will receive in England.

IN HER *Grateful Negro,* Edgeworth also presents and politicizes the simple "one good turn" precept in a racialized Jamaican plot wherein a Negro slave, Caesar, avoids being sold away from his lover, Clara, by a benevolent master, Mr. Edwards, who buys the couple from their owner, Mr. Jeffries. For this act of kindness, Caesar repays Mr. Edwards by notifying him of a murderous slave rebellion led by Hector, another of Jeffries's slaves. But where interracial coupling in the earlier texts is a nonsexual attempt to forge a connection between black and white people in England who will, together, reproduce a dynamically reciprocal and mutually supportive society dedicated to freedom, interracial coupling in *The Grateful Negro* is read as part of a political allegory about creating a society dedicated to colonial slavery in a text meant for "different ages, sexes and situations in life" (preface to *Popular Tales*). To market her support for this society, Edgeworth designs two types of interracial couplings for her adult readers to consider—one rational, the other emotional.

Edgeworth's sources for "the ruling passion of Hector," a belligerent slave who "would sacrifice his life to extirpate an enemy" (406), come from the illustrations of the mad dog and the enraged bull that kill indiscriminately in the earlier 'grateful Negro' stories. Hector's animalistic compulsion to satiate his passions even at the expense of his own life shows a self-centeredness that is also present in his master, Mr. Jeffries, a character whose "thoughtless and extravagant temper" (399) almost leads to the sale of his most productive slave, Caesar, in order to cover his debts. Hector and Mr. Jeffries are connected by the fact that the force of their intemperate emotions leads to the same end: extreme violence and destruction on the plantation. Jeffries's financial extravagance is sustained by the work of slaves like Hector who are routinely beaten by the overseer, Durant; and Hector's emotional intemperance against such conditions leads to a rebellion and murderous rampage against whites like Jeffries. In comparison to the simple precept that the earlier 'grateful Negro' stories politicized, Jeffries and Hector offer indications that no good emotional turns by the master produce no good emotional returns from the slave, and the violence, disharmony, and destruction that they collectively reproduce in Jamaica indicate that this nonsexual, interracial coupling of colonial intemperance is a dynamic failure of reciprocity.

The contrast to this all-feeling, unthinking interracial coupling comes from Caesar and Mr. Edwards and their reasonable approach to slavery.

Unlike the foundational 'grateful Negro' texts where pecuniary assistance was immediately provided to the African, Mr. Edwards does not take as instant a reaction to the distressing sight of Caesar and Clara's separation by sale. We are told, "[he] was moved by [Caesar and Clara's] entreaties, but he left them without declaring his intentions [to buy them both]" (402), and he only does so after he has discussed their situation with Mr. Jeffries. Similarly, Caesar's decision to act on his new master's behalf and reveal Hector's plan to kill whites during the rebellion occurs only after three separate deliberations concerning his allegiance to Hector, his Koromantyn tribe, and Clara. Thus, well-reasoned acts by the master produce well-reasoned responses from the slave that take into account the best interests of the whole Jamaican society.

By aligning Hector's animalistic passion with Jeffries's equally destructive indifference, and contrasting these negative examples of emotion with Caesar's and Mr. Edwards's abilities to temper their emotional reactions to slavery with reason, Edgeworth shows that her *Grateful Negro* isn't interested in using nonsexual, interracial coupling to market a message about the collective humanity of blacks and whites as detected in her literary forebears. Instead, she wants her readers to develop a preference for, and recognize the legitimacy of, reasonable acts performed by black and white men from unreasoned and emotionally self-centered ones performed by men of the same colors. The former coupling produces the dynamic reciprocity that is necessary for collective societal happiness, while the latter does not.

The pointed historical names that Edgeworth gives to these examples of gratitude, revenge, thoughtlessness, and benevolence appear to reinforce her desire to market the appeal and legitimacy of a certain type of male leadership. The name 'Jeffries' evokes the memory of George Jeffreys, a figure of injustice long connected to, and reviled for his association with, rebellion. In *The History of England from the Revolution to the Present Time,* Catherine Macaulay admonishes "the execrable Jeffries" as a "detestable citizen,"[29] after Smollett had already called him "inhuman" in his own *Complete History of England.*[30] The reasons for such enmity arise from Jeffreys's behavior after the Monmouth Rebellion in 1685 when, as Lord Chancellor, his impartiality as a judge was put in doubt after he personally organized the executions of hundreds during the Bloody Assizes. This illegitimate paternalist, thoughtless to anyone else's advancement but his own, is emotionally paired with the rebellious slave, 'Hector,' whose name refers to the greatest Trojan warrior prince. Like his namesake, who donned Achilles' armor and thought himself indestructible, Edgeworth's Hector uses obeah as a means to both protect

---

29. Vol. 2 (Bath: Cruttwell, 1778), 11–12.
30. Vol. 3 (London: Rivington and Fletcher, 1762), 507.

himself and enable his destruction of his white enemies. However, Hector's downfall comes about when obeah, like Achilles' armor, is exposed as flawed. Thus, emotional overconfidence and invincibility affect the leadership styles of these historical figures. This is not the case for the most recent historical figure Edgeworth evokes. As many critics have already observed, 'Edwards' is Edgeworth's open homage to Bryan Edwards, who died in 1800 but had been an important part of the colonial assembly in Jamaica, the administration charged to judge the rules and practices of the country. The evocation of his name only two years after his death might be Edgeworth's attempts to keep his ideas about amelioration alive. He is paired with 'Caesar,' a name that recalls the great military tactician and political dictator who played a critical role in transforming the Roman Republic into the Roman Empire.

These historical names reinforce the didacticism of Edgeworth's political allegory. For adult readers, *The Grateful Negro* is an exercise in distinguishing between the dynamic reciprocity of leaders recognized for their improvements to society from the dynamic disparity of leaders who, though arguably great, have flaws in their abilities to lead. Under the right black and white leadership, Jamaican society will be preparing itself for the experience of freedom that Britons of all colors ostensibly enjoy in England. This is how "*The Grateful Negro*" markets the amelioration of slavery, or what Aravamudan calls "proslavery reformism," as a legitimate *antislavery* position:[31] it is against slavery as it is currently practiced, but instead of emancipating slaves, the text offers reasonable leadership as the immediate solution to problems of slavery experienced by slaves.

The Grateful Negro's positions on amelioration and colonial leadership make for an interesting contrast with the Leeward Islands Amelioration Act of 1798. Its official title—"An Act more effectually to provide for the support, and to extend certain regulations for the protection of slaves . . . "—articulates its humanitarian goals very clearly. Under it, slaves had specific entitlements to clothes, food, and even an elementary education, and they were to be financially compensated for work. The act also advocated for slaves' moral improvement by promoting marriage, but it prohibited them from observing the Christian marriage ceremony.[32]

Despite articulating these goals, however, the colonial leaders who cre-

---

31. In 1802, the amelioration of slavery in the colonies would be considered a valid antislavery position, since early abolitionist societies such as the *Society for the Abolition of the Slave Trade* (1787) were committed to the abolition of the trade and would have considered amelioration part of a long-term goal.

32. For more on the Amelioration Act of 1798 see David Barry Gaspar, "Ameliorating Slavery. The Leeward Islands Slave Act of 1798," chapter 13 in *The Lesser Antilles in the Age of European Expansion* (Gainesville: University Press of Florida, 1996); and Cecilia Green, "A Civil Inconvenience'?" 22.

ated the Amelioration Act appear to have been inspired more by political maneuvering than by humanitarian aid. Prompted by "forced and abrupt" efforts in England to abolish the slave trade, members of the General Council and Assembly of the Leeward Islands appear to have acted out of the fear that the English metropole was taking control of the situation, and their efforts in the Amelioration Act were geared toward taking that control back to their advantage. In his wonderfully precise work on the act, David Barry Gaspar reveals that this advantage was "to modify or improve the conditions under which slaves lived in order to promote natural increase and reduce reliance on the slave trade." The reproduction of slaves by "natural increase" "emerged as the overriding concern of the General Council and Assembly,"[33] and "managerial efforts shifted slowly from 'buying' to 'breeding' as a labour supply strategy."[34] Concerns about natural reproduction were timely since Hilary Beckles and Trevor Burnard both show infant mortality rates were high and birth rates low throughout the century.[35] Colonial legislators couched their policy as one that would improve the future lives of slaves who would then improve their own lives through the reproduction of family units, thereby providing a prime illustration of the dynamic reciprocity demonstrated in "The Grateful Negro" and *Sandford and Merton* that a society needs to thrive. Black African women were, implicitly, the backbone of this policy since it was only through their successful reproductive efforts that this ameliorative society could succeed.

Although "natural increase" appears to be the hallmark of ameliorative efforts undertaken by colonial leaders in the 1798 act, *The Grateful Negro* shows no interest in it when marketing its own ameliorative position. Biological pregnancy and motherhood are remarkably absent in the depictions of Esther, Clara, Hector's Wife, and Mrs. Jeffries.[36] Instead, the text articulates and markets as natural the reproductive appeal of a harmonious society dedicated to slavery under black and white male leadership. This difference between the reproductive positioning of the Amelioration Act and *The Grateful Negro* opens up an important question about Edgeworth's text: if it is arguing that Jamaica's stability, continued improvement—indeed its very existence—depends, exclusively, on the reproductive efforts of a reasonable, and dynamically reciprocal, interracial coupling of black and white male leaders rather than the efforts of black women, what role does the black

---

33. Gaspar, "Ameliorating Slavery," 244.
34. Hilary Beckles, *Centering Woman* (Kingston: Ian Rand, 1999), 159.
35. Trevor Burnard, *Mastery, Tyranny, and Desire* (Chapel Hill: University of North Carolina Press, 2004), 220–27; Beckles, *Centering Woman*, 159.
36. A slave boy is mentioned in the text, but he is not biologically connected to any of the named characters, his father being one of the anonymous slaves beaten by Jeffries's overseer, Durant.

African woman play in the ameliorative slave society that Edgeworth imagines and markets in her text?

RATHER THAN a biologically reproductive role within *The Grateful Negro*, the African woman plays an ideological one that begins to take shape when we examine two of Edgeworth's important literary and editorial forebears. According to Sharon Murphy, Edgeworth's "writing is hugely influenced by the ideological formulations, or cultural romances, with which the late-eighteenth-and-early-nineteenth century British nation tried to (re)negotiate its relationship to slavery,"[37] and Murphy turns to Behn's *Oroonoko* as a structural source for Edgeworth's reading of the master–slave relationship. Given its long history and literary notoriety as one of the first modern novels and one of the most popular plays ever in British literary history, *Oroonoko* is, undoubtedly, the most representative text about African characters and slavery in the eighteenth-century British canon. So Murphy is right to choose it as a foundation for Edgeworth's thoughts on slavery. Edgeworth must have known both the drama and novel versions of this story, but she refers explicitly to Behn's version in *The Grateful Negro* when she names her Koromantyn hero 'Caesar,' a pointed reference to Behn's 'Coramantien' hero, Oroonoko, whose name changes to 'Caesar' in Surinam.

A 1777 edition of Behn's *Oroonoko* edited by Mrs. Griffith leads me to further contend that Edgeworth was not only well acquainted with Behn's novella but that she also sought to improve upon this female author's ideological and fictional response to the problem of slavery. Griffith's edition of *Oroonoko* includes a preamble on Oroonoko's character in which she states: "yet I should hope, for the honour of human nature in general, and of our countrymen in particular, that the author has a good deal exaggerated the cruelties which she reports to have been exercised upon the gallant Moor who is the subject of the piece."[38] This "hope" sounds remarkably similar to Edgeworth's own in the first footnote of *The Grateful Negro* in which she, first, praises August Von Kotzebue's *The Negro Slaves* as a "fine drama" and then questions its credibility with this comment: "It is hoped that such horrible instances of cruelty are not now to be found in nature" (399). Given that another edition of Griffith's *Oroonoko* appears in 1800,[39] Edgeworth might well have known it. Indeed, the echo of Griffith's "hope"

---

37. *Maria Edgeworth and Romance*, 110.
38. *A collection of novels, selected and revised by Mrs. Griffith*, vol. 1 (London: Kearsly, 1777), 210.
39. *English Nights Entertainments. The History of Oroonoko; or, the Royal Slave. Written originally by Mrs. Behn, and revised by Mrs. Griffiths* (London: Maiden, 1800).

in Edgeworth's footnote implies that the younger female writer might well have been inspired by Griffith's editorial license to expurgate the "horrible instances of cruelty" in *Oroonoko,* and used this as a model for *The Grateful Negro* and its attempt to rewrite the "horrible instances of cruelty" Edgeworth witnessed in *The Negro Slaves* (a drama which is written in the *Oroonoko* tradition).

The "hope," then, of marketing a British colonial society that is less barbarous at present than in the past is the emotion by which Griffith and Edgeworth convince themselves of the propriety of editing scenes of violence in slave literature. With this license, Griffith tones down the massacre of Oroonoko at the end of the novella, and makes no mention of his "members" being cut off first. Edgeworth's acts of censorship involve improving upon the characterization of Behn's hero by having her own Caesar embody all the virtues that were invested in Behn's original, except two: the desire for revenge and rebellion against colonial leaders. As I have already shown, these emotional qualities are reserved for Caesar's tribesman, Hector. By demonstrating a Koromantyn's ability to shirk off emotional temptations to commit violence in Jamaica, and instead, commit to a reasonable course of action on slavery, Edgeworth's Caesar transforms into what Edward Long would call a "Creole Black"—a de-Africanized African in the colonies.

Because Edgeworth makes such obvious attempts to present her Caesar as an improvement upon Behn's, it seems natural to assume that Caesar's betrothed, Clara, is a refined reinterpretation of Behn's Imoinda. Initially, it appears that these African women share many of the same fundamental characteristics. Clara is "a young and beautiful female negro" (401), an image that has parallels with Imoinda's youthful representation as a "beautiful *Black Venus*" (14). The Latinate origins of Clara's name connote words like 'famous,' 'brilliant,' 'clear,' 'bright,' and 'luminous'—words that could equally apply to Imoinda's dazzling celebrity in the African King's court, where "nothing else was talked of, no other sound was heard in every corner where there were whisperers, but Imoinda! Imoinda!" (15). The implied celebrity of these women, however, seems to belie their significance in each text. They are not mentioned in either title—*The Grateful Negro*'s pointed gesture to only one admirable male figure—Caesar—reminding us of Behn's title and its exclusive focus on Oroonoko. Moreover, the bodies of each text contain only fleeting glimpses of these African women. Behn's most descriptive comment about Imoinda says more about her bloodline than her body: she is "delicately Cut and Rac'd all over the fore-part of . . . [her body] . . . that it looks as if it were Japan'd" (40), a process that announces Imoinda's noble birth among the Coramantien tribe, and in turn, her distinction from ordinary female slaves in Surinam. For her heroine, Edgeworth provides her own distinguishing detail. We are told, "Clara was an Eboe" (404) (Igbo in modern parlance), an African from Benin.⁴⁰

If, as I have been arguing, Edgeworth not only knew Behn's *Oroonoko* but also improved upon its ideological representations of African male heroism, then this brief evocation of Clara's Eboe-ness is jarring. What does it mean that Clara is "an Eboe" and Caesar is not? Why does Edgeworth choose to construct a heroine from the sinews of *Oroonoko* only to disassociate her from the impression that "Koromantyns are frank, fearless, martial, and heroic" (404)—qualities that Imoinda had embodied for over one hundred years? Since her efforts on Caesar's part are clearly designed to improve upon Behn's portrayal of Oroonoko, is Clara's Eboe identity an improvement of Behn's Imoinda, or not?

IN CLARA, Edgeworth puts her heroine's tribal identity to a different ideological use than her hero's. To unearth these ideological ends we must turn to the authoritative text about Africans in the West Indies from which she "adopted" many of her ideas. Bryan Edwards's descriptions of Koromantyns in his *History* provided Edgeworth with a source for the admirable traits of her hero,⁴¹ but his description of "Eboes" is far less complimentary. He states that Eboes

> In complexion . . . are much yellower than the Gold Coast and Whidah negroes; but it is a sickly hue, and their eyes appear as if suffused with bile, even when they are in perfect health. I cannot help observing too, that the conformation of the face, in a great majority of them, very much resembles that of a baboon. I believe indeed there is, in most of the nations of Africa, a greater elongation of the lower jaw, than among people of Europe; but this distinction I think is more visible among the Eboes, than in any other Africans.⁴²

---

40. Here, Edgeworth departs radically from Behn's Imoinda, who we assume is from Coramantien since her father fought as a subject of Oroonoko's grandfather's court.

41. Edwards distinguishes "the Koromantyn, or Gold coast negroes, from all others, [for their] firmness both of body and mind; a ferociousness of disposition; but withal, activity, courage, and a stubbornness, or what an ancient Roman would have deemed an elevation of soul, which prompts them to enterprises of difficulty and danger." *The History, Civil and Commercial, of the British Colonies in the West Indies*, vol. 2 (London: Stockdale, 1793), 63.

42. Ibid., 73–74. To his credit, Edwards does add this qualifier to this description: "I mean not however to draw any conclusion of natural inferiority in these people to the rest of the human race, from a circumstance which perhaps is purely accidental, and no more to be considered as a proof of degradation, than the red hair and high cheek bones of the natives of the north of Europe," 74.

Olaudah Equiano, himself an Eboe, had already refuted these pejorative descriptions of his people in his *Interesting Narrative* (1789), published four years before Edwards's *History:*

> Deformity is indeed unknown amongst us, I mean that of shape. Numbers of the natives of Eboe, now in London, might be brought in support of this assertion; for, in regard to complexion, ideas of beauty are wholly relative.... Our women too were, in my eyes at least, uncommonly graceful, alert, and modest to a degree of bashfulness; nor do I remember to have ever heard of an instance of incontinence amongst them before marriage.[43]

Though Edgeworth does not cite Equiano's text as a source, her description of the "young and beautiful" Clara is similar in its intent to redeem the virulence of what Equiano implies are widely dispersed reports of the Eboes' physical inferiority. But the brief, nominal way that Clara's beauty is evoked—without any of Equiano's passionate vindication or Behn's pointed parallels (Imoinda as "the beautiful *Black Venus*")—indicates that Edgeworth's aim is not to cement her black heroine's beauty for her readers as these writers have done. Rather, she creates the spectacle of a "yellower" Eboe Clara set against a darker "Gold Coast" Caesar—impressions which, in skin color, present this couple as an intertribal version of the interracial and intratribal Africans seen in dramatic and novel versions of *Oroonoko*. I have already pointed out how Caesar is an improved and appealing Oroonoko; yet, the impression that Clara's "yellower" Eboe complexion has a "sickly hue" implies that Eboe beauty is much less appealing than Behn's beautiful black, and Southerne's beautiful white, Coramantien beauties. This impression of Eboe inferiority is calculated and deliberate.

I want to contend that Edgeworth is being strategic about constructing Clara as a reflection of, yet a departure from, the ideal African heroine, Imoinda, especially Behn's version of this character. For instance, once Imoinda arrives in Surinam, Janet Todd reveals that the Latinate foundations of her new name, 'Clemene,' connote gentleness.[44] In Jamaica, Clara displays the 'Clemene' temperament: Edgeworth writes that "Eboes are soft, languishing, and timid" (404). However, "constitutional timidity" is "The great objection to the Eboes as slaves," Bryan Edwards reports, since "They require... the gentlest and mildest treatment to reconcile them to their

---

43. Equiano, *Interesting Narrative* (Norwich, 1794), 14–15. This narrative was first published in 1789.

44. In her edition of *Oroonoko* (London: Penguin, 2003), Todd writes, "The name is possibly derived from the Latin *Clementia*, meaning 'clemency' or 'gentleness'" (87, note 73).

situation."[45] Since gentleness is Clara's overriding—indeed, from Edwards's perspective, her most dominant—characteristic under slavery, it offers a way to transform her into a black Creole slave who poses no physical threat to the society. In Surinam, Behn's Imoinda is the complete opposite in this respect. Armed with her bow and poisoned arrows, Imoinda represents an active threat to both the Deputy Governor and the institution of slavery when she fires this weapon and almost kills him. Moreover, the fact that the name 'Clemene' is hardly used in the Surinam section of Behn's text leads Todd to conclude that Imoinda resists being assimilated to European culture in a way that Behn's 'Caesar' does not.[46] By making Clara an Eboe whose temperament adheres to the gentle spirit of the creolized black woman but eschews the active spirit of rebellion, aggression, and resistance that formed an important part of Imoinda's original identity, Edgeworth constructs Clara as a reflection of, yet a departure from, the idealized temperament of the popular African heroine.

Edgeworth continues to differentiate Clara from Imoinda by drawing directly from the tone that Edwards's *History* conveys toward Eboe religious practices. He writes: "Of the religious opinions and modes of worship of the Eboes, we know but little; except that . . . they pay adoration to certain reptiles, of which the guana (a species of lizard) is in the highest estimation" (282). Edwards's attention to the "little" that is known about Eboe religion implies that ridicule should be shown to all Eboes absurd enough to pay "adoration" and "the highest estimation" to "a species of lizard." Similarly, Edgeworth decries religious superstition in *The Grateful Negro,* as seen in the disparaging tone with which she describes "The enlightened inhabitants of Europe" smiling "at the superstitious credulity of the negroes, who regard those ignorant beings called *Obeah* people with the most profound respect and dread" (403). Clara is one of these "superstitious . . . negroes" who thoroughly believes in the power of the obeah woman, Esther. For paying such homage, Edgeworth involves Clara in the ridicule that Edwards implies should be shown to all such superstitious Eboes. She ridicules this Eboe woman at a time where Equiano has already made suggestive religious parallels "between the Eboan Africans and the modern Jews"[47] and without any attempt to underscore her potential civilization through religious conversion as Behn's narrator does to Imoinda, entertaining her with "Stories of Nuns . . . endeavouring to bring her to the knowledge of the true God" (41).

---

45. *History*, vol. 2, 74.
46. *Oroonoko*, ed. Todd, 87.
47. *Interesting Narrative*, 27 and 20–25. Also see Peter J. Kitson's discussion of Equiano, Eboes, and Jews in *Romantic Literature, Race, and Colonial Encounter* (Hampshire: Palgrave, 2007), 117–18.

Edwards points out another Eboe trait that connects yet distinguishes Clara from Imoinda when he reveals that the Eboes' "despondency of mind [is] so great as to occasion them very frequently to seek, in a voluntary death, a refuge from their own melancholy reflections."[48] This propensity for depression and suicide brings to mind Trefry's description of Clemene as she "languish'd" (38) for Oroonoko in Surinam as well as Imoinda's own honor killing where she is "faster pleading for death than [Oroonoko] was to propose it" (60). Because it is an Eboe propensity, depression and suicide also provides a new understanding of what Clara means when she asserts that she will "Never! Never" (407) be the wife of anyone but Caesar: if they are separated, she'll kill herself. But whereas Imoinda's depression and suicide are both badges of African female honor, Clara's has an inauspicious claim to fame that Edwards draws attention to:

> The depression of spirits which these people seem to be under, on their first arrival in the West Indies, gives them an air of softness and submission.... Nevertheless, the Eboes are in fact more truly savage than any nation of the Gold coast, inasmuch as many tribes among them ... have been, without doubt, accustomed to the shocking practice of feeding on human flesh.[49]

From this historical understanding, Clara's "soft, languishing, and timid" air is due to a "depression of spirits" about being in Jamaica, but it should not be mistaken for female sensitivity because beneath it lies the cannibalistic savagery that is endemic to Clara's tribe.

Thus, Edgeworth uses Clara's Eboe-ness—her "air of softness and submission"—to form, in Edwards's words, "a striking contrast to the frank and fearless temper of the Koromantyn negroes."[50] Within this contrast, Clara embodies none of the exemplary reason and virtue displayed by her Koromantyn partner, none of the heroism associated with the Coramantien, Imoinda, and many of the perceived Eboe vices documented in Edwards's

---

48. *History,* vol. 2, 74. William Beckford confirms Edwards's point when he writes: "The Eboe negroes are particularly addicted to suicide, and a very trifling anticipation of misery will make them rush, almost by families at once into eternity." *Remarks upon the situation of negroes in Jamaica* (London: Egerton, 1788), 23.

49. Edwards is at great pains to attest to the veracity of this point, claiming, "This circumstance I have had attested beyond the possibility of dispute, by an intelligent trust-worthy domestic of the Ebo nation, who acknowledged to me, though with evident shame and reluctance (having lived many years among whites), that he had himself, in his youth, frequently regaled on this horrid banquet." *History,* vol. 2, 75.

50. Ibid. In *Practical Education,* the Edgeworths use this exact quote to describe Africans who have not been inured to slavery. I believe that Caesar is Edgeworth's attempt to create a creolized Negro who can also develop a "frank and fearless temper" while being inured to the slave institution (212).

History. As a fully realized 'Clemene'—a passive African Creole who, in temperament and character, is also the complete opposite of her Koromantyn lover—Edgeworth achieves a strategic act of refinement in her construction of the African heroine in *The Grateful Negro:* the 'creative defamation' of Clara's role *as* heroine.

I may be the first to use such a term in relation to Edgeworth but I am not the first to accuse her of this kind of strategic prejudice leveled at a particular type of fictional character. In a letter dated August 7, 1815, Edgeworth's contemporary Rachel Mordecai genteelly compliments "the good sense and candor of Miss Edgeworth," but nonetheless, proceeds to chide the author about her fictional representations of Jews:

> How can it be that she, who on all other subjects shows such justice and liberality, should on one alone appear biased by prejudice: should even instill that prejudice into the minds of youth! Can my allusion be mistaken? It is to the species of character which whenever a Jew is introduced is invariably attached to him. Can it be believed that this race of men are by nature mean, avaricious, and unprincipled? Forbid it, mercy.[51]

Although Julie Nash has written that Edgeworth "had a number of prejudices"[52] common to her class, Susan Manly locates the specific nexus of Mordecai's critique "in the anti-Jewish stereotypes deployed in stories meant for children."[53] Mordecai is aghast at the way in which Edgeworth connects the "nature" of Jewish men with all villainy, thereby denying the fact that Jewish men are actually "in most instances liberally educated, many following the honourable professions of the Law, and Physick, with credit and ability, and associating with the best society our country affords."[54] In her American community Mordecai views Jewish men as societal heroes, and she is affronted by Edgeworth's creative efforts to defame them in didactic tales that confirm the prejudices of Edgeworth's class and nation, and reproduce these prejudices as justifiable modes of behavior for minors to believe and be influenced by. Mordecai's gentle critique has a creative effect. *Harrington* (1817) is Edgeworth's adult response to the charge of prejudice in tales for children, and her attempt to atone for her textual bias against Jews.

---

51. "From Rachel Mordecai's First Letter, 7 August 1815," "Appendix A" in *Harrington*, ed. Susan Manly (Peterborough: Broadview, 2004), 298.
52. Julie Nash, "Standing in Distress Between Tragedy and Comedy: Servants in Maria Edgeworth's *Belinda*," *New Essays on Maria Edgeworth*, 161.
53. *Harrington*, 8.
54. Ibid., "Appendix A," 298.

In *The Grateful Negro,* Edgeworth encourages readings of her African hero and heroine within the realm of the *Oroonoko* legend; but she, deliberately, moves Clara away from the appealing role of heroism that Imoinda had evoked for over a century in order to disparage a particular type of colonial African. In Behn's *Oroonoko,* Imoinda's African-ness is indisputably appealing, dynamic and heroic in Surinam. She is Oroonoko's equal: the "beautiful *Black Venus* to . . . young *Mars*" (14)—the woman warrior who, with the flash of an eye, conquers the hearts of men, black and white, young and old, and casts the most valiant blows against slavery when she wounds the Deputy Governor with her bow and arrow, and willingly accepts her own death. In Clara, however, African-ness is astoundingly unthreatening, horribly savage, and superstitiously irrational—in all, completely unheroic. And this impression is not only established in relation to the Coramantien, Imoinda.

In Edgeworth's text there are at least two types of Africans in Jamaica, and they are ideologically distinct. Clara's Eboe-ness with its attachments to superstition, savagery, and passivity corresponds to static African primitivism—one that confirms Edwards's belief that "West Indian Eboes . . . in general . . . appear to be the lowest and most wretched of all the nations of Africa."[55] Caesar's Koromantyn identity with its attachment to reason and commitment to nonviolence represents the dynamic potential that Edward Long identifies when he asserts: "Creole Blacks differ much from the Africans, not only in manner, but in beauty of shape, feature, and complexion. They hold the Africans in the utmost contempt . . . but value themselves on their own pedigree, which is reckoned the more honourable, the further it removes from an African, or transmarine ancestor."[56] By creatively defaming Clara's African-ness and establishing Caesar as an African figure of black Creole refinement, Edgeworth reinforces division in this African romance and identifies this couple as dynamically disparate.

THE GRATEFUL NEGRO reinforces the primacy and the appeal of the "plantocratic romance" not only by contrasting it with a dynamically disparate African romance; Edgeworth also uses the discourse of marriage to tip the scales in the black and white male Creoles' favor during three distinct textual moments.

In the first, Clara embodies the ideal of fidelity with zeal. At the beginning of the text, Durant tells Mr. Edwards, "'They [Caesar and Clara] were

---

55. *History,* vol. 2, 73.
56. *History of Jamaica,* vol. 2, 410.

to be married; but we'll find Clara another husband . . . and she'll get the better of her grief, you know, sir, as I tell her, in time.'" "'Never! Never!'" (401) an incensed Clara exclaims, indicating her steadfast fidelity to Caesar with the same enthusiasm that Ada expressed in Chapter One.[57] Clara's unyielding attachment is, ostensibly, a refutation of Edwards's assertion that Negroes have "an almost promiscuous intercourse with the other sex; or at least in temporary connection, which they form without ceremony, and dissolve without reluctance."[58]

However, the "plantocratic romance" trumps the African one by the power of its fidelity. Although Mr. Edwards "Willingly paid several dollars more than the market price for the two slaves" (404), appearing to endorse their fidelity with hard cash, Edgeworth makes it clear that he buys them for practical rather than sentimental purposes. He "had often admired [Caesar's] industry" (401), and when he

> took his new slaves home with him, desired Bayley, his overseer, to mark out a provision-ground for Caesar, and to give him a cottage. . . .
>
> "Now, my good friend," said he to Caesar, "You may work for yourself, without fear that what you earn may be taken from you; or that you should ever be sold to pay your master's debts."

In other words, if Caesar vows to work hard on Mr. Edwards's plantation, Mr. Edwards vows to ensure that Caesar can provide for himself and not be sold away from the woman he loves. Given this dynamic exchange of vows, Clara's expression of fidelity ("Never! Never!") is sentimentally meaningless since it is vow based only in feeling, and thus, has no power to achieve anything pragmatic, where Mr. Edwards fulfils the role that colonial masters were required to play under the Amelioration Act. As Gaspar notes,

> To improve morals, they enacted that within two months of the publication of the amelioration act . . . planters should assemble their slaves to determine which were linked as husband and wife. Slaves having more than one mate were to be persuaded to choose one. The choice was to be recorded; and once a year the planter should read out the list of who was connected to whom before the assembled slaves, praising those who behaved well and censuring those who did not. Masters were required to do their best to keep husbands and wives together. . . .[59]

---

57. See Chapter One, 27.
58. *History,* vol. 2, 81.
59. Gaspar, "Ameliorating Slavery," 254.

In this description, the colonial master is responsible for reinforcing slave fidelity by persuasion, record, annual declaration, praise, and censure. These sustained psychological efforts attempt to ensure the continuance of African fidelity as well as a plantation's productivity. In *The Grateful Negro*, Edgeworth privileges this idea of fidelity as a pragmatic achievement orchestrated by white men rather than a romantic emotion expressed by African women.

In addition to privileging the fidelity of the white Creole master, Edgeworth also privileges his version of love over the African expression of it. On the question of a slave's capacity to feel love, Edwards states, "The poor negro has no leisure in a state of slavery to indulge a passion which, however descended, is nourished by idleness."[60] By this definition, Clara is fully dedicated to love. Her love "idleness" appears on Mr. Edwards's plantation when she becomes distracted by the thought that the obeah woman, Esther, will do harm to Caesar, and thus, "seemed to take no interest in anything" else, while "Caesar was indefatigable in his exertions to cultivate and embellish the ground near his cottage, in hopes of making it an agreeable habitation for her" (410). Here, Caesar's enthusiasm and Clara's apathy even goes against Edwards's idea that "The females of this [Eboe] nation are better labourers than the men."[61] Edgeworth's deliberate act of polarizing her African couple shows that she favors the greater love Caesar has for the society at large because his industrious efforts to improve the land on Clara's behalf are in line with his master's efforts to establish a cohesive society. Their selfless care of the land marks them as the leaders she intends for readers to recognize, just as she means for Clara's romantic love—an idleness that puts her own emotional needs above those of the society she lives in—to be seen as unproductive.

Last, the "plantocratic romance" tops the African one in terms of legal ratification. Edgeworth is aware that a West Indian society cannot survive on the reproductive ideologies of reasonable black and white men. As the Amelioration Act commands, it must be peopled by the next generation of slaves such as Caesar. To achieve this, African coupling must be encouraged. Along those lines, Clara's coupling with Caesar—to "Never! Never!" marry anyone but him—is a clear improvement over Edwards's idea of slaves governed by "visions of romance" (75), and "licentiousness and dissolute manners." He continues, "Any attempt to restrain [this], by introducing the marriage ceremony among them, as is strenuously recommended by many persons in Great Britain, would be utterly impractical to any good purpose."[62] Beilby

---

60. *History*, vol. 2, 80.
61. Ibid., 74.
62. Ibid., 81.

Porteus, Bishop of Chester, was one of those strenuous recommenders. His *Sermons on Several Subjects* (1783) remarks,

> If ever then we hope to make any considerable progress in our benevolent purpose of communicating to our Negroes the benefits and the blessing of religion, we must first give them some of the blessing of society and of civil government . . . inform their minds, correct their morals, accustom them to the restraints of legal marriage . . . and even allow a certain number of the most deserving to work out their freedom by degrees.[63]

The Grateful Negro tries to strike a balance between these two positions in its depiction of the African romance.

Edgeworth encourages Clara's "visions of romance" for Caesar—visions that suggest the successful reproductive future of a stable slave-family unit because Clara will not randomly reproduce a family "with anyone but him." However, her text still keeps alive the spirit of Edwards's legal opinion against formal Christian marriages for real slaves by deliberately resisting any reference to formal marriage at the very end of the text even though, as a romance, readers are led to expect it. Amidst all the other climactic retributive judgments—Esther's capture, Durant's murder, Caesar's stabbing, Clara's awakening, Mr. Jeffries's bankruptcy—Edgeworth never actually acknowledges the act of consummation for her African couple that centuries of romantic conventions demand for the type of story that she has written about them: Caesar's marriage to Clara as a just reward for his service to Mr. Edwards. Her resistance to marriage at the end of *The Grateful Negro* is strategic. With the 1798 Amelioration Act's prohibition against formal Christianized slave marriages as a backdrop, Edgeworth deliberately fails to reproduce the happy-nuptial ending that her African romance demands in order to market what she believes to be a more important message: Caesar's deference to Mr. Edwards is ratified in an ameliorative policy in which his relationship with Clara is not.

Thus, the appeal of amelioration in *The Grateful Negro* depends on Edgeworth's ability to construct an African romance that defies romantic conventions, and instead, voices a political one. Instead of promoting Clara and formalizing her values of fidelity and love in a recognized marriage to Caesar, Edgeworth privileges these values in Caesar's relationship with Mr. Edwards and presents them in *The Grateful Negro* as a fictionalized idealization of the Amelioration Act. To put this point in context, where the *Oroonoko*s I discussed in Chapter One showed a gap in legislation capable of protecting

---

63. "Sermon XVII" from *Sermons on Several Subjects* (London: Payne, 1783), 398.

slaves in the colonies, Edgeworth shows colonial paternalists—benevolent men such as Mr. Edwards, his namesake Bryan Edwards, and the legislators on the Council and Assembly of the Leeward Islands—filling that legal gap by providing a plan of stability that will allow all African couples of any tribe to create coupling conditions so that they may love freely with almost the same protections of marriage, but without any of its legal complications that are so ill-suited to the lives of slaves and so not in the interests of masters or the societies in which they live. In effect, she has solved the legal problem about slave couplings that I exposed in Chapter One. Where the absence of a legal policy regarding slave couplings gave colonial masters the freedom to impose, in its stead, a suicidal practice that saw slaves working to death, Edgeworth's *The Grateful Negro* provides an ideological template, not for the making of legal slave marriages but for slave couplings that mimic but do not replicate the Christian types of marriage favored in England. In this way, *The Grateful Negro* and the Amelioration Act both offer themselves up as romanticized, colonial versions of the Hardwicke Marriage Act, since both are bereft of this act's legal rigor and its Christian and contractual regulations yet both present slaves' lives and couplings as wholly dependent on the good will and trust of the benevolent paternalist. But how trustworthy is this figure?

EDGEWORTH makes two moves in her first footnote that attempt to contextualize the benevolent paternalist's trustworthiness. First, she points to "The Negro Slaves—a fine drama, by Kotzebue" (399) to establish a context for the worst type of violence on the plantation; then she qualifies this violence with this statement (as if a generation and not 6–7 years separates Kotzebue's text and her own[64]): "It is to be hoped that such horrible instances of cruelty are not now to be found in nature. Bryan Edwards, in his *History of Jamaica,* says that most of the planters are humane; but he allows that some acts can be cited in contradiction of this assertion" (399). Edgeworth uses contemporary history to qualify contemporary fiction's representation of plantation violence, minimizing the planters' involvement in it by reducing violence to either the colony's uncivilized past ("It is . . . hoped . . . that . . . instances of cruelty are not *now* to be found") or to an uncivilized minority ("*most* of the planters are humane"; only a few, aren't) as reported by *the* historical expert on the subject. All this effort is designed to convey the idea that planters are, generally, trustworthy.

And yet, both of Edgeworth's sources were skeptical about this trust-

---

64. If she read it in the German original it would have been about 12–13 years.

worthiness, especially as it related to white men and black women. Edwards explains that women of color "are over all the West Indian islands maintained as kept mistresses to white men. But if we examine the situation of these unfortunate women, we shall find much more reason to blame the cruelty of the keepers, in inviting them to this disgraceful life, than of their imprudence in accepting the offer."[65] A white male planter's sexual and psychological tyranny over four black African women marks the essence of the plot in Kotzebue's play. John brags about his torture of one of them, stating: "I once made a wild girl tame . . . [by having] her whole body pricked with needles; then cotton dipped in oil was twisted round her fingers, and lighted—Three days after she loved me most tenderly" (I.ii). This open declaration of cruelty presents an ominous foreshadowing for the heroine, Ada, who is introduced in the first act, "working at a cotton gin" (I.i), essentially producing the instrument of torture involved in her own potential sexual violation. Violence on John's plantation also influences the psychological and emotional decline of the two other black slave women: Lilli, who, in the beginning, uses humor as a defense against the violence of slavery, but by the end, has been reduced to tears because of the horrible instance of cruelty that John threatens to enact on Ada; and an African woman, referred to only as the "Negro Woman," who enters the stage carrying a dead baby in her arms and delivers an affecting soliloquy in which she recounts her experiences of miscarriages, being sold, forcibly married, and also her reasons for putting a nail into her dead baby's heart.

With such vivid depictions foregrounded in the historical and literary sources that Edgeworth acknowledges that she read and admired, "horrible instances of cruelty" against black women could not have escaped her attention. Yet, despite reading about them, she felt no desire to respond to, or acknowledge, a black woman's experience of sexual violation in either the heroine's characterization or the plot of *The Grateful Negro*.[66] Given her footnote's inclination to veer on the side of promoting the benevolence rather than the malevolence of the planter class, this approach is, certainly, expected. The inclusion of sexual violations against black women would have exposed the less than humane behavior of real planters in the colonies and sullied the appeal of her ameliorationist stance in the text. This is the kind of pointed critique that will eventually finds its way into *The Horrors of Slavery* (1824), in which the biracial radical Robert Wedderburn expresses

---

65. *History of the West Indies (Abridged)* (London: Crosby, 1798), 133.
66. Incidentally, another edition of Kotzebue's *Negro Slaves* appears in 1800 alongside Mrs. Griffiths's edition of Behn's *Oroonoko* and the anonymous version of "The Grateful Negro," a good indication that Edgeworth's views about colonial slavery were being established by these particular texts at this time.

"abhorrence and indignation at the conduct of [his] father" and reveals: "By him my mother was made the object of his brutal lust, then insulted, abused, and abandoned."[67] But Edgeworth's footnote and its attempts to redeem a planter class that Edwards, Kotzebue, and (later) Wedderburn are interested in exposing for the violent and cruel ways they treat black women, is particularly disingenuous, not because she simply ignores Edwards's and Kotzebue's representations of violated black women; its infelicity lies in the fact that she turns their victimized figures into her victimizers by involving them in the most extreme acts of violence on the plantation. As a final covert attempt to shield the male plantocracy from all associations with sexual and physical acts of violence, Edgeworth pairs black and white women in African and interracial couplings which strategically divert attention from the paternalists' violent role on the plantation.

The first indication of this strategy appears in Edgeworth's deliberate construction of a female interracial coupling. It involves the violation performed on the body of a black woman by a villainous white *woman*, a significant departure from Edwards and Kotzebue, who focus on white men in this tyrannical, usually sexual role. Marietta Morrissey calls this "A lore . . . that European women, bored and jealous, were more cruel to their slaves than white men,"[68] and Edgeworth provides an episode that illustrates it. When a slave woman was "taking out one of the gowns" that had "just arrived from London" in a large chest, "it caught on a nail in the lid, and was torn. [Mrs. Jeffries], roused from her natural indolence by the disappointment to her vanity, instantly ordered that the unfortunate female slave should be severely chastised. The woman was the wife of Hector" (414–15). The severe chastisement that Mrs. Jeffries enacts on Hector's wife over such a trivial incident ostensibly shows Edgeworth taking a nuanced and gendered approach to the cruelty witnessed in Kotzebue's play, pointing out that white women of the planter class are just as implicated as, if not more than, white men in the physical violation and torture of black women.

However, before lauding Edgeworth for casting a discerning eye on the domestic acts of violence that affected black women on the plantation in the manner that Morrissey discusses in *Slave Women in the New World* (1989), her representation of the African woman's experience of violence is shockingly vague and unsympathetic. The act of being "severely chastised" implies that Hector's wife experiences some kind of extreme punishment. But what kind of punishment exactly? Physical? Verbal? Both? Neither? And how severe? Vagueness pervades another important facet of this African woman's characterization. For instance, it is not unusual that a slave woman does not

---

67. Ed. Iain McCalman (New York and Princeton: Markus Wiener, 1991), 45.
68. *Slave Women in the New World* (Lawrence: University of Kansas Press, 1989), 149.

have a last name despite being a "wife" since slaves routinely did not have surnames, and if they did, they usually assumed their master's last name. But Edgeworth does not even personalize this African woman's identity by giving her a first name; instead, referring to her as "the wife of Hector," a phrasing that places more emphasis on this character's marital status than on her spouse's possession of her. Since I have already argued that Edgeworth and Edwards are averse to the idea of formal Christian slave marriages, this emphasis on "wife" could be pointing to a dangerous level of attachment between Hector and his spouse which competes with, and threatens to supersede, the influence of their master, and therefore creates instability within the slave society. But the vagueness surrounding the depiction of this African female victim of slavery makes one thing clear: if Edgeworth's aim in *The Grateful Negro* is to creatively defame African-ness, the African heroine, and the African romance as I have been arguing in relation to Clara, then this victimized African woman's vague characterization also contributes to all of these goals.

Hector's wife's experience of violence and her relationship with her African husband are far less important than her involvement in another kind of strategic coupling. The fact that Edgeworth only refers to her and Mrs. Jeffries by their marital designations indicates that Hector's wife and Mrs. Jeffries are a female iteration of the male interracial coupling that I discussed earlier in this chapter which illustrated the emotional selfishness, the failure of dynamic reciprocity, and the resultant societal destruction that Hector and Mr. Jeffries reproduce. In these areas, these women are even more influential than their husbands. Once Hector's wife is "severely chastised" on Mrs. Jeffries's orders, "this fresh injury worked up [Hector's] temper, naturally vindictive, to the highest point. He ardently longed for the moment when he might satiate his vengeance" (415). The severe chastisement Mrs. Jeffries sanctions for Hector's wife proves to be the tipping point for rebellion. Edgeworth associates these married women with instigating extreme violence in *The Grateful Negro,* thereby taking off the fictional spotlight that Kotzebue shines on the tyrannical male planter class who, in real life, are directly responsible for instigating plantation violence in general, and violence against the black women in particular.

Where Edgeworth's representation of Hector's wife is riddled with strategic vagueness, her representation of the obeah woman, Esther, is strategically specific yet equally distracting. Her proper name is the first indication of this specificity; the third, and extremely extensive, footnote that describes Esther's practice of obeah in Jamaica is another. Although Edgeworth may have been influenced by other accounts,[69] her footnote includes references

---

69. John Fawcett's pantomime *Obi; or, Three Finger'd Jack*, for instance, a theatrical sensation

to obeah people from Edwards's *History*, among them, "an old Koromantyn negro" whom Edwards identifies as "the chief instigator" (408–9) in a 1760 Jamaican uprising known as Tacky's Rebellion.[70] Edwards reveals that this "old Koromantyn negro . . . was fortunately apprehended, convicted, and hung up with all *his* feathers and trumperies about *him*" (408–9; my emphasis). Edgeworth reiterates Edwards's language when she refers to Esther as "the chief instigator of the intended rebellion" (410). By doing so, she regenders the role of "chief instigator," establishing Esther in the violent role associated with the male African who opposed the ameliorationist society of Jamaica. Esther's influence is confirmed when we are told: "It was she who had stimulated the revengeful temper of Hector almost to frenzy" (410).

Esther and Mrs. Jeffries are, thus, identified as another important female interracial coupling since they are both directly responsible for stimulating Hector. As chief instigators of the rebellion that he leads, Esther and Mrs. Jeffries represent an ideological attempt to gender the causes of violence. Their characterizations lead us to assume that violence is caused by primal feminized emotions (materialism) and primitive masculinized beliefs (obeah), none of which account for the master's direct involvement in the act of causing violence. Creating these women as the chief instigators of Hector's violence is a gendered act of distraction in *The Grateful Negro* designed to create a buffer between the slave and the real causer of violence: the colonial master.

While Edgeworth's female interracial couplings distract her readers from imagining the white male acts of violence usually associated with plantation life, her pairing of the African women, Clara and Esther, also has an important distracting effect of its own to play in the text. When Clara tells Caesar to "avert the wrath of the sorceress, by obeying her commands, whatever they might be," Caesar responds, "[Esther] shall not succeed, even though she speaks with the voice of Clara" (411), literally marking his lover as the mouthpiece for Esther's violence. Esther's ventriloquism is physically reinforced in a scene in which she gives Clara "a preparation of deadly nightshade" and displays her "stretched on the ground, apparently a corpse":

> Caesar, in a transport of rage, seized [Esther] by the throat: but his fury was soon checked.
> "Destroy me," said the fiend, "and you destroy your Clara." (416)

The vocal and physical coupling of this Koromantyn woman and her Eboe

---

during the summer of 1800.

70. See Srinivas Aravamudan's "Introduction" and Appendix B of *Obi; or, the History of Three Fingered Jack* for more information on Tacky's Rebellion.

counterpart presents them as a feminized version of the African coupling between Caesar and Clara. These women appear to act with one voice and body controlled by Esther and dedicated to aims that she is quite clear about: "victory, wealth, freedom and revenge" (417). Curiously missing from this list, however, is any explicit acknowledgement of sexual violence as a specific reason for female involvement in rebellion. In yet another creative act of distraction, Edgeworth makes her composite African woman speak with one voice articulating a list of ideals that generalize a slave's desire for freedom but this figure does not respond to the specific acts of sexual violence that African women experience under colonial white men.

Collectively, then, the female interracial and African couplings in *The Grateful Negro* appear to provide gendered and emotional distractions that take the text's focus away from the violence performed by colonial tyrants and that experienced by African women on the plantation. The need for these types of distractions speaks to the instability at the heart of the "Creole Realism" that Edgeworth attempts to construct in *The Grateful Negro*. In order to make sure that benevolent paternalism and its corollary—the Amelioration Act—appear in as strong and appealing a light as possible, Edgeworth shows she is quite prepared to not only market Caesar's submissive Creole heroism and his relationship with Edwards, but also creatively defame Clara's African-ness, subvert her role as heroine and her romantic compatibility with Caesar, regender and overdramatize Esther's involvement in violence, and unsympathetically diminish Hector's wife experience of it. By denying her African women any kind of sympathetic role as objects of Creole paternalist violence and illustrating them primarily as major instigators of violence equal to a white female counterpart rather than the violated victims who were, more often, victimized by male and female members of the white planter class, Edgeworth does not merely contradict Kotzebue and his attempts to court sympathy for the African female victims of slavery in *The Negro Slaves*. She also presents these African women with a power to incite violence that belies their actual historical experience on the plantation.

I make this point in full recognition of the fact that actual black women negotiated power on and off the Jamaican plantation. Thomas Thistlewood's voluminous diaries detailing his life as a plantation owner provide clear evidence that the black bondswoman, Phibba, wielded considerable influence over him, and Jenny Sharpe has written persuasively about Nanny and her legendary powers as "the most celebrated woman from the era of slavery in Jamaica"[71] and leader of a band of maroon slaves. But Sharpe also notes that "Nanny is relatively unknown in Britain,"[72] and the same is true for Phibba.

---

71. *Ghosts of Slavery*, xvi–xvii.
72. Ibid.

Unlike the Jamaican folk hero Jack Mansong, no pantomime, melodrama, newspaper reports, and novel popularized the existence of these women or lionized their heroism in Britain. So it is more than likely that Edgeworth did not encounter them in her research and use them to inform her representation of the African woman. But in relation to the African women she *did* encounter—Imoinda, Ada, the "Negro Woman," Lilli, the woman tortured with cotton—her representations of the African women Clara, Esther, and Hector's wife are so far removed from these earlier expressions of African heroism and victimization that one can only conclude that *The Grateful Negro* creatively defames African women's experiences on the plantation in the service of benevolent paternalism and the "plantocratic romance."

IN THIS CHAPTER, I have shown that Edgeworth's literary work has a tendency to favor the racial interests of paternalists far earlier than her 1810 letter to Barbauld and alterations to *Belinda* reveal. The strategic authorial attempts to distract and defame, market and privilege in *The Grateful Negro* lead to the conclusion that this is a text that speaks with a particularly resonant voice—a soft, strategic voice of paternal tyranny. Its ameliorative call censors the "horrible instances of cruelty" that black women experience on the plantation, and eclipses the African woman's concern about rape privileged for over a century in Southerne's *Oroonoko*. Edgeworth's text even appears to eclipse Behn's Imoinda in its depiction of Mr. Edwards.

In the first days after Caesar has been bought by Mr. Edwards and given his plot of land to work, Caesar returns from his morning's work to find "his master pruning the branches of a tamarind tree that overhung the thatch."

> "How comes it, Caesar," said [Mr. Edwards], "that you have not pruned these branches?"
>
> Caesar had no knife. "Here is mine for you," said Mr. Edwards. "It is very sharp," added he, smiling; "but I am not one of those masters who are afraid to trust their negroes with sharp knives."
>
> These words were spoken with perfect simplicity. . . . (412)

Handing Caesar a weapon that could, potentially, result in his own death is a suicidal gesture that brings to mind a scene from Behn's *Oroonoko* that also involves a Caesar, a knife, a romantic coupling, a potential death by suicide, and a smile pregnant with meaning. Behn writes: "[Caesar] drew his Knife to Kill [Imoinda,] this Treasure of his Soul, this Pleasure of his Eyes; while Tears trickled down his Cheeks, hers were Smiling with Joy she should die by so noble a Hand" (60); and when he "gave the final stroke" and severed "her yet smiling face from that delicate body, pregnant as it was with the fruits of tenderest love" (61), Imoinda falls dead, a death "the Heroick wife [was] faster pleading for . . . than he was to propose it" (60).

When the smiling, ascendant figures in these two romantic scenes are juxtaposed in this manner, the larger implications of Edgeworth's acts of textual violence become clear. The smiles from these figures represent two dichotomous futures: Imoinda's, the morbid and sentimental appeal of a free life beyond the grave; Mr. Edwards's, the rational and pragmatic appeal of an enslaved life in Jamaica. The smile on Mr. Edwards's face and the benignity of his ameliorative call offer so bright and appealing a future that readers and critics are quite easily led to forget the violent tyranny against black women enacted by other presumably benevolent men within slave societies that would make suicide a preferable future—men such as Thomas Thistlewood. Of his relationship with his black "wife," Phibba, Hilary Beckles writes, "while her family life with Thistlewood was set within the frames of an authoritarian, but flexible white patriarchy . . . she knew, and was often reminded by Thistlewood, of the limits slavery placed upon it."[73] In other words, Thistlewood's acknowledgment of Phibba as his "wife" did not in any way contradict the sexual permissiveness that slavery allowed him to openly negate the marriage bond and frequently engage in consensual and forced sex with other slave women under his authority. While his journals indicate that he felt perfectly free and entitled to do this under the institution of slavery and still maintain a reputation for being a good master and "husband," enslavement meant that Phibba and the other African women under Thistlewood's influence had to accept and could only mildly protest his sexual tyranny. Thus, certain in the belief of their own goodness despite the tyrannical actions that they and their peers are responsible for, men such as Thistlewood and Mr. Edwards present a life under slavery that eclipses not only the interests of the enslaved African women who share her violent experience on the plantation but also the luster of Imoinda's "yet smiling face" as she gracefully makes the ultimate sacrifice. But fictional African women can be heard speaking out against this colonial tyranny despite literary attempts to overshadow their experience. To witness this, we must turn to *The Negro Slaves* and to William Earle's *Obi*.

---

73. Beckles, *Centering Woman*, 57.

CHAPTER 3

"Between the saints and the rebels"[1]

Imoinda and the Resurrection of the Black African Heroine

> *Heroick Imoinda;* who, grown big as she was . . . having a Bow, and a Quiver full of poyson'd Arrows, which she manag'd with such dexterity, that she wounded several, and shot the *Governor* into the Shoulder; of which Wound he had like to have Dy'd. . . .
>
> —Aphra Behn, *Oroonoko*, 55[2]

APHRA BEHN must have been well aware that she was establishing a rather unusual prototype for the ideal African heroine when she created "*Heroick* Imoinda." In particular, the startling description of this "big" black woman using a poisonous weapon to ward off the rapidly advancing colonial militia in Surinam brought an original display of bravery, fortitude, and heroism to Restoration literature that had no precedent in the representations of African women from romances and dramas of the past.[3] As if to confirm her new heroine's importance, Behn hopes that the "Glorious Name" of "the Brave, the Beautiful, and the Constant *Imoinda*" can "survive to All ages" (65)—the capitalized list of qualities that precede Imoinda's "Glorious Name" enunciating reasons why this atypical black African woman should be established within the pantheon of British literature's feminine ideals.

---

1. Gelien Matthews, *Caribbean Slave Revolts and the British Abolitionist Movement* (Baton Rouge: Louisiana State University Press, 2006), 9.

2. Ed. Joanna Lipking (New York: Norton, 1997). All subsequent references are to this edition.

3. For a brief overview of the types of African female characters who appeared in romances and masques prior to 1688, see Lynda Boose's "The Getting of a Lawful Race."

But Behn could not have known how far the task of popularizing this ideal African woman's name and character would stray outside "the Reputation of [her own] Pen" (65). The eighteenth century's male dramatists, theater owners, critics, commentators as well as the actresses who, collectively, kept the name 'Imoinda' prominent in the public eye by altering the *Oroonoko* story, capturing Imoinda's essence onstage, or discussing her virtues in their writing can justly lay claim to dispersing and popularizing Imoinda's reputation far wider than Behn's prose fiction could have done on its own. However, this popular Imoinda was not circulated in the way that Behn had originally imagined. It is Behn, alone, who appears to write with an explicit interest in promoting a black African woman as a central heroic fixture in British literature, an interest that most of the century's dramatists and prose fiction writers did not share.[4]

The black Imoinda's ability to "survive to All ages" is, certainly, a primary source of inspiration for this book and its quest to pursue, through the motif of "Imoinda's shade," the visibility, viability, and ascendancy of this black heroine's influence as an imaginative concept in the constructions of African heroines who appear in British literature well beyond 1688. However, so far, I have shown that despite an anonymous author's attempt to privilege the spirit of the African Imoinda and advance a more aggressive antislavery stance in the 1760 anonymous version of *Oroonoko*, a prominent writer could also consciously resist attempts to render a contemporary black African heroine within "Imoinda's shade." In the previous chapter, I argued that one of Maria Edgeworth's strategies for promoting amelioration in *The Grateful Negro* relied on her intertextual knowledge of Imoinda as the representation of the ideal black African heroine and Clara's failure to measure up to this ideal. Edgeworth's deliberate acts of what I call 'creative defamation' toward Clara are an authorial attempt to undermine Clara's relationship with Caesar, thereby establishing it as a less idealized version of the iconic African romance between Oroonoko and Imoinda, and thus, a less attractive and less important contrast to the fraternal relationship between Caesar and Mr. Edwards—a coupling that Edgeworth privileges as an idealized romance about the benefits of ameliorating slavery in the colonies. Because *The Grateful Negro* justifies its conservative, proslavery, reformist agenda by establishing a distance between the idealized and the common African woman, it is logical to turn, once again, to Behn's heroine for cues to understanding the other side of this equation: how did other popular

---

4. Behn's particular interest in "big" black women appears again in her posthumously published prose fiction *The Adventure of the Black Lady* (1697). See the collection *All the histories and novels written by the late ingenious Mrs. Behn in one entire volume* (London: R. Wellington, 1700) for this short novel and Chapter Five of this book for a discussion of this text.

late-eighteenth-century writers establish connections between idealized and common African women in ways that promoted far more aggressive and progressive positions against slavery than are taken in either *The Grateful Negro* or the anonymous *Oroonoko*? Or, to put it another way, what texts resurrect the spirit of the black African Imoinda, and how are the fictional women portrayed in them challenging the soft, strategic voice of paternal tyranny and the appeal of its ameliorative call?

In this chapter, I focus on two texts and authors that provide answers to these questions by utilizing a familiar strategy: altering and reinterpreting *Oroonoko* for a contemporary audience. I argue that the diachronic references to rebellion and sainthood, maternalism and matrimony that are present in Behn's representation of Imoinda provide a template for understanding Ada, the African wife from August von Kotzebue's drama *The Negro Slaves* (1796), and Amri the widowed mother in William Earle's novel *Obi; or, The History of Three Fingered Jack* (1800). By embodying Imoinda's maternal and matrimonial qualities as well her reputations as a saint and a rebel, these fictional African women do not merely resurrect Imoinda's spirit; they are also involved in their own pivotal battles with paternal tyrants in Jamaica. It is during these moments of confrontation that Kotzebue's and Earle's texts are seen forcefully rejecting the conservative approach to antislavery depicted in proslavery texts such as the 1760 altered *Oroonoko* and *The Grateful Negro*.

Speaking of the initial stages of antislavery history, the contemporary historian Gelien Matthews notes that

> The British antislavery movement was marked by four recognizable phases. The first began around 1783, when the initial attacks against the servile regime were heard in Britain, and included the period from 1787–1807, which concentrated on the abolition of the slave trade . . . abolitionists fought the first leg of the campaign without being too seriously concerned about rebellious slaves.[5]

The Negro Slaves and *Obi* were both published within Matthews's first phase of the British antislavery movement. Yet each author uses Imoinda and her confrontation with tyranny as a template from which he presents his own fictional representation of a common black African heroine and establishes her at the forefront of proposing solutions to the problem of slavery in the shape of immigration and gynecological rebellion that go far beyond the mere "abolition of the slave trade" that Matthews's first wave of abolitionists sought.

---

5. Matthews, *Caribbean Slave Revolts*, 15.

However, each text's schizophrenic ending undermines these two realistic and radical interventions into the discourse of antislavery activism. At once sentimentally *Oroonoko*-esque and unequivocally emancipatory, the climaxes of *The Negro Slaves* and *Obi* reveal an authorial hesitancy about completely casting off the long-held influence of Behn and Southerne to promote the idea of complete emancipation. This means that, as progressive as Kotzebue's and Earle's heroines are when resurrected in "Imoinda's shade," the texts that house them are neither pliable nor assertive enough to imagine their radical antislavery agendas as actual lived realities for real black African women.

THE RIGHTS OF MAN discourse emerging from the French Revolution and championed by radicals such as Thomas Paine offered black and white activists in the eighteenth century accessible language to advance their cases against various forms of inequality. Through reason, sentimentality and bombast in speeches, literature, pamphlets, narratives, and the like, black men and white women such as Ottobah Cugoano, Olaudah Equiano, Mary Hays, and Mary Wollstonecraft used Paine's discourse to challenge contemporary paternalist opinions about, and approaches to, the rights of blacks and women. However, black women are never singled out as active contributors to this kind of political agitation because of the absence of substantive source material written by them from the period that reveals how they politicized their own particular experience of slavery, gender, and race. Important stories of women such as the Hart sisters do not contain as much political insight as critics would like, and the first-known British slave narrative written by a woman does not appear until 1831.[6]

While eighteenth-century first-person narratives by black women may be lost or merely undiscovered, Kotzebue's and Earle's texts provide an opportunity to observe the political agitations that fictional black African women are generating in the literature published at this time. In the field of antislavery literature, these fictional representations are as important as first-person narratives because the effect they are designed to have on the national psyche is no less profound. While white female and black male activists are talking and writing about freedom and equality in speeches and published texts, Kotzebue's and Earle's fictional black women are also depicted as aggressively using their bodies to fight for both ideals in their battles with paternalists, and until other first-person African women's narratives surface, these fictional black female bodies can speak to their concerns. They are not created

---

6. Moira Ferguson, ed., *The Hart Sisters* (Lincoln: University of Nebraska Press, 1993). Mary Prince narrates the first female slave narrative.

in a vacuum, however. I contend that Kotzebue and Earle are actively resurrecting two impressions about Behn's "*Heroick* Imoinda" that are gleaned by examining the epigram I include at the beginning of this chapter, specifically Behn's comments about Imoinda's disposition, marital status, martial spirit, and, in particular, the growth of her body.

Imoinda's advanced pregnancy while engaged in battle is, certainly, one of the epigram's most striking details. Behn draws attention to her heroine's "big," presumably cumbersome, state that, to the narrator's evident amazement, does not impede the "dexterity" of her handling of "a Bow, and a Quiver full of poyson'd Arrows." With equal amazement, however, one might ask where this "dexterity" of hand came from? The African section of Behn's novella makes no mention that Imoinda knew anything about archery much less how to handle "a Bow, and a Quiver full of poyson'd Arrows" with "dexterity." Yet the fact that Imoinda's father was an African "General" leads to the assumption that her toxophilite "dexterity" was not a random trait: it was bestowed, most likely, by diligent paternal instruction. Connections between the martial behavior of this father and daughter become even more deliberate once Behn indicates that the General "was kill'd with an Arrow in his Eye, which the Prince *Oroonoko* . . . very narrowly avoided; nor had he, if the General, who saw the Arrow shot, and perceiving it aim'd at the Prince, had not bow'd his Head between, on purpose to receive it in his own Body, rather than it shou'd touch that of the Prince, and so saved him" (12). The General uses his body as a defensive weapon—a human shield—that not only screens Oroonoko from certain death but also sets in motion Oroonoko's future visit to the General's house, where he sees Imoinda for the first time, and where she becomes an alluring, offensive weapon, putting "on all her Additions to Beauty . . . for nothing more than so glorious a Conquest" (15) of becoming Oroonoko's wife. As stout human shield and alluring weapon, this African father and daughter are the martial tools that work in tandem, marshalling Oroonoko to his matrimonial fate.

In the complete absence of any authorial interest in her maternal line, Imoinda's "dexterity" at archery suggests that she has inherited her father's martial spirit, and her heroism is confirmed when Behn describes her using a bow and poisoned arrows to wound and almost kill the Deputy Governor. By deploying these weapons against Surinam's leading paternalist figure, Imoinda continues the legacy work her father established on the African battlefield; like him, she demonstrates her commitment to protecting noble African masculinity of the present (Oroonoko), and the future (the possibly male heir she carries). But on the Surinamese battlefield she might even be said to exceed her father's martial efforts by defending African masculinity, not through the self-sacrifice of suicide, but through outright physical rebellion against the state and the paternalist figure that deny the legitimacy of her marriage to Oroonoko. Success in the form of the Deputy Governor's death would have essentially destabilized the power structure in Surinam, thereby securing for this rebellious woman an opportunity to be with her husband forever.

Rebelling against the state in order to secure her marriage to Oroonoko was not Imoinda's original modus operandi, however. In Africa and during her early days in Surinam, particular emanations from her body—"the strength of her Charms," "the sweetness of her Words and Behaviour," her disarming "Modesty and Weeping"—in all, the softer aspects of Imoinda's feminine wiles, are the things that the "beautiful Black *Venus*" uses as weapons in her dexterous attempts to either dominate, resist, or subdue paternalist figures such as the Coramantien King and the European Trefry, and hence, control the terms by which she is able to preserve herself inviolate for Oroonoko. In this, she has some success. When Imoinda arrives in Surinam, her soft weapons disarm Trefry, thereby allowing for her unsullied reunion with Oroonoko and a "Celebration of [a] Wedding" in which "*Caesar* took *Clemene*[7] for his Wife, to the general Joy of all People" (40). Before long, Imoinda "began to shew she was with Child" (51), and it is this new development to her body that adds another layer to her role as a rebellious wife.

To the colonial paternalists, Oroonoko—the hero that Srinivas Aravamudan has identified as little more than a petted possession[8]—is far less valuable than his wife. They are prepared to mercilessly whip and ultimately kill him for inciting rebellion, but they "carry'd her down to *Parham,* and shut her up; which was not in kindness to her, but for fear she shou'd Dye with the Sight [of a whipped Oroonoko], or Miscarry; and then they shou'd lose a young *Slave,* and perhaps the Mother" (57).[9] Imoinda is fully aware of her value on the plantation. Once she "began to shew she was with Child . . . [she] believ'd, if it were so hard to gain the Liberty of Two, 'twou'd be more difficult to get that for Three" (51). Her emphasis on the compounding difficulty of gaining freedom with a baby imminent displays her awareness of the fact that each time she begins to "shew," the more the stock of her body rises as a source of additional revenue for the master, and the less inclined he will be to emancipate her, Oroonoko, and their expanding brood. 'Shewing' is, thus, not only a mark of the urgency of reestablishing her former rank, it is also the starkest of stark reminders that future Africans will lose control over the disposal of their bodies in the face of absolute colonial authority.

---

7. "Clemene" is Imoinda's colonial name. See Chapter Two (88, n. 44).

8. *Tropicopolitans,* 29–70.

9. Children born under slavery always took the social role of the mother.

Therefore, when Imoinda attacks the Deputy Governor in Surinam, Behn implies that this battle is not only a critical opportunity for the black African rebel-wife to fight for the legitimation of her marriage; her pregnant body also stands as an emblem for the two meanings of motherhood that Adrienne Rich distinguishes in *Of Woman Born:* "the *potential relationship* of any woman to her powers of reproduction and to children; and the *institution,* which aims at ensuring that that potential—and all women—shall remain under male control."[10] Either this African mother-to-be wins the battle, thereby ensuring that her future African offspring regain complete control over the disposals of their bodies, or she loses, consigning them to a future of perpetual enslavement under colonial male control. By using an African woman's martial and pregnant body as an emblem for the future of African slavery and freedom in the British Empire, the "big" Imoinda stands as an aggressive maternal alternative to the proslavery paternalism privileged in *The Grateful Negro.* Imoinda rises above her soft role as the "beautiful Black *Venus*" in Africa to become the embodiment of this bigger maternal cause in Surinam when Behn says that her heroine does "nothing but Sigh and Weep for the Captivity of her Lord, her Self, and the Infant yet Unborn" (51). Here, Behn elevates one of Imoinda's bodily emanations into a resonant pseudoreligious symbol. Imoinda's "Sigh" is venerated and presented in a markedly different way from that of Trefry, who "had done nothing but Sigh for her ever since she came [to Surinam]" (38). While his sigh is, undoubtedly, due to some combination of passion and frustrated lust, hers expresses anxiety about the future freedom of a particularly resonant whole composed of herself as wife and mother, Oroonoko as "Lord," and the (presumably male) "Infant" offspring—a royal, African, familial trinity. Imoinda's "Sigh" is an African expression of the Judeo-Christian Holy Spirit, an ethereal evocation of future concern for the spirit of freedom denied to this royal African father and future infant. By evoking it, Behn transforms her heroine's bodily quest for freedom into a pseudoreligious symbol that privileges the liberation, instead of the enslavement, of these exceptional living gods who so resemble "Mars" and "Venus," and establishes Imoinda as a matron (rather than patron) saint of freedom for future Africans.

This preliminary discussion suggests that Behn's abolitionism, traditionally read as ambiguous because she withholds her own opinion of Oroonoko's enslavement, is more definitive when explored through Imoinda. But primarily, I am claiming that Imoinda's aggressive confrontation with the Deputy Governor establishes her, diachronically, as a rebel-wife willing to kill and be killed to secure the freedom to live with her ideal husband, as

---

10. (New York: Norton, 1976), 13.

well as a saint-mother martyred for valiantly trying to secure freedom for future Africans.[11] This composite image of the "big" black African woman attacking British-colonial paternalism is an important moment from Behn's *Oroonoko* not only because it shows the fictional African woman rather than the African man at the forefront of overthrowing tyranny and rejecting any benevolent claims colonial authorities might make about ameliorating slavery, but also because it presents her body as most actively involved in the African's fight for an imagined future without slavery. This image is replicated in the battles against Creole tyrants that later fictional black African heroines of "Imoinda's shade" engage in.

ALTHOUGH AUGUST von Kotzebue achieved acclaim in Britain for plays such as *The East Indian* (1789, 1796 English translation) and *Lover's Vows* (1780, 1798 English translation), *The Negro Slaves* was, actually, his first work anonymously translated into English in 1796, and one of a dozen of his plays that were never performed for English audiences.[12] Its nonperformance is, itself, a revealing fact and may be attributed to its tone. At a time in which antislavery sentiment in new dramas appears to have been largely buried in comedies and farces[13] (a point I develop further in the next chapter), *The Negro Slaves*' serious approach to the issue of slavery is a theatrical anomaly. Its serious tone puts it on par with the list of altered *Oroonoko*s that began appearing in 1759, but its graphic scenes of work, torture, infanticide, and murder on a slave plantation—so clearly not designed for all adult audi-

---

11. Southerne constructs his Imoinda with some knowledge of these factors in mind. For instance, he costumes his African heroine with a bow and quiver, indicating her desire to fend off, and rebel against, the state. However, the fact that we never see her onstage with a "big" pregnant body (as demonstrated by the frontispieces of actresses who performed the role) or in a scene in which she is directly attacking the Deputy Governor ensure that this dramatic white Imoinda is far less recognizable as the aggressive composite of the rebel-wife/saint-mother that Behn originally intended.

12. See L. F. Thompson's *Kotzebue: A Survey of his Progress in France, & England, Preceded by a Consideration of the Critical Attitude to him in Germany* (Paris: Librarie Ancienne Honoré Champion, 1928), 57–60, for a list of Kotzebue's plays that were either performed and/or published in England. In his "survey," Thompson dismisses *The Negro Slaves*' importance in building Kotzebue's reputation in England and affords the text only a passing mention. My approach is more in line with that of W. Sellier (*Kotzbue in England* [Leipzig, 1901]), who, Thompson writes, "is of opinion that this play was the foundation of Kotzebue's fame" (60). As I will show, despite never being performed, *The Negro Slaves* publicly influenced some prominent British writers in their own literary works. For more on Kotzebue's other work published during this time and contemporary considerations of his work, see "August von Kotzebue and Polynesia" in George Steinmetz's *The Devil's Handwriting* (Chicago: University of Chicago Press, 2007), 272–78.

13. For instance, see Colman's Inkle and Yarico, McClaren's *The Negro Slaves*, Bickerstaff's *Love in the City* and *The Romp*, Dibdin's *Fashionable Lovers*, Macready's *The Irishman in London*, and Pratt's *The New Cosmetic*.

ences[14]—actually identify a new and extreme approach to representing the issue when compared with Southerne's and all of the other comparatively ungory *Oroonoko*s. In the following two sections, I contend that Kotzebue consciously develops the genre of the exclusively read, intertextual, antislavery prose drama that I originally discussed in Chapter One,[15] and appears to turn it into a new and more extreme political tool, informed, but not encumbered, by the legacies of Behn and Southerne, their texts, or the conservative liberalism that limited antislavery thought in the anonymous *Oroonoko* and *The Grateful Negro*.

As a serious piece of historically based antislavery propaganda, *The Negro Slaves* is far more definitive about freedom than *Oroonoko* and *The Grateful Negro*—texts that, I have shown, support ameliorative approaches to the problem of slavery, justified, in the latter text's case, by Bryan Edwards's *History*.[16] In *The Negro Slaves*' "Dedication," Kotzebue eschews both Edwards and amelioration by recording and celebrating a definitive antislavery policy recently enacted by Denmark's Regent, Fredrick VI. The edict for the abolition of the Danish slave trade was passed on March 16, 1792, a significantly different outcome from William Wilberforce's attempt to pass a similar act in England only a year earlier. Even though the Danish edict did not become law until January 1, 1803, Denmark was still the first country in the world to enact it, and Kotzebue's "Dedication" minces no words about his admiration of this effort: "I have fixed on the Negro-slaves as the vehicle . . . because the Danes were the first who dissolved the fetters of this unfortunate race, and because I am ambitious of making known my gratitude as a citizen of the world . . . to the whole Danish nation."[17] Composing his play in honor of a nation that has palpably demonstrated its dedication to the abolitionist cause shows that Kotzebue is using his drama to challenge, rather than succumb to, the soft, strategic voice of paternal tyranny and its ameliorative call. Moreover, he takes a more comprehensive historical view of slavery than Edgeworth, openly admitting that he extracts, sometimes verbatim, from French, German, Danish, and other European antislavery authorities and tracts.[18] This expansive approach allows him to move his

---

14. In his "Dedication," to the 1796 version of *The Negro Slaves*, Kotzebue states: "Many traits in this piece are too horrible, and therefore, in the representation, several of them were omitted."

15. See Chapter One, 45 and 63–67.

16. See Chapter Two, 87–92 for more on how Edgeworth is using Bryan Edwards.

17. For more on Danish involvement in slavery, particularly from a black woman's perspective, see Eddie Donoghue's *Black Women / White Men: The Sexual Exploitation of Female Slaves in the Danish West Indies* (Trenton, NJ: Africa World Press, 2002).

18. In his "Dedication," Kotzebue states that "Raynal's *Histoire Philosophique*, Selle's *History of the Negro-Trade*, Sprengel on *Negro-Trade*, Isert's *Travels into Guinea*, the famous Black Code, and several scattered tracts in periodical works have fully supplied him with the materials" to create his drama (vii).

own text beyond the conservatism that was familiar to texts like *Oroonoko* and *The Grateful Negro*, which were focused on Britain's involvement with slavery, and towards a European perspective where the radical idea of abolition was not merely a future possibility, but a lived actuality.

Alongside the "Dedication," *The Negro Slaves'* title page (figure 9) provides more evidence of Kotzebue's intent to present a more progressive stance against slavery. In keeping with contemporary conventions of Romanticism that utilized the ordinary man as a worthy site for poetic examination, and in contrast to titles such as *Oroonoko* and *The Grateful Negro* that privilege one extraordinary male African hero, Kotzebue's title evokes a plurality of non-gender-specific "Negro Slaves," and he is very particular about the genre he uses to represent this amorphous group.

Kotzebue "entreats his readers, spectators, and critics, not to consider this piece merely as a drama"; the hyphenated moniker "dramatic-historical" indicates his intent to blend, in real space and time onstage, the conditions of black slaves as they have been presented over the expanse of European history. Of course, using the space of, and time on, the stage to represent serious concerns about slavery was hardly a new proposition. By the time *The Negro Slaves* was published, Southerne's *Oroonoko* had been rewritten at least five times, with John Ferriar's *Prince of Angola* (1788) standing as the most recent example of an *Oroonoko* altered to appeal to contemporary British audiences' burgeoning interest in antislavery. But the success, ascendancy, and frequency of these altered *Oroonoko*s reveal a significant historical problem. Southerne's play had, for decades, stood as the nation's preeminent drama about slavery, and the altered *Oroonoko*s that follow in its wake appear to popularize slavery's injustice. By doing so, such works create the impression that altering *Oroonoko* is the best way for a serious dramatist to politicize antislavery injustice in the legitimate theater at the end of the eighteenth century. But the political usefulness of these altered *Oroonoko*s is historically problematic since they did not alter the legend's focus on an interracial relationship between slaves formerly of high rank and, thus, did not reflect the historical or contemporary experience of black African slavery.

Kotzebue seems well aware of this problem and keen to correct it in his own "dramatic-historical" antislavery drama. His *Negro Slaves* focuses on common, rather than royal, Africans in its title, and the historical focus of his genre hints that his text veers well away from the sentimental conventions that made dramatic *Oroonoko*s appealing yet less-than-credible reflections of contemporary slavery.

However, the title page and genre choice are not the most important indications that he is redesigning elements from *Oroonoko* to make his own drama a politically and socially relevant experience of antislavery injustice.

THE
NEGRO SLAVES,

A

DRAMATIC-HISTORICAL PIECE,

IN THREE ACTS.

TRANSLATED FROM THE GERMAN

OF

THE PRESIDENT DE KOTZEBUE.

Form'd with the same capacity of pain,
The same desire of pleasure and of ease,
Why feels not man for man?
                    THE WRONGS OF AFRICA.

LONDON:

PRINTED FOR T. CADELL, JUNIOR, AND W. DAVIES,
(SUCCESSORS TO MR. CADELL) IN THE STRAND;
AND J. EDWARDS, IN PALL-MALL.

1796.

Figure 9.
Title page, *The Negro Slaves*, 1796, August Von Kotzebue (1761–1819)

To achieve this focus, Kotzebue consciously produces two versions of *The Negro Slaves*, both of which are designed "to represent ... the horrible cruelties which are practiced towards our black brethren," but only one of which expresses these "horrible cruelties" all "at one view."

> Many traits in this piece are too horrible, and therefore, in the representation, several of them were omitted. This might be attended with advantage on the theatre; but in the publication, the author has been obliged to restore the omissions, otherwise his piece would not have had any claim to the title of an Historical Piece. (x)

Distinguishing between theatrical "representation" and read "publication" of the same antislavery piece, Kotzebue confirms the distinction I established in Chapter One between the exclusively read and previously performed versions of *Oroonoko*.[19] The exclusively read dramatic text can do harsher, more historically accurate and affecting antislavery work than the performed one because, in this case, it allows the reader to become imaginatively immersed in all the "too horrible" traits that this dramatist deems necessary. Because he openly announces that his text intends to go beyond the experience of injustice common to staged adaptations of *Oroonoko*, Kotzebue distinguishes his drama. In contrast to Edgeworth and her efforts of 'creative defamation' in *The Grateful Negro*, I want to bring Kotzebue's *The Negro Slaves* and the efforts it makes to redesign and imbue an exclusively read antislavery drama with social credibility and political relevance for the contemporary reader under a rubric that I will, henceforth, refer to as 'creative reformation.'

THE "DEDICATION" is the most obvious textual space where Kotzebue puts creative reformation directly into action. It describes him writing *The Negro Slaves* from a position of comfortable isolation—a "rural solitude at a distance from all that can be justly or unjustly called great" but "where love, friendship, independence crown [his] head daily with fresh flowers" (vi). From this position of extreme comfort and isolation, Kotzebue tells his dedicatee, the "Danish Counsellor of Justice and King of Denmark's agent at the Russian Court": "I will stretch out my hand to my brave friend and intreat him in the midst of his more public walk, sometimes to cast an eye on the peaceful shore, where his friend has raised himself a cottage under shady elms" (vi). This image of Kotzebue's "peaceful shore" contrasts so starkly with the textual description he gives of Jamaica as "the island of tears"

---

19. See my discussion of the anonymous 1760 *Oroonoko* in Chapter One, 45, 63–67.

where "everything should grow green and prosper but cheerfulness" (41) that it cannot simply be read as a friendly request to be remembered enjoying the idyllic perks of rural sublimity. Such extreme differences in personal, geographic, and textual landscapes suggests that they are, in fact, interdependent; Kotzebue is only able to imagine Jamaica in his antislavery text by, first, recounting how far he is psychologically and physically removed from it in his "Dedication." "Rural solitude" is, then, the ideal reflective space for this writer to imagine colonial horror, and he "is not ashamed to confess that while he was writing this piece he shed a thousand tears"—an emotional reaction that he, no doubt, expects to be repeated by readers reading his exclusively read drama in their own spaces of reflective solitude.

Contextualizing the author's interdependent state of mind during the construction of *The Negro Slaves* also gives perspective to his outstretched, entreating hands. They are, undoubtedly, textual reconfigurations of those emblazoned on contemporary abolitionist paraphernalia wherein a male slave's outstretched, pleading, and shackled hands ask to be remembered as "a man and a brother" (figure 10).[20] Writing his antislavery "piece" from a space of reflective seclusion, Kotzebue in his "Dedication" presents his own comfortable hands alongside those of the shackled slaves he advocates for in the body of his text to actively connect himself to, yet acknowledge his difference from, this iconic image, and to claim an explicit identification with the common, rather than the royal, slave. In this way, Kotzebue's "Dedication" creatively reforms an authorial problem that beset the altered *Oroonoko*s and made them less effective portrayals of contemporary antislavery sentiment. His insightful identification with the common slave shows that he is politicizing drama where *Oroonoko*s were romanticizing a royal interracial couple, and his sensitive authorial positioning alongside this common slave contrasts with the insensitivity of writers such as Edgeworth whose *The Grateful Negro* voices the combined interests of colonial paternalists and deliberately eclipses those of the black female slave.[21]

The three-lined inscription on the title page offers another indication that Kotzebue is trying to creatively reform another of the authorial limitations that made *Oroonoko* less convincing as an antislavery drama. Excerpted from William Roscoe's poem *The Wrongs of Africa* (1787), the inscription is quite pedestrian in its expression of a monotheistic belief in a single humanity. However, Kotzebue's decision to use Roscoe's poem as the ideological motif for his drama offers an additional source of evidence for continuing to think of *The Negro Slaves* as a creative reformation of contemporary anti-

---

20. Quakers associated with the Society for Effecting the Abolition of the Slave Trade came up with the design of the chained, supplicating Negro in 1787.

21. Chapter Two, 76, 102–3.

Figure 10.
"Am I Not a Man and A Brother?"
Cameo marketed and popularized by Josiah Wedgwood (1730–95)

slavery drama. For when Roscoe's speaker attacks "the meretricious glare / Of crowded theatres, where . . . Sits Sensibility, with wa'try eye / Dropping o'er fancied woes her useless tear,"[22] he is, clearly, critiquing the role that the theater and, by extension, dramatists such as Southerne played in catering to the viewer's experience of seeing pain over the reality of its existence outside the theater.[23] By evoking Roscoe's poem, Kotzebue implies that he is aware of, and at least tacitly agrees with, its critique of the genre he excelled in.

22. William Roscoe, *The Wrongs of Africa* (London: Faulder, 1787), 2.
23. Southerne was known to cater to audience interests. See the introduction to Novak and Rodes's edition of *Oroonoko*.

To overcome both the speciousness and overt sentimentality of theatrical representation, his "Dedication" claims to document for "readers, spectators, and critics, all of the horrible cruelties which are practiced towards our black brethren" (vii). Unlike *Oroonoko* and *The Grateful Negro,* which, I have shown, are capable of articulating the "horrible cruelties" done to white women under the Hardwicke Act as well as privilege the benevolence of the white men responsible for the Amelioration Act, *The Negro Slaves*' explicit focus on "horrible cruelties" done to blacks aligns it with Roscoe's *Wrongs of Africa* not only in focus, but also in effect. Kotzebue intends to present in an exclusively read historical piece images that can shock consumers of literature with the force of poetry by graphically confronting cruelties in ways that will have a lasting impression in the theater of the mind.

The Negro Slaves shows no interest in considering the "horrible cruelties" that were practiced *by* blacks *against* whites, however, a bias that his contemporaries did not share. *The Grateful Negro* and the anonymous *Oroonoko* both make much of the fear of violence that white colonists lived under in Surinam[24] and Jamaica, and as Victor Hugo's *Bug Jargal* (1818), Heinrich Von Kleist's *The Betrothal in Santo Domingo* (1811), and Claire de Duras's *Ourika* (1823) show, such fears were at a peak when incidents such as the Haitian Revolution, the Great Maroon War, and Tacky's Rebellion took place.[25] But even this failure to address black violence against whites stands as another of Kotzebue's authorial acts of deliberate creative reformation. His focus on the horrors experienced by "our black brethren" shows him using his exclusively read play to creatively reform the nature of the reader's dramatic experience. It is not designed for the viewer to empathize with individuals who look and act like them—a theatrical experience that *Oroonoko* encouraged and Roscoe vilified; rather, Kotzebue wants his readers to fully imagine the horror and pain of those who do not look like them. His drama encourages reflection on the constant state of fear under which blacks lived as well as the "horrible cruelties" that were far more prevalent in their lives on a daily basis than were intermittent revolts and insurrections. By locating fear and violence as African rather than European experiences, the exclusively read edition of *The Negro Slaves* distinguishes itself from *Oroonoko* and *The Grateful Negro* because it creatively reforms the theatrical experience of reading, moving it more toward educating about difference and away from using slavery as a motif for European sentimental entertainment.

---

24. Southerne's *Oroonoko* has an early scene where the colonists are afraid of the blacks joining an Indian rebellion.

25. For a brief history of the Jamaican revolts, see Aravamudan's edition of *Obi*. Also see Richard Hart's *Slaves Who Abolished Slavery* (Kingston, Jamaica: University of the West Indies, 1980).

Thus, Kotzebue's pretextual identification, authorial positioning, narrative focus, and editorial effort all reveal his intentions to use *The Negro Slaves* as an opportunity to advance a more progressive antislavery stance in ways that will overcome some of the structural, social, political, and authorial shortcomings that previous attempts at progressive antislavery drama fell into and future antislavery texts would not necessarily correct. His *Negro Slaves* is a text in which the horrors of slavery are not held back, the characters are not royal and not primarily male, and the pain they experience is gruesome, unromanticized, historically credible, and primarily focused on illuminating the life of the slave and not merely the sensibility of the reader.

However, I have not yet pointed out Kotzebue's two most important acts of creative reformation as he turns his *The Negro Slaves* into an appropriately politicized antislavery drama. They appear in his plot and dramatis personae. Set in the British colony of Jamaica, the play takes place on what seems to be a huge slave plantation where coffee, sugar, and cotton are all produced. Two Englishmen—John, "a rich planter," and William, "his [younger] brother"—inherit the plantation after their father dies. William, however, has been getting an education in Europe and he returns to the plantation to find John (who, it seems, has never left Jamaica) committing heinous acts of cruelty to his slaves. Paul, "the superintendent or overseer of the slaves," executes John's cruelties on an assortment of slaves, notably Truro, "an Old Free Negro," and Lilli, an unmarried Congolese woman, and one of "two young female Negro slaves" mentioned in the dramatis personae. The play's central narrative, however, revolves around the other black African woman, Ada, who faces the most threatening malevolence because John owns, covets, and is intent on forcing her to accede to him sexually. Ada, however, resists his demands because she still acknowledges her marriage to Zameo, whom she thinks she has left behind in Africa but who, unbeknownst to her, resides on the same plantation.

In this play wherein young and old, male and female, enslaved and free, married and single, separated and reunited, European, African, and Creole characters all coexist, Kotzebue creates a plantation society that is a far more diverse, realistic, and complex sampling of slave life than is depicted in *Oroonoko* or *The Grateful Negro*. Moreover, the plot device wherein two idealized black African lovers are each separately enslaved in Africa only to be reunited in a British West Indian colony where they attempt to reconstruct their former marriages under the new conditions of colonial slavery dominated by Creole tyrants underscores that *The Negro Slaves* is an antislavery drama that readers and spectators both are completely familiar with: it is none other than a structurally, politically, and creatively reformed adaptation of *Oroonoko*.

But one figure's absence is noticeably glaring from the dramatis personae: the white woman. Kotzebue's decision not to include this figure as a heroine or even as a character in his play could well be a tacit reminder of the "shortage of white women in eighteenth century Jamaica" that Hilary Beckles believes "explains in part the rapid rise of the mulatto population."[26] However, in his analysis of Thomas Thistlewood, the Jamaican slave-holder, prolific diarist, and serial rapist of black slave women, Beckles also points out that this shortage alone may have played little part in a white planter's attraction to black slave women: "While [Thistlewood] indicates, by his silence [in his diaries], the infrequency of social contact with white women, no statement is made to the effect that black women were targeted because of a shortage, or absence of white women."[27] Kotzebue's decision to exclude the white woman, then, could be an attempt to capture, historically, the real absence of white women from Jamaican plantation life; but by doing so, his play also focuses attention on the threat of rape that African women experienced under planters such as Thistlewood.

Resurrecting the African heroine's black skin color in a dramatically altered version of *Oroonoko* are Kotzebue's two most important acts of creative reformation. Thomas Bellamy's *The Benevolent Planters* (1787) and Archibald MacLaren's *The Negro Slaves* (1799) are indications that Kotzebue's *Negro Slaves* was not the first or even the only attempt during the 1790s to present a common black African heroine on the English stage. But by excising from the *Oroonoko* legend the white yet familiarly English woman that, for an entire century, had embodied the female African slave experience onstage, and replacing her with not only one black African woman but three additional ones in a play whose business is to promote all the "horrible cruelties" done to our black brethren, Kotzebue's drama bolsters its reputation as the most politicized version of the *Oroonoko* legend in the eighteenth century, and the one most likely to resurrect, in a new light, the spirit of the black African heroine, Imoinda.

OF THE MANY textual indications that Kotzebue's *Negro Slaves* is a more politically relevant and socially credible illustration of the *Oroonoko* legend, then, I am suggesting that none is more purposeful than his characterization of the drama's heroine, Ada, as a creatively reformed Imoinda. I have already discussed how Southerne's and the anonymous *Oroonoko*s use textual categories of difference (religion, dress, marriage) to underscore Imoinda's

---

26. Hilary Beckles, *Centering Woman*, 64.
27. Ibid., 41.

African-ness despite her white complexion, thereby making these heroines Africans along the lines of Behn's original black heroine.[28] In his textual resurrection of the *Oroonoko* legend, Kotzebue continues in this tradition of exploiting the African-ness of his heroine. After one hundred years of exposure to the *Oroonoko* legend, contemporary readers would have known the African heroine for her beauty, integrity, and fidelity to Oroonoko, and Kotzebue evokes these qualities, explicitly, in his Ada.

Kotzebue constructs Ada's black African beauty by referring to, yet building upon, one of the odd characteristics that made Behn's "Black *Venus*" beautiful. Lilli refers to it when she makes a comment about African women's unique deformity: "the scars on our faces add to our beauty" (I.vii). But where Behn states that those, like Imoinda, "who are Nobly born of that Country, are so delicately Cut and Rac'd all over the fore-part of the Trunk of their Bodies" (40), Lilli refers to it as a sign of the common African woman's beauty since neither she nor Ada are "Nobly born." Their master, John, appears to agree; he calls Ada "a beautiful woman" despite her implied African scars. By describing the deformity that exoticizes these women as typically, rather than uniquely, African and appealing, Kotzebue makes the idea of scarification less horrific, less exclusive, and more egalitarian than Behn, thereby leading to his creation of an appealing, rather than repulsive, common black African slave woman as a heroine.

Beauty of any kind has its privileges, and despite her common slave status, Ada still has the power to partake of them as she is observed to "gormand at a dainty table . . . [and] stretch [her] limbs on a soft mattress" (I.ii). Such perks come with a price, however. Truro reminds her that by encouraging John's advances, she can "lessen the severity of both [her] fate and [the other slaves]; of [hers] by submission, of [theirs] by gentle entreaties" (I.ii). Where Behn and Southerne restrict Imoinda's sexual and reproductive struggles only to the burden of keeping her own beautiful royal body inviolate from the unwanted sexual advances of men, Kotzebue suggests that Ada's virtue could potentially lie not in keeping her body inviolate, since Truro reminds her, "you are not . . . a king's wife that according to our laws, to touch you is death" (I.ii), but in the sacrificial way she chooses to use it for the larger good of the black slave collective.[29] Ada refuses to compromise her marriage vow, however, proclaiming, "it is love alone not royal dignities that can make a woman faithful" (I.ii). By depicting her taking this determined stance on marital fidelity, Kotzebue delivers another of his pointed and egalitarian

---

28. See Chapter One, 54–57.
29. Historically, Thomas Thistlewood's mistress, Phibba, could be seen as one such woman. See Douglas Hall's *In Miserable Slavery: Thomas Thistlewood in Jamaica, 1750–86* (London: Macmillan, 1989) for more on her.

creative reformations of Imoinda's spirit. Rather than using her African beauty for sexual bartering, a horrible cruelty that enslaved black women are known to have done at this time,[30] Ada demands the same rights to acknowledge and vindicate the virtuous hand she gave in marriage as her famous literary forebear, Imoinda. In his construction of a common yet uncompromisingly virtuous and beautiful black African heroine, Kotzebue creatively reforms the contemporary view of black African woman who falls within "Imoinda's shade" by underscoring that she need not be "Nobly born" to be morally noble. Sexual integrity and marital fidelity are other Imoinda-esque qualities that combine with African beauty to make Kotzebue's common black African slave woman the equal of Behn's heroine.

But of all the acts of creative reformation that Kotzebue establishes between them, their heroic parallels are most important because they contain the most affecting examples of antislavery injustice, and thus, the most potential for challenging the soft strategic voice of paternal tyranny and its ameliorative call.

To eighteenth-century readers, Imoinda would have been known not merely for her beauty and virtue but also for the two heroic acts that most attest to her unique brand of resistance to both paternalism and the institution of slavery: attacking the Deputy Governor, and accepting her own death by suicide. Kotzebue creatively reforms the spirit of these heroic acts in his representations of Ada and her battle with John. Where Behn makes Imoinda's confrontation with the Deputy Governor about marriage and reproductive freedom, Southerne and Kotzebue make their respective African women's battles with paternalists about marriage and sexual freedom. Southerne introduces the Deputy Governor as a sexual predator who is keen to dispose of Oroonoko so that he can satiate his lust for Imoinda. Kotzebue creatively reforms the dynamics of this sexual encounter between the white man and the married black woman to make this a harsher moment of crisis than his contemporary readers had encountered in any of the altered *Oroonoko*s. Even worse than the Deputy Governor, who at least allows Oroonoko and Imoinda the chance to reunite as a couple once they discover each other in Surinam, John has no intention of letting Ada reconnect with her husband once she reencounters Zameo in Jamaica. He immediately divides them, locking Ada up in a prisonlike room and tying Zameo to a tree where, from a window, Ada is able to witness him about to be beheaded. John then gives her an ultimatum: she must agree to willingly submit to him sexually, thereby saving her husband's life, or refuse to submit, whereby her husband will die and she will be forcibly raped. He has already demonstrated his

---

30. See *History of Jamaica* (London: Lowndes, 1774), 328–36, for Edward Long's discussion of the ways in which women of color are involved in sexual bartering.

ability to "tame" an unnamed "wild girl" (I.ii). John uses her husband's beheading as the torture designed to "tame" her into sexual compliance. These are the explicit sexual terms in which the battle between the common African woman and the paternal tyrant over the control and disposal of her body are laid out in *The Negro Slaves*.

Kotzebue goes to great lengths to establish a connection between Ada and Imoinda's spirit of heroism. In response to John's threat, Ada begins to display the belligerent spirit of Behn's rebel-wife. She becomes physically and mentally aggressive with respect to herself and the paternalists who oppress her, telling Lilli:

ADA: Furnish me with a knife
LILLI: A knife? For what? . . .
ADA: Whether this arm is to save my innocence, or whether God has ordained me to be the avenger of thousands, I know not; but let me have a knife that I may feel composed. (III.iii)

Her request for a knife to commit either suicide or vengeance against "thousands" recalls both the knife that Imoinda used against herself in Southerne's *Oroonoko* as well as the bow and arrow that she used against the British militia in Behn's novella.

In addition, after feigning submission to John's sexual demands, Ada convinces him to relent and grant her one final meeting with Zameo. During this meeting, Ada tries to convince Zameo to kill her: "give me death!" she tells him, "Death by thy hand! . . . Take this knife and plunge it in my breast" (III.viii).[31] Ada's request conveys the spirit of scenes from both Behn's and Southerne's *Oroonoko*s in which the "Heroick Wife" is "faster pleading for death than [her African husband] was to propose it" (60). Like Oroonoko, Zameo is hesitant. To convince her husband, Ada conjures up a graphic image of rape and emasculation: "A few more minutes and he [John] will come to take me away; you will hear my groans—you will hear the last sigh of my dying innocence—with insulting smiles will he present himself before your eyes—triumphantly exclaiming 'Tis over! . . . Will you deliver me yourself to the tiger's mouth?" (III.viii). Ada forces Zameo to experience both thoughts with references to her "groans," "last sigh of innocence," and John's "smiles." The effect is immediate. Zameo agrees to kill her. Kotzebue creatively reforms this scene by making a common black slave wife the prime agent, orchestrating an honor killing as her own rather than her husband's choice, as it appears to be in Behn's *Oroonoko*.

---

31. "Which way wou'd you dispose me?" Imoinda asks Oroonoko. "I must die" (V.iii).

Firm in her resolve to die, Ada's virtuous body also undergoes a drastic enlargement: "Ah what slumbering vigor has awakened in me! I am no more what I was, my heart expands, my bosom swells" (III.ii). Here, her expanding heart and swelling bosom are different manifestation of Imoinda's "big" body on the Surinam battlefield, representing the heroic expansion of the common black African woman's capacity for feminine virtue.

Clearly, Kotzebue's explicit parallels are designed to resurrect in Ada the heroic spirit of the "Constant" rebel-wife Imoinda and her quest for freedom in order to magnify the common black African woman's femininity for politicized ends. African women employed alongside men on the plantation fields were not always viewed according to their gender. As Hilary Beckles notes: "the predominate image associated with the representation of the black woman was that of great strength—the symbol of blackness, masculinity and absence of finer feeling. Her sexuality was projected as overtly physical (no broken hearts here!) . . . social immorality, perversity and promiscuity were maintained by her."[32] Instead of this kind of masculinized superwoman or the extremely violent representations of plantation women that Edgeworth creates, Kotzebue's Ada is a more progressive construction of a big black woman because she resurrects Imoinda's heroic role as a legitimate female heroine of virtue and counteracts the genderless and violent contemporary impressions of actual black women on Jamaican plantations.

However, explicit physical, mental, and heroic parallels between fictional common and the noble black African slave women do not, by themselves, make *The Negro Slaves* a radical intervention into the antislavery discourse that *Oroonoko* dominated in the eighteenth century. They merely reinforce the fact that the spirit of *Oroonoko*'s Imoinda is being resurrected in *The Negro Slaves*' Ada in order to raise the profile and importance of the common married black woman so that she may be seen within the heroic context of "Imoinda's shade," thereby politicizing the contemporary black slave woman's experience of violence.

The Negro Slaves makes its radical intervention into the discourse of slavery only seconds before Zameo is about to execute Ada. Truro arrives with emancipating news: "You are free," he proclaims to Ada, "(*pointing to William*) Thanks to him." John's estranged brother has "given up half his fortune" (III.ix) to secure her freedom. With this last-minute reprieve, the play creatively reforms the *Oroonoko*-esque ending that Kotzebue had meticulously set up and makes a radical emancipating gesture toward freedom and marriage. Zameo and Ada's relationship will not merely be reestablished in Jamaica under the aegis of William's benevolent paternalism. Having

---

32. Beckles, *Centering Woman*, xx.

previously attained his freedom from John, Zameo was committed to leaving Jamaica with William, telling Ada during their final meeting: "From the coast of Europe my eyes will wander over the ocean, and seek thy dear image in every cloud that rises from the sea" (III.viii). Now that William has successfully bought and freed them both, the climactic assumption is that both she and Zameo will go somewhere in "Europe" where they will be free to live as husband and wife.

This is the radical antislavery message about freedom that *The Negro Slaves* markets. By explicitly connecting Ada with Imoinda but refusing to allow his heroine to complete the honor killing that Imoinda popularized as a macabre liberation from slavery, Kotzebue creatively reforms the depiction of the common black African heroine and provides his readers with a solution to the problem of slavery that *Oroonoko* and its many alterations did not imagine and that Edgeworth considered and then dismissed in the 1810 *Belinda*. The death of an idealized black African couple is not the means of truly achieving a psychological and political victory over slavery; their immigration to Europe—to an enlightened place such as Denmark or even England—is. Each of the three chapters in Part Two of this book explore how contemporary writers take this radical idea of freedom through immigration into account and apply it to Britain in a series of marriage plots involving black women in England who confront paternalists and promote abolition on Britain's own terra firma. But with respect to *The Negro Slaves*, Kotzebue makes the common yet beautiful, morally big with virtue and rebellious African wife the most heroic illustration of resistance to the sexual will of John, and then rewards her with marriage, guaranteed freedom, and presumed independence for her valiant display of African heroism. This move presents Ada as a more socially victorious and politically conscious version of the rebel-wife, Imoinda. It is Kotzebue's decision to creatively reform *Oroonoko*'s African romance as a drama that promotes marriage and freedom for African slaves in *this* life and not the afterlife that makes his *Negro Slaves* a radical intervention into antislavery discourse. But his efforts in this vein don't end with Ada, however; they also involve William.

He is a staunch abolitionist who recoils at John's abuse of slaves and openly admires William Wilberforce and the King of Denmark for their fervent commitments to abolition.[33] But William is still guilt-ridden about his financial connections to slavery. His own luxurious maintenance, including an elaborate liberal education in Europe, has depended on the profits of slavery and he is ashamed of it, blushing "for every shilling in my pocket! Every

---

33. The English translator includes a personal dedication to Wilberforce, and within the text, William praises Wilberforce as one who "defends [Negro] rights with fervid eloquence" (II.iii) and as "that man, whose noble heart has made him an orator in the cause of humanity" (II.i).

morsel put into my mouth [which] is embittered by the tears of suffering human nature" (I.vi). With this depiction of the sympathetic and conflicted Englishman, Kotzebue creatively reforms the liberal conservative stance of proslavery advocates such as Maria and Blandford in the anonymous *Oroonoko*, and (later) Mr. Edwards in *The Grateful Negro*, who represent a Creole society that would rather slavery did not exist but are not emotionally conflicted by their positions of financial and social superiority in relation to slaves in a colonial society. William's shame and guilt is a pointed critique of the self-interest and hypocrisy of this advantageous position that sympathetic colonial whites held. By renouncing most of his fortune to buy this idealized African couple and taking them to a free Europe, William endorses immigration as an expensive yet viable solution to the problem of colonial slavery. If antislavery is to be a successful venture, Britons must be willing to sacrifice future profits and fully commit to the ideal of freedom for all as William is beginning to do.

The Negro Slaves represents a pinnacle of radical antislavery drama because it uses a common black African heroine and an enlightened white Englishman to justify its politically extreme position on immigration at a time in which Britain had not even successfully taken up the charge of abolishing the slave trade. And there is evidence that at least one British dramatist is inclined to follow Kotzebue's lead. Archibald MacLaren's one-act drama, *The Negro Slaves* (1799), has a Jamaican slave, Quako, proclaim to his African bride, Sela, "Then we shall go to England, and be free Britons" (I.v.23).[34] Immigration is only one of the two possible endings that Kotzebue provides to his play, however. The other is also liberating but not anywhere near as radical, and this fact connects it to the ending of William Earle's *Obi*, another text which resurrects the African heroine yet splits its ending. Before I discuss the effects that these endings have on the resurrected African heroine, however, I want to, first, outline the way *Obi* is similar to *The Negro Slaves* in its approach to antislavery, Imoinda, and *Oroonoko*.

WHERE *The Negro Slaves* creatively reforms an *Oroonoko*-esque marriage plot, offering immigration rather than death as a radical solution to the common Africans' experience of slavery, the African widow Amri from William Earle's novel *Obi; or, the History of Three Fingered Jack*, is involved in another kind of radical antislavery intervention during this period that begins to take shape in the scant details of what is known about the author's life.

---

34. Thompson believes that Kotzebue influenced Archibald Maclaren's hero and heroine. *Kotzebue: A Survey*, 60.

In the tremendously informative and detailed introduction to the most recent edition of Earle's novel, Srinivas Aravamudan reveals that there is very little known about the life of this young author, who was a mere nineteen years old at the time of *Obi*'s publication.[35] But one of the few surviving facts about him revolves around the accusation that his play *Natural Faults* (1799) was a plagiarized version of Marie Thérèse De Camp's *First Faults*. In the preface to *Natural Faults*, Earle acquits himself of this charge by counterclaiming that De Camp had actually built her play upon the foundations of his original script, which had been sent to her by another hand. He also declares that his play was founded primarily on Henry Mackenzie's *The Man of Feeling* (1771), but that it also owed its influence to "an old newspaper, in which [he] read an account of a meeting in Hyde Park between a father and a seducer, each of whom, equally unwilling to wound his antagonist, fired his pistols in the air. I caught hold of the idea," Earle remarks, "and instantly dramatized it. All the rest is my own" (vi, preface). Clearly, he provides this information, and indeed, publishes *Natural Faults,* to counter the charge against him and take direct public action against De Camp for staging his play as her own.[36] Scant though this information is, it presents Earle as a conscious and conscientious intertextualist who demands the right to be acknowledged and credited for his creative work.

This fleeting glimpse of the young Earle as an outraged, earnest, and original intertextualist aggressively pursuing a public act of revenge on a woman who not only uses his labor without credit, but profits from it, makes for an interesting ideological insight into the mind of this young author one year before he publishes his novel about revenge and slavery in Jamaica. Earle's novel does not contain a host of pretextual indicators that spell out his interest in, and reasons for, entering the antislavery fray; yet, it does include an "Advertisement" at the very beginning of the text in which he personally applauds Jack for "[standing] alone a bold and daring defender of the Rights of Man" (68). "Bold and daring" were certainly not the usual adjectives writers had used to describe Three Fingered Jack in earlier historical accounts.[37] Thus, Earle's use of them, alongside his obviously aggrieved mindset over the plagiarism charge, offers the first indications that this young author is ideologically contradicting the stance on this notorious figure held by his contemporaries at the same time that his personal life is consumed

---

35. *Obi; or, The History of Three Fingered Jack*, ed. Srinivas Aravamudan (Peterborough: Broadview, 2005), 15. All subsequent references are to this edition.

36. Preface to *Natural Faults* (London: Earle and Hemet, 1799), iii–iv. Earle claims that De Camp "intended to have [*Natural Faults*] performed for her benefit" (viii).

37. See Benjamin Moseley's *Medical Tracts* (London: Nichols, 1800), 197–205. Also see Aravamudan's introduction to *Obi*, 10–17.

with notions of individual rights and revenge. *Obi* offers a way to bring his personal and ideological positions together.

Alan Richardson has noted that Obi or Obeah—a term that Aravamudan defines as "a set of practices and beliefs produced by the cultural synthesis of enslaved populations drawn from a number of African locations" (8, *Obi*)—was all the rage in British literature between 1797 and 1807;[38] but the period 1800–1802 is an especially rich time for literature that focused on this theme, with John Fawcett's pantomime *Obi; or, Three Finger'd Jack* appearing in 1800 to be followed, almost immediately, by Maria Edgeworth's *Belinda* (1801) and *The Grateful Negro* (1802), both of which contain significant Obi episodes. Advertisements for Earle's *Obi* appear on October 31, 1800,[39] a few months after Fawcett's pantomime made its first run at the Haymarket theater with no less than nineteen performances during the course of the summer season. The close proximity between the two publications suggests that Earle may have written his novel to capitalize on the popularity that the Obi theme had generated during this period, not to mention the public success that Fawcett had already garnered in the theater that year. The affronted mind-set displayed by this young author after his public spat with De Camp suggests that Earle was probably not inclined to plagiarize Fawcett's pantomime, yet he may have seen in it a way to express his own personal and ideological frustrations.

Jeffrey Cox believes that pantomime might actually have been the perfect genre for a play such as *Obi* because its "unconventional form provided an opportunity to put on stage some potentially radical material. This is not to suggest that Fawcett's play embraces Jack," Cox qualifies; but "there are . . . features of the play that work against its overarching conservatism."[40] Some of these features include having a famous actor such as Charles Kemble or Ira Alrdrige play the part of Jack, thereby giving the title role a gravitas that allowed the villainous black to be recognized as something more than merely base. Music was also used to influence the way a viewer experiences Jack in a particular scene. But gesture is, perhaps, the most important device in a pantomime genre deprived of words, because it makes the body speak. For example, in the scene in which Jack appears loaded with Captain Orford's "sash, epaulettes, gorget etc. of which he has robbed him" (10), audiences would have recognized this as a villainous gesture since this young,

---

38. "Romantic Voodoo: Obeah and British Culture, 1797–1807," *Studies in Romanticism* 32 (1993): 3–28.

39. P. D. Garside, J. E. Belanger, and S. A. Ragaz, *British Fiction, 1800–1829: A Database of Production, Circulation & Reception*, designer A. A. Mandal, http://www.british-fiction.cf.ac.uk, [10 October 2008]: DBF Record No. 1800A028.

40. "Theatrical Forms, Ideological Conflicts, and the Staging of *Obi*," Romantic Circles Praxis Series (online), paragraphs 5, 6, and 7.

white Captain has been acknowledged from the very beginning of the play as the betrothed husband of Rosa, the Planter's daughter and heroine of the drama. But the fact that Jack steals Orford's military insignia rather than any material goods implies that he is interested more in robbing the authority of those men of power charged with maintaining the status quo of white ascendancy in Jamaica. In Fawcett's pantomime, Jack's gestures against the colonial paternalists contain within them the marks of a simple robber *and* an avenger of slavery, establishing his own power by stripping white men of theirs.

Despite such "bold and daring" gestures, however, Jack is completely vanquished at the end of Fawcett's play when three enterprising slaves—Quashee, Tuckey, and Sam—kill him. In a scene reminiscent of the climax to Shakespeare's *Macbeth*, "Two Slaves bearing Jack's Head and Hand" participate in the "Grand March and Procession" around the stage as the entire company—a mass of actors comprising in excess of eighty-three people—assembles for the final song and dance to celebrate Jack's physical destruction. The "bells," "triangles," "streamers," "illuminated lanterns," "green leaves," "poles," and the like that litter the stage give it an overwhelming spectacle of carnival and jubilation, drowning out any sense of loss or tragedy for the fallen slave. The overall effect of this highly orchestrated "Finale" is sheer appreciation that Jack's presence has been extinguished from this society, complete adulation for the slaves who achieved this feat, and relief that order has been reestablished in this colonial slave society. Fawcett's *Obi* is ultimately, then, a text that clearly acknowledges Jack's "bold and daring" gestures against the institution of slavery but ultimately refuses to vindicate or validate them as heroic.

In his novel, Earle does not change the essentials of Jack's story and character as seen on Fawcett's stage; however, his *Obi* does explain the African's "bold and daring" gestures as viable heroic responses to the problem of slavery. This novelistic effort to reframe Jack's villainy as heroism relies heavily on Earle's connections to three women and one text: Behn, Imoinda, Amri, and *Oroonoko*.

THERE IS ENOUGH circumstantial evidence contained in the scant details of Earle's known life to propose that he had probably read *Oroonoko* as well as seen it performed before he began to write *Obi*. His preface to *Natural Faults* mentions his great interest in writing for the theater, a fact that would make seeing plays and reading them part of his informal apprenticeship,[41] and his audacious claim that Mackenzie's *The Man of Feeling* is "that perhaps

---

41. *Natural Faults*, v–vi.

best novel in the English language"[42] suggests that he had probably perused enough novels as the son of a London bookseller to make this claim with some credibility. One of them might well have been Behn's *Oroonoko*.

With his access to both versions easily within his grasp, there is every reason to believe that Earle's familiarity with *Oroonoko* formed part of his thinking for his own slavery novel, just as *The Man of Feeling* had previously influenced his *Natural Faults*.[43] However, I want to make the case that Behn's *Oroonoko* had a particularly strong influence on Earle's *Obi*. Proof for this comes out not only because they are both marketed as historical novels in their titles but also in the textual parallels between Jack's and Oroonoko's portrayals at crucial moments in each novel. These African men are from different ranks and tribes—Jack is a common Feloop; Oroonoko a royal Coramantien (Koromantyn)—yet, Aravamudan notes that "There are parallel thoughts in the speech that Jack makes . . . and the well-known speech of Oroonoko rousing his countrymen."[44] Another example of this kind involves Jack "clasping the infected bodies" of his mother, Amri, and his best friend, Mahali, "already putrid from the heat of the climate" (150), a scene that recaptures Oroonoko "mourning over the dead Idol of his heart [Imoinda]," whose body "smelt a Stink that almost struck [those assembled round her] dead" (62). However, it is not the parallels between Behn's and Earle's heroes that I want to focus on, but on the experiences of their heroines. In what I am going to read as a politicized act of creative reformation, Earle builds on Behn's Imoinda by presenting Amri as an intriguing mother figure who embodies two types of maternalism—one that the "big" Imoinda made famous in the wilds of Surinam, the other that Behn and her *Oroonoko* made famous in the world of British literature.

The first act of creative reformation involves constructing the fictional African, Amri, in the role of historical storyteller about slavery. Earle makes her deliver an "African tale," the synopsis of which is as follows. She and Makro are ideal lovers living a blissful married existence in Africa until the day they find two white men, Captain Harrop, and a young boy, William Sebald, shipwrecked off the coast. They are rescued by the African couple and nurtured back to health. After converting the Africans to a vague form of Christianity, Harrop, the elder of the two white men, plans to return to Jamaica via a slave ship that docks at the African harbor. He trepans Amri

---

42. Ibid, iv.

43. Indeed, *A New Catalogue of the Extensive and Well-Chosen Collection of English books; being part of Earle's original French, English, Spanish and Italian Circulating Library* (Nichols, 1799) lists both Behn's collected novels and Southerne's collected plays as part of Earle's father's collection (24, 67).

44. *Obi,* 110, note.

and Makro and sells them into slavery. In Jamaica, Harrop's villainy shifts its focus. Through devious machinations, he also manages to marry William's rich sweetheart, Harriet Mornton, an event that causes William to turn savage and take to residing in the hills of Jamaica, away from civilization. The Jamaica romance involving William and Harriet is important and I will return to it at the end of this chapter, but it is not a part of Amri's "African tale." While on board the slave ship, Jack's father, Makro, eventually dies after receiving five hundred lashes for insubordination. But before his death, he issues a chilling request to his wife: "Oh! Amri, I beseech you, live. . . . Take this girdle from my loins, and keep it in your possession. If the being to whom you are to give life, be male, let him wear it from his earliest birth, and whisper in his ear, till manhood dawns, what he owes to his country. Inspire his young bosom with revenge" (90).

One can view Amri's "African tale" merely as the frame story to Jack's being and purpose in the novel; but the fact that Earle purposely makes a common black woman deliver this fictional "African tale" involves it, and her, in an actual history of antislavery narratives created by women. Amri literally conceives this tale with Makro during the middle passage, carries it into Jamaica, and gives birth to it when she narrates it to Jack as an adult. Behn provides an intriguing parallel to Amri's reproductive act of oral storytelling since she, too, conceives the *Oroonoko* story allegedly on a trip to Surinam, carries it for twenty-five years, and literally gives birth to it in 1688. For her effort, Algernon Swinburne heralded Behn as "the first literary abolitionist—the first champion of the slave on record in the history of fiction; in other words, in the history of creative literature."[45] Despite such accolades, critics have traditionally interpreted Behn's antislavery stance in *Oroonoko* as, at best, ambiguous; yet its ambiguity does not negate the narrative's political significance. *Oroonoko* may have been Behn's strategic opportunity to draw attention to events of the Glorious Revolution and articulate her rebellious support for the dethroned King James II. Giving birth to the text in 1688 certainly gives credence to the idea that she used the *Oroonoko* narrative as a strategic political weapon.

The fictional Amri and the literal Behn can be viewed, equally, as figures of a kind of strategic narrative maternalism, one that corresponds with Andrea O'Reilly and Silvia Caporale Bizzini's notion of "maternal autobiography," a term that politicizes "mothers' experiences as they are storied and narrated."[46] Although their print and oral tales are delivered at deliberate points in time in order to influence political events, Behn and Amri's acts

---

45. "Social Verse," *Studies in Poetry and Prose* (London: Chatto & Windus, 1894), 95.
46. *From the Personal to the Political: Toward a New Theory of Maternal Narrative* (Selinsgrove, PA: Susquehanna University Press, 2009), 12.

of creation also politicize each narrative mother's autobiographical experience. In creating *Oroonoko,* Behn politicizes her personal frustrations as a woman writer as much as she conveys her royalist sympathies. But in *Obi,* Earle politicizes more than the black woman's ability to tell her story. In addition to giving Amri an oral tale, Earle also makes her an expectant mother, one whose body stands as another evocation of the battle that the fictional Imoinda had originally fought against Creole tyranny. In that episode, Imoinda used poisoned arrows to oppose the Deputy Governor. In *Obi,* Amri's body is, itself, the loaded weapon: she must reproduce a male child to carry out Makro's dying request. Identified as "the only offspring of the loins of Makro" (74), Jack is live ammunition housed in Amri's womb, waiting for the spark of her "African tale" to aim his vengeance on Harrop. Jack's actual birth, then, creatively reforms the context of the representative battle between the African mother and the white colonial tyrant illustrated in *Oroonoko* and resurrected in Jenny Sharpe's research on the indomitable figure, Nanny, "the most celebrated woman from the era of slavery in Jamaica" who, Sharpe says, "is remembered as a symbolic fighter as well as a symbolic mother" to a "group of rebellious maroons."[47] No longer must the black African mother fight on behalf of her child's future, as Imoinda does; instead, this mother and child are locked together in a coterminous, symbiotic fight against colonial tyranny. In Amri and her "African tale" and in the absence of actual African women writers of slave narratives, Earle creatively reforms Imoinda's spirit of antislavery aggression against Creole paternalists by bringing together and politicizing the black African woman's roles as both narrative and biological reproducer.

USING EARLE'S *Obi* and Behn's *Oroonoko,* I have been arguing that narrative maternalism is about women authors strategically reproducing tales to influence political events, and Amri's literal maternalism is about reproducing individuals to participate alongside her in one specific political event. If we combine these two maternalist roles, as I think Earle intends that we do, the full extent of Amri's strategic role in the novel emerges. The narrative and literal elements of her maternalism are brought together in *Obi* to form a malevolent attack that destabilizes Creole ascendancy from two hate-filled directions.

"Torn from the arms of her husband, her family and friends, while in the may-day of her life, from her native Africa," the "beautiful slave," Amri, "had vowed to curse the European race forever; and had a son, in whose

---

47. *Ghosts of Slavery,* xvi–xvii; 7; 1.

breast she never failed to nurture the baneful passion of revenge" (71). Jack is, essentially, an empty vessel within which Amri transfers her resentment for "the European race," and he is nurtured on this psychological diet of hate. Far from completely ruining him, however, Earle suggests that this diet of hate actually improves Jack's disposition in substantive ways. To elevate her son's mind, Amri teaches Jack "to despise his groaning companions," the other slaves—to be "superior to [their] whining," thereby ensuring that their victimized slave mentality will never define him. Hate is also presented as the psychological motivation for an African's love of self, continent, country, and tribe. Even though he was born in Jamaica, Amri tells Jack: "My son, your country borders on the Gambia, and its inhabitants are distinguished from all others by the name of Feloops. Remember that the spirit of our nation is, Never to forget an injury, but to ripen in our breasts the seeds of hate for those who betray us" (74). In her eyes, hate is a retaliatory process of African duty and honor, and after twenty-two years of instructing him in it, Amri ensures that her son is not the servile black Creole slave he was destined to be but a virtuous black African man free in mind if not in body or location. At a time where Edward Long's *History of Jamaica* states that masters as well as slaves are stigmatizing Africans as primitive,[48] Earle deploys African hate as the dynamic source for the African's liberty under slavery and privileges Amri as one of the "mainly African born women" Richard Burton identifies who "were among [Creolization's] most active opponents, clinging to ancestral beliefs, customs, and memories… 'singing [their] country'…in anger and anguish at what they had suffered." [49]

Where Amri deploys African hate in order to reproduce a new kind of virtuous African man free of the stigmas of slavery, her "African tale" deploys hate to produce a new kind of virtuous and liberated European man. This "African tale" takes up only a minor amount of narrative space in the entire *Obi* text, which is, essentially, an epistolary novel that presents Jack's life story in a series of letters written by George Stanford, an enlightened Englishman living in Jamaica, and sent to his friend, Charles, in England. These letters are presumed to be Stanford's own testament of the deplorable practice of slavery in Jamaica as he sees it. Yet Amri's "African tale" completely dominates Stanford's emotions, letters, opinions, and voice. He claims to "set down in her own words as near as [his] memory can trace. *MAKRO and AMRI, AN AFRICAN TALE*" (73), essentially using his letters as a vehicle for Amri's "own words" of hatred for "the European race." In this combined text, Amri and Stanford speak, symbiotically, as one

---

48. See *History of Jamaica*, vol. 2, 423–96. See also Burton, *Afro-Creole* (Ithaca, NY: Cornell University Press, 1997), 26–27.

49. Burton, *Afro-Creole*, 32.

literary body ideologically opposed to one specific type of European. It is "in the narrative of Amri" that Stanford "[proceeds] to delineate [the base] character of an European West-Indian" (82), and Amri's views about them cause him to exclaim: "Those are not my countrymen whose inhumanity is the subject of my pages. They may be Britons born, but are not Britons at heart, and I disclaim them." Amri's "African tale" is, thus, the vehicle by which sympathetic white men are made to both identify with her hate and use it to "disclaim" or liberate themselves from a monolithic conception of Britishness. This hatred of Creoles is, in turn, transferred to England via Stanford's body of letters where hate is conveyed as a national virtue. Stanford remarks, "so much for the tale of Amri; read it Charles, and blush for your countrymen" (103). The "blush" of anger, shame, embarrassment, and hate for the Creole is the mark of virtuous indignation and liberated Englishness.

Amri's "African tale" does not only reproduce a virtuous Englishman free of the stigmas of white colonial ascendancy, it also liberates his thinking about the most hate-filled actions of the worst slaves. After Jack witnesses the deaths of Amri and his best friend, Mahali, at the hands of Europeans, he becomes completely enraged and embarks on a murderous rampage: "Let me pass over the unheard-of-cruelties that succeeded," Stanford writes, but he briefly indicates that a "poor woman felt the sharpness of [Jack's] poignard; numbers of innocents fell beneath his rapacious sword, and black men alone were spared" (150). The "poor woman" mentioned is the unnamed white wife of an unnamed white English guard that Jack had formerly killed while escaping from prison. She is fully aware that Jack killed her husband, yet she still seeks him out to offer him help after his mother's and Mahali's deaths because she believes Jack is a good man at heart. By including the murder of this English female Samaritan, Stanford dehumanizes Jack, describing him "with all the savage fury of a beast of prey" (149). However, Stanford's conscious decisions to "pass over the unheard-of-cruelties" that Jack commits, in additional to his terse and unsympathetic depiction of the poor white woman—not even bestowing on her or her husband names or sentimental death scenes[50]—and his suggestion that Jack's murderous rampage is reasoned rather than deranged (Europeans are murdered; "black men alone were spared") all indicate that active attempts are being made to gloss over Jack's villainy and deliberately deemphasize its harshness, presumably to uphold Amri's statement that Jack's hate-filled behavior is a retaliatory and virtuous, rather than inherently malicious, African characteristic.

---

50. See Chapter Two (96–98) for my discussion of the ways in which Edgeworth engages in a similar type of censorship and also appears to gloss over the planters' heinous colonial behavior.

Like Esther in *The Grateful Negro*, Amri is the "chief instigator"[51] of Jack's and Stanford's individual experiences of hatred in Jamaica, and the "African tale" that she delivers is the spark that ignites them both into physical and textual activism. It motivates them both to the actions of fighting and writing with a pointed call to arms: "Now is the time when you should contend for the rights of yourself and mother. Now is the time when you should revenge my cause. You are arrived to maturity, and, to inspire you to revenge my injuries, I will relate the misfortunes of my life" (73). By establishing the notion that Amri's literal and narrative maternalism produces black and white male activists—sons who, together, mount a challenge against slavery, Earle creatively reforms the representative battle scene first exemplified in *Oroonoko* between the black African woman and the white colonial tyrant.

However, he employs Jack's African and Stanford's English hate for much bigger ends than a mere battle against Harrop. Collectively, *Obi*'s hate-filled activism seeks to physically and ideologically undermine the entire framework of slavery. Amri tells Jack: "I beheld you, while yet an infant on my knee, the avenger of Makro's wrongs . . . and then the idea recurred to my heart: 'may he not be the saviour of our country!'" (95). From the very beginning of his existence, the hate for Harrop that Amri imparts to her son is infused with the higher aspiration that he will be the African "abolisher of the slave trade!" (95). In addition, the hate for Creoles that she is able to inspire in Stanford also allows for a more nuanced ideological critique of slavery in general. When Stanford exclaims: "who worked [Jack's] passion to a pitch? Who drove him to the deeds of desperacy and cruelty?" (157), he is not merely taking aim at European West Indians; his rhetorical questions are vague enough to also hold Britain accountable for establishing the institution of slavery that cause Jack and others like him to avenge themselves.

In his *Rights of Man* (1791) response to Edmund Burke's *Reflections on the Revolution in France*, Thomas Paine argued that the French Revolution was permissible because it aimed to restore citizen's natural rights and national interests. One year later, Thomas Clarkson appears to be making the same justification on behalf of the black Jacobins of St. Domingue. Using the language that Paine's polemic popularized, Clarkson asserts that West Indian insurrections are caused by an inhuman slave trade in which "thousands are annually poured into the Islands, who have been fraudulently and forcibly deprived of the Rights of Men."[52] In *Obi*, Earle anchors his opposition to colonial slavery in the British Empire using the ideologies of these two

---

51. Edgeworth, *Tales and Novels*, vol. 2, *Popular Tales*, 408.
52. *The True State of the Case, Respecting the Insurrection at St. Domingo* (Ipswich: J. Bush, 1792), 3. By St. Domingue I am, of course, referring to the French colony on the Island of Hispanola that became Haiti in 1804.

English men. Stanford's belief that Jack is a "noble fellow" who "deserves the admiration of all free born men" (112) resonates with Paine's text; but Stanford's acceptance of Jack's hate-filled attempt to dispatch Harrop and dismantle the slave trade justifies violent behavior in the British colonies within the same "Rights of Men" discourse that Clarkson leveled at the men of African descent involved in the 1791 insurrection in St. Domingue. This would have put Earle at major odds with his contemporaries, for the idea that slaves could revolt and determine their own futures, as the Haitian Revolution made evident, was met with horror in England and its colonies. As David Brion Davis points out: "for numerous whites, the Haitian Revolution reinforced the conviction that emancipation in any form would lead to economic ruin and to the indiscriminate massacre of white populations."[53] Yet, Earle clearly views the idea of violent revolution differently.

Where Paine celebrates the French constitution's proclamation that "There shall be no titles," a prohibition by which "*nobility* is done away, and the peer is exalted into MAN,"[54] Earle makes his white protagonist, Stanford, acknowledge and legitimate the violence of the most hate-filled of slaves and exalt *this* lowly slave figure into "Man." Through this sympathetic white perspective, Earle merges Clarkson's ideas about St. Domingue with Paine's ideas about France to advocate for a revolution from the bottom up that includes those who are seen as beyond the pale of humanity. But rather than replicate this paternalist, French-inspired, ideological notion of revolution from the bottom up in his novel, Earle regenders the ideological focus to make Amri and her "African tale" the stimulus for popular revolutionary action and thought.

As a biological and ideological reproducer of sons who each demonstrate their humanity by vigorously opposing the institution of slavery, Earle aligns Amri's fictional "African tale" with the polemics that Clarkson and Paine produce. They have a shared hate of tyranny and a belief in freedom that they are prepared to justify to the white paternalist societies in which they exist. In effect, Earle is romanticizing an ideological coalition between a black African mother and two white English fathers wherein sons "themselves, each in his own personal and sovereign right, entered into a compact with each other"[55] to justify the freedoms that each of their forebears have brought to light. The "African tale" that Amri narrates to English readers through Stanford's letters and the Rights of Men polemics that Clarkson and Paine write for Britons are ideological tools that encourage Earle's fictional and Britain's real black and white male children to think and act in collective

---

53. *Inhuman Bondage* (Oxford: Oxford University Press, 2008), 158.
54. *The Rights of Man*, ed. Hypatia Bradlaugh Bonner (London: Watts, 1906), 35.
55. Ibid., 29.

opposition to tyrannical thought both at home and abroad, thereby making them ideological precursors to Robert Wedderburn's pamphlet *Axe Laid to the Root* (1817), which, Iain McCalman argues, represents a "sustained attempt to integrate the prospect of slave revolution in the West Indies with that of working-class revolution in England."[56]

This is the nature of the radical spirit underpinning Earle's *Obi*. He brings together the enlightened white Englishmen Stanford, Clarkson, and Paine and the revolutionary black slaves Amri and Jack as an antislavery family united, not by blood, but by this unique ideological understanding that challenges to contemporary slavery in the British colonies are a unique opportunity to fight for the reestablishment of the essence of British liberty. Their unity is, clearly, an ideological alternative to the ameliorative male coupling for which Edgeworth advocates in *The Grateful Negro*. The dependence and infantalization that benevolent paternalists such as Mr. Edwards encourage in slaves such as Caesar is challenged by the independent maturity that the malevolent maternalist Amri nurtures in Jack and Stanford, who liberate themselves physically and psychologically from the enslavements that consume their peers. In particular, Jack and Stanford's interracial coupling challenges the soft, strategic voice of paternal tyranny and its ameliorative call by presenting an alternative voice that loudly calls for revolution as the viable end black and white leaders should be working toward. And unlike Edgeworth's "chief instigator" of violence, Esther, Amri instigates violence *in conjunction with* white men rather than *in opposition to* them. In this way, Earle breathes new life into the idea of black female activism in the decade of the 1790s, creating a fictional black slave woman who is connected to the Rights of Man discourse and who nurtures others to revolt against the status quo in support of an ideal of freedom that *all* Britons, and not just African women, should hold dear. This, in itself, is a radical proposition in 1800. For as Cecelia Green notes, even as late as 1816, "outright abolitionism, which stressed the inherent inhumanity of slavery and the natural right to freedom of the enslaved, was still the purview of a few radicals among whites, including some liberal intellectuals, political firebrands, and religious groups like the Quakers, who, since 1761, had taken a principled stance against the trafficking in human flesh."[57]

Stanford calls Amri "self-deluded" (105) for having the temerity to think that she and her son can overthrow the entire institution of slavery. Yet, he also twice refers to her as the "heroic woman" (120, 147) because of her valiant resistance to slavery. It is this heroism that Earle vindicates at the end

---

56. *Horrors of Slavery*, 18.
57. Cecilia Green, "'A Civil Inconvenience'?" 14–15.

of Amri's life by giving it a religious validation that is designed to elevate her from the common African woman she is to the Imoinda-esque heroine she will be. Amri sends prayers to the "God of Africa, [to] hear it, revenge" (76), and her father, Feraurue, is an Obi man (97), who gives Jack the "Obi horn" which she "herself slung . . . round [Jack's] neck" (105) as he embarks on his quest to avenge her, yet Amri's connections to the occult practice of obeah do not affect her credibility as a heroine. Neither does her ambiguous practice of Christianity. Following her conversion in Africa, Stanford remarks that Amri "sent up prayers to heaven for the protection of her son" (116), yet she also "blessed the Almighty providence that protected" (117) Harrop so that she would be able to satiate her vengeance on him. Again, this mixture of sincere and vengeful Judeo-Christian worship presents no contradiction in Stanford's estimation of her. As soon as she physically expires, he writes, "Heaven received her amidst a choir of angels" (148). Amri's swift and immediate ascent to heaven upon her death despite her conflicting religious prayers and practices effectively canonizes this malevolent maternalist for her heroic efforts against slavery, confirms that she is a martyr for the cause of freedom, and consolidates the impression of her as a saint-mother created in "Imoinda's shade."

TOGETHER, the rebel-wife, Ada, and the saint-mother, Amri, resurrect elements of *Oroonoko*'s Imoinda, elevate the role that the common black African slave woman plays in attacking slavery, and move the antislavery debate into the radical realms of immigration and gynecological rebellion. However, despite being politically astute, socially conscious, and surprisingly progressive treatments of antislavery, both texts have schizophrenic endings that bring conservative elements from the altered *Oroonoko*s back to the fore.

Ada's representation as the rebel-wife advocating for a literal form of freedom through marriage and immigration is undermined by a second, alternative ending to Kotzebue's play. The very last scene of the final act is divided into two halves of the page. I have already analyzed the top half, in which William gives up half his inheritance to liberate Ada and enables her and her husband to depart for Europe and freedom. However, on the bottom half of the page, Kotzebue presents an alternate ending in which Zameo executes Ada, loses his senses, and kills himself with grief. In shock and disbelief, John, William, and Paul stare down at Zameo's dead body, and William, overcome with grief at two needless African deaths, "hastily advances towards John," screaming, "Curse upon thee, Murderer!" "The curtain falls."

Clearly, the tragic murder-suicide of this ideal African couple fulfills the *Oroonoko*-esque plot that Kotzebue had meticulously crafted up to this point.

However, the idea that African emancipation can only be achieved through death makes this ending more dissatisfying and less progressive than the first because it stimulates the emotions of viewers and readers alike, as my earlier discussion of Roscoe's poem pointed out, without providing either of them an opportunity to reflect on their contemporary involvement with the problem of slavery or to imagine ex-slaves living within their midst once the drama ends. In addition, the reference to the financial sacrifice Britain must make if it is to support antislavery efforts is also lost in this alternate one, since William is no longer required to lose half his fortune freeing Ada. Instead, William calls John a "murderer" and articulates the same sort of accusation witnessed in Hawkesworth's and Gentleman's *Oroonoko*s, wherein a Briton points his moral finger at a tyrannical Creole without taking any responsibility for his or his country's own collusion in the practice of slavery and the deaths of slaves.[58]

The *Obi* ending is also split into two parts that, together, show a distinct ideological parallel with the 1760 anonymous version of *Oroonoko*. Earle's first tragic ending involves Jack's valiant yet unsuccessful battle against three black adversaries, Quashee, Sam, and an unnamed boy. Stanford laments, "Thus died as great a man as ever graced the annals of history, basely murdered by the hirelings of Government" (157), a statement that vividly evokes echoes of Oroonoko's death at the hands of the Irishman, Bannister, and the rest of the British militia in Behn's novella. Like Oroonoko, Jack dies without successfully overthrowing the slave society that oppressed him, but he does manage to fulfill his father's and mother cause. Prior to his death, Jack had successfully kidnapped "the wretched Harrop" (119); but once Jack is killed, Harrop is left alone in the cave where Jack imprisoned him, and he eventually dies of hunger.

Harrop's death also facilitates another, decidedly more positive, ending that involves William Sebald, the young white man whom Harrop cheated in order to marry the Jamaican heiress, Harriet. Harrop's death paves the way for the reunion of these thwarted lovers, who have also suffered because of Harrop's villainy. Stanford's last line of the novel notes that "William Sebald and Harriet were at length united, and have for many years enjoyed the sweets of a happy union" (158). Directly after Jack is killed, Earle suggests that this married couple becomes part of the new, presumably enlightened ruling class in Jamaica since their own experiences with Harrop will make them more sympathetic to the misfortunes of black slaves oppressed by similar tyrants. This view of a new, enlightened, and sympathetic white Jamaican leadership brings to mind the similarly enlightened white Creoles, Maria and

---

58. See Chapter One, 60–61, 63.

Blandford, from the anonymous version of *Oroonoko*, whose marriage at the end of that play also inferred that they are dedicated to ameliorating rather than liberating slaves from slavery.[59] William and Harriet's marriage and the continued productivity of their union suggest that a similar move to understand but not liberate Africans is being made. In this new sympathetic era of Jamaican paternalism at the end of *Obi*, efforts to ameliorate slavery have intensified under a sympathetic white Creole society but not to the extent of overthrowing the institution or completely emancipating Africans.

Thus, the endings of *Obi* and *The Negro Slaves* still contain the same echoes of conservatism about slavery that *Oroonoko* and its altered versions never managed to overcome. Despite their use of common black African women who advocate radical ideas about freedom that are more expansive than *Oroonoko*s of the past, both texts still seem to be ultimately trapped in the *Oroonoko* mold and message. In Part Two of this book I discuss the texts that can actually overcome this dilemma, transcend the *Oroonoko* mold, and use fictional black women as abolitionist advocates in England. But as colonial fictions, *Obi* and *The Negro Slaves* must be remembered for two things: first, for their use of the fictional rebel-wife and the saint-mother at a time in the antislavery movement where the concerns of these common black African women are usually forgotten, overlooked, or ignored, to promote radical solutions to the problem of slavery that were well outside the mainstream; and second, the fact that the common black slave woman's freedom is, ultimately, just as elusive for them as it was for Imoinda. For this reason, *Obi* and *The Negro Slaves* mark the point in British literature where Imoinda's literal influence has, perhaps, reached the zenith of effectiveness in championing antislavery. Since the idea of freedom is not completely achievable in the British colonies, "Imoinda's shade" needs to move overseas in search of full emancipation—to places where freedom is more of a possibility and where women of African descent are actively involved in petitioning for it. Places like England, and women like Cubba, Savanna, and Olivia Fairfield.

---

59. See Chapter One, 68.

PART TWO

Imoinda's Shade Extends

Abolition and Interracial Marriage in England

... [S]he is a negro-driver's frow, fresh from Demarara; she had married Monsieur Heureux, but he dying, and leaving her very rich, she married the person with her, John Dulman, Esquire, as he now styles himself, who wanted dame Heureux's money, in order to pay debts he had incurred to a very expensive mistress, and to be able to indulge her extravagance. John Dulman and his dame taking a fine house in London, tried to become people of fashion; gave concerts, parties, routes. The dame endeavoured to learn drawing, music, and all fine accomplishments, but nothing could whitewash the negro.
—Robert Bissett, *Douglas; or, The Highlander* (1800)

CHAPTER 4

Creoles, Closure, and Cubba's Comedy of Pain

Abolition and the Politics of Homecoming in Eighteenth-Century British Farce

> *Imoinda, Indiana, Belvidera,* no longer please ... Pantomime and Farce bear all before them—
> —Anne Oldfield, *Theatrical Correspondence in Death,* in *An Epistle from Mrs. Oldfield, in the Shades, to Mrs. Br—ceg—dle, upon Earth* (1793), 14

> Belcour: 'Tis upon English ground all my difficulties have arisen.
> —Richard Cumberland, *The West Indian* (1771), I.i.

> Mungo: My pain is dere game.
> —Isaac Bickerstaff, *The Padlock* (1768), I.vi

FOR FOUR NIGHTS in December 1759, David Garrick[1] put on John Hawkesworth's new adaptation of Thomas Southerne's popular old play *Oroonoko,* and in the process, transformed the contemporary landscape of British theater. As I explain in Chapter One, this updated *Oroonoko* excised all of the comic elements from Southerne's original, and in their stead, Hawkesworth presented the play as a pure tragedy centered on the eponymous hero and his enslaved wife, Imoinda. However, for those who still yearned for a little of the slapstick colonial humor that Charlotte et al. had provided, Garrick didn't disappoint on those four December nights. The spirit of the theatrical afterpiece that followed *Oroonoko* more than compensated for their absence.

---

1. *The London Stage* (4:II, 760–61) lists these dates in December 1759: 4, 6, 8, and 10.

143

James Townley's farce *High Life Below Stairs* had originally introduced "a young West Indian of fortune,"[2] Peregrine Lovel, to the stage on October 31, 1759. But during this premier performance, uproar ensued. Members of the audience roundly "hiss'd" the play.[3] Yet their dissension was brief. The *London Stage* reveals, "The farce [was] not so much hiss'd"[4] during its second performance the very next day, and within five weeks of its ostensibly inauspicious beginning, the afterpiece was paired with well-established tragedies such as *The Mourning Bride*, *Isabella, or The Fatal Marriage*, and *Oroonoko*, on its way to becoming one of the most celebrated British farces over the next hundred years.[5]

While English spectators would have thoroughly enjoyed a night of West Indian entertainment that paired Hawkesworth's *Oroonoko* with Townley's *High Life*, these staged depictions of white Creole tyranny and buffoonery might have offended some white Creoles in the audience because they openly ridiculed and disparaged this figure despite his significant role in establishing Britain's empire.[6] Edward Long reveals that "most of the old Creole families are allied, by their inter-marriage among their ancestors, before the island was populously settled"[7]—a time when, Catherine Hall has observed, "Jamaica was Britain's 'Wild West' of the seventeenth century, a frontier society."[8] From such an inauspicious beginning, West Indian planters banded together and worked long and hard in difficult climates to make themselves wealthy, and their ultimate "aim . . . was to acquire fortunes to enjoy at home"[9] in England. So wealthy white Jamaicans in the audience must have felt that the assurance of a financially secure homecoming was a testament to their ancestors' heroic history of taming and conquering this British outpost and transforming it into a wealthy addition to the empire. Once they returned home, Creoles even changed themselves. Hall asserts that "absentee planters liked to present themselves as English property-

---

2. James Townley, *High Life Below Stairs* (London: Newberry, 1759), 2. All subsequent references are to this edition.

3. *The London Stage* (4:II, 753).

4. Ibid.

5. For further discussion of the play's immense success and popularity, see Gillian Russell's "'Keeping Place': Servants, Theater and Sociability in Mid-Eighteenth-Century Britain," *Eighteenth Century Life* 22 (2001): 21–42; and Lynn C. Bartlett's "High Life Below Stairs or Cribbage in the Kitchen," *English Language Notes* 23 (1985): 54–61.

6. For a farce that featured Creole heroism and romance, see the plot outline to Margaret Cheer's *West Indian Lady's Arrival in London* (1781) in Richardson Wright's *Revels in Jamaica 1682–1838* (New York: Dodd, Mead, 1937), 155. See also Errol Hill's *The Jamaican Stage, 1655–1900* (Amherst: University of Massachusetts Press, 1992), for more discussion about Cheer and Jamaican theater in general.

7. *History of Jamaica*, vol. 2, 266.

8. *Civilising Subjects*, 69.

9. Ibid., 72.

holders rather than slave-owners, distancing themselves from what went on in the colonies,"[10] and they also became active participants in British parliament and political life in general, forming what Peter Fryer refers to as the influential "West India Lobby"[11] in London.

But this history of labor and financial success is not conveyed in *High Life*. Instead of engendering the audience's admiration, the play depicts the wealthy white Jamaican man coming home to England as an influential figure to ridicule. This tendency—punctuated by the laughter of the English members of the audience—might have been the most painful part of the evening for white Creoles, since it must have brought home to them, in stark terms, that although "they thought of England . . . as home . . . they were no longer English."[12] They were different. Perhaps inferior. Wholly Creole.

My brief attempt to imagine the thoughts of Jamaican spectators as they watch white West Indians onstage at the Drury Lane in 1759 reveal that a tension exists between the English perception of the stage Creole and his homecoming and the Creole's perception of these things. It also raises some intriguing questions about the political and social ramifications of homecoming that will form the basis of the argument I advance in this chapter. When the white West Indian comes home to England, is he still an Englishman as Creoles generally thought, or is he wholly different as Lovel's onstage persona suggests? Moreover, if English "metropolitans argued . . . that slavery was alien to the free soil and pure air of Britain, repugnant to the spirit and genius of the British constitution and the Christian religion,"[13] as Cecilia Green attests, then, when a wealthy white West Indian brings home a black slave, does this make him "alien" and less English in "spirit"? And what of the slave? Does mere residence in England make her an English citizen despite her prior legal status as property in the colonies? In short, if Britain's political position on the issue of domestic slavery is so opposite to the West Indian way of life and being, can slaves and slaveholding figures come home to be recognized as English men and women, or do the attachments to slaves and slavery make these figures homeless presences in English society?

THIS CHAPTER explores representations of West Indian blacks and whites in comedies whose plots feature stage Creoles returning home to England, specifically comedies that employ African characters to reflect on the white

---

10. Ibid., 107.
11. See *Staying Power*, 44–50, for a great discussion of the West India Lobby and their political influence in London.
12. *Civilising Subjects*, 75.
13. Green, "'A Civil Inconvenience'?" 12.

Creole's difference from the English. Cecilia Green asserts that although English "metropolitans may have accepted some notion of the settlers as extensions of themselves, they also saw the colonies as whole social formations that were essentially . . . marked by difference, indelibly so in the case of the overwhelming African majorities of the West Indian territories."[14] However, where these Creole differences are deliberately effaced in, perhaps, the most popular sentimental comedy of this genre, Richard Cumberland's *The West Indian* (1771)—humor that has been characterized as a comedy of tears[15]—I turn to a series of comedies that exacerbate the white Creole's difference from the English: Townley's *High Life Below Stairs,* Isaac Bickerstaff's *Love in the City* (1766), and William Macready's *Irishman in London; or, The Happy African* (1793)—farces which this chapter brings under the rubric comedies of pain.[16]

Much of this chapter focuses on the wealthy white West Indians in these farces—Peregrine Lovel, Priscilla Tomboy, and Mr. Frost—because their fish-out-of-water experiences establish a Creole-in-London template, later popularized in *The West Indian,* wherein newly arrived Creoles experience, firsthand, the pain and ridicule of adapting to English metropolitan society. Each farce's conclusion depends on each author's ability to relieve the pain and ridicule experienced by these colonial outsiders, and this relief is usually evoked in a climax which signifies that the stage Creole is no longer an outsider but a fully assimilated part of English culture. However, where Cumberland's sentimental comedy privileges the relief of the white Creole's pain and establishes him as a reborn and reformed English returnee, the farcical black characters and wordplay present in *High Life, Love in the City,* and *Irishman in London* appear to do the opposite: they focus the reader's attention on African pain in ways that destabilize, rather than affirm, the recognition of wealthy white Creoles as bona fide English men and women.

However, before indiscriminately lauding them as equally progressive antislavery texts for refocusing their emphases on pain from the white Creole to the black African, *High Life* and *Love in the City* are far less progressive in their depictions of the relief from pain that Africans can expect to receive in England. In Chapter Three of this book, I argue that *The Negro Slaves* presents marriage and immigration to a European place of freedom as a radical relief from the pain of slavery for the common black African heroine. Yet

---

14. Ibid., 8–9.
15. Stanley Thomas Williams states that Cumberland's "*The Jew* dissolved its audiences into tears." *Richard Cumberland* (New Haven, CT: Yale University Press, 1917), 231.
16. Isaac Bickerstaff, *Love in the City* (London: Griffin, 1767); William Macready, *The Irishman in London; or, The Happy African* (London: Woodfall, 1793). All subsequent references are to these editions.

of the three farces I consider here, only one of them—*Irishman in London; or, The Happy African*—uses the homecoming and marriage plot as an abolitionist expression of complete relief for the African's pain by establishing a female ex-slave as a potentially married British resident.

I argue that, in its attempt "to establish a basis for merging or marrying two unlike entities so that they would become part of a national or imperial whole,"[17] as Mary Jean Corbett writes, *The Irishman in London* involves the African woman, Cubba, and the white Irish man revered in the farce's main title in an intriguing and elaborate politics of homecoming that aligns with what Isaac Land calls "street citizenship." Their interracial relationship is a joint opportunity for members of the empire's underclass to wed two expressions of activism into one abolitionist whole: complete relief from the pains of colonial slavery in the colonies, and poverty in Ireland. Through this London alliance, Cubba is established as another fictional African woman who expands the parameters of freedom for women under "Imoinda's shade."

IN ORDER TO explore the connection between comedy, pain, and what Roxann Wheeler calls categories of difference in England, I want to examine the comedic genre known for making audiences take pleasure in viewing bodies in pain. Thomas Shadwell captured farce's painful, slapstick side when he described the "putting out of candles, kicking down of tables, falling over joynt stools" as some of its most recognizable qualities.[18] These clumsy physical antics force viewers to focus on actors' bodies and take pleasure in the actors' abilities to simulate painful experiences in the exaggerated physical style that farcical humor relies on. However, because it puts pain on display with an emotional detachment that Henri Bergson has called "anaesthesia of the heart,"[19] farce has long been considered the lowest and most base form of comedy especially in relation to high, romantic, or sentimental comedy, all comic art forms that Jessica Milner Davis says engage our "intelligent critical faculties."[20] "When empathy takes hold," Davis continues, "then the farcical-type characters begin to display self-consciousness and become more human, the consequences of fooling become more serious, and sentimental or romantic comedy is quickly at hand."[21] The implication here is that

---

17. *Allegories of Union in Irish and English Writing, 1790–1870* (Cambridge: Cambridge University Press, 2000), 44.
18. Thomas Shadwell, "Dedication to Charles Sedley," from *A True Widow* (London: Tooke, 1679).
19. Henri Bergson, "Laughter," in *Comedy*, ed. Wylie Sypher (Baltimore: Johns Hopkins University Press, 1956), 64.
20. *Farce* (New Brunswick, NJ: Transaction, 2003), 13.
21. Ibid.

farces lack the sophistication witnessed in other comic genres, an idea that Maurice Charney agrees with when he defines farce as "comedy . . . in which anything can happen. The characters are developed by quirks and eccentricities rather than according to any believable, psychological truth."[22] Despite generating a "comic alienation from the actions on stage"[23] and nullifying a viewer's ability to take representations of pain too seriously, farces' outrageous plots and unbelievable characterizations can still be wholly "diverting" in the memorable stock "types"[24] they reproduce.

"Talking of the Farce of 'High Life below Stairs,'" Samuel Johnson "said, 'Here is a Farce, which is really very diverting when you see it acted; and yet one may read it, and not know that one has been reading anything at all.'"[25] Here, Johnson confirms the critical understanding that farces are quick and light yet visually impressionable theatrical experiences. Farce is always understood and privileged from this visual perspective even though, as Johnson himself reveals, eighteenth-century farceurs also made their work readily available to readers at the same time as, or shortly after, its performance on the stage. In 1759, *High Life Below Stairs* went through at least five editions, all within two months of its premiere (figure 11); *Love in the City* went through two editions in London and Dublin in 1767 (figure 12), the year of its premier; and although it first appeared in English theaters in 1792, *Irishman in London* went through two printings in London and one in Dublin in 1793 (figure 13). Although Johnson doesn't find "anything at all" in the farcical text, the fact that they are circulating at the same time as farcical performances forces me to revisit the argument that I originally established in Chapter One that underscored the difference between seeing the role of an African performed onstage by white actors and reading about African-ness on the published pages of the *Oroonoko* text. In that chapter, I followed Peter Holland's *The Ornament of Action* to argue that there is an essential difference between the reader's and the viewer's experience of Imoinda's African-ness. The published text privileges marriage, dress, and religion as categories of difference that contextualize Imoinda's African-ness on the pages of the *Oroonoko* text, whereas the actresses' whiteness, dress, and celebrity are privileged in staged depictions of Imoinda, making this character seem more English to the viewer than African. I want to extend this prior argument about the importance of reading African-ness to my current examination of Africans in eighteenth-century farces.

---

22. Maurice Charney, *Comedy High and Low* (Oxford: Oxford University Press, 1978), 97. See also Jessica Milner Davis's *Farce: The Critical Idiom* (London: Methuen, 1978) for a pithy potted history of the term and its usage.
23. Davis, *Farce*, 10.
24. Ibid.
25. James Boswell, *The Life of Samuel Johnson LLD*, vol. 2 (London: Baldwin, 1791), 332.

HIGH LIFE
BELOW STAIRS.

A

F A R C E

OF

T W O   A C T S

As it is performed at the

THEATRE-ROYAL in *Drury-Lane.*

O *imitatores, Servum pecus!* HOR.

The THIRD EDITION.

LONDON:
Printed for J. NEWBERY, at the *Bible* and *Sun* in St. *Paul's Church-Yard*; R. BAILYE, at *Litchfield*; J. LEAKE and W. FREDERICK, at *Bath*; B. COLLINS, at *Salisbury*; and S. STABLER at *York.*
MDCCLIX.

[Price One Shilling.]

Figure 11.
Title page, *High Life Below Stairs*, 1759, James Townley (1714–78)

Love in the City;

A
COMIC OPERA.

As it is Performed at the

THEATRE ROYAL
IN
COVENT-GARDEN.

The Words Written, and the Music Compiled

By the AUTHOR of

LOVE IN A VILLAGE.

THE SECOND EDITION.

LONDON:

Printed for W. GRIFFIN, in Catharine-Street,
in the Strand.

MDCCLXVII.

[P. 1s. 6d.]

Figure 12.
Title page, *Love in the City*, 1767, Isaac Bickerstaff (1735–1812)

THE IRISHMAN IN LONDON;

OR,

THE HAPPY AFRICAN.

A FARCE.

IN TWO ACTS.

WRITTEN BY

Mr. *WILLIAM M^cCREADY.*

PERFORMED AT THE

THEATRE ROYAL,

COVENT-GARDEN.

DUBLIN:

PRINTED BY G. PERRIN,

For the Company of Bookfellers.

1793.

Figure 13.
Title page, *The Irishman in London; or, The Happy African*, 1792,
William Macready (d. 1829)

I contend that readers of farces are not always intended to be as emotionally detached from the African bodies in pain they read about on the pages of published farces as viewers accustomed to laughing at bodies in pain were expected to be. After all, in this era of the slave trade where skin color eventually becomes the predominant category of difference, African bodies in pain appear with undoubted frequency in numerous printed media. Poems such as Thomas Day's *The Dying Negro* (1773), Hannah More's *The Black Slave Trade* (1788), John Jamieson's *The Sorrows of Slavery* (1789), and the anonymous "The African's Complaint Aboard a slave Ship" (1793) make serious work of the black body in pain, and they are joined in their efforts by other genres: political propaganda such as Thomas Clarkson's *Essay on the Slavery and Commerce of the Human Species, Particularly the African* (1786), religious tracts such as John Wesley's *Thoughts Upon Slavery* (1774),[26] and illustrations such as those in John Gabriel Stedman's *Narrative of a Five Years' Expedition, Against the Revolted Negroes of Surinam* (1796) (Figures 14 and 15).[27]

Even proslavery advocates were obliged to account for the black body in pain. Whether it was to profess knowledge of a more cruel experience of pain in Africa as the Antiguan planter, Samuel Martin, attempts in *An Essay Upon Plantership* (1750),[28] or to claim to have "never known, and rarely heard, of any cruelty either practiced or tolerated by [Creole gentlemen] over their Negroes,"[29] as Edward Long does in his *History of Jamaica*, late-eighteenth-century readers were literally bombarded with the black body in pain. As such, I want to consider black characters that appear in farces at this time as operating under a dialogic plane: they are at once, and simultaneously, deemphasizing the African's pain by allowing English viewers to laugh at black bodies onstage, but in the reader's mind, they are also part of an extended body of printed media that draws attention to the African body experiencing the pain of slavery. It is this dialogic perspective that this chapter addresses.

Isaac Bickerstaff's dialect-speaking stage black, Mungo, claims, "E'en from my tongue some heart felt truths may fall,"[30] indicating that even his humorous broken vernacular is designed to create a little disturbance about slaves and slavery within the plot of the play, and, by extension, within the mind of the reader in a way that had the potential to be lost on viewers distracted, as they constantly were, by laughter, hissing, people-watching,

---

26. (London: Hawes, 1774), 46–47.
27. (London: Johnson, 1796).
28. *An Essay Upon Plantership* (London: Cadell, 1773), iv–v.
29. *History of Jamaica*, vol. 2, 269.
30. Epilogue from Isaac Bickerstaff's *The Padlock*.

Figure 14.
A Female Negro Slave, with a Weight chained to her Ancle,
John Gabriel Stedman (1744–97) in his *Narrative of a Five Years Expedition
against the Revolted Negroes of Surinam* (1796)

Figure 15.
A Negro Hung alive by the Ribs to a Gallows, John Gabriel Stedman (1744–97) in his *Narrative of a Five Years Expedition against the Revolted Negroes of Surinam* (1796)

conversations, interruptions, and audience comings-and-goings that regularly took place in the theater, reducing the dramatic force of what was occurring and being said onstage. As Janet Todd points out, "By modern standards [eighteenth-century] spectators were still rowdy . . . and there was much complaint by theatre people about inattention."[31] The same cannot be said for readers. In fact, William Hogarth's inclusion of blacks in farcical scenes of everyday British life, such as "Noon" in the *Time of Day* (1736) series (figure 16), visually illustrates that the process of reading blackness in eighteenth-century narratives demands attention in order to fully understand and appreciate the social commentary being made, as David Dabydeen has demonstrated in *Hogarth's Blacks* (1987). By reading the Africans in *High Life Below Stairs, Love in the City*, and *The Irishman in London; or, The Happy African* with a serious Hogarthian eye of social commentary and critique, I will demonstrate that buffoonery was a significant part but not the whole of the African's function within farce. When African-ness is actively imagined rather than merely reproduced cosmetically on the bodies of the white actors and actresses onstage, the farcical African is read as a dramatic "type" whose blackness offers some commentary about slaves and/or slavery as the contemporary writer saw it. In the absence of evidence that speaks to each dramatist's particular stance on the issue, staging, dialogue, and wordplay offer another way to determine if and how the dramatist's construction of African-ness was designed to establish some sort of emotional connection to the slew of printed media outside the theater that were collectively responsible for influencing Britons and politicizing the experiences of black bodies in pain.

I AM ARGUING, then, that humorous depictions of blacks onstage that also claim a reader's attention to this mournful theme of African slavery on the pages of their published editions are sometimes designed to be at the root of a British viewer's comedic pleasure *as well as* provide the British reader with an opportunity to reflect on the pain that the British Empire exacts. This dialogic plane is completely avoided, however, in one of the most famous comic representations of a white stage Creole in England: Richard Cumberland's *The West Indian*.

As his French-sounding name implies, Belcour, the West Indian of Cumberland's title, has a 'good heart' (Belle Coeur), but he also has an impetuous, extravagant manner that Wylie Sypher identifies as a trait commonly

---

31. Janet Todd, *Sensibility: An Introduction* (London: Methuen, 1986), 34.

Figure 16.
"Noon," 1736, from *The Four Times of Day*,
William Hogarth (1697–1764)

applied to literary depictions of wealthy white West Indians.[32] To see the full extent of this personality, Stockwell, a prosperous English merchant and Belcour's long-lost father, decides to postpone revealing his paternity to his son until he has time to observe this son's "disposition: this can only be done by letting his spirit take its course without restraint" (I.i). Belcour's "spirit" of impetuosity, however, involves the "outlandish spark" in a violent altercation upon his arrival at the London port. Before he makes his "passage from the riverside" (I.v) to the town for his introduction to Stockwell, Belcour became "out of patience with the whole tribe of custom house extortioners, boatmen, tide-waiters and water bailiffs, that beset [him] on all sides," and he "proceeded a little too roughly to brush them away with [his] rattan" (I.v). Being "accustomed to a land of slaves" (I.v)—subordinates who, he implies, would never dare to question and plague a man of his class with restrictions and costs associated with citizenship—the West Indian violently attacks all the pesky English functionaries who have the temerity to "beset" him, impeding his smooth transition into this society. His violence toward them, however, meets with equal force. "A furious scuffle ensued; in the course of which, [Belcour's] person and apparel suffered so much that [he] was obliged to step into the first tavern to refit" (I.v) before arriving for his first meeting with Stockwell. Recounting this whole incident in the town office of the man he does not yet know to be his father, the white West Indian says he still feels "the effects of it in every bone of my skin" (I.v).

In London, Belcour's body is in pain[33]—pain resulting from an incident in which his old colonial assumptions about class clash with the resistant forces of a new metropolitan society where his rank, privilege, and citizenship status are not as assured as he thought. If he is to avoid further cultural clashes of this kind and alleviate the pain of his arrival, Belcour must learn not only to temper his wild West Indian ways but also to transform them into moderate English ones. The imagery surrounding his arrival attests as

---

32. For a specific examination of this white West Indian stock character, see Wylie Sypher's "'The West-Indian as a 'Character' in the Eighteenth Century," *Studies in Philology* 36 (1939): 503–20. For a broader examination of the West Indian's relationship to slavery and abolition see his *Guinea's Captive Kings*.

33. My use of this term is informed both by Kristina Straub's "Bodies in Pain: The Subjection of Players," in *Sexual Suspects* (Princeton, NJ: Princeton University Press, 1992), 151–73; and the introduction to Elaine Scarry's *The Body in Pain* (Oxford: Oxford University Press, 1985), 3–23. Where Straub skillfully discusses the pains of players/actors in the eighteenth century, I restrict my analysis to the pains that drama itself, and Farce, in particular, seeks to convey as it relates to the West Indian and slavery. This chapter is an attempt to refute Scarry's "complaint" (taken from Virginia Woolf) "about the absence (or what should be designated the 'near absence') of literary representations of pain" (10). As I will argue, farcical humor, in general, has many depictions of bodies experiencing pain. And when those bodies are from the West Indies, I contend that this literary discourse surrounding bodies in pain sometimes revolves around antislavery and even abolition.

much. Making his way from the amniotic security of privileged citizenship that both the West Indian island and ship provide him, through the stifling experience of the vaginal "passage from the riverside" to the town where he must fight his way through perceived impositions and impediments to arrive, newly attired, into the arms of the English father he has never before seen, the body of Cumberland's Creole experiences a violent rebirth in London. This is only the beginning of his redevelopment, however. Belcour's survival in his new metropolitan environment depends on his ability to learn and adopt the well-stocked, "temperate and restrained authority" that his English father, Stockwell, exemplifies. After he has thus re-formed himself, the community at the end of *The West Indian* rewards Belcour with marriage to Louisa Dudley, a virtuous English woman.

This marriage does more than provide a harmonious conclusion to Cumberland's comedy; it also relieves the stage Creole from the stigma of colonial incongruity that initially plagued him. Belcour becomes part of a dynamic of assimilation in which his marriage to an Englishwoman as well as his reunion with his biological father are the remedies that complete his transformation from outlandish Creole to refined English resident. This transformation also reveals a potent strand of nationalism lying at the heart of Cumberland's text. Belcour minimizes the distance between the Creole onstage and the English spectator by transforming into the ideal representation of the figure audiences know well—a reformed "Christian Englishman" (I.ii) as well-stocked in English morality and respectability as his English father, Stockwell. Stockwell's biological recognition of, and reunion with, his son is, then, mimicked by the English spectator's recognition of Belcour at the end of the play. Because of his reformed values, both recognize Belcour as their own and welcome him back home to the English fold.

However, the relief from the pain of colonial incongruity that Belcour's successful act of homecoming affords him at the end of the play elides a contentious relationship that contemporary white Creoles, in general, had with the experience of pain itself. Throughout the course of the play, *The West Indian* does not include any direct scene and only the most indirect reference to the pain that the Creole had previously inflicted on Africans during his time as a West Indian slaveholder. Although they are as much associated with the West Indies as any white Creole, Africans have no speaking parts in *The West Indian* and are only tacitly evoked onstage once: "*A Sailor enters, ushering in several black Servants, carrying portmanteaux, trunks etc.*" and delivers an inventory of Belcour's goods; these include "two green monkeys, a pair of grey parrots, a Jamaican sow and pigs, and a Mangrove dog" (I.ii). Lumped together with the animals, the "black Servants" are implicitly animalized themselves, and as such, their presence lends little to understanding Belcour's character or the play's plot; they are, merely, additional examples of Belcour's excessive exoticism and wealth—trinkets that attest to his circumstance and locate his origins in an exotic Caribbean clime. Cumberland's strict avoidance of black characters onstage seems all the more deliberate considering contemporary precedent had already made the African in England a viable comedic presence on the British stage. For instance, only three years before *The West Indian,* Isaac Bickerstaff's extremely popular comic opera *The Padlock* (1768) became a sensation largely because of its representation of the black male, Mungo.[34]

In light of Bickerstaff's evident success with this figure, Cumberland's refusal to privilege blacks in his own popular West Indian play suggests that another dynamic may be at work in this text—one that works in tandem with its dynamic of assimilation—a dynamic of denial. *The West Indian* denies the significance of the humans that Belcour depends on for his existence as "a young West Indian of fortune" in an effort to distance him from them—slave master from slaves—as the Creole goes about the business of emotionally connecting with the British audience and transforming himself into a reformed and refined Englishman. And this distancing is not only visually reinforced onstage. Cumberland's use of the euphemism "Servants" rather than slaves in the play's stage directions to refer to Belcour's blacks offers a brief yet potent linguistic indication that he intends to deflect overt discussions of slaves and slavery away from his published text as well.[35] This deliberate distancing of black slaves and slavery from the visual and textual dynamics of *The West Indian* and from direct association with the white Creole hero encourages both British viewers and readers to gloss over the dark vices of the man "accustomed to a land of slaves" and, instead, to focus solely on the way in which his painful introduction to England is ultimately relieved through marriage and paternal recognition. However, their delight in Belcour only comes about because the dramatist has expedited the Creole's appeal and obviated the potentially repugnant view of his character by deliberately minimizing the existence of black pain.

Cumberland's redemptive literary and social work on behalf of the white stage Creole is replicated much later in his play *The Jew* (1794), another

---

34. Thomas Davies writes, "*The Padlock* is a pleasing musical performance.... The music was composed by Mr. Dibdin, who played the part of Mungo with much satisfaction of the audience." *Memoirs of the Life of David Garrick,* vol. 2 (London, 1780), 164. Errol Hill also points out that *The Padlock* was popular in Jamaica during the late eighteenth and early nineteenth centuries (*The Jamaican Stage,* 78).

35. Another interesting scene of this nature occurs in *The Woman of Colour* when the heroine, Olivia Fairfield, defends her black servant, Dido, to a little boy named George and tells him that "her father and her mother were slaves, or, as *you* would call them, servants to [Olivia's father]" (80). Here, the biracial woman articulates the polite difference between "servants" and "slaves."

popular sentimental comedy that, in this instance, aimed at redeeming the social reputation of the religious figure that Shakespeare's Shylock (among others) had turned into an accepted site of public scorn.[36] But in 1771, the year that Belcour first appears on a London stage, *The West Indian* might have deployed its dynamics of assimilation and denial for a very specific political purpose. During this year, the white slaveholding Creole class in England was the target of significant reproach and condemnation from the Englishmen Granville Sharp and Francis Hargrave, who banded together to legally challenge Charles Stewart's attempts to regain control of his former slave, James Somerset, two years after Somerset had left his master's service. If he legally regained ownership, Stewart aimed to transport Somerset to Jamaica and have him resold there. His efforts, however, were unsuccessful. Rather than being remanded to the Caribbean, Somerset was discharged in the 1772 ruling that came to be known as the Mansfield Judgment. It is unknown whether Cumberland's efforts at shielding Belcour from the stigmas of slaves and slavery were deliberately designed to garner public support for slaveholding men such as Stewart as opinion against them mounted during the year leading up to Mansfield's judgment in the Somerset case. However, his sentimental comedy made some things very evident to his contemporaries: *The West Indian* is designed to court favor for the white Creole in England, soften the portrayal of this proslavery figure, and encourage his continued improvement by divorcing him from the practice, the people, the place, and the pains that threaten to define him as unscrupulously harsh, and by marrying him to a virtuous Englishwoman, an act that endears him in the hearts of the English viewers and establishes this character as a national symbol of pride. In short, in the pre–Mansfield Judgment environment in which *The West Indian* appeared, Cumberland reveals that the Creole can come home again and be ultimately recognized as an Englishman, but only if the playwright is able to navigate an elaborate politics of homecoming that maximizes the redemptive Creole's process of assimilation in England while minimizing, or even denying, the existence of black pain.

WHEN CUMBERLAND'S sentimental comedy is considered alongside the farces *High Life Below Stairs* and *Love in the City*, the emphases on the white Creole's colonial incongruity, domestic pain, transformation, and assimilation are pronounced even more forcefully. *High Life*'s action takes place, primarily, within the domestic underworld of Lovel's home—the kitchen—

---

36. For more on this, see Michael Ragussis, *Figures of Conversion* (Durham, NC, and London: Duke University Press, 1995).

where the servants exhibit astoundingly egregious behavior. The head houseservants, Philip and Kitty, organize a party to take place while their master is away, and they are joined by Lady Bab's and Lady Charlotte's maids, and Sir Harry's and the Duke's man-servants—domestics who "have the honour to serve the Nobility" (I.ii) and think of themselves so far "above the common forms" (I.ii) that they all adopt the airs, graces, and even the names of their employers. During the party, these servants aim to enjoy the full bounty of Lovel's wine cellar, accompanied by the best musical entertainment his money can provide. But this night of extreme revelry is only the latest depredatory act. Kitty tells Philip that he should "set up a chocolate house" "with the five hundred pounds which [he has] already saved in this extravagant fellow's family" (I.iii), and she and Philip "cheat him wherever [they] can lay [their] fingers" (II.i); Cook disposes of some of her master's "perquisites" to the tallow chandler; and Coachman and Kingston, the black male servant, raid the wine cellar to drink "their master's good journey" (I.iii) as soon as he ostensibly departs for Devonshire. With these depredatory domestic goings-on it's little wonder that Lovel's "expenses often made [him] stare" (I.i)! Without regulation, his servants take pains to help themselves to everything at their disposal, consuming or disposing of his goods with a reckless abandon that threatens to financially destroy him while their noble guests affect the manners of their employers. "High life" in terms of extravagant living, rank impersonation, and general revelry is literally being had with all abandon "below stairs."

These domestics are not the most egregious transgressors of rank, respectability, and temperance in the domestic society Townley creates onstage, however. Lovel's contrasts with his English friend, the older gentleman, Charles Freeman, reveal how thoroughly this West Indian man clashes with the ideals of responsible rank and respectable English masculinity. As soon as he enters the play, Lovel displays all of the negative traits that Wylie Sypher has identified as typical of the eighteenth-century stock West Indian. Ostentatious displays of wealth and luxury enthrall him; Freeman recounts, "You Gentry of the Western Isles . . . love Pomp and Parade—I have seen it delight your Soul, when the People in the Street have stared at your Equipage; especially if they whispered loud enough to be heard, 'That is Squire Lovel, the great West Indian'" (I.i). Exposing his excessive love of vanity and superficiality, Freeman puts Lovel in contrast and warns him that his typical West Indian passion for self-indulgence will eventually take as peremptory and premature a physical toll on him as it has on all his race: "you [West Indians] consume so fast that not one in twenty of you live to be fifty years old" (I.i). Freeman's perceptive critiques indicate that Lovel is completely oblivious to the way the extreme passions of his own soul delights yet imperils his body.

Indeed, Lovel is oblivious to the pain he inflicts on his own body, because he is intoxicated with conspicuous acts of consumption and displays of wealth. His name—an obvious wordplay on the phrase 'love all'—emphasizes just how completely overconsumption defines him. From the beginning, *High Life* establishes that this wild West Indian is painfully at odds with a critical, sober, experienced, and enlightened English Freeman.

Assembling an amalgam of domestics who transgress rank and temperance in the home of a Creole man whose name and body epitomizes both these acts of transgression, Townley not only makes Lovel's domestic household reflect the pains of which Lovel's own body suffers, he also blames the West Indian for allowing his colonial sensibilities to take hold in the metropolis, creating a space for domestics to mindlessly inflict a multitude of pains on him, themselves, their profession and the respectability accorded to notions of rank. For so egregiously transgressing the mores of rank and respectability in the metropolis, the Creole in London is recognized as a dangerously destabilizing presence who threatens to inspire pain and dis-ease at every level of British society. However, *The West Indian* reminds us that this wild man is capable of being reformed in England if the distance between his behavior and that of a representative Englishman can be breached. For this to happen, Lovel's home and body must be both reborn and reformed in London.

Townley begins outlining Lovel's rebirth once the master pretends to leave his London house for Devonshire, only to return to it cleverly disguised as a "country boy" named "Jemmy" who is seeking to be trained up in service. With country clothes, a coarse carrot-red wig, and a rustic accent, Lovel infiltrates the ranks of the servant class on the night of their party to find out, firsthand, whether his own domestics are cozening him. His rebirth in London occurs literally and painfully at the hands of one of the servants whom Lovel is convinced "is a rogue among my folks . . . that surly Dog Tom" (I.i). Prior to the party, the more perceptive Freeman observes that Tom "has a good deal of surly *honesty* about him" (I.i; my emphasis). "Jemmy" aims to put Tom's honesty and Freeman's perception to the test. A stage direction states that "Jemmy" "[*Goes up to Tom*]" (II.i) in a threatening posture accompanied by the pilferers, Philip and Kitty, in order to find out where Tom's allegiances lie. "What do you know?" (II.i) they each ask Tom in turn. "I know that you two are in Fee with every tradesman belonging to the House," Tom snaps at Philip and Kitty, "and that you, Mr. Clodpole, are in a fair Way to be hang'd. [*Strikes Lovel*]" (II.i). Assured of Tom's honesty by his angry retort and the indignation he expresses about the servants' depredatory behavior, Lovel calls Tom's strike "an honest blow" (II.i), a particularly resonant phrase. "An honest blow" refers to a strike from an honest man, a blow that hits a target directly, or a well-deserved reprimand. When applied to newborns, "an honest blow" is also the crucial slap that brings them into life. All of these connotations relate to Lovel as he immediately disabuses himself of his initial assumption and cries, "the fellow I thought a rogue is the only honest servant in my house" (II.i). Repeating the word "honest" twice to refer to Tom after Freeman has already used it in relation to this servant confirms that Lovel not only begins to see his own household through Freeman's eyes but also to see how painfully at odds he had been in relation to this perceptive Englishman. His rebirth in the metropolis has commenced. Next up, the reformation of his home and his body.

After Lovel receives Tom's "honest blow" and begins to see the error of his ways, his reformation depends on his active attempts to reestablish the boundaries he has allowed to be so freely transgressed. This message is also brought out by Townley's skillful use of wordplay at the end of the farce. During the party "Jemmy" becomes "free of the cellar" (II.i) when Philip gives "him a smack of every sort of wine from humble port to imperial Tokay" (II.i). "Yes, I am free—I am very free" (II.i), Lovel remarks after drinking the wine, his repetition a performative way of signaling "Jemmy's" apparent drunkenness from having imbibed these fine wines. Lovel's use of this emancipatory phrase also resonates, somberly, throughout the remainder of the farce, however. "Jemmy" frees himself from the party only to reappear, moments later, reclothed as Lovel pretending to have returned home from Devonshire, very early and completely drunk. Where the old vice-ridden Lovel entered his home disguised as the naïf, "Jemmy," and discovered how easy it is to become "free of the cellar," a new, completely sober and enlightened Lovel returns to the flagrant site of transgression disguised as his old vice-ridden self and reveals how easy it is to become free of these intoxicating forces. He divests himself of all vestiges of vice when he discharges the ringleaders, Philip and Kitty, and expels the noble domestics from his home. With these acts of closure, Lovel restores order to his household and his body; he alleviates his own pain and ridicule by getting rid of the domestics who illustrate the extreme West Indian vices that put him so painfully at odds with the sober English Freeman. Lovel's decision to reenter his home initially pretending to be drunk but ultimately showing himself completely sober and enlightened has a greater significance, however, because it is an act of homecoming that attests to the transformation of his soul and, in turn, his national identity. He has freed not only his house of vice but also his body of the intoxicating delights of consumption that had, heretofore, corroded it. Onstage, this reformed and liberated West Indian has returned to his London home and remade himself—mind, body, and spirit—into another appealing, critical, sober, and enlightened English free man.

WHERE THESE climactic acts of homecoming and identification with the older paternal surrogate relieve the West Indian from the stigmas of his Creole identity and allow him to be recognized onstage as a completely reformed Englishman, the domestic sphere takes on a decidedly economic air in the staging of Isaac Bickerstaff's[37] comic opera *Love in the City*. It opens with two women, "Priscilla and Penelope: one seated, and holding a skein of silk, while the other winds it off on a ball." This genteel work is not taking place within the "back parlor" of a house, as viewers would expect, but "nearer the front" of "a grocer's shop with a compting house"[38] owned by Penelope's brother and Priscilla's cousin, Young Walter Cockney, who sells "tea, sugar and other things" there. In a clear effort to merge the circulation of exotic colonial goods with women marketing the domestic talents that will make them profitable in the marriage trade, Bickerstaff's farce perhaps anticipates Adam Smith's *Wealth of Nations* (1776) and its argument that societies benefit more from free market economies. Bickerstaff, however, sets the farcical tone for his play by focusing on the pain of homecoming as it relates to a Creole female recently liberated from the confines of both a West Indian colony and an English school.

As its title suggests, Bickerstaff's drama can be read as an eighteenth-century rendition of the hugely popular Home Box Office (HBO) comedy *Sex and the City*, wherein four single white women from different backgrounds—in this case, one French woman, one West Indian woman, and two Englishwomen (one young, the other older)—are looking for love amidst the hustle and bustle of a major metropolitan city. London is their home, and it is hailed in song as the "noblest mart on earth, / Unrival'd still in commerce reign" (I.i). But instead of viewing Londoners purely as the "nation of shopkeepers"[39] that Smith would eventually envisage, Bickerstaff presents them as a diverse nation of social climbers who use love and marriage to trade themselves up in English society.

The Creole, Priscilla Tomboy, is the richest and most independent of this London-based foursome, but also the most in need of elevation because of her volatility. She has been "sent to England for [her] education" (I.ii).[40] Yet she seems totally incapable of being formally educated in the traditional manner of an English lady, a point underscored by Walter, Priscilla's

---

37. For more on Bickerstaff, see Bell's *British Theatre. Consisting of the most Esteemed English plays* (London, 1797), 8; Judith Milhous and Robert D. Hume, "Isaac Bickerstaff's Copyrights—And a Biographical Discovery," *Philological Quarterly* 83 (2004): 259-73.
38. *Love in the City*, 9.
39. *Wealth of Nations*, vol. 2 (Dublin: Whitestone et al., 1776), 483.
40. Bickerstaff defined his work as "Comic Opera," but I include it within the field of Farce because it contains the same slapstick humor and basic characterizations with the added benefit of music.

cousin and potential suitor, who reveals that she "was turned out of Hackney boarding-school for beating the governess" (I.i). Priscilla's impatience with English functionaries and her penchant for retaliatory violence toward them brings to mind Belcour's violent behavior at the English wharf because he is a West Indian "accustomed to a land of slaves." Walter believes that her violence derives from the same source: "the breeding [she] got in the plantations." This was a common view taken of Creoles. Only two years earlier, the English physician John Fothergill had described them as "bred for the most part at the Breast of a Negro slave; surrounded in their Infancy with a numerous Retinue of these dark attendants, they are habituated by Precept and Example, to Sensuality, Selfishness, and Despotism."[41] The privilege of complete ascendancy over slaves in the West Indies allows Creoles such as Priscilla to be "free to act as they pleased towards blacks,"[42] as Trevor Burnard has asserted, and it is this history of despotic ascendancy that explains Priscilla's penchant for violence in England. To increase the comic effect of this West Indian girl going wild on the British stage, Bickerstaff also includes a verbal dimension to Priscilla's violence. She announces that she would rather "spit in [the] face" of the man her guardian, Uncle Barnacle, "has a mind to marry [her] to" than "kiss him" (I.ii). And when she pretends to imagine domestic bliss with Walter she tells him, "If you come to Jamaica with me, I'll raise the Negers for us—It's only giving them a few yams and licking them" (II.iv).

Violence is, clearly, Priscilla's defining characteristic, and its emphasis indicates not only her colonial incongruity in London but also that she is in desperate need of a finishing education in feminine refinement before she is forever set down as a "romp,"[43] the term Samuel Johnson uses to define as "a rude, awkward, boisterous, untaught girl." Indeed, Walter emphasizes her need for change when he remarks, "I believe you think you have got among your blackamoors. But you are not got among your blackamoors now Miss" (I.i). Implying that she is too accustomed to savagery, Walter insinuates that Priscilla must be civilized now that she is no longer living in the colonies. The classroom has failed to produce this transformation into a refined white femininity. But Bickerstaff's title and wordplay indicate that another transformative process is available to Priscilla. Her surname, "Tomboy," implies that the penchant for violence which so completely defines her is, actually, only an awkward intermediary phase in her female development—the growing pains of a female adolescent used to an unregulated West Indian life. Actively getting rid of this name provides a way to relieve these adolescent

---

41. *Considerations relative to the North American colonies* (London: Kent, 1765), 41–42.
42. Trevor Burnard, *Mastery, Tyranny, and Desire*, 32.
43. In fact, *Love in the City* was actually altered and retitled *The Romp* in 1786.

growing pains, and as the title of the play suggests, love, marriage, and the prospect of a London home and husband's surname are vehicles by which the female growing pains of Miss "Tomboy" will be reborn and reformed into a refined example of English femininity.

Despite her adolescence, Priscilla is a most aggressive marriage negotiator. She tells her cousin, Penelope, "I am neither in leading strings, nor hanging sleeves. Why should not I please myself?" (I.ii),[44] clearly indicating that, relieved of the physical trappings of infancy and childhood, she is aware of, and intent on using, her mature body for her own pleasurable ends. These pleasurable ends involve social elevation by marriage: "why should I marry a tradesman," she tells Penelope, "when I can have a gentleman?" (I.ii). Her preference for an independent man of wealth indicates that she intends to exchange her considerable West Indian wealth for the prestige accorded to rank and respectability in England. To this end, she rejects the wealthy grocer, Walter, and sets her sights on Mr. Sightly, "the sweetest, prettiest gentleman you ever set your eyes on" (I.ii). Where bodily self-indulgences expressed by the Creole men in *High Life* and *The West Indian* illustrated the vices that Lovel and Belcour must eschew in order to move forward with their transformations into refined Englishmen, Priscilla's self-indulgent quest to find love in the city with this English gentleman not only drives the premise behind the plot but also underscores her own active intent on being transformed from the wild adolescent "Tomboy" that she is into "the sweetest, prettiest [gentle*woman*] you ever set your eyes on."

In short, Priscilla's impending marriage means that she is destined to become a Mrs. "Sightly," as in, worth seeing, English woman—as potentially worthy an example of marital admiration as her cousin, Penelope, whose name is an explicit evocation of Odysseus's faithful wife[45] and whose engagement to "a [poor] young mercer, just set up in business" (I.iii), is a testament of her lack of materialism and her true feeling. In his *History of Jamaica* (1774), Edward Long comments on the potential benefits of a Creole woman's transformation into an Englishwoman when he observes that "The [Creole] ladies . . . who live in and about the town, being often in the company with Europeans, and others brought up in Great Britain, copy imperceptibly their manner and address; and become better qualified to fill the honourable station of a wife."[46] Through marriage to Mr. "Sightly,"

---

44. Ann Morse Earle writes, "The use of the word hanging sleeves in common speech and in literature is most interesting. It had a figurative meaning; it symbolized youth and innocence. This meaning was acquired, of course, from the wear for centuries of hanging sleeves by little children, both boys and girls." *Two Centuries of Costume in America, MDCXX–MDCCCXX* (New York: Macmillan, 1903), 286.

45. In Homer's *Odyssey*, during her husband's long absence, Penelope kept suitors at bay.

46. Long, *History of Jamaica*, vol. 2, 278–79.

Priscilla seeks to relieve the growing pains of colonial incongruity that plagued her in London, and this act of closure transforms her, onstage, into as striking a domestic copy of the admirable, English, faithful wife, Penelope, as *High Life*'s stage transforms Lovel into another English free man.

HIGH LIFE and *Love in the City* introduce the Creole template that *The West Indian* popularized wherein a white stage Creole is reformed and relieved of pain through a process of rebirth and reformation that sees the Creole change into an appealing copy of the comedy's idealized English character who has served as the Creole's more respectable foil at home in the English metropolis; however, these farces challenge, rather than reproduce, the politics of homecoming detected in *The West Indian* by exacerbating, rather than occluding, the African's experience of pain for readers.

Although Edward Long "rendered all due praise to the Creole ladies for their many amiable qualities"[47] in his *History of Jamaica,* and Thomas Atwood claimed in his *History of Dominica* (1791) that "the English white women in the West Indies are as lovely as in any part of the world besides, make as good wives, tender mothers, and as agreeable companions,"[48] factual and literary accounts often distinguished between two types of white Creole women. J. B. Moreton's *West India Customs and Manners* (1793) attests that white Creole women "who are educated properly from their infancy are as chaste and well bred women as any in the world" but, like Fothergill, Moreton distinguishes these "chaste" ones from those "who receive their education amongst negroe wenches, and imbibe great part of their dialect, principles, manners and customs."[49] Helena Wells echoes Moreton's distinction when she describes her eponymous heroine's education in *Constantia Neville, or the West Indian* (1800): "The pains taken to keep Constantia from the negroes (Mrs. Neville always having an English women in her nursery) added to the society in which she was permitted to mix in her father's house, gave her at twelve years old a fluency of speech, and correctness of language, which many of her seniors would have been proud to possess."[50]

In contrast to such prodigies, Creole women who associated with blacks offered British writers opportunities to creatively explore white female degeneracy. Before Priscilla marries Mr. Sightly, her aggressive method of pursuing him—becoming acquainted with him in Miss La Blond's shop, writing to him, and offering to run away with him—suggests that Fothergill

---

47. Ibid., 276.
48. *History of Dominica* (London: Johnson, 1791), 211.
49. *West India Manners and Customs* (London: Parsons, 1793), 121.
50. Vol. 1 (London: Whittingham, 1800), 77.

and Moreton were right: associating with "blackamoors" has made Priscilla into as sexually rapacious a Creole woman as Thomas Dibdin's Lady Selina Sugarcane from *Family Quarrels* (1802)—a Creole woman with a black maid (Betty Lily) who "made a tour of the whole village, Crossed two ploughed fields, and, after wandering in the church-yard . . . overtook [Charles Supplejack]" (II.iii) in her own aggressive sexual pursuit of her intended suitor.[51]

However, it is emotional intemperance and degeneracy that most defines the fictional Creole woman connected to blacks. I have already discussed how Mrs. Jeffries from Edgeworth's *The Grateful Negro* severely chastised Hector's wife in a fit of pique over a torn dress. This type of emotionally extreme and extremely unfeeling behavior is also displayed by the first Mrs. George Ellison in Sarah Scott's historical novel of that name, whose outpouring of sympathy for an injured lapdog exceeds the level of compassion she shows for a whipped slave. But Bickerstaff's stage visually reinforces these textual impressions of the female Creole's emotional intemperance and degeneracy when Priscilla becomes extremely abrasive to her black maid, Quasheba, ordering her to "bring down my catgut. Why don't you make haste? See how she lets it fall: take it up again—Here threadle my needle—where are you going now? Stand behind my back" (I.ii). Priscilla's aggressive manipulation of Quasheba's body is humorous onstage because her rapid sequence of orders prevents the maid from doing any of them correctly. One can imagine her black body flailing from task to task in a frantic silence, making viewers laugh at her exaggerated physical responses to Priscilla's rapid sequence of commands. But in the published version of the text, the reader's focus is drawn more to two serious acts of extreme immobilization that Priscilla enforces over her black maid: "stand behind my back," she commands, and "if ever I hear, hussy, that you mention a word of what I am going to say to any one else in the house, I will have you horse-whipp'd till there is not a bit of flesh left on your bones" (I.ii). Where Quasheba's silence onstage was a way to focus on her farcical body movements, the silence and immobilization that Priscilla enforces on the pages of the published text with the threat of extreme bodily pain if Quasheba transgresses is read as an example of the white Creole's despotic and malevolent nature which Fothergill, Moreton, Wells, and others reviled. By identifying, within the same scene, the despotic environment under which the silenced black body exists as well as this silenced black body's humorous potential, *Love in the City* exposes the dialogic plane under which it functions, and it makes an active connection to other print media that identified the African experience of pain even as it

---

51. Thomas Dibdin, *Family Quarrels* (New York: Longworth, 1806).

encourages viewers to laugh at this abused black woman. Bickerstaff's textual critique of Priscilla does not stop there, however.

"Oh, poor creature!" Penelope exclaims, incensed and alarmed at Priscilla's brutality toward Quasheba. The Creole woman answers dismissively,

> PRIS. Psha,—what is she but a Neger? If she was at home at our plantations she would find the difference, we make no account of them there at all: if I had a fancy for one of their skins I should not think much of taking it.
> PEN. I suppose then you imagine they have no feeling?
> PRIS. Oh! We never consider that there. (I, ii)

Penelope's sensitivity toward Quasheba is hardly extensive. She never makes any overt gesture to end or relieve the black woman's pain; yet, the idea that this English woman imagines slaves in the colonies with "feeling" similar to her own shows that she is capable of narrowing the emotional distance between the colonial slave and herself. Not so Priscilla, who issues three astoundingly extreme examples of her emotional distance from the pain of African slaves: "we make no account of [Negers] there at all"; "I should not think much of taking [a Neger's skin]"; "we never consider that [Negers have feelings] there." On the issue of pain, her pronouns indicate that she speaks for the entire white Creole nation.

It is this complete lack of tempered humanity and empathy for the African's pain that ultimately undermines Priscilla's transformation in English society. Instead of transforming from Miss "Tomboy" to Mrs. "Sightly"— a copy of English femininity worth seeing—the intent behind the textual wordplay of Priscilla's surnames before and after marriage suggests more the unchanging transformation she makes from one ghastly, intemperate spectacle of femininity to another. Despite the onstage spectacle of her intended marriage, at the play's end, Priscilla is exposed as a textual failure of transformation—a Mrs. "Sightly" who will be as garish a wife as she was an adolescent "Tomboy." On paper, this Creole woman is, essentially, unchanged in London.

WORDPLAY IS the specific device Bickerstaff uses to present Priscilla's faux transformation, thereby establishing her as one who is not and cannot be reborn or reformed in the metropolis because physical intemperance and emotional degeneracy toward Quasheba disqualify her from being recognized as English. Although Townley employs the same device to the same end in *High Life Below Stairs,* it operates on a different dialogic plane.

During the humorous onstage climax where the "sober" Lovel symbolically purged and "punish'd the bad" servants, rewarded "the good," honest one (II.i), and is recognized as a reformed English man, the reader recognizes that Lovel is anything but a free man because his black servants, Kingston and Cloe, remain with him. They have also participated extensively in the abuse of Lovel's home, yet they are noticeably missing during the climax, an absence that implies they have somehow escaped punishment. But I want to suggest that, of all Lovel's domestics, it is most important that Kingston and Cloe face punishment because of what the farce implies that they and their blackness represent.

At the beginning of the play, Lovel's confident and unequivocal assertion that "I will swear for [the integrity of] my blacks" (I.i) suggests that a high level of familiarity exists between him and the slaves he has brought with him from his Jamaican plantation. But disguised as "Jemmy" during the servants' party, Lovel finds out their real identities: Kingston is a drunk and Cloe is a whore—both examples of the kinds of delightful yet imperiling consumption that Freeman has previously critiqued in Lovel. During the course of the play, Lovel does administer some admonishments to his black servants when "Jemmy" roughly handles Kingston by his nose to wake him up from his drunken stupor and ridicules Cloe's beauty and sexual worth with the implication that her interest in him is far from "A very pretty Amour" (I.iii). Yet such punishments are too mild for blacks whose sexual and bacchanalian tendencies reflect the immoral urges inherent in Lovel's own West Indian body and soul, and threaten not merely the financial, but also the moral tenor of his home. Without a doubt, Kingston and Cloe *must* be dismissed with the other major ringleaders so that Lovel can remake himself into another English free man.' Indeed, his complete reformation *depends* on their dismissal. And yet, *High Life* resists showing this particular act of purging blackness because it is an act of closure that the text is unable to countenance in 1759.

In that year, British law had not yet settled on a definitive statement about the legal status of slaves brought to Britain by their West Indian masters, and thus, the informal Yorke–Talbot decision of 1729 was the accepted practice on this issue: baptism and residence in England did not alter a colonial slave's enslaved status.[52] So in 1759, there is high degree of uncertainty as to the citizenship status of Kingston and Cloe, who inhabit the nebulous position between slaves and servants in England. The assurance behind Lovel's transformation into an English free man hits a roadblock at the end of the play because of this uncertainty, one that is more evident to a reader attuned to Yorke–Talbot than to a viewer dazzled by the farce's climactic act

---

52. Shyllon, *Black People in Britain*, 20.

of purging. If Lovel merely dismisses Kingston and Cloe from his home and employ, he wouldn't be punishing these blacks; technically, he'd be freeing them as well as granting them de facto citizenship status by allowing them to hunt for jobs elsewhere in England. In fact, the only punishment this white Creole slaveholder can enact on his slaves is to send them back to Jamaica and to slavery, an act that *Staying Power* (1984), Peter Fryer's marvelous history of black people in Britain, shows was not unprecedented.[53] However, the prospect of reenslavement might have been too extreme a punishment for an English audience to take pleasure in, especially with *Oroonoko* as this farce's backdrop. So Townley's farce avoids detailing Lovel's judgment over the black servants who illustrate the worst of his own faults by not having them return during the climax. Yet their absence is a palpable and serious textual moment. The continued presence of Kingston and Cloe in Lovel's home and life that the published text draws attention to reveals Lovel's homecoming as a sham. Until he discharges Kingston and Cloe, the reader recognizes that Lovel can never be recognized as another sober English free man because his connection to slaves and slavery still defines him and maintains a presence within his home and identity in England. This will forever make him different, perhaps inferior, wholly Creole, and never English.

Thus, despite humorous climaxes involving marriage and the divestment of vice-ridden employees that, together, create impressions, onstage, that Priscilla and Lovel have transformed into refined English residents, textual wordplay coupled with the palpable presence or absence of black pain in *High Life* and *Love in the City* serve to reinforce the unchanging nature of the white stage Creole and confirm for English readers of these farces that Lovel is no English Freeman and Priscilla is no English Penelope. Creoles ultimately lack the humane feeling, action, and sensibility that is a mark of true Englishness; their homecomings in these farces are not welcoming acts of national recognition and reception but politicized acts of national distinction that combine English xenophobia with antislavery criticism. These farces privilege the purity of the English spirit of freedom by excluding Creoles from legitimate English recognition because of their either emotional attachment to or emotional detachment from slaves and slavery. Farces are able to make a subtle political protest against white Creoles, on behalf of slaves, and against slavery by highlighting the Creoles' exclusion from the spirit of Englishness.

But what of the farcical stage Africans themselves? Does either farce make any conscious effort to relieve the pain of Africans by incorporating them in this spirit of English freedom?

---

53. See Fryer's discussion of "the profligate Duchess of Kingston" and her black servant Sambo. *Staying Power*, 73.

PRIOR TO 1772, "from about the middle of the eighteenth century," Peter Fryer states, "there is evidence of cohesion, solidarity, and mutual help among black people in Britain."[54] Fryer's work, alongside that of Folarin Shyllon, Nancy Myers, and Gretchen Gerzina, shows that there was already a thriving community of black people who had made a home in eighteenth-century England and had done so since as early as 1505. The majority were young, working-class metropolitan Africans employed in the domestic trade. They had their own societies and, as Myers shows, were frequently recorded among the nation's birth, death, marriage, baptism, and criminal records. Inclusion in the day-to-day documents and activities of life in London indicates that England was already a home for black people and a place that relieved them from the pain of slavery, to a certain degree, by allowing them to freely intermingle and marry among themselves as well as whites of their respective classes. This made England, and London in particular, an ostensibly welcoming place for black slaves who came there from the slave colonies.

However, this progressive view of England as a home and potential haven for a new community of Africans from the West Indies cannot be detected in either *High Life* or *Love in the City*. The African characters in these farces make their presences felt in ways that undermine the Creole's English transformation, but they are never seen as integral parts of the social fabric that coheres at the end of each farce since their lives as slaves are not transformed in any of the finales. For instance, although all of Bickerstaff's white characters—male and female—are trying to find love in a London society where marriage is a strategic opportunity for social and financial advancement, Bickerstaff never makes the "Black Girl," Quasheba, involved in this business. He is prepared to use Quasheba's silenced black body to provide slapstick humor onstage, and to emphasize Priscilla's despotic Creoleness on the pages of the published text. But he shows no interest in using "Christian marriage" as a vehicle for imagining Quasheba's freedom in England even though a black or white husband would have freed her from Priscilla's despotic clutches, thereby establishing this version of the marriage plot as a politicized recourse to freedom for the African in England. His decision to include her in his text but not explore the political ramifications of an African woman seeking "love in the city" draws attention to the limits of the dialogic plane on which his text operates. Because it, ultimately, shows no interest in relieving the despotism under which Quasheba's silenced body exists by giving her the freedom to be exchanged or negotiated for on her own terms in the manner that the four white women in the text enjoy, *Love*

---

54. Ibid., 67.

in the City is noticeably silent on the relief of African woman's pain even as the text actively exposes it.

As a pair of formerly enslaved blacks now living in England, Kingston and Cloe might appear to offer up the idea of an intraracial marriage in England as a symbol of freedom along the lines of Ignatius and Anne Sancho.[55] But *High Life* is aggressive in its refusal to involve its black characters in an emancipating marriage plot because it garners more laughs by involving them in a hypersexual one. In one of his most revealing stage directions, "[*Kingston kisses Cloe heartily*]" after being her partner during a dance scene, causing Philip to exclaim, "See how the Devils kiss!" (II.i). Philip's comment draws attention to, exaggerates, and marks as diabolic the blacks' excessive sexual exuberance even though all the other white servants are involved in the "[*kissing round*]" (II.i). But Townley does not stop there. Black sexual exuberance is grossly intemperate. In a drunken stupor, Kingston and Coachman refuse to allow Cook to help them to bed:

COACHMAN: She shan't see us to bed—we'll see ourselves to bed
KINGSTON: We got drunk together, and we'll go to bed together. (I.iii)

Kingston's earlier enthusiasm for Cloe is matched, here, with a suggestive homoerotic enthusiasm to "go to bed *together*" with Coachman. And Cloe shows a similarly untoward enthusiasm for interracial sex. Enraptured by the "pretty boy" "Jemmy," she brazenly offers herself to him, openly asserting that he "shall be in love with me by and by" (I.iii). Townley makes rampant heterosexual, implicit homoerotic, and potential interracial sex the overriding functions of his black characters. Their hypersexualized bodies provide bawdy, titillating physical humor that typical farce relies on. However, because they are only read as hypersexual, and because Quasheba's marital desires are not read at all, these Africans in England continue to suffer the pain not only of slavery under their respective masters, but also of exclusion from the spirit of English freedom that permeates each text.

Relief for the African's painful exclusion from a harmonious London life does come in the shape of William Macready's *Irishman in London; or, The Happy African*. This farce premiered at Covent Garden on April 21, 1792, the same year that the House of Commons voted to gradually abolish the slave trade within four years. This was also the year in which the Irish politician Hercules Langrishe introduced an act in parliament that allowed Catholics

---

55. Ignatius Sancho was a celebrated eighteenth-century black man of letters who corresponded with a wide variety of people, including Lawrence Sterne. His collected letters were published posthumously in 1782. He married Anne Osborne, a black woman of West Indian origin, on December 17, 1758, in St. Margaret's Church, Westminster.

to practice law in England for the first time.[56] Langrishe also supported the 1793 Catholic Relief Act that gave Catholics the right to vote as well as hold most civil and military offices. Thus, Macready's play comes out in a year in which it appeared that English politicians were making some real progress in jointly relieving the pains experienced by both Irish Catholics and slaves.

In contrast to *High Life* and *Love in the City,* however, *Irishman in London*'s plot takes a multiple approach to homecoming by combining the metropolitan experiences of different colonial types who all meet in London. In Macready's plot, Mr. Frost, an English-Jamaican Creole, returns to England with his daughter, Caroline, and her black maid, Cubba, in an attempt to sever her relationship with the army captain, Seymour, and to arrange her marriage to a rich Irishman, Patrick Colloony. Colloony arrives in London to meet his intended bride, and his servant, Murtoch Delany, accompanies him. In a London street, however, Frost unexpectedly runs into Seymour, who learns of the Creole's intention to marry his daughter to the Irishman she has never met. Acting as an intermediary, Seymour's valet, Edward, finds out that Caroline still loves Seymour and will refuse the Irishman. But Caroline's fears about being forced to marry Colloony prove groundless. On the two occasions that Colloony meets with Frost's family, he mistakenly takes the Englishwoman, Louisa, Caroline's impoverished and orphaned friend, for his intended bride. Frost, himself, has actually made an offer of marriage to Louisa, but his advances are characterized as untoward because he is of an age where he should be acting as Louisa's surrogate father and not her lover (Frost rather ambiguously refers to his age as "fifty or so" [I.i]). The play ends with Frost blessing Caroline's marriage to Seymour, and renouncing his claim to Louisa, freeing her to marry Colloony. In this way, the old Creole assumes a role in aiding the happiness of young lovers rather than impeding it.

Macready's play, then, brings another type of Creole—an old lecherous one—to London in an effort to reform his attitude to romance and restrain his untoward and outdated libido. But even though *Irishman* follows the template witnessed in other farces and transforms the stage Creole into a responsible English patriarch, the title indicates that he is certainly not Macready's main focus. The question of who the focus *is* becomes complicated by the fact that there are two Irish men in London—Colloony and his Irish servant, Delany. By referring to a singular "Irishman" in his title, however, Macready appears to privilege one Irish man's experience in London over the other. But which one, and why does he privilege it?

---

56. The parliamentary vote was 230 to 85. It was nullified a year later by the Commons's refusal to take the bill up again after it was turned down in the House of Lords. Langrishe issued his act on January 25, 1792.

Christopher Flynn's wonderful work on this text answers this question by identifying one Irish man's "ability to see others and himself" as the factor that determines "*the* Irishman of the play's title."[57] However, his essay privileges this particular Irishman as the exclusive "spokesman for cultures . . . that served as a unified challenge to Englishness by their common exclusion from the marketplace" even though the African woman, Cubba, is just as much of a dominant spokesperson within the drama. To provide some balance, then, as well as expand the political activism that Flynn identifies in the text, the remaining two sections of this chapter will not only identify this Irishman but also reveal how the wordplay evoked by him and the African mentioned in the play's subtitle operates on a dialogic plane that provides, as well as politicizes, comic relief.

FROM THE VERY beginning of Macready's play, experiences of pleasure and pain in London serve to distinguish the two Irish men politically. Colloony, "an elegant young fellow from Ireland" "with a fine fortune" (I.i), enters in Act One marveling and apostrophizing about the metropolis: "Oh London, London, dear London as Ercher says; had I millions I'd spend it all there—it's the mert for enjoyment" (I.i). Delany enters immediately after Colloony, singing a song: "We Irishmen both high and low, we are both neat and handy / The ladies everywhere we go allow we are the dandy" (I.i). The difference is revealing. Colloony's soliloquy describes him taking personal pleasure in the attractions of the metropolis; as a "mert for enjoyment," London relieves all his possible pains. Indeed, he finds "everything so captivating" that he exclaims, "I wish from my heart I may never leave it" (I.i). Delany's song, on the other hand, takes pleasure in all Irish male bodies, "both high and low," as international attractions themselves, and he unequivocally believes that Ireland is "the sweetest little place in the world" (I.i), telling Colloony "worrow do, sir, send me home" (I.i). Politically, then, the wealthy Irishman enters the play happily announcing himself as an avowed assimilationist, whereas his servant-countryman takes pleasure in his identity as a staunch Irish loyalist.

This difference is underscored more forcefully in another humorous yet politicized scene. After enquiring about their journey from the riverside to the town, the Creole, Frost, asks his prospective Irish son-in-law: "But . . . are not the towns through which you came worthy of observation?" Colloony replies: "Certainly sir your manufactories are so astonishingly greet, they prove at once the wonderful industry and wealth of your nation" (II.i).

---

57. Christopher Flynn, "Challenging Englishness from the Racial Margins: William Macready's *Irishman in London; or. The Happy African,*" *Irish Studies Review* 16 (2008): 169.

Delany, however, thinks otherwise: "I could see three times as much as maister Pat . . . and the devil a manufactory I saw equal to our own. Och! If you could only look at the oyster beds in pooibeg, the Foundling of the Lying-in Hospital at Dublin, they are the right sort of manufactrys" (II.i). The conflation of "oyster beds" and orphanages as "the right sort of manufactrys" is enough to make readers and viewers as well as the other characters laugh at Delany's absurdity while they all critique him as uncouth for deriding his English host's country, especially when contrasted with Colloony's complimentary response. But Delany defends himself against this laughter and critique with the surprising retort "there can't be better manufactories in the world, than those that provides comfortable lodgings, and every sort of bread and meat for poor creatures that can't provide for themselves" (II.i). Where Colloony sees London as a "mert for [his own individual] enjoyment" as well as the place where his marriage to a Creole heiress will continue to provide him even more means to enjoy life there, Delany uses his voice in London for an aggressive type of Irish activism. He articulates a need for alleviating Irish poverty by remembering the pains of the helpless people he has left behind. While an audience would laugh at his brogue, rabid nationalism, tendency to exaggerate, and refusal to ingratiate himself to the English, the concern he expresses toward the Irish Catholic poor differentiates him, politically, from the obviously self-centered Colloony.

Aspects of Delany's characterization call to mind the political platform held by the United Irishmen. Founded in 1791 and grounded in what Jill Marie Bradbury and David Valone call "commonwealth principles of limited monarchical rule, equal rights for all men, and religious toleration,"[58] the United Irishmen were actually a radical offshoot of the Volunteer movement, a group that became actively involved in political reform in Ireland in the early 1780s. However, the issue of Catholic emancipation caused the United Irishmen to splinter from this original group: "Fundamentally, the language and platform of the Volunteers assumed the continuance of Protestant political and social dominance," whereas the spokesmen for the United Irishmen issued a "bold call for the equal treatment of 'all sects and denominations of Irishmen' in political, legal, and social structures."[59] With this political schism providing a contemporary context, it appears that Delany and Colloony confirm Flynn's belief that "Macready's play depicts Irishness as a divided identity, or as a set of interdependent but distinct identities."[60] In their connection to, or disconnect from, Irish pain and pleasure, these Irishmen embody the debate over whether the future of Catholic relief in

---

58. *Anglo-Irish Identities 1571–1845* (Lewisburg, PA: Bucknell University Press, 2008), 18.
59. Ibid., 19.
60. Flynn, "Challenging Englishness from the Racial Margins," 164.

Britain will be achieved through the attachment to an Irish national identity as Delany embodies, or in the submission to a metropolitan force as Colloony represents.

Ultimately, textual wordplay reveals the political position that *Irishman in London* privileges for its readers. Colloony's name is not simply a reference to an Irish town; it is also, presumably, a play on "colony," a word Samuel Johnson defines as "a body of people drawn from the mother-country to inhabit some distant place." Johnson's reproductive image conveys the idea that a colony produces a new individual, and the metonymic phrase "body of people" suggests that anyone can be a part of a colony. In short, a colonist is, simply, anyone of any class who inhabits any distant locale connected to a metropolitan realm. But as an avowed assimilationist who not only praises London but also wishes to "never leave it," Colloony belies Johnson's understanding of a colonist as one who "inhabits some distant place" because of his preference for a metropolitan home. Macready's negative attitude toward this Irishman surfaces in the word "Loon" that transforms colony into Colloony. According to Johnson, a "loon" is "a sorry fellow; a scoundrel; a rogue." By combining these two Johnsonian expressions, Macready gives the impression that the wealthy Irishman is "a sorry fellow; a scoundrel; a rogue" for transforming from a new Irish representative of a colony to a sycophantic Colloony in London, attracted more to the bodily pleasures he can selfishly experience there rather than using his wealth to relieve the pains of other Irish colonists at home. Remember, had he millions, Colloony says he would spend it *all* in the metropolis.

The textual wordplay involving Delany's experience of being renamed in London further substantiates this negative impression of Colloony. When Colloony calls him "Dill," an epithet describing a simpleton or fool, Delany retorts: "Don't be calling me Dill, myself can't bear it, it's making so little of one. My name is Murtoch Delany" (II.i). He also chastises Colloony for critiquing Ireland (II.i). "Och! Maister Pat," Delany exclaims, "don't be running down oer country: myself can't bear it" (II.i). Delany "can't bear" Colloony demeaning either himself or his home country. Both acts pain him. And because he feels and articulates the pains of his home in a way that Colloony does not, Macready aligns Delany's farcical body with a distinct political agenda.

Colloony may "wish to prove by actions instead of words that Ireland is the soul of virtue not vice to flourish in" (I.i), but his affected "actions" onstage are those of a flatterer willing to pander to, and merge himself with, the Protestant majority. Delany's "words," on the other hand, when read on the published pages of Macready's text, identify his commitment to promoting and defending Ireland and the people most commonly defined by it: the

Irish Catholic underclass.[61] His characterization reveals that the complete relief of pain for oppressed colonial bodies will not come about through the assimilation of the wealthy Irish male body in the English metropolis, as the absentee landlord, Colloony, represents. Instead, *Irishman in London* reveals a level of skepticism about Catholic relief acts such as those in 1792 and 1793 that enable Catholics of a particular class to openly participate in British political and social life but do nothing for the Irish underclass at home. As Bradbury and Valone state: "The Relief Act . . . failed to bring real emancipation or to redistribute social and political power . . . since the act depended on the willingness of Protestant gentry and corporations to grant life leases to Catholic tenants, open guilds to Catholic members, and accept Catholics as jurors."[62] With Colloony more inclined to side with Protestants for his own pleasure than to advocate for the relief of the Catholic poor like Delany, *Irishman in London* critiques the contemporary steps forward on behalf of Catholic relief as entirely insufficient. In reminding readers of the literal pains of poverty experienced by the Irish underclass, Delany pushes for a more expansive approach to complete relief at home in Ireland. This leads me to the same conclusion as Flynn but from a different source. Of the two Irishmen in London, Delany is the *Irishman* whose metropolitan experience Macready privileges in his title. He is an Irish hero because he represents the pains as well as the humor of his home country and its people.

IF THERE IS some confusion about the Irish man privileged in Macready's main title, there is none concerning the identity of the figure mentioned in his subtitle. Without a doubt, *The Happy African* refers to Caroline Frost's maid, Cubba, the play's only African character, who asks her employer, "why everybody no be happy like me?" (I.ii). Given my earlier discussion of print media's obsession with black bodies in pain, this textual interest in privileging an African's happiness is extremely anomalous. What is the nature of Cubba's happiness in London? How has her pain been relieved there?

Cubba's condensed slave narrative articulates her own history of pain and happiness under slavery:

> CUBBA: me only so many year old (*holding up her fingers*) when cross Bochro man catch me—me going walk one day, did take me from all my friend—me shall never see dem again—but missee so good since she buy me, me no wish to go back, though my fader great king. (II.i)

---

61. This idea is complicated even more by the fact that Macready played the part of Colloony himself.

62. *Anglo-Irish Identities*, 19–20.

Unlike Phillis Wheatley's speaker in "On Being Brought From Africa to America," who attributes her relief from the pain of the middle passage to God's "Mercy," the mere act of being purchased by Caroline relieves the pain of Cubba's initial enslavement, and for this act of kindness she expresses the kind of gratitude that Oran displays in Thomas Bellamy's *Benevolent Planters* (1787) when he proclaims that "Slavery is but a name"[63] under the subjection of a benevolent planter. In fact, Flynn has revealed that this was exactly how Macready originally conceived her:

> When asked why she won't accept freedom in England, she explains—or would have if the official censor, John Larpent, hadn't banned this part of her self-representation: "No; den me great slave, if missa forsake me—every body use me ill, me beg—Now, when me hungry—dry—missa feed me—give me drink—Cloaths—every thing me wish—me be very happy—no want free."[64]

In this purged speech, Cubba's happiness is an infantilized expression of dependence that can be easily read and dismissed as textual approval for the policy of amelioration and even support for the African's continued enslavement in England.

However, in the actual published version of the farce, Cubba's happy African-ness is as dialogically politicized for readers as Delany's humorous yet politicized expression of Irishness. Like his, Cubba's role is seen as farcical, but it is read with serious implications about the home and people she has left behind in the West Indies. "Nobody ought to be merry when missee frettee" (I.ii), she tells Mr. Frost, completely identifying with the pains of her mistress, Caroline, in a broken English akin more to doggerel than true feeling. But this humorous identification with the white woman's romantic pain does not prevent Cubba from privileging the actual pain experienced by African slaves at home in the colonies. When Caroline evokes pity for Colloony, Cubba interjects with the incredulous assertion, "Missee, you pity great man? He no good—me pity poor black, he no do good—run away—he get whip and chain" (I.ii). By distinguishing between the sentimentalized pain of a "no good" absentee landlord and the physical pain experienced by enslaved black men, the happy African uses her humorous voice in the metropolis to contextualize and visualize rather than elide or ignore the colonial vice of which West Indians such as Belcour, Lovel, and Tomboy are all guilty. Rather than using the metropolis as these white Creoles do, to satisfy their own

---

63. (London: Debrett, 1789), I.iii.
64. Flynn, "Challenging Englishness from the Racial Margins," 164.

pleasures and progressions into English men and women, Cubba uses London as a powerful opportunity for the type of political activism that she would not have had at home in the colonies—activism that absentee landlords such as Priscilla, Lovel, Belcour, and Colloony are completely opposed to. Part of Cubba's happiness, then, involves the pleasure of being able to articulate and validate to others in England the existence of black colonial pain that white Creoles, selfishly consumed with their own pains and pleasures, routinely elide.[65]

Cubba's West Indian language is, thus, a dialogically politicized expression of activism in London. Like Delany's raw Irish brogue, Jamaican English is the basis of Cubba's inferior, farcical voice in the play since it distinguishes her from all the other characters that speak Standard English. But unlike the silenced Quasheba, Cubba gets to speak extensively, and her broken form of English achieves the same humorous yet politically progressive effect of Delany's Irish brogue. Just as his farcical comments about "manufactories" draw serious attention to Irish bodies in pain, Cubba's Jamaican English also makes serious political interventions on behalf of African slaves when she says:

> CUBBA: Good, bad, all colors.—Bochro read great big book, tell him how he can be good—for all dat, some do very bad—poor black no understand read—how they know good from bad, when them massa no show them good zample? (I.ii)

This is a black Creole reevaluation of Lovel's speech at the end of *High Life:*

> LOVEL: If persons of rank would act up to their standard, it would be impossible that their servants could ape them—But when they affect everything that is ridiculous, it will be in the power of any low Creature to follow their example. (II.i)

Rather than simply blaming "ridiculous" "persons of rank" for being poor role models, Cubba refashions Lovel's critique by calling out the Creole tyrants who "read great big book" of religious words—the Bible—but do not perform its moral acts: men who speak with the soft, strategic voice of paternal tyranny. Cubba's critique is a distinctly antislavery call for planters to either be more responsible role models or educate slaves so that they can learn to be responsible to a higher authority. The ability to convey this pro-

---

65. At the end of her *History,* Mary Prince asserts that an opportunity to advocate is her main motivation for narrating her life story.

found message in her own tongue and not that of an assimilated Englishman offers another reason for Cubba's happiness: the broken English she excels in conveys as active—if not more powerful—a message for relieving the problem of slavery as any other standard form of speech.

Cubba's African-ness is also dialogically politicized by its location. Frost tells "her every hour that she is in a blessed land of liberty, that she is her own mistress, Free as air in hopes of getting rid of her; but she won't stir—no she sticks like bird lime" (I.ii). Referring to the Mansfield Judgment and its presumption of freedom for slaves as soon as they arrived on British soil, Frost reveals that Cubba is legally emancipated in a way that Kingston, Cloe, and Quasheba were not. But why would he be "in hopes of getting rid of" a free labor source faithfully devoted to his daughter? One possible answer? Money. Under Mansfield's judgment, Frost knows that he must pay Cubba a salary; perhaps he resents the fact that she enforces this by sticking with this family like "bird lime"—the sticky substance that hunters use to ensnare birds in trees. Clearly unflattering and definitely intended to be humorous, Frost's use of the simile places agency solidly in Cubba's hands now that she is an English resident. For it implies that Cubba fully understands her freedom but uses her fidelity to Caroline as the emotional currency that ensures her employment, employment that financially entraps Frost. This proves to be a remarkable reversal of the entrapment that initially brought her from Africa to Jamaica. At the ends of their respective texts, Kingston, Cloe, and Quasheba are all trapped within their masters' respective households, and they have no choice over where and with whom they stay since they are completely at the whim of masters who bring them to England and can just as easily whisk them back to the colonies again. By contrast, Macready politicizes Cubba's stubborn choice to stay in the Frost home; she is an African in the happy position of being able to choose to give financial pain to a white Creole master in London, where Africans like her have only formerly received it with no pay from Creole tyrants in the colonies.

The dialogically politicized language, speech, and actions of the Irishman and the African, then, prove crucial to understanding how Macready's text changes the popular farcical template about colonial figures being transformed into pure English men and women in the metropolis. By using a main title and a subtitle that, together, draw more attention to the empire's underclass than to its wealthy, in a genre that purports to be just another quick and light look at how funny outlandish colonial figures can be when they exhibit behavior that makes them painfully at odds with English notions of rank and respectability, Delany and Cubba are revealed as the hero and heroine of a dialogically politicized comedy—one that presents lower-class figures of empire actively identifying themselves as much more than comic relief in the metropolis. They do not selfishly advance or pleasure themselves as their wealthier colonial counterparts do onstage; on the pages of the published text, the African and the Irishman avoid the pains of colonial incongruity that plague wealthy white colonials in the metropolis because they revel in the presumed inferiority of their national difference. Instead of experiencing the embarrassing pains of rebirth and reformation that their Creole and Irish upper-class counterparts do as they seek to transform into English residents, Cubba and Delany are incapable of making this kind a transformation as their speech, actions, and mannerisms make patently clear. They are unchangeably African and Irish. But unlike that of the white stage Creole whose unchanging West Indian-ness heralded his/her exclusion from England, Cubba and Delany's unchangeable identities are patriotic expressions of abolitionism.

With their unchangeable identities firmly fixed in their raw languages, these lower-class figures of empire are driven by, and are articulating desires of, a more progressive, political nature, and their articulation of these desires is the key to their inclusiveness within British society. By uniting the Irish Catholic underclass with the African slave in the titles and the main performances of his farce, Macready presents them both as activists who use their metropolitan voices to demand the complete abolition of pain for their respective peoples. In essence, he redefines the politics of homecoming involving colonials in London from being concerned with the transformation of the colonial individual to being concerned with the transformations of the oppressed figures of empire. In coming to London and articulating the pains experienced by the people they have left behind, Cubba and Delany are identifying themselves as part of a politics that Isaac Land has termed "street citizenship." In his reading of the black street entertainer Joseph Johnson, who "sang patriotic songs in the streets of London with a model ship bound to his head,"[66] Land shows that "Britishness, was not beyond [the] reach" of common blacks who "engaged in what might be called citizenship from the bottom up"[67] when, like Johnson, they made concerted attempts to identify themselves with the country. "Wearing a ship," Land believes, "served as a comprehensive statement of who Johnson was [a seaman on a merchant vessel], where he was from, what he had done, where he belonged."[68] In short, Johnson confirms that "Britishness was about behavior, not birthplace or bloodline."[69] Street citizenship, then,

---

66. Land, "Bread and Arsenic: Citizenship from the Bottom Up in Georgian London," *Journal of Social History* 39 (2005): 90.
67. Ibid.
68. Ibid., 100.
69. Ibid., 90.

is "an approach which recognizes the power of ordinary people to contest and reshape society's assumptions about who people are and who belongs where."⁷⁰ In the published versions of Macready's play, Cubba and Delany are also actively contesting and reshaping readers' assumptions about African slaves and the Catholic underclass by presenting them as humorous activists who, in using the metropolis to petition for the complete abolitions of pain for the oppressed people of empire, are claiming a right, as Britons, to speak freely on behalf of these Other underprivileged people who claim the British Empire as home.⁷¹

MACREADY'S PLAY encourages readers to accept this couple as British street citizens during a comic resolution that brings the Irishman in London and the happy African together in an interracial union. Delany has romantic aspirations: "I wish I had something to do ... or a fine young lady would fall in love with me or any diverting incident of that nater" (II.i), he remarks, and Cubba answers his call, saying, "you want speak a wi me?" (II.i). Macready appears to make the idea of interracial marriage seem taboo with Delany proclaiming to Cubba, "Honey, it won't do—now don't think of it," and Cubba telling him "me no want you love me—dat be very bad thing—your face white, me poor Negro" (II. i). But despite these objections, "the milk of compassion rises within [Delany] for poor Cubbagh," (II.i) and Cubba tells him, "Me love a you dearly," and she asks him to "tell a . . . fine story about your country, me like to hear" (II.i). Her interest in Delany as the person and Ireland as the place that could both potentially give her pleasure implies that she is being silently seduced by an imagined future of domestic happiness away from the Frosts.

In drama, the marriage of the hero and heroine symbolizes a harmonious relief from any former pains that the play, itself, has generated, and Macready's play is no different in this respect. Just as Frost is about to give Caroline's hand to Colloony in marriage:

[*Edward takes Cubba's hand, slips Caroline's gently away, and puts Cubba's in its place under Frost's arm.*]
MURTOCH: Arrah! Is it my own little daffy down dilly you want, Maister Pat, to bring home! O thunder! Arrah be asy. (II.ii)

---

70. Ibid., 104.
71. "An Irishman said, he was very fond of the women in general; but that an African girl, with whom he got acquainted upon the gold coast, pleased him better than all the rest of the fair sex together." *Garrick's Complete Jester* (London: Oxlade, 1779), 13.

With Cubba mistakenly presented as Colloony's bride, Murtoch Delany claims ownership of his "own little daffy down dilly," and his "Arrah[72] be asy" is an indignant warning to Maister Pat not to encroach on his chosen partner and future bride. Amidst the humor, then, Macready clearly invites Cubba and Delany to partake of a harmonious London life where two other wealthy colonial marriages are openly ratified, and the West Indian, Mr. Frost, who ratifies all of these climactic marriages, confirms the validity of this interracial coupling. Frost has stated that Cubba is entirely free in this land of liberty. Unlike his farcical Creole forebears, he has completely renounced slavery in England and, thus, completely reformed himself into a true English patriarch. If Cubba wants to marry, then, she has the complete freedom to do it. It's her choice. *Irishman in London; or, The Happy African* concludes with this suggestion that the pain of this formerly enslaved black woman can, and almost definitely will, be completely relieved by the happiness of an interracial marriage and a great British home.

RATHER THAN the "horrors" of social degeneration imagined by Richard Edgeworth and other English gentlemen of his ilk, Macready's play presents interracial marriage in England as a positive, politicized articulation of underclassed peoples of empire banding together as activists. His efforts mark a turning point in our approach to the fictional women of "Imoinda's shade." Where the Imoinda-esque heroines in the colonies were employed by British writers in colonial texts to literally fight tyranny with their bodies, Cubba indicates that the African woman becomes involved in a different type of activism in fictions set in England: that of merging with other oppressed groups and articulating their joint oppression as a means of attaining abolitionist relief for all. Unity also forms the basis for understanding the black woman's activism in *Adeline Mowbray* (1805).

---

72. "Arrah" is only used as an expression of surprise or excitement.

CHAPTER 5

"'What!' cried the delighted mulatto, 'are we going to prosecu massa?'"

Adeline Mowbray's
Distinguished Complexion of Abolition

> Liberty by the English law depends not upon the complexion; and what was said even in the time of queen Elizabeth, is now substantially true, that the air of England is too pure for a slave to breathe in.
>
> —Sir William Blackstone, vol. 1 of *Commentaries on the Law of England* (1800), 425.

THE BLACK SHADE of a mulatto woman's complexion makes a dramatic entrance midway through *Adeline Mowbray* (1805),[1] Amelia Opie's third long-prose fiction. At this point in the tale, Opie's eponymous heroine has become a pariah in English society for steadfastly refusing to marry her domestic partner, Frederic Glenmurray. She believes that a "pure and honourable union" (I, 77) will naturally form between them without the need of an official ceremony, and she lives by this principle despite the fact that it does not provide her with legal recognition or social respect. Adeline's family and friends are outraged. They ignore her principled stance and ostracize her for leading what they perceive to be a life of brazen infamy. At this same time, the couple's finances abruptly dwindle, and Glenmurray's terminal illness noticeably worsens. It is while they are, thus, poised on the brink of imminent disaster that a curious and apparently trivial incident occurs—an incident that transforms the tale's political scope: Glenmurray exhibits an

---

1. (New York: Woodstock Books, 1995). This is a reproduction of the 1805 edition. All subsequent references refer to this edition.

insatiable craving for a pineapple. To appease his whimsical appetite, the cash-strapped Adeline pawns her veil in order to buy the sweet treat. But en route to the "fruiterer's" (II, 154) she happens upon, and becomes embroiled in, another incident wherein a mulatto woman makes a dramatic entrance into the narrative and her black complexion compels Adeline to forgo her primary objective.

Assembled at the door of a "mean-looking house" (II, 154), a crowd watches the mulatto woman's sick husband, William, being dragged to prison for debt while Savanna, the equally ill mulatto woman, tries, unsuccessfully, to prevent his arrest.

> A surly-looking man, who was the creditor himself, forcing a passage through the crowd, said, "why, bring him along and have done with it; here is a fuss to make indeed about that idle dog and that ugly black b—h!"
>
> Adeline till then had not recollected that she was a mulatto; and this speech, reflecting so brutally on her colour,—a circumstance which made her an object of greater interest to Adeline,—urged her to step forward to their joint relief with an almost irresistible impulse. . . . (II, 157)

Up until this point, Opie's narrative had only concerned itself with Adeline's activism as a virtuous proponent for the abolition of marriage. But Adeline's urge "to step forward" clearly introduces a new discussion about activism on behalf of people of African descent. While it is possible to discuss, individually, either of these modes of activism in the text, the fact that Adeline defends Savanna from the creditor's harsh racial epithet ("ugly black b—h!") at the same time that she is defending herself for stepping forward as a virtuous proponent for the abolition of marriage implies that Opie is actively merging these modes of activism for a specific end. In this chapter, I propose that Opie consciously unites, yet ultimately distinguishes between, Adeline and Savanna and the activist discourses that they inspire in *Adeline Mowbray*, and by doing so, provides another way to consider its theme of abolition—a reading that offers an especially triumphant view of one of these women's complexions.

CONTEMPORARY REVIEWS of Opie's tale missed the resonance of the Adeline and Savanna union as well as the tale's discourse of abolition.[2] As M. O. Grenby attests: "*Adeline Mowbray* . . . could only have been interpreted by

---

2. Contemporary reviews of the novel make no reference to this as an antislavery/abolitionist tale, and very few make any reference to Savanna at all.

contemporaries as an inquest into both the practicalities and morality of cohabitation and childbearing without marriage."[3] In exploring this theme, modern critics such as Roxanne Eberle and Gary Kelly have brought out the tale's biographical foundations both as a "roman à clef about Mary Wollstonecraft and William Godwin" (who were known by, and friendly with, the author), and as an illustration of Opie's political ideology after her marriage to the painter John Opie and before her conversion to Quakerism.[4]

Recently, however, Eberle and others have also taken more notice of Savanna's role in order to further probe the tale's abolitionist politics. To this end, Eberle reads *Adeline Mowbray* as a novel that "explicitly addressed many 'Jacobin' concerns: free love, free speech and abolition," ultimately ending in a "powerful 'world of obligation' which brings together women of different races."[5] But at the end of her essay, Eberle is skeptical of this exclusively female "world of obligation," asking whether it is "an entirely positive alternative to inherently flawed heterosexual union."[6] Carol Howard offers more skepticism about the novel's liberating potential. In her perceptive and persuasive reading, she also recognizes the scene that opens this chapter (she calls it "The Story of the Pineapple") as an important barometer for understanding Savanna;[7] however, she interprets Adeline's "step forward" as a gesture that may liberate Savanna from debt, but in the process, reenforces the mulatto woman's containment since the money that Adeline pays to settle the couple's debt allegorically simulates a white mistress stepping forward to purchase a mulatto woman's fierce allegiance and unlimited service for a paltry price, much as a slave master might do.[8] Howard also expresses skepticism about Savanna's maternal role and liberation in the tale, a concern shared by Susan Greenfield, who reads Savanna as "the ultimate representative of the dark underclass, the servant [who] provides a point of contrast against which Adeline's superior status can be distinguished."[9] Reading Savanna only as a foil, Greenfield concludes that although the novel "derides slavery . . . it also sentimentalizes a maternal servitude grounded in racial difference," making "the political outcome . . . ambiguous."[10]

---

3. M. O. Grenby, *The Anti-Jacobin Novel* (Cambridge: Cambridge University Press, 2001), 89.
4. Gary Kelly, "Amelia Opie, Lady Caroline Lamb, and Maria Edgeworth: Official and Unofficial Ideology," *Ariel* 12 (1981): 3–34; and Roxanne Eberle, "Amelia Opie's *Adeline Mowbray*: Diverting the Libertine Gaze; or, the Vindication of a Fallen Woman," *Studies in the Novel* 26, no. 2 (1994): 121–52.
5. Eberle, "Amelia Opie's *Adeline Mowbray*," 3, 21.
6. Ibid., 22.
7. Carol Howard's "'The Story of the Pineapple': Sentimental Abolitionism and Moral Motherhood in Amelia Opie's *Adeline Mowbray*," *Studies in the Novel* 30, no. 3 (1998): 355–76.
8. Ibid., 10.
9. Susan Greenfield, *Mothering Daughters* (Detroit: Wayne State University Press, 2002), 126.
10. Ibid., 128.

Persuasive as these critical stances are, I want to challenge their collective skepticism about Savanna's social, political, and maternal roles as well as her liberation within the text by proposing alternative readings of both Savanna's characterization and the tale's abolitionist discourse—readings that take into account the important role that *Imoinda's Shade* has been ascribing to a fictional line of African women that are actively involved in promoting progressive antislavery and abolitionist positions in British literature by intervening in marriage plots.

In Chapter Three, I outlined the manner in which the fictional African saint-mother and rebel-wife that originated in Behn's characterization of Imoinda challenged the institution of slavery by being the focuses of radical alternatives to ending it through immigration to a free European territory (as Ada demonstrates during one of the endings of Kotzebue's *The Negro Slaves*) or active gynecological rebellion (as Amri demonstrates through literal and narrative acts of maternalism in *Obi*). Chapter Four shows the imaginative manner in which the African heroine, Cubba, builds upon these radical foundations by relocating the antislavery battle to English shores and uniting two activist appeals for the relief of pain on behalf of the oppressed black and white underclasses who live in Irish and West Indian homes. *Irishman in London* also demonstrates that the African can experience complete relief, in the form of the abolition of pain, not simply through interracial marriage, but through the opportunities to enjoy freedoms of speech, citizenship, residence, activism, and inclusion in Britain that Cubba's impending marriage to Delany signifies.

Given this trajectory, I want to propose that Savanna is the latest in this line of fictional African women who fall under "Imoinda's shade." Her depiction as a free woman, wife and mother in England builds upon Ada's, Amri's and Cubba's representations by presenting England not as a potential haven of freedom for an African female slave, but more so, this woman's already established homesite of affirmed residence. Savanna threatens to politicize interracial marriage even more than the African woman in London because interraciality refers not merely to her marriage with her white husband, William, but also to their son, the Tawny boy, as well as to Savanna's own identity as a mulatto. My discussion of Maria Edgeworth's 1810 *Belinda* has already shown that even the most trivial representation of a fictional interracial relationship between an African man and English woman was treated as an alarming threat that needed to be contained. So the idea of an interracial woman, couple, and family making England their already established homesite is, undoubtedly, emblematic of the horrors about interracial marriage and African freedom that men such as Richard Edgeworth are becoming increasingly anxious about by 1805.

Adeline Mowbray could have, quite easily, united the threat of Savanna's degenerative influence as a mulatto woman, wife, and mother in English society with the degeneration of morals that Adeline signifies as a proponent for the abolition of marriage and pandered to those contemporary fears. But instead, its white and mulatto women meet as mutual victims of harsh societal forces (the creditor and society itself) that seek to subdue them. Such moments of confrontation are customary for all the fictional African women discussed in *Imoinda's Shade:* Ada's confrontation with John, Amri's with Harrop, Clara's African romance competing with Mr. Edwards's plantocratic one, Cubba's marriage to Delany—all of these are derivations of Imoinda's confrontation with the Deputy Governor on the battle field of Surinam, fighting for a future of freedom.[11] Although this moment of confrontation did not end victoriously for Behn's Imoinda, another big black lady from Behn's literary oeuvre experiences a far more successful outcome to her own confrontation with the tyrants that attempt to subdue her. But this Imoinda-esque confrontation takes place in a site far removed from Surinam, and because it does, it resonates with Opie's *Adeline Mowbray.*

The Adventure of the Black Lady (1697)[12] was published in a posthumous collection of Behn's work years after her death in 1689; however, Margaret Ferguson believes that it was actually written in 1688, the same year as the publication of *Oroonoko.*[13] In this novel, Behn introduces the heroine Bellamora, a young, middle-class white woman who travels to London from Hampshire, eight months pregnant, unmarried, and in desperate search of her cousin, Madam Brightly. "Unacquainted with the neat practices of this fine city" (492), the naïve heroine promptly loses her trunk containing all her valuables when she asks a "strange porter" (492) to deliver her goods to Brightly's lodgings on Bridges-Street, a place Ferguson identifies as a "notorious haunt for prostitutes."[14] Brightly does not live at the Bridges-Street address, however, and no one has any concrete knowledge of her present whereabouts. This leaves Bellamora in a bind. Homeless, destitute, and impoverished, all within a few hours of coming to town, not to mention unmarried and heavily pregnant, Bellamora is brought face-to-face with a certain and imminent demise in the big city. Until, that is, an unnamed landlady described as a "good, discreet, ancient Gentlewoman" (493) takes an interest in her situation, and along with another unnamed lady (who

---

11. See Chapter Three, 111.
12. (London: Wellington, 1705). All subsequent references refer to this edition.
13. Margaret Ferguson's essay "Conning the 'Overseers': Women's Illicit Work in Aphra Behn's 'The Adventure of the Black Lady,'" Early Modern Culture. An Electronic Seminar, 5 (2006), paragraph 13.
14. Ibid., paragraph 10.

turns out to be Bellamora's seducer's sister) they contrive to get Bellamora's valuables back as well as to orchestrate her marriage to her seducer, Fondlove, the imminent child's biological father.

The outlines of Behn's plot establish it as a narrative forebear of William Hogarth's *A Harlot's Progress* (1731–32) (figure 17). Like Hogarth, Behn is clearly interested in exploring a naïve woman's confrontation with, and negotiation of, big city life. But whereas Hogarth's first plate goes to great lengths to visually emphasize Moll's purity and innocence by depicting her with a demure, downcast look, a plain white country dress, closed bonnet, and useful sewing implements, the use of blackness in Behn's suggestive title has the opposite effect, immediately casting the "black lady" it refers to in a negative stereotypical light. Roxann Wheeler's discussion of *Spectator 262* shows that "Addison . . . refers to a wicked man" when he writes: "If I write any thing on a black Man, I run over in my Mind all the eminent Persons in the Nation who are of that Complection";[15] Behn appears to do the same in her construction of her "black-haired lady" (500). Beauty may be implied in the heroine's name, "Bellamora," an Italianized reference to a beautiful Moor (Bella Moor-a); however, Anthony Barthelemy's work on Shakespeare's *Othello* identifies religious difference, evilness, licentiousness, and foreignness as stereotypically Moorish traits.[16] A beautiful "black-haired lady" making a surreptitious and hasty dash to London while pregnant and unmarried is a seemingly blatant indictment of vice that the 'mora' part of her name confirms. At least the London authorities think so. Once they hear that an unmarried, pregnant "young black-haired lady (for so was Bellamora) . . . was either brought to bed, or just ready to lie down" (499–500) within their parish, they aggressively seek her out, presumably to make an example of her as a model of infamy. It is here, writ large, that Behn sets up an English-based moment of confrontation between a big black woman and the forces that seek to subdue her.

Behn, however, resolves this confrontation in the "big" black woman's favor. Referring to the authorities, derisively, as "The vermin of the Parish (I mean, the overseers of the poor who eat the Bread from 'em)" (499), she identifies them as tyrants and ensures that the "good, discreet, ancient" landlady thwarts them in their witch hunt. This landlady feigns ignorance about Bellamora and presents the authorities with a black cat that had lately littered as the presumed pregnant "black lady" that they seek. Her humorous sleight of hand here clearly undermines the intentions of the parish authorities, but it also stigmatizes her because the "ancient" adjective used

---

15. Roxann Wheeler, *The Complexion of Race*, 3.

16. See chapter one of his *Black Face, Maligned Race: The Representation of Blacks in English Drama from Shakespeare to Southerne* (Baton Rouge: Louisiana State University Press, 1987).

Figure 17.
Plate 1 of *A Harlot's Progress*, 1732, William Hogarth (1697–1764)

to describe her, coupled with the textual implication that she has the power to make Bellamora disappear and reappear as a black cat, connect her to witchery. In addition, Ferguson has pointed out that the landlady's ability to reach back to that "strange porter" to demand the return of Bellamora's valuables shows that she is a well-established member of the illicit group of black-market traders in London.[17] The woman connected to powerful black practices of magic and crime is, thus, the most active participant in the black lady's vindication and victory over the societal forces that seek to subdue her.

In this moment of confrontation between pregnant and powerful black English women joined in opposition to tyrannical parish authorities, Behn orchestrates a pointed moral victory for socially stigmatized women. The parish authorities that seek Bellamora out and use their power to establish her as a model of infamy are themselves morally suspect, since they are more concerned with seizing easy opportunities to make their exploitative livings off the poor and vulnerable, like "vermin," rather than truly exposing social immorality. If they were sincere about this issue, they would have taken the time to find out, as the landlady does, that the young and "foolish" (493) Bellamora has fallen pregnant more out of a naivety about sex than a vice-ridden attraction to it. The landlady's black power, then, provides a "good, discrete," and morally just way to assist Bellamora, preventing this naïve innocent from becoming a fallen woman as lost in London as Madam Brightly, and their joint triumph also lays bare the hypocrisy of societal forces that are intent on subduing vulnerable women without accounting for the self-interest of their intentions.

My analysis of Behn's *Adventure of the Black Lady* contextualizes this chapter's discussion of *Adeline Mowbray* in two ways. First, Behn's novel reveals that the stigma of blackness functions actively and metaphorically as a trope in the lives of white English women. Opie also uses blackness as a gendered trope in her English tale; however, she uses it literally as well as metaphorically in her representations of Savanna and Adeline. Second, Behn involves Bellamora in an English-based moment of confrontation with paternalist forces that differs from the experiences of the other fictional African women who fall under "Imoinda's shade" in one important respect: the big "black lady" is liberated from the stigma of sexual infamy that the parish authorities are determined to assign her. By the efforts of two creative storytellers (Behn and the landlady), Bellamora emerges the victor in her confrontation with tyranny. Similarly, *Adeline Mowbray* involves its literal and metaphorically blackened women in English-based moments of confrontation with tyrannical forces that seek to subdue them. But only one of these women emerges from this battle triumphant.

---

17. Ferguson, "Conning the Overseer."

THIS CHAPTER proposes that *Adeline Mowbray*'s primary focus on Adeline and the abolition of marriage is challenged by another discussion about abolition that takes into account Savanna's role as a free yet impoverished woman, wife, and mother in England. These two abolitionist discourses are structured around Opie's deft use of literal and figurative blackness in the lives of both female characters. For the most part, the tale uses blackness as a gendered trope that focuses on two types of transgression, social and sexual: as a mulatto woman in England Savanna represents the former, and Adeline the latter as a virtuous proponent for the abolition of marriage. Like Bellamora and Imoinda before them, Savanna and Adeline are involved in orchestrated moments of confrontation with English tyrants who seek to stigmatize and subdue socially and sexually transgressive women. Where colonial tyrants are usually constructed as planters or slaveholders, tyranny in England appears in other guises: a creditor, an English gentleman, a fruiterer, a libertine, and even a kept mistress. The confrontations that these tyrants have with stigmatized women generate discussions about extending sexual and social freedoms to blacks and women in England. But Opie presents the principles behind each of the social and sexual transgressions that Savanna and Adeline stand for as worthy. The fugitive slave, Savanna, has a natural mulatto complexion that can be read as England's commitment to the abolition of prejudice and poverty within its borders, and the equally fugitive fallen woman, Adeline, can be seen as a radical yet virtuous woman petitioning for the right to abolish marriage and champion a rational heterosexual union free from the legal ties that Sarah Chapone and Mary Astell had long identified as enslaving for women.[18]

But rather than equalizing these two intersecting black female quests for liberation, Opie brings their abolitionist discourses and experiences together in England to distinguish them and their activist agendas from one another. This difference is also illustrated through the deft manner in which the tale distinguishes the legal implications of each woman's black complexion. Where the novel looks with complete legal disdain on the blackness that Adeline signifies as a sexual transgressor, it looks much more favorably on the legal establishment of Savanna's mulatto complexion within British society. In other words, despite metaphorically intersecting the abolitions of prejudice, poverty, and marriage in Savanna's and Adeline's black complexions, *Adeline Mowbray* claims the legal right of a foreign black woman to be free and British while denying the legal right of a radical English woman to be free and black. This distinguishes Savanna's complexion as the only viably acceptable measure of freedom for a female transgressor in the novel because

---

18. Sarah Chapone, *The Hardships of the Laws in Relation to Wives* (1735); and Mary Astell, *Some Reflections Upon Marriage* (1700).

it privileges the legal conditions of freedom available to blacks in Britain from those not available to white women. The most privileged example of an African woman's negotiation of freedom occurs when Savanna advocates for the legal prosecution of Adeline's tyrannical and errant husband, Berrendale. I argue that Savanna's desire to "prosecu massa" (III, 155) not only offers the most viable "step forward" in confronting Berrendale's brutal behavior to her and Adeline, it also represents the most triumphant outcome that the African women of "Imoinda's shade" could have against the tyrannical forces that seek to subdue them in England.

IN THE SCENE from *Adeline Mowbray* that I reproduce at the beginning of this chapter, Opie presents blackness in three ways. Literally, it refers to the racial victimization that people of African descent experience in England with the creditor's dehumanizing reference to Savanna and her color clearly bringing this out. In addition, as I mentioned earlier, Adeline's "greater interest" in a poor mulatto woman's experience of prejudice at a time when she, herself, is an impoverished victim of prejudice establishes a metaphorical connection between victimized people of African descent and radical English women. But Adeline also puts her scant resources where her feelings are, escapes the Mandevillian charge that sympathy is a loud-sounding nothing, and saves Savanna's white husband from being arrested. As such, the scene idealizes a favorable response to victimized people of black and white complexions and both genders. And, as a way of emphasizing this fact, I will henceforth refer to it as 'the arresting scene,' a phrase that not only describes with accuracy what the "creditor" intends to do to William but also refers to the way the scene draws the reader's sympathetic attention to all victimized people who fall under the legal and social judgment of England and its laws.

Alongside the facts that blackness in the arresting scene is an umbrella term for blacks, stigmatized women and the victimized poor in general, Savanna's specific type of blackness—her mulatto-ness—brings up another signification about interracialism in England. Instead of fulfilling Glenmurray's request for the pineapple, Adeline steps forward to help not simply a biracial woman, but an interracial couple, and a multiracial family. Such behavior raises a question. Do the combined needs of this interracial collective in England deserve to outweigh those of an English gentleman, a terminally ill one at that? Maria Edgeworth would definitely answer 'no.' In Chapter Two, I discussed the manner in which she expunges the interracial marriage between Juba and Lucy from *Belinda* to satisfy her father's "great delicacies and scruples" about such marriages. For these kinds of English gentlemen, interracial couplings represent social degeneration, and thus do not deserve to be validated. But what of the interracial people themselves? Do their needs deserve recognition and validation in England, as Adeline's behavior seems to suggest?

West Indian historians and commentators are mostly responsible for popularizing impressions of interracial people from the British colonies. "Among the tribes which are derived from an intermixture of the Whites with the Negroes, the first are the *Mulattos*," writes Bryan Edwards; his *History* continues: "the descendants of Negroes by White people, entitled by birth to all the rights and liberties of White subjects in the full extent, are such as are above three steps removed in lineal digression from the Negro venter. All below this, whether called in common parlance Mestizes, Quadrons, or Mulattoes, are deemed by law Mulattoes."[19] Edwards presents mulattos as one undifferentiated mass of people of color who encompass a wide range of biological connections to whiteness. Other writers' observations about class and gender, however, distinguish the mulattos within Edwards's large group. Edward Long sarcastically comments on the way in which the "tawney breed" of upper-class mulattos transgress social boundaries when they return to Jamaica after being educated in England. One example is a mulatto "Miss [who] faints at the sight of her relations, especially when papa tells her that black *Quasheba* is her own mother."[20] Long believes that "a well educated Mulatta must lead a very unpleasant kind of life"[21] in Jamaica because her wealth and education makes her ill-reconciled to the fact that, despite all her efforts, she will never be accepted among refined, white Jamaican society. He also makes an alarming claim about mulattas' reputations for licentiousness, suggesting that "the major part, nay almost the whole number, with very few exceptions, have been *filles de joye* before they became wives."[22] J. B. Moreton adds to this impression by berating "Mongrel women" for being "extremely proud, vain and ignorant," and "though the daughters of rich men, and though possessed of slaves and estates, they never think of marriage; their delicacy is such . . . that they despise men of their own colour; and though they have their amorous desires abundantly gratified by them and black men secretly, they will not avow these connections."[23] "As for the lower rank, the issue of casual fruition," Long remarks, "they, for the most part remain in the same slavish condition as their mother; they are fellow-labourers with the Blacks and are not regarded in the least as their superiors. . . . The lower classes of these

---

19. *The History, Civil and Commercial, of the British Colonies in the West Indies*, 17–18.
20. *History of Jamaica*, vol. 2, 329.
21. Ibid.
22. Ibid., 337.
23. *West India Customs and Manners* (London: Parson, 1793), 124–25.

mixtures, who remain in the island, are a hardy race, capable of undergoing equal fatigue with the Blacks. . . ."[24]

In the West Indies, a female mulatto such as Savanna had to contend with all of these aspersions of sexual and rank transgression. But Adeline's triumphant action on the couple's behalf and the generally favorable response to Savanna and William's relationship suggest that *Adeline Mowbray* attempts to counter negative impressions about both mulattos and interracial coupling in England. Despite Sander Gilman's belief that common contemporary prejudice stigmatized all black women as naturally promiscuous and degenerate,[25] Opie appears to be actively undermining the licentious stigma that Long and Moreton promote about mulatto women by deliberately underplaying them in Savanna. As Howard asserts: "despite the potency of such colonial myths, the dominant discourses of the novel actually work to suppress the discourse of black (or mixed raced) women's sexuality."[26]

However, where the mulatto woman's sexual threat to England is downplayed in the novel as a whole, the social threat attributed to ex-slaves in England is played up significantly in the arresting scene. By making Savanna's black color and the depressed financial state of her interracial relationship and family equal parts of Adeline's cause célèbre, *Adeline Mowbray* puts a black face to the domestic problem of poverty as well as prejudice. This problem concerned blacks and whites equally; yet it became politically tethered to blacks at the end of the century after black ex-slaves from the colonies, black ex-sailors out of work, and black ex-soldiers who had fought for the British in the American War of Independence appeared on the streets of London, visibly racializing the sight of poverty. Action was taken to address this issue. During the lead-up to the 1787 Sierra Leone colonial experiment, the Committee for the Relief of the Black Poor was responsible for providing financial assistance to blacks living on London streets, and their financial payouts were ultimately part of an ill-fated scheme to encourage black people to willingly move to Africa and establish a new colony on its west coast. Isaac Land has shown that "the black poor were simply defined by their common 'black' color, and their presence in London was treated as an aberration in need of correction."[27] In other words, philanthropy was merely

---

24. *History of Jamaica,* vol, 2, 332.
25. "Black Bodies, White Bodies: Toward an Iconography of Female Sexuality in Late Nineteenth Century Art, Medicine and Literature," in *"Race," Writing, and Difference,* ed. Henry Louis Gates, Jr. (Chicago: University of Chicago Press, 1986), 223–61.
26. Howard, "'The Story of the Pineapple,'" 371.
27. Isaac Land, "Bread and Arsenic: Citizenship From the Bottom Up in Georgian London," *Journal of Social History* 39 (2005): 94.

a mask for prejudicial attempts to get rid of people whose complexions as well as their poverty made them figures of social transgression. Widespread skepticism about this scheme ensured that many of the black poor did not board the ship to Sierra Leone and remained on the streets of London, continuing to be "treated as an aberration" and seen as a most visible instance of social transgression in England.

Adeline's philanthropy, inspired as it is by Davis's brutal reference to Savanna's blackness, can be read as a private pecuniary response to this public history of British philanthropic help in combating the problem of black poverty. But where the efforts of the Committee were designed merely to rid the country of poor blacks, Adeline's intention in financially assisting Savanna is the opposite. She offers Savanna domestic assistance to reestablish her footing at home in England, and this assistance also makes some kind of atonement for the skin-color prejudice she experiences from the creditor. In effect, Adeline liberates Savanna from the stigmas of poverty and prejudice that forces like the Committee and the creditor enact. Savanna's mulatto-ness has a dual social purpose, then. It, at once, connects her to the generic "black poor," but it is also a specific reminder that, as a part white woman, she is also connected to the English nation. This connection is made even more evident with her marriage to William. Just as he and other poor white vulnerables like him need assistance, Savanna's mulatto-ness is a specific reminder that the black poor in England are also equally deserving of some kind of liberation from poverty as well as skin-color prejudice that allows them to regain their footing at home rather than abroad.

With this understanding, *Adeline Mowbray* seems much more aware of, and involved in, a discourse that is best discovered by adjusting the historical lens to look backward in English abolitionist history. If, as I am arguing, Opie's focus on mulatto-ness in English society is a part of a specific contemporary discussion about British activism in favor of the abolition of prejudice against the poor in general but specifically the black poor who chose to remain on English shores, then a pivotal event in this history comes in the form of the Yorke–Talbot decision of 1729, which essentially established blacks as property in England and denied them rights to citizenship by baptism or residence there. The first legally documented attempt to counter this prejudice appears in Sir William Blackstone's *Commentaries on the Laws of England*. By reading the first two editions of these *Commentaries* alongside the legal and commercial dynamics Opie stresses in the arresting scene, the next section argues that there is an English ambivalence about citizenship rights for poor slaves in England that Opie wants to identify and correct in her novel.

IN 1706, magistrate John Holt[28] asserted that the English air liberated slaves. But my discussion of Kingston and Cloe's nebulous position at the end of Townley's *High Life Below Stairs* demonstrates that this pronouncement was not necessarily true in 1759.[29] Prior to 1772, J. C. Oldham contends that popular knowledge of laws on this issue did not receive wide publication until the first edition of Blackstone's *Commentaries* (1765).[30] In it, we are told:

> And the spirit of liberty is so deeply implanted in our constitution, and rooted even in our very soil, that a slave or a Negro, the moment he lands in England, falls under the protection of the laws, and with regard to all natural rights becomes eo instanti a freeman.

Blackstone uses the phrase "a slave or a Negro" in this first edition as shorthand for acknowledging black slaves and slaves of any other complexion.[31] The law protects this racially amorphous slave with regard to all "natural rights" presumably enjoyed by Caucasian English people at large. Thus, Blackstone's representation of English law in 1765 recognizes the humanity of all individuals petitioning before it, and it especially acknowledges slaves of any color as the epitome of its avowal that one's racial and class designations are immaterial in establishing these inalienable "natural rights" to freedom.

However, in the second edition of Blackstone's *Commentaries* published the following year, the term "natural rights" is replaced with a new phrase:

> And the spirit of liberty is so deeply implanted in our constitution, and rooted even in our very soil, that a slave or a Negro, the moment he lands in England, falls under the protection of the laws, and so far becomes a freeman; though the master's right to his service may possibly still continue.[32]

---

28. See Gretchen Gerzina's *Black London: Life before Emancipation* (New Brunswick, NJ: Rutgers University Press, 1995), 120–21, for discussion of this 1706 John Holt statement outlawing slavery in England.

29. See Chapter Four, 169–73.

30. See James Oldham's essays on Lord Mansfield and slavery in *Mansfield Manuscripts and the Growth of English Law in the Eighteenth Century* (Chapel Hill: University of North Carolina Press, 1992) and "New Light on Mansfield and Slavery," *Journal of British Studies* 27 (1988): 45–68.

31. See Jonathan A. Bush's "The First Slave (and Why He Matters)," *Cardozo Law Review* 18 (1996): 599. Bush shows that the phrase "England was too pure an air for slaves to breathe in" comes from this 1567 case of "One Cartwright brought a slave from Russia." So legal antislavery challenges in England were initially conceived with a white and not a black complexion in mind.

32. These passages are both taken from Oldham's discussion of this inconsistency in his "New Light" essay (60–61). He demonstrates that Blackstone was prompted to clarify the 1765 position not as a complete reversal on his part but possibly after consultation with Mansfield himself. But

Appending the fact that a "master's right" to the "service" of "a slave or a Negro" "may possibly" outweigh their "natural rights" to freedom in England, the law changes its stance on domestic slavery. It diminishes its concern with recognizing the "natural rights" to humanity and freedom for slaves of any complexion as soon as it acknowledges a colonial master's continued rights within the metropolis. Black complexions actually motivate this shift from the absolute to the tepid support of the racially amorphous slave's freedom because property rights—specifically the rights to use and dispose of black slaves' "service"—become a hotly contested issue that the law was increasingly called upon to deal with. As Lord Mansfield himself pointed out: "The setting 14 or 15,000 men at once loose by a solemn opinion, is very disagreeable in the effects it threatens."[33] Those "very disagreeable" and threatening "effects" are none other than the loss of millions of pounds in property.

In one year, then, the British paternalist palate for lucre reveals itself in the complexion of English law. Black people go from being read legally as on a par with Britons of other complexions in Blackstone's first edition to being distinguished as different in the second because of the legal privileging of the master's right to property. This legal shift with regard to black complexions creates a number of questions that reverberate as part of the discussion about black people in Britain toward the latter end of the eighteenth century. Should black slaves purchased outside the metropolis and brought to Britain have a moral right to freedom, or not? And what are the financial and social implications of having "natural (human) rights" that outweigh a "master's (legal) right" to property, and vice versa?

In the arresting scene, Opie stages this discussion through the moral and commercial questions that Glenmurray and Mr. Davis generate. Within the scene, she appears, at first, to support a "master's (legal) right" to property over "natural (human) rights" to freedom when we consider the terms with which she legitimates the property claims that these English men are entitled to. For not taking William's obvious illness into account as he mercilessly sets about sending him to debtors prison for a "trifling" six pounds, Mr. Davis is called "a hard-hearted, wicked wretch" (II, 156). This impression is supported further by his false gesture of benevolence mentioned by the same anonymous crowd member: "if they will pay half he will wait for the rest, but then he knows they could as well pay all as half" (II, 157). Another

---

surely his need to clarify was made so that the law wouldn't be misconstrued as granting immediate freedom to slaves. Therefore, although the liberal spirit of the 1765 edition may have been unintentional, it is still evident as a legal possibility. And, moreover, Hargrave (chief advocate for Somerset) invoked the 1765 argument of immediate freedom on his client's behalf.

33. Oldham, *Mansfield Manuscripts*, 1223.

crowd member predicts the inevitable outcome for Savanna and William if Davis succeeds in getting him jailed: "He'll die, and she'll die, and then what will become of their poor little boy?" (II, 156). Yet amidst all of these sentimental concerns and dire predictions, Opie includes the fact that Davis has an indisputable right to seek legal recourse against William for defaulting on the couple's debt repayments: "not but what it is his due, I cannot say but it is" (II, 156), another crowd member states.[34] This combination of sentimental and legitimating crowd opinions puts this English creditor's character in context. He is clearly a tyrant, yet the law gives him a legitimate right to act in this way.

Opie's specific use of the term "creditor" further legitimates Davis's right to claim his money because it can be directly connected to a proslavery, biblical validation made at the same time of the novel's publication. In an era in which the validity of slavery was a hotly contested issue, the contemporary proslavery movement in England sought to extend and legitimize creditors' indisputable property rights with scripture. For instance, William Cobbett's "Slave Trade" in the *Political Register* (1802) uses the Old Testament to argue "that the selling of the debtor and his family to satisfy the creditor, is a very ancient usage."[35] With this use of a biblical-historical substantiation, Cobbett validates the legitimacy of a creditor's right to property, and his use of the term also involves Opie's own "creditor" in this proslavery rhetoric as he sets about sending William to debtors' prison. Opie's Mr. Davis, then, can be read as one with Cobbett's colonial creditors: they all feel divinely and legally entitled to trade in human flesh for their own financial needs. Moreover, because he makes no attempt to specify the race of "the debtor and his family," Cobbett's interpretation of scripture allows creditor Davis to legitimately extend his influence so far as to sell individuals of any complexion in order to "satisfy" all debts owed to him. Tyranny, it appears, can be legally as well as biblically legitimated in England as well as the colonies.

Opie also legitimizes the actions of the other Englishman, Glenmurray, who is not physically present in the arresting scene but whose influence is evoked through his connection to the pineapple. Glenmurray, we are told, "was a man of family, and of a small independent estate" (I, 52), and as a member of the landed gentry and, moreover, a nobleman with a reputation for "active virtue," courteous manners," and "blamelessness of . . . life" (I, 53), Glenmurray has earned a legitimate right to consume the best that this

---

34. A couple's debts were always incurred against the man in a married relationship.

35. Preface taken from Cobbett's essay reprinted in *Slavery, Abolition, Emancipation,* 373. He is probably referring to II Kings 4:1–2. Incidentally, in his proslavery article, Cobbett also refers to the Mansfield Judgment, showing that the issue of slavery in England was still contemporaneous in 1802 while Opie is writing *Adeline Mowbray.*

English society has to offer because of his superior conduct as an English gentleman.[36] Yet, his right to consume in the novel is presented as more than a mere reiteration of Bernard Mandeville's belief that the private consumption of colonial produce creates the public benefits of trade and industry. Opie raises the tenor of Mandeville's self-interested consumer position by imbuing a private and whimsical consumer impulse with sentimental credibility. Glenmurray doesn't simply *want* a pineapple, he is shown to *deserve* one. Having already demonstrated that she is able to "please the capricious appetite of decay" (I, 24) during her grandmother's terminal illness, Adeline feels equally compelled to accommodate the pineapple given Glenmurray's own terminally ill condition, and people of African descent are as intimately involved in his desires being met as Adeline. Opie's specific use of a pineapple, a fruit grown and cultivated by workers of color in the Caribbean that Carol Howard calls a "symbol of nobility, decadence and the unusual"[37] for its elite status among sweet luxury goods in England, not only answers his capricious appetite, it also stands as a testament of his status as a good English gentleman savoring the sweet taste of his privileged, noble, and virtuous life as death imminently consumes him.

Thus, legal, biblical, sentimental, and rank justifications are used to invest Glenmurray's and Davis's business and consumer rights with credibility as well as to acknowledge the institutions that are designed to put a respectable face on Britain's involvement in trade. For if all 'Williams' did not pay their debts, and all 'Savannas' were liberated from the colonial lands of the English gentry, then English paternalists such as Davis and Glenmurray would not only suffer, they would also be deprived of money and goods that they are legitimately entitled to. Moreover, the country's involvement in trade would crumble. Justifications such as these are designed to keep 'Williams' and 'Savannas' bound to support the master's commercial activities ahead of their own. This reading of the commercial and moral dynamics contained in the arresting scene shows a clear connection with the ethos contained in the second edition of Blackstone's *Commentaries:* a master's legitimate right should always trump the natural sentimental rights of individuals in England.

Instead of completely justifying these masters' rights, however, Opie makes her readers view them with skepticism when the appetites that drive

---

36. Charlotte Sussman's *Consuming Anxieties* (Stanford: Stanford University Press, 2000) reveals the importance attached to consumer rights such as those expressed by Glenmurray. In fact, according to Bernard Mandeville's *Fable of the Bees,* Glenmurray has a duty to consume because his consumerist tastes support business interests in the country without requiring him to engage in the dirty business himself.

37. Howard, "'The Story of the Pineapple,'" .362

the English gentleman and the creditor are exposed as too egregious and tyrannical for Britons to admire. In the arresting scene, Opie explicitly connects Glenmurray's "appetite" for the pineapple with the oppression of slavery. For his attraction to the pineapple's sweetness, after expressing "a sort of distaste" (II, 152) for the grapes that Adeline initially buys for him, implies that Glenmurray is a "slave"[38] (II, 162) to a "diseased appetite" that will be appeased only by "the gratification of eating one" (II, 152).[39] Charlotte Sussman's book *Consuming Anxieties* describes English abolitionists leading successful boycotts of colonial sugar through popularizing the macabre impression that consuming sugar in tea was akin to drinking the blood of slaves involved in producing the sweet flavor. Thus, Glenmurray's insatiable attachment to the pineapple's reproduces this "diseased appetite" for slave blood—an immoral craving far removed from the biblical blood suggested in the presence of Adeline's grapes. Through the evocation of Glenmurray's diseased appetite, Opie exposes the English consumer's tyrannical taste for sweetness.

Opie's examination of Mr. Davis's appetite is metaphorical. Cobbett's "Slave Trade" has already exposed him as a thinly veiled cousin to the colonial slave master. A "creditor," like a slave master, buys interest in an individual's life, and his financial investment grants him the right to legally dispose of them, or his interest in them, if they financially default or personally displease him. William has done both. Aside from the unpaid debt, someone in the crowd also reveals that Davis also owes William a "grudge" (II, 156) over an unspecified incident. It is this "grudge," perhaps, that explains Davis's insatiable appetite for revenge toward the couple and his aggressive pursuit of a sick man over a "trifling . . . six pounds" (II, 156–57). When "another man" in the crowd canonizes the couple as "hard-working, deserving persons" (II, 158), it is Davis's "grudge" that elicits a brutal parody of this man's opinion: he delivers a caninization of William and Savanna as "that idle dog and that ugly black b——h."

Davis's caninization calls to mind two different kinds of prejudice. First, it reflects the way in which financially solvent Londoners continued to see and despise the black poor and the London poor in general, a tension that is clearly understood by Edward Long, who states: "history evinces, that, in

---

38. We're also told that Lawyer Langley "was formed to be the slave of women" (III, 109). Interestingly, Savanna is never actually called a slave and is only obliquely referred to as escaping slavery very late in the third volume (III, 102). By resisting the definition of slave for Savanna and bestowing it on two English men, Opie associates slavery with unquestioning subservience to powerful visceral forces (sweet foods / loose women) that can completely master the senses.

39. See Sussman's introduction to *Consuming Anxieties* for discussions about the ways consumption of certain products (sugar, tea, etc.) was viewed as drinking the blood of slaves who were forced to produce them.

all ages ... the rich are the natural enemies of the poor; and the poor, the rich; like the ingredients of a boiling cauldron, they seem to be in perpetual warfare, and struggle which shall be uppermost."[40] Davis's caninization of the couple suggests that poverty marks blacks and their white counterparts equally as figures of a degeneracy that is unattractive and lackadaisical. In effect, he seeks to elevate his own humanity by denigrating theirs. His prejudice may also be due to that fact that he thinks William's marital association with a mulatto woman is "indelicate and almost unnatural,"[41] like Sarah Scott's Sir George Ellison. Indeed, his response to the interracial couple is a dynamic reversal of the English-based 'grateful Negro' scenes that I discussed in Chapter Two, wherein Thomas Day and an anonymous author sought to acknowledge the humanity of slaves in England by distinguishing them from the wild beasts that sought to destroy white benefactors.[42] Davis's canine references connect him with men such as Maria Edgeworth's Jamaican slave-holder, Mr. Jeffries, who considers African slaves "a race of beings naturally inferior," as well as J. B. Moreton, who describes all mulattos as "mongrels."[43] Like them, he is a legitimate middle-class benevolent tyrant who dominates a diverse group of working poor people in England whom he thinks of, collectively, with the enmity and superiority that white Creoles held over black slaves and mulattos.

Pitting Glenmurray's craving for sweetness alongside Davis's bitterness toward the poor interracial family, Opie shows how the colonial taste for tyranny coalesces on the palates of metropolitan paternalists who revel in their own diseased appetites to exploit the poor and people of African descent for their own personal needs. The forcefulness and brutality of these appetites—Glenmurray's insatiable desire for the pineapple, Davis's merciless desire to send William to jail for a trifling debt—is challenged by Adeline's "irresistible impulse" to "step forward" prompted by the reference to Savanna's complexion, at the expense of her prior commitment to Glenmurray, and in opposition to Davis. Adeline's philanthropy enacts a literal triumph over the forces that seek to subdue Savanna by openly questioning the moral legitimacy of English commercial practices and nullifying the tyranny of a domestic "creditor" and domestic partner. With Adeline's action, Opie suggests that no matter how respectable and legitimate commercial practices look at face value, English paternalist rights should not be akin to those that colonial paternalists enjoy in which humans are treated like dogs for money. In the spirit of the law granting "natural rights" to humans of all

---

40. Long, *History of Jamaica*, vol. 1, 25.
41. *The History of Sir George Ellison*, 139.
42. See Chapter Two, 79–81.
43. Maria Edgeworth, *The Grateful Negro*, 404.

complexions in the 1765 *Commentaries*.[44] Opie appears to believe that "in England [everyone should] have the enjoyment of our benevolent, liberal and impartial legislation, without regard to men's complexions,"[45] and the triumph she orchestrates for Savanna and William suggests that, for the deserving poor of any color, inalienable "natural rights" to freedom are in the national interest ahead of commercial concerns.

MY READING of the arresting scene aligns Savanna's experience with Bellamora's in *The Adventure of the Black Lady*. In Opie's text, a stigmatized woman (Adeline) confronts the tyrannical forces (Glenmurray's and Davis's appetites) that seek to subdue a black woman (Savanna), and she uses the means at her disposal to liberate this vulnerable black woman from the exploitation of those paternal forces. This is, undoubtedly, a triumphant act. After Adeline pays their debt, Savanna and William improve in health and looks, obtain jobs for themselves, and a situation for their son, and they begin to thrive. The abolition of poverty and prejudice put into action by Adeline's philanthropy eschews the impression of social degeneracy that their poverty represented and allows this interracial couple to be seen, triumphantly, as productive members of English society.

The arresting scene also enacts a vindication of the original stigmatized woman just as Behn did for the landlady in her text. This second confrontation involves the white heroine and another tyrannical figure. On her initial trip to the "fruiterer's," the mistress of the shop (unbeknownst to Adeline) says to her maid that she should have "asked another person only a guinea [for the pineapple]; but as *those sort of women* [referring to Adeline] never mind what they give, I asked two, and I dare say she will come back for it" (II, 151; my emphasis). Given that Adeline's reputation as a kept woman ultimately stretches into continental Europe, it is probable that the "fruiterer" knows about her relationship with Glenmurray and responds to Adeline as if the shade of ill repute is inscribed on her body. She feels entitled to exact the extra "guinea" from Adeline because of presumed extravagant spending habits of women who are kept by English gentlemen.

The "fruiterer's" prejudice toward Adeline's reputation as a kept woman is strikingly similar to the "creditor" and his justification for persecuting

---

44. In this, Opie agrees with Mary Wollstonecraft: "There is one rule relative to behaviour that, I think, ought to regulate every other; and it is simply to cherish such an habitual respect for mankind as may prevent us from disgusting a fellow creature for the sake of a present indulgence." *Vindication of the Rights of Women*, 248.

45. *Morning Herald*, January 2, 1787.

Savanna for a "trifling . . . six pounds" because of his prejudice against the working poor. In other words, women of both complexions face financial exploitation because Adeline's reputation signifies sexual transgression while Savanna's complexion signifies a prejudicial response to the social transgression of poverty. The syllabic, rhythmic, and rhyming assonance of "fruiterer" and "creditor" signifies how harmoniously aligned Opie thinks these professional business people are. Like the parish vermin from Behn's *Adventure of the Black Lady,* commercial traders enjoy powerful opportunities to financially exploit vulnerable women with stigmatized reputations and complexions.

Adeline's "step forward," then, can be read not merely as a reaction to the prejudice that Davis holds over members of the working poor. By not returning for the pineapple and using the money for social philanthropy, Adeline escapes the charge that would indelibly mark her as this common "sort" of sexual transgressor who frequents the fruiterer's business, undermines the fruiterer's physical assessment of the "sort" of woman she is, and challenges the stigma that the fruiterer attributes to her reputation. She unknowingly saves her own reputation by confirming that she is not the "sort" of spendthrift sexual transgressor that the fruiterer expected, but another kind of transgressor—a *virtuous* advocate for the abolition of marriage whose actions are separate from the *notorious* "sort" of kept lady commonly known to the fruiterer. Mixing two pro-abolitionist discourses within the same action in the arresting scene, Adeline's "step forward" triumphantly defends her own position as a sexual transgressor while consciously and triumphantly acting on behalf of Savanna's position as an impoverished social transgressor in English society.

Adeline, however, does not act for their "joint relief" until Davis blasts Savanna's blackness; until then, "Adeline . . . had not recollected that she was a mulatto." In this sentence, Adeline recollects that Savanna's blackness carries with it an oppressive stigma about poverty which her "step forward" determinedly challenges. Yet the suggestive, and I would add deliberately confusing, pronoun also includes the possibility that Adeline does not remember that "*she* [*too*] was a mulatto."[46] Of course, Adeline is, undeniably, Caucasian. But I think Opie's delightfully suggestive syntax presents the possibility that this virtuous English woman's sexually ambiguous position as an advocate for the notorious idea of abolishing marriage is metaphorically hybrid at the same time that she presents Savanna as a literal one. Indeed, the impression of her as a metaphorical mulatto is strengthened by the fact

---

46. Susan Greenfield has found another important instance of this syntactic ambiguity in her chapter "Mother, Daughter and Mulatto: Women's Exchange in Adeline Mowbray," thereby suggesting that this is not an isolated case but a deliberate literary device employed by Opie.

that she is read with the same sexual stigmas that Long and Moreton leveled at West Indian mulatto women.

Because the "creditor" and "fruiterer" both react physically and with exactly the same financially exploitative prejudice toward Adeline and Savanna, Opie gives the impression that these metaphorical and literal mulatto women intersect in, to borrow Mary Louise Pratt's term, the "contact zone"[47] of conjoined exploitation under commercial oppressors as their stigmatized bodies circulate in England. However, despite both of their triumphs over the tyrannical forces that seek to exploit or subdue them, Adeline and Savanna inhabit mulatto space dialogically. Adeline's "greater interest" in remembering and reacting to the social stigmas associated with Savanna's complexion offers her an excuse to focus on philanthropy while ignoring the stigmas implicit in her own morally ambiguous stance against marriage—a stigma tangibly witnessed in the fruiterer's physical and negative reaction to her reputation. Hence, Adeline's philanthropy on behalf of the poor occurs at a time that she recollects and acts against the social stigmas surrounding Savanna's blackness and poverty but forgets, or at least fails to acknowledge, that her own reputation carries stigmas of a mulatto complexion. Savanna, however, is brutally reminded of her connection to stigmatized blackness when Davis blasts her complexion. In other words, while Savanna *knows* that she is a literal mulatto consigned to the stigmatized space that has been designated for people of her color and rank, Adeline *does not recollect* that she is a metaphorical one whose actions place her in the same sexual space of infamy as the literal mulatto women from Long's and Moreton's West Indian texts. In *Adeline Mowbray*, then, the mulatto contact zone that each woman inhabits is distinguished by the level of awareness each woman has about the understanding of the blackness she embodies. Interrogating the difference between Savanna's conscious position as a literal mulatto and Adeline's unknowing metaphorical one leads to a dialogic understanding of Opie's use of the term "mulatto," the shade of blackness so unjustly victimized by English commercial interests because of a prejudged association with sexual and social transgression in England.

IN ORDER TO contextualize the sexual and social transgressions that are literally and metaphorically inscribed in Savanna's and Adeline's mulatto complexions, it is necessary, first, to examine the way social and sexual transgressions are reflected in the complexions of the novel's English men and

---

47. "'Contact zone' is an attempt to invoke the spatial and temporal copresence of subjects previously separated by geographic and historic disjunctures, and whose trajectories now intersect." Mary Louis Pratt, *Imperial Eyes* (London and New York: Routledge, 1992), 7.

women as a whole. Two scenes involving males provide the first examples of the ways in which Opie links complexion with a discussion about sexual and social transgression in England. The first scene occurs in Lisbon, Portugal, where Adeline flees with Glenmurray after her stepfather, Sir Patrick O'Carrol, attempts to rape her. While "sitting on a bench in one of the public walks" (I, 189), the unmarried couple happen upon Mr. Maynard, an old acquaintance of Glenmurray's who is vacationing there with his sisters. Mr. Maynard has a "sun-burnt complexion" from having "gone to seek his fortune in India" (I, 189), and he returns to England a "Nabob" (I, 189)—a title that, in conjunction with his complexion, identifies him as cultural transgressor against Englishness. "Certainly by the turn of the century, nabobs were widely being censured," writes M. O. Grenby. "The idea of the nabob, the lowly man who had gone away to India . . . only to return with a fortune, possibly got by means the most nefarious, was a very serviceable figure for novelists wishing to show the dangers of new and unmerited social standing."[48]

The second scene occurs after Adeline and Glenmurray return home to England and settle in Richmond. While out walking and admiring the scenery, Adeline happens upon "some well-dressed boys at play" and she begins "darkly brooding over the imagined fate of her own offspring" (II, 133). One boy, in particular, catches her attention: "she saw [him] standing at a little distance from the group, and apparently looking at it with an eye of envy" (II, 134). The other boys have rejected this one because he is an illegitimate child—a "little bastard"—whose "sunburnt neck and hands" are so "very very clean" (II, 135) but still not socially clean enough to allow him access to the playgroup composed of his upper-class peers. Even though he is "better dressed than the rest" (II, 134), the expensive clothing that his mother buys for him is like another layer of stigmatized skin visually confirming that she is not the social equal to the parents of the other boys but one of "those sort of women [who] never mind what they give" (II, 151) for commodities. Maynard's and the rejected playmate's sunburned complexions both suggest that English culture and morality are threatened by "Nabobs" and rich "little bastards" whose wealth mistakenly places them in a class that should epitomize sexual and cultural propriety.

The complexions of two women are presented in a way that identifies them as sexual and social transgressors of a different kind. The first, an unnamed woman described only as the "very showy woman" (III, 35), is the mistress of an eminent lawyer, Mr. Langley, "celebrated for his abilities as a chamber counselor" (III, 30), and the man whom Adeline consults

---

48. M. O. Grenby, *The Anti-Jacobin Novel*, 147–48.

after Glenmurray's death to try obtain a nearly three-hundred-pound inheritance that Glenmurray had bequeathed to her in his will. Mary Warner is initially introduced to the novel as Adeline's servant, but after Adeline fires her for insolence and she loses another job with the Quaker, Mrs. Pemberton, Mary becomes Langley's second kept mistress. She and the "very showy woman" both display artificially colored complexions: the very showy woman's "highly rouged" (III, 35) face parallels Mary, near the end of the novel, "rouged like a French countess of the ancien regime" (III, 108). Rouge obviously attempts to replicate the blooming complexion of the contemporary English Rose ideal of beauty.[49] But Opie critiques these women, not so much for their use, but their overuse of it. Excessively coloring themselves, Mary and the very showy woman physically adulterate the English Rose idea of beauty and, in turn, ideologically contaminate the virtuous ideals embodied in this characteristic representation of English femininity. Mary's foreign, regal, and anachronistic appearance speaks particularly to this adulteration as rouge replaces any wholesome impressions she may have as an English "village" (III, 1) inhabitant with the stamp of despotic, artificial, and alien femininity. This is, surely, Opie's critique of Jacobin politics and its radical way of breaking down hierarchies, leading people such as Mary to believe that they are equal to aristocrats. But with bodies trapped "in the extremity of fashion" (III, 35), Mary and the "very showy woman" are only marked as theatrically excessive women who so alarm Opie that she stages them in a tyrannical guise that is familiar yet unusual for these "rouged" women. Because they make such gross exhibitions of ordering the eminent lawyer Langley about, Opie concludes, "he was formed to be the slave of women" (III, 109); and with this pointed reference to their aggressive and dominant personalities, *Adeline Mowbray*'s "rouged" women are unexpectedly aligned with colonial tyrants, and, as such, are threats to traditional ideals of English femininity.[50]

Thus, the complexions of English men and women in the novel are used to code Opie's views on social and sexual transgression in England. The "sunburn" accounts for Maynard's role as a "Nabob" and the rejected playmate's position as a "bastard," while rouge brands the theatrically tyrannical

---

49. For a definition of the "English Rose," see Fenja Gunn's *The Artificial Face* (Worcester: Trinity Press, 1973), 110.

50. This theatrical threat is very real, as Gunn reveals in this 1770 act of Parliament, taken from *The Artificial Face:* "All women of whatever age, rank, profession, or degree, whether virgins, maids, or widows, that shall, from and after such Act, impose upon, seduce, and betray into matrimony, any of his Majesty's subjects, by the scents, paints, cosmetic washes, artificial teeth, false hair, Spanish wool, iron stays, hoops, high-heeled shoes and bolstered hips, shall incur the penalty of the law in force against witchcraft and like misdemeanours and that the marriage, upon conviction, shall stand null and void" (124).

women whores. All of them are depicted as grossly contaminating upstanding notions of Englishness and destabilizing two important foundations of English society: social hierarchy and sexual propriety. However, the consequences of their behavior are quite different.

In Mr. Maynard's description, Opie stresses his "irreproachable character" (II, 189); despite his "Nabob" complexion, his reputation is impeccable. The same can be said about the rich "little bastard." Adeline asks his peers,

> "Is he ill-natured?"
> "No."
> "Does he not play fair?"
> "Yes"
> "Don't you like him?"
> "Yes." (II, 136)

Reputations for irreproachableness, fairness, good nature, and likeableness are all commendatory, and the scrupulousness of the rich little bastard's expensive clothing and Mr. Maynard's character suggest that they are both trying hard to fit in despite the stigmas that define them. Sir Egerton Brydges's preface to his novel *Arthur Fitz-Albini* (1798) offers a clear condemnation of transgressive figures such as Mr. Maynard and the rich "little bastard":

> So long as mere wealth, without consideration by what means it was acquired, or regard to the birth, or education, of the possessor, shall be an introduction into all society, and all places of trust and respect, the ties of harmony and goodwill, by which a government is supported, must every day be growing looser; subordination must become insufferable to its natural defenders; morals must daily deturpate.[51]

Yet Opie's transgressive males represent a decidedly different societal outcome from Brydges's dire predictions of societal decay. Her use of the sunburn suggests that the commendatory reputations of these men, will, in due time, be relieved of the stigmas associated with their sexual and social transgressions once they become more acclimatized to the society that their finances allow them access to, and when that society becomes so accustomed to them that it excuses their slight deficiencies and allows them to blend in. Opie uses the sunburn, then, to exonerate as well as label the sexual and social transgressions English men perform.

---

51. "Preface to the Second Edition," *Arthur Fitz-Albini* (London: White, 1799), xiv.

Exoneration is not the point of order for "rouged" women, however. The natural, possibly permanent, yet excusable discoloration belonging to these "sunburned" men of color contrasts obviously with the unnatural, temporary, and inexcusable overcoloration of the "rouged" women of color. Generally, cosmetics and costumes are applied with the intention of improving a woman's physical appearance, but Mary employs both of them as a means of social mobility. Her emphasis on showiness arises out of pique over a comment she had overheard Adeline make about how "plain" (III, 110) looking she was as a servant. "I suppose you are quite surprised to see how *smart* I am!" (III, 110; my emphasis), she triumphs to Adeline, reveling in her transformation from plain servant to "French countess." The double meaning of "smart" indicates not only Mary's belief that she has physically improved by becoming Langley's mistress but also that she has been clever enough to exploit herself in this way.[52] Consequently, Opie associates extreme makeup with a misguided female intent to radically improve her financial and social appearance through independent and intellectual initiative. But cosmetic excesses only establish Mary's and the very showy woman's infamous reputations.

Clearly, a social double standard is reinforced through the complexions of these men and women of color. Where sunburned men such as Maynard and the rich "little bastard" will eventually be allowed to participate in society despite their reputations for social and sexual impropriety, rouged women cannot expect to do the same because, as Mary shows, they are performing the aristocratic role with such excessive failure. At least the males naturally look and act the part of the class that they aspire to be. Mary and the "very showy woman" are only farcically performing it.

IT IS COLORED female complexions in *Adeline Mowbray*, then, that are most indicative of the extreme kind of social and sexual chaos apparent in England, and it is from this general discussion of complexion in the text that Adeline's reputation as a metaphorical mulatto must be read. On three occasions, English women explicitly make her up as a black sexual transgressor akin to Behn's Bellamora and as licentious as one of Long's colonial mulattos. The first blackening reference comes indirectly from Mrs. Mowbray. When her young, "penniless profligate" husband, Sir Patrick O'Carrol, absconds with her fortune, Mrs. Mowbray exculpates her own recklessness of marrying him without "writings or settlements ... drawn up" (I, 135) by accusing

---

52. Although Eberle reads Opie's novel as a vindication of Mary Wollstonecraft, I read *Adeline Mowbray* as a blatant albeit sympathetic denouncement of Wollstonecraft that emerges in Mary Warner's first name, initials, and her representation as a harlot with "smart" pretensions.

Adeline of seducing him away from her. Dr. Norberry, a family friend of the Mowbrays, incensed by Mrs. Mowbray's scapegoating, renounces his friendship with her, telling Adeline: "when she whitewashed herself [she] blackened you" (II, 77). Dr. Norberry's colored analogy would only appear incidental if direct attempts to sexually stigmatize Adeline as a black female transgressor were not made by both of lawyer Langley's mistresses. "Is not that black mawkin gone yet?" (III, 37) the "very showy woman" jealously asks Langley, piqued by his attentions to Adeline as he escorts her to the downstairs door of his office. This woman views Adeline as Mrs. Mowbray does: a sexual intermediary who threatens her relationship with a man. By contrast, Mary views Adeline as a black intermediary who facilitates her relationship with Langley, legitimizing it with an air of intellectual respectability, and it is from her that the most damaging blackening reference comes. "You taught me that marriage was all nonsense," she tells Adeline, "and so thought I, miss Mowbray is a learned lady, she must know best . . . so I followed your example" (III, 111). She tries to credit Adeline's principled stance against marriage as the facilitating factor in her vice-ridden decision to become a kept mistress, and she makes a concerted effort to imply that she and Adeline share the same ideological view against marriage by using the popular black analogy "Twas the kettle . . . calling the pot" (III, 110). In short, when Mary utilizes Adeline's reputation as a "learned lady" to validate her own "smart" decision to be a woman of ill repute for financial gain, she confirms Adeline's position as a metaphorical mulatto—a virtuous advocate for a seemingly immoral act.[53] Like a literal mulatto, Mary, the fruiterer, and the society at large see only the immoral and physical side of Adeline's stance against marriage and ignore the virtuous principle within it.

The "Nabob," the rich "little bastard," and the "rouged" women all confirm that characters with colored complexions are, in Opie's mind, intimately connected with contaminating some aspect of English culture. And while men may escape censure for this contamination, women with notoriously colored reputations—even virtuous ones such as Adeline—do not. This point is emphasized in two of the novel's pivotal confrontations involving Adeline and Mary.

The first confrontation aligns Mary with the creditor, Davis. Mary's aggression and dominance over Mr. Langley has already identified her as an exploitative tyrant of Davis's ilk. Prior to her appearance in Langley's office, she also reenacts many of his other vices. When she is employed as Adeline's servant, Mary harbors a grudge toward her mistress for calling her "plain"

---

53. One contemporary critic fears that this will be the effect produced by throwing appealing colors over Adeline's character.

that turns into an insolence that gets her discharged, and later, develops into an unbridled desire to persecute Adeline, especially when her former mistress opens a school in Mary's native village. "So much was she piqued at the disbelief which she met with" (III, 2) when she calls Adeline a "kept" lady that Mary demands the right to expose Adeline at church in as aggressive an act of public persecution as Savanna experienced under Davis. Mary, "proud of her success" (III, 4) at exposing Adeline, uses the church setting to legitimize her social position in her native society by sullying Adeline: she "looked triumphantly at [the crowd], and was resolved to pursue the advantage which she had gained" (III, 4). Once again, Opie draws attention to a tyrant's right to oppress a stigmatized woman, but in Adeline's case, a "rouged" woman rather than a male "creditor" exercises this right. Yet in this confrontation, the tyrant is thwarted from pursuing her moral "advantage" when an anonymous man hastily "stepped forward" (III, 5) to offer Adeline assistance, thereby liberating Adeline from Mary's tyranny as Adeline herself had liberated Savanna from the creditor. Adeline's second confrontation with Mary does not end as triumphantly.

Where the church setting of their first confrontation illustrated Adeline's moral victory over Mary, Opie constructs their second one in another symbolic space. After Glenmurray's death, Adeline marries his cousin, Berrendale, and they have a daughter, Editha. But Berrendale leaves his family for the West Indies, forcing Adeline to take steps to prove herself Berrendale's legal wife and "substantiate Editha's claim to his property" (III, 104). So she consults with the "very great lawyer" (III, 104), Mr. Langley, who had behaved terribly to her when he thought she was Glenmurray's mistress and continues to do so now that he thinks she belongs to Berrendale. It is in his law office that she meets Mary dressed like a "French countess." Within this space, it is Mary, not Langley, who dominates. She claims an ideological affinity with Adeline, telling her former mistress, "no ceremony, you know, among friends and equals" (III, 109), and she berates Langley when he attempts to silence her. But Mary's composure is momentarily shattered when news is brought that her son has perished of smallpox. To comfort her, Adeline embraces Mary until she realizes that she is endangering her own child with a potential smallpox infection. When she attempts to end this dangerous embrace, Mary "kept her arms closely clasped round Adeline's waist" (III, 116), "hugged her the closer," and "was the more eager to hold her fast." Adeline, then, forcefully "endeavoured to break free from the arms of her tormentor" (III, 117), but Mary is formidable: "she parried all Adeline's endeavours to break from her" (III, 118). Despite Adeline's "strength of phrensy and despair . . . a fatal control [is irrevocably] exercised over her" (III, 118) by Mary.

Opie presents this physically violent and sexually charged confrontation with tyranny in lawyer Langley's office—a presumed hall of judgment and justice. In the arresting scene, Adeline's step forward resulted in a financial triumph over tyranny for the poor in England. Outside the village church, an anonymous man stepped forward to enact a moral triumph over tyranny during Mary's first confrontation with Adeline. However, in Langley's law office, it is noticeable that the only one capable of stepping forward to protect Adeline from Mary's violence *is* lawyer Langley, who, we're told, "was formed to be the slave of women, and had not the courage to protect another from the insolence to which he tamely yielded" (III,109). Langley's sexually suspect behavior with women identifies him as a weak judge of character and an ineffective defender of virtue. Whether they are rouged or metaphorically mulattoed, he views all colored women as equally stigmatized in his office and judges them accordingly.

In lawyer Langley's office, then, in the absence of an effective legal defense and in the presence of the domineering tyrant, Mary, Opie renders defeat on Adeline's idea of abolishing marriage with a smallpox disease that permeates Adeline's body and irreversibly ravages her English Rose complexion. Mary's infection ultimately ends Adeline's life. But before it does, Adeline realizes something about herself that she had been oblivious to earlier. The mulatto reputation that she upholds, metaphorically, by her virtuous adherence to the infamous principle of abolishing marriage only serves to embolden infamous women such as Mary while it weakens the influence of principled ones such as Adeline. The ease and swiftness with which Mary's infection eviscerates Adeline stands as a metaphor for the way in which Adeline's principle is easily corrupted; and because the beauty of her principle lay in its purity, Opie kills off her heroine. She does not want Adeline to live as the face of a hybrid principle, cosmetically enhancing her blighted reputation as contemporaries infected by smallpox scars routinely did with red and black patches.[54] Adeline's facial disfigurement and physical demise symbolize the ultimate fate facing women who champion hybrid principles that provide them with no defense before the law. Savanna's mulatto complexion, however, is viewed differently in the novel, largely because of the law.

THE LEGAL ambivalence surrounding the status of black slaves in England witnessed in Blackstone's two interpretations was, ostensibly, reconciled by Lord Chief Justice Mansfield's 1772 ruling in the Somerset case that mas-

---

54. Gunn's *The Artificial Face* (110–14) discusses the way that women wore red and black patches over pockmark scars in the eighteenth century.

ters could not forcibly send ex-slaves who arrived in England back to the colonies. But Mansfield's judgment was a narrowly defined ruling with a practical application that left a lot to be desired since it failed to conclusively pronounce or even safeguard the abolition of slavery in England.[55] After the Mansfield Judgment, Folarin Shyllon, Peter Fryer, and Gretchen Gerzina have convincingly proved, slaves were frequently bought and sold in English newspapers well into the 1820s.[56] In popular print culture, slavery within England was an all too common reality for an extended period after Mansfield's judgment.

However, despite its insufficiency in guaranteeing freedom, the principle behind the Mansfield Judgment found an outlet in English literature and culture at large. In the wake of Mansfield's judgment a myth is produced— a myth of the *supposed* freedom of black slaves in Britain—a Mansfield myth that Shyllon calls "quite untrue."[57] Maria Edgeworth's Juba in *Belinda* (1801) is part of a strong contemporary literary movement popularizing it after 1772. Thomas Day's "The Dying Negro" (1774) encourages sympathetic support for the Mansfield semblance of freedom by harshly portraying the real-life impressment of a male Negro slave from Bristol in 1773 and his subsequent suicide to avoid being sold in the colonies. More explicitly, William Cowper proclaims, "We have no Slaves at home" in *The Task* (1785), and Archibald MacLaren's one-act drama *The Negro Slaves* (1799) has a Jamaican slave, Quako, tell his African bride, Sela, "Then we shall go to England, and be free Britons" (I.v.23). Immigration to a free European nation is also the radical solution to the problem of slavery proposed as one of the endings to Kotzebue's *The Negro Slaves*. Opie evokes the Mansfield myth herself in "The Negro Boy's Tale,"[58] published three years before *Adeline Mowbray*. Zambo, the poem's enslaved Jamaican protagonist, imagines England as a "sweet land / . . . Vere, soon as on de shore he stand, / De helpless Negro slave be free" (54).[59]

Zambo's fictionalized idea of immediate freedom was even a lived reality

---

55. To examine this debate see Edward Fiddes, "Lord Mansfield and the Sommersett Case," *Law Quarterly Review* 50 (1934): 499–511; William M. Wiecek, "*Somerset*: Lord Mansfield and the Legitimacy of Slavery in the Anglo-American World," *University of Chicago Law Review* 42 (1974): 86–146; David Brion Davis, *The Problem of Slavery in the Age of Revolution, 1770–1823* (Oxford: Oxford University Press, 1999), chapter 10.

56. See Shyllon's *Black People in Britain* and Gerzina's *Black London*.

57. Shyllon, *Black People*, 25.

58. For analysis about the importance of the use of the word 'Tales' in Opie's oeuvre, see Gary Kelly's "Discharging Debts: The Moral Economy of Amelia Opie's Fiction," *Wordsworth Circle* 11 (1980): 198–203. Roxanne Eberle makes a similar point in "'Tales of Truth?': Amelia Opie's Antislavery Poetics," in *Romanticism and Women Poets*, ed. Harriet Kramer Linkin and Stephen C. Behrendt (Lexington: University Press of Kentucky, 1999), 71–98.

59. *Poems, by Mrs. Opie* (London: Longman, Hurst, Rees, and Orme, 1806).

for some blacks in Britain. In a letter to Charles Stewart written three weeks after the Mansfield Judgment was passed, John Riddell writes:

> But I am disappointed by Mr. Dublin who has run away. He told the servants that he had rec'd a letter from his Uncle Sommerset acquainting him that Lord Mansfield had given them their freedom & *he was determined to leave* me as soon as I returned from London which he did without even speaking to me.[60]

Publicly acknowledging Mansfield as his excuse to "run away," Dublin evokes the myth of instantaneous freedom and leaves Riddell's establishment "without even speaking to" his former master, presumably to prevent the myth of indigenous freedom that he relates to the other servants from being refuted.

So from all of these literal and fiction evocations of freedom under the Mansfield myth, it would seem that the fictional Savanna, who "had escaped early in life . . . to England" (II, 110), should realize Zambo's vision of immediate emancipation once she arrives there. Yet her determination to stay with and serve Adeline years after the Mansfield Judgment seems so much like a domestic form of benevolent enslavement that Cubba privileged in the Larpent manuscript of *Irishman in London*.[61] She willingly accepts a life of servitude under Adeline when she makes a determined vow to serve her for a subsistence of "nothing but my meat and drink" (II, 175) out of gratitude for the three guineas' worth of kindness meted out during the arresting scene. And Adeline apparently consolidates Savanna's reenslavement when she refers to her as "my property" (III, 84) and bequeaths Savanna to her mother in her will—language and gestures expected more from slave-holders such as Riddell or even tyrants such as Davis. The fact that this woman liberated under the Mansfield myth would willingly choose to attach herself to Adeline in a relationship that appears to mimic benevolent slavery presents a level of skepticism about the text's position on the mulatto woman's freedom. If Savanna's emancipation in England is not the novel's aim, what does her dependence on Adeline mean, and how does it affect the novel's abolitionist stance?

I want to suggest that the myth of freedom popularized by the Mansfield Judgment informs Opie's depiction of Savanna and offers another way to think about how Opie's novel attempts to promote the liberty of Africans in England as a triumph over tyranny. Although Eleanor Ty concludes, "Opie's novel eschews radical solutions,"[62] her conclusion does not take into account the radical idea of granting citizenship status to poor black ex-slaves at a time

---

60. Quoted in Oldham, "New Light on Mansfield and Slavery," 65–66; my emphasis.
61. See Chapter Four, 179.
62. Eleanor Ty, *Empowering the Feminine* (Toronto: University of Toronto Press, 1998), 160.

in British history when organizations such as the Committee for the Relief of the Black Poor were viewing poor blacks as foreigners and actively working to get rid of them.[63] My earlier reading of the arresting scene argued that Opie shows support for the black poor who choose to remain on English shores when she distinguishes between natural and commercial rights. All Britons, irrespective of color, should have access to the former. Specific support of citizenship status for Savanna emerges when Opie states that Adeline "had not recollected that [Savanna] was a mulatto" until Davis berates her blackness. This is, perhaps, Opie's tacit way of saying that one should see Savanna as Adeline does, first and foremost, as a free British woman, and only secondarily as black. This kind of reading is supported in other areas of the novel.

Carol Howard reads Savanna and Adeline's relationship within "the nostalgic language of fealty"[64]—a sentimental pledge of allegiance—and this perspective proves helpful in reexamining the novel's abolitionist politics. By accepting a subservient role in British society, Savanna is seen as upholding the feudal order. Her deference to Adeline is an articulation of the conservative response to authority that Edmund Burke valorized in his *Reflections on the Revolution in France* (1790). Yet, if this is the case—if Savanna is an illustration of the kind of ennobling deference to authority that, Burke suggests, distinguishes the British from the French—then her deference to Adeline is a patriotic act that adheres to British principles, and, thus, distinguishes her admirably when viewed alongside the foreignness embodied in figures such as the "French Countess" Mary Warner, the nabob Mr. Maynard, Adeline's sexually abusive stepfather, the Irish peer, Sir Patrick O'Carrol, and other contemporaries such as the rich "little bastard" who are intent on knocking down British society by their socially and sexually transgressive behavior. Savanna's willing act of deference is a performative act of patriotism—one that identifies her as another of Isaac Land's "street citizens." Of these individuals, Land writes: "The reward for patriotic service was a rough-and-ready inclusiveness around the edges of the conveniently undefined category of 'Briton.'"[65] In a society of individuals who continually misread Adeline's principle as vice, Savanna's deference to Adeline, both when she is unmarried to Glenmurray and when she is legally married to Berrendale, shows that she is able to recognize, and is prepared to attach herself to, the ideal British principle of virtue that Adeline stands for in a way that other Britons are not. In the spirited attachment to Adeline and the principle of pure virtue, then, Opie identifies Savanna as a pure British subject.

---

63. Shyllon, *Black People*, 103.
64. Howard, "'The Story of the Pineapple,'" *367*.
65. Land, "Bread and Arsenic," 90.

There are other reasons for considering Savanna as a black British street citizen in the novel. Contemporary proslavery critics falsely claimed that the Mansfield Judgment had created this poor black problem when bondsmen such as Dublin peremptorily absconded from their masters without subsequently securing other means of subsistence.[66] This was a false claim. But after 1772, a black slave's abrupt determination to leave a former master was not necessarily the most pragmatic solution to the problem of poverty for the black working class in England. As Felicity Nussbaum observes: "Lord Mansfield ... extended the protection of habeas corpus ... to the slave James Somerset in 1772, and thus to all black people in England—though he did not extend that privilege to grant them wages or poor law relief."[67] Neither the Mansfield Judgment nor the myth surrounding it guaranteed black people job security or state protection if they asserted their freedom under them. And as Gretchen Gerzina's *Black London* points out, of the black men who had fought alongside the British during the American War of Independence in return for the promise of freedom and assistance in England, "most were still penniless slaves ... highly visible on English streets,"[68] and very few of them actually received financial remuneration for the loyalty they showed to the British during the war.[69]

Hence, one must consider Savanna's relationship with Adeline as a negotiation of the precarious consequentiality of asserting freedom in a society that cared little for the subsequent protection of the lives of the black poor who chose to remain in England after the 1787 Sierra Leone expedition. Viewed within this context, Savanna's allegiance to Adeline can be read as a reflection of the type of assistance that Britain should have provided for the black poor who had demonstrated their loyalty to support and fight for British principles. Serving Adeline allows Savanna to aspire within English society. "But, lady," Savanna explains to Adeline, "you break my heart ... if you not take my service. My William and me too poor to live togedder of some year perhaps" (II, 177). Aside from the grateful appeal from her "heart" to repay Adeline for her kindness, Savanna underscores a practical need for subsistence because William cannot afford to support them both. It is noticeable that she makes no comment about being forced into poor-law assistance, perhaps knowing that her foreign black complexion excludes her from it. But in pursuing work under Adeline, Savanna displays "a determined enthusiasm of manner" (II, 178) that is in the service of being self-sufficient

---

66. Ibid., 118–19.
67. "Women and Race: 'A Difference of Complexion'" in *Women and Literature in Britain, 1700–1800*, ed. Vivien Jones (Cambridge: Cambridge University Press), 69.
68. Gerzina, *Black London*, 136.
69. Shyllon, *Black People*, 117–58.

even if it is ostensibly utilized with the intention of staying with, and repaying, Adeline. Savanna is, thus, an indication that the opportunity to work is what the black poor need,[70] and Adeline is the principled British subject who provides it.

Savanna's dedication to the principle of marriage accompanies her dedication to the principle of work and reflects more on her Britishness. "I should have let [Glenmurray] go to prison, before disappoint my William" (II, 176), she states, revealing that an unswerving determination to satisfy her husband in the face of Adeline's distress would not have caused her to aide Adeline and forgo her prior commitment to him. Savanna is obviously committed to her husband; however, Howard skeptically cites the fact that they only meet once in the novel as an indication that their relationship takes second place to Savanna and Adeline's. In actuality, Savanna's determination to see and nurse William once he falls ill while working in Jamaica offers an instance of her marital fidelity. Despite her vow of allegiance to Adeline, Savanna secures a free passage to Jamaica one full day before she secures her employer's permission to leave: "[A ship's captain] tell me yesterday that he let me go for noting" (III, 86–87), she tells Adeline, indicating that she has already explored a viable way of seeing William and she has the means to potentially use it whether or not Adeline agrees to her departure. The fact that she travels to Jamaica after having "escaped, early in life, with her first husband" (III, 102), to nurse William as any wife would do, without any fear of the consequences as to her status, suggests that she has established a free mind-set as a British woman. Savanna's initial escape to England "early in life, with her first husband" offers just enough information to suggest that she has been breathing the pure air of English liberty for a while—perhaps, breathing it so much that she has imbibed the principle of freedom and forgets the fact that outside of England she is still perceived as a slave.

The reader, socially attuned to the legal and moral legitimacy of the text's view on indigenous freedom for people of all complexions, is expected to view and accept Savanna's capacity for pure British working-class virtue despite her black, fugitive, and socially transgressive skin because she embodies the British principles of rank deference, industry, constancy in marriage, and dedications to virtue and freedom. Where Adeline's ideological hybridity as a virtuous proponent of an immoral act completely destroyed her good reputation, Savanna's literal complexion effects the opposite. Opie constructs Savanna as an intriguing and perhaps shocking illustration of the idea that a street citizen does not have to have an English Rose complexion to live up

---

70. Mary Prince makes a similar statement at the end of her *History*. *The History of Mary Prince*, ed. Sarah Salih (London: Penguin, 2000).

to the reputation of ideal British femininity. As Land puts it: "British-ness was about behavior not birthplace or bloodline."[71]

I HAVE BEEN arguing that the abolitionist discourse in *Adeline Mowbray* is not about liberating people of African descent from slavery. In England, the Mansfield myth had ostensibly established that. Rather, Opie's portrayal of Savanna shows that the abolition of prejudice and poverty leveled at the black poor allows them the freedom to be seen as pure black British citizens.

The most triumphant instance of Savanna's use of her citizenship status comes in a comment she makes as she and Adeline contemplate legally confronting a colonial tyrant. Ever since his tryst with a house-servant, Savanna resolves to "thwart" (III, 54) the villainous Berrendale for his tyrannical treatment of Adeline. But this determination is never more so apparent than when she returns from Jamaica. The most revealing instance of Savanna's dedication to the pursuit of freedom from her position as Adeline's employee appears when she escapes from the enslavement that Berrendale returns her to and travels back to England to inform Adeline of his bigamous marriage to a West Indian heiress. Adeline "desired [Savanna] to proceed to business" (III, 155). Incredulously interpreting "business" as a call to arms protected by rights of habeas corpus, "the delighted mulatto" cries, "'What! . . . are *we* going to prosecu massa?'" (III, 155; my emphasis). Adeline, however, comes

> "to a *determination* to take no *legal steps* in this affair, but leave Mr. Berrendale to the reproaches of his own conscience."
> "A fiddle's end!" replied Savanna, "he have no conscience, or he no leave you: better get him hang; if you can den you marry de colonel."
> "I had better hang the father of my child, had I, Savanna?"
> "Oh! no, no, no, no,—me *forget* dat." (III, 155–56; my emphasis)

In this scene, Opie provides another of those pivotal moments of confrontation between a woman of African descent and a colonial tyrant. But in this moment, Savanna is more defensive in her actions. One asks, what exactly *is* the fugitive slave *remembering* as she proceeds to determine the expediency of not only prosecuting Adeline's errant husband but hanging him too?

Clearly, from her response, she remembers that Berrendale has abandoned his wife; but is that all? Does she recall her own reenslavement because of him? Does she also recall his ubiquitous position as a "massa" like Davis—a businessman involved in the exploitation and oppression of mulatto women

---

71. Land, "Bread and Arsenic," 90.

like herself as well as Adeline? The "delighted" way she invokes the all-inclusive pronoun "we" suggests that she does. For Savanna knows Adeline will get material justice and perhaps a new husband from Berrendale's legal demise, but including herself in the prosecution process underscores the vindication she also expects to receive under English law because of his behavior toward her. Adeline, reluctant to take any further action "which might injure her reputation" (III, 155), is determined to take no "legal steps" in this affair. She abandons both of her assertive abolitionist positions taken during the arresting scene now that Mary has made her understand the negative consequences of her actions. But Savanna's desire to "prosecu massa" reveals her understanding of, and hidden determination to use, the "legal steps" forward established by Mansfield's 1772 decision. In a gesture that purports to exclusively aide Adeline, Savanna wants to take "legal steps" that also "prosecu massa" Berrendale for forcibly returning her back into Jamaican slavery, an act that she seems to recollect would be her "business" to prosecute under the Mansfield Judgment if perpetrated in England. And from her vantage point as a black British employee, she tries to utilize Adeline to achieve this end.

Proposing, justifying, and including herself in "legal steps" forward using the English courts, Savanna alone presents a way to tangibly provide "joint relief" from the unjust commercial oppressions that sexually and socially stigmatized women of *all* complexions experience in England. Committing bigamy in Jamaica purely for profit and returning Savanna to slavery purely to protect it, Berrendale violates Savanna's freedom and Adeline's nuptial vow by exploiting the former's black complexion and the latter's notorious reputation. Such behavior associates him with the fruiterer, the kept mistress, Mary, and the creditor, Davis. In fact, given his impending marriage to a Creole heiresses, Berrendale is the literal embodiment of the colonial tyrant from which these indigenous characters are derived. Hence, Savanna's desire to "prosecu massa" Berrendale strikes at the heart of actions that need to be taken collectively against him, and all tyrants like him.

Taking "legal steps" to "prosecu massa" Berrendale relates, then, to all confrontational scenes where powerful displays of bigotry and exploitation are aimed exclusively and unfairly against "mulatto" women with stigmatized (black) complexions. It calls for a legal reevaluation of the moral foundations underlying the commercial rights displayed in the arresting scene, where the creditor and the fruiterer persecute Savanna and Adeline over a pineapple and a "trifling . . . six pounds" with powerful displays of bigotry and exploitation because of a prejudged association with sexual and social transgression. It also relates to Mary's position in Langley's office, calling for the strengthening of laws that counter the kept mistress's reign as the advocate for the abolition of marriage. In effect, Savanna's question retaliates against all unjust persecutions and prosecutions of unjustly stigmatized women of all complexions by proposing the following to Adeline: 'aren't we going about the "business" of avenging the creditors'/fruiterers'/kept mistresses' abilities to exploit us because of our 'black' complexions? Aren't you and I—"we" (mulatto women)—going to use the morally legitimate principle of "natural rights" to legally "thwart" these tyrants?' In paraphrasing the implications behind Savanna's desire to "prosecu massa," I am suggesting that her desire to take "legal steps" forward provides the most pragmatic solution to address the violations against freedom and marriage that Berrendale and other tyrants such as the prostitute, the creditor, and the fruiterer commit. But she lacks the assistance of her benevolent benefactor to make these prosecutions happen. In my last chapter, *The Woman of Colour* offers a chance to see if such an empowering representation of black femininity by a rich mulatto advocate for the abolition of slavery can actually come to fruition in England. But from her limited position as a scantily waged but fully protected black British employee, Savanna's articulation of legal steps forward against English tyrants has a triumphant effect on English society, identifying the main legal avenue by which the black poor in England can protect their freedom to be British.

THIS CHAPTER resituates the current skeptical approach to abolition in Opie's work. She encourages a favorable response to the discussion about the legal status of black people in England popularized under the Mansfield myth when she vindicates one woman's form of blackness while pointing out the vice of the other. She is at least one British author who counters Moira Fergusson's claim that eighteenth-century British women writers "misrepresented the very African-Caribbean slaves whose freedom they advocated."[72] By producing a text that imagines the Mansfield Judgment as a legal reality that promotes a woman of color's freedom to be British, *Adeline Mowbray* evokes the spirit of the most abolitionist of English abolitionist tales. Its vindication of the rights of a woman of African descent's entitlement to fall under English laws and legal protections shows the level of assistance that was denied Imoinda in Surinam. Thus, the spirit of "Imoinda's shade" extends from the wilds of Surinam to shake the foundations of England's judicial system with Savanna's attempt to "prosecu massa."

In presenting Savanna as a free British woman who is, ultimately, left to the "joint care" of Mrs. Pemberton, the Quaker, and Mrs. Mowbray, the landed widow—women with the religious and financial weight to continue

---

72. Moira Fergusson, *Subject to Others* (New York: Routledge, 1992), 3.

the protracted fight against tyranny in England—Opie ends the novel by conveying the spirit of the natural. Natural rights for all English people are ostensibly contained in Blackstone's 1765 *Commentaries* and reinforced in *Adeline Mowbray*. The Mansfield myth purportedly allows black slaves to naturally join the ranks of the English working classes. And Savanna's natural complexion is purged of any sexual and social stigmas and welcomed into the Rosevalley estate—a place where a diverse group of individuals live together, each having lost a spouse to death by natural causes. Rosevalley is also the place where the future reputation of English Rose femininity, Editha Berrendale—Adeline's daughter—resides. Editha's future reputation in England depends upon a more socially successful nurturing of her femininity there than her mother experienced, and she has a balanced cadre of people capable of making this happen. Dr. Norberry, the man of feeling, caters to her physical well-being while Mrs. Pemberton, the highly principled Quaker woman, caters to her spiritual salvation and Mrs. Mowbray, the propertied landowner, her material wealth. However, the mulatto woman's role in Editha's nurturing is not immediately clear. Of the four, Savanna has been the only one consistently present in the child's life. She is also the only living reminder of Adeline herself—her complexion the living remembrance of Adeline's unfortunate demise as a women's rights activist as well as an example of another way of championing freedom in England that elevates an advocate's reputation without losing her station in the world. Savanna's shade of complexion is, then, a warning to as well as an outlet for Editha's burgeoning femininity at Rosevalley, the place where English Roses like herself and her mother bloom and die, and bloom again. With the demise of the advocate for the abolition of marriage, the aftermath of the text makes one thing sure about the mulatto woman's influence in Editha's life: the nurturing of enlightened English femininity—the future English Rose that blossoms in this retired landscape depends entirely upon the way it and the pure English soil of liberty at Rosevalley negotiate the natural presence of Savanna.

CHAPTER 6

"An unportioned girl of *my* complexion can . . . be a dangerous object."

Abolition and the Mulatto Heiress in England

Oroonoko: No, let the Guilty blush,
The white man that betrayed me. Honest Black
Disdains to change its Colour.
    —Thomas Southerne, *Oroonoko* (1696), I.ii.242–44

Lord Ogleby: You are right, Brush.—There is no washing the Blackamoor white.
    —George Colman and David Garrick, *The Clandestine Marriage* (1766), II.i.138–39

"I rejoice to hear it. We'll make her blush for herself. Her fine olive complexion, you know, is changeable enough."
    —Anonymous, *The Fair Cambrians*, vol. 1 (1790), 109

But after all, since there will be some *womaniz'd Fools* of our own Sex, that can't be kept from running mad for the *outside* of a *Skin*, and doating on a *fine Complexion*, I shall *prove this Paradox to mortify their Pride and yours, that a despis'd Mooress* is really a greater *Beauty* than all your finical chalky-fac'd European Ladies: The *Sun* has but *half-bak'd you*, you are not arriv'd to the perfection of *Mulattos* . . .
"*That* a Black-a-moor Woman is the *greatest* Beauty; *in a Letter* to a *Lady exceeding Fair*"
    —John Dunton, *Athenian Sport* (1707), 103

For most certainly, there are Beauties that can charm of that Colour.
    —Aphra Behn, *Oroonoko* (1688/1997), ed. Joanna Lipking, 11

ON OCTOBER 30, 2005, in a *Washington Post* op-ed titled "Guess Who? You Can Ask Me, but Don't Expect an Answer," Monica Bhide, an Indian critic who writes about "food, culture and their influence on our lives," narrates several scenes of racial misreading—some disturbing, others amusing—in which she is mistaken for an Arab, a Brazilian, a Mexican, and a Pakistani. One of these misreadings stands out more than the rest, however, because it is more than just a case of national misrecognition:

> When I was living in Lynchburg, Va., many years ago, I was babysitting for a 4-year-old. His parents were Caucasians, well educated and very kind. (Why do I bother mentioning their skin color? Because it's important to understanding the scene I'm about to describe.) When the boy first saw me he asked, "How come she is not brown?" Apparently the only two colors he knew were white and brown, and I did not match either. His parents explained that people come in many colors and then sheepishly left to go to dinner.
>
> We played outside for a bit. I then turned to him and said, "Honey, you are so dirty playing in this mud, you need a bath." He came up to me and began furiously rubbing the back of my hand. "You need a bath more than I do." When my skin color did not change, he said, "Oh, it does not come off. I just thought you looked like that because you need a bath."

Though she never intended to have her body used in this way, the little "Lynchburg" boy's furious attempts to wash Bhide as white as he sees himself and his parents ends up being a useful exercise. His experiment on Bhide's body proves to his satisfaction that her complexion "does not come off"—that people of colors other than brown and white *really do* exist—and it does so in a far more concrete way than his sheepish parents attempted to do with their brief and embarrassed precept.

This use of a racialized female body as a didactic tool has roots in a literary incident that occurred two hundred years ago and over three thousand miles away. Early in the plot of the intriguing anonymous[1] novel *The Woman of Colour* (1808),[2] a young white English boy runs to an assembled group of adults gathered in a London drawing room with a complaint about Dido, a Negro maid recently arrived from Jamaica. "Oh, mamma! Mamma," he

---

1. For the debate about the novel's author, see *The English Novel 1770–1829*, vol. 2, *1800–1829*, ed. Peter Garside, James Raven, and Rainer Schowerling (Oxford: Oxford University Press, 2000), 69–70 and 265.

2. *The Woman of Colour, A Tale in Two Volumes* (London: Black, Parry and Kingsbury, 1808). All subsequent references are to this edition. Also, see my 2007 Broadview edition of the novel. For more insight into the term's usage and the lives of Jamaican people of color in general, see Gad Heuman's *Between Black and White* (Westport, CT: Greenwood Press, 1981).

exclaims, "that nasty black woman has been kissing me and dirtying my face all over!" (I, 91). Dido's mistress, Olivia Fairfield, a Jamaican mulatto heiress[3] with "a dower of nearly sixty thousand pounds" (I, 25), witnesses the boy's outburst. But seeing "something bewitchingly charming in [his] infantine simplicity" (I, 92), she decides to correct his prejudice using her body as the example.

> I took him on my lap, and holding his hand in mine, I said,—"You see the difference in our hands."
> "Yes, I do, indeed," said he, shaking his head. "Mine looks *clean,* and *yours* looks *not* so very dirty."
> "I am glad it does not look so *very* dirty," said I; "but you will be surprised when I tell you that mine is quite as clean as your own, and that the black woman's below, is as clean as either of them. . . . God chose it should be so, and we cannot make *our* skins white any more than you can make yours black."
> "Oh! But *I* can make mine black if I choose it," said he, "by rubbing myself with coals."
> "And so can I make mine white by rubbing myself with *chalk,*" said I; "but both the coal and the chalk would be soon rubbed off again."
> "And won't *yours* and *hers* rub off?" said he.
> "Try," said I, giving him the corner of my handkerchief; and to work the little fellow went with all his might. (I, 93–96)

When he equates mulatto and black pigmentation with filth and his own whiteness with purity, the little English boy exhibits the same sign of racial naivety as the "Lynchburg" boy. In this case, however, he assumes that rubbing himself with "coals" will make his white skin "black" like Olivia's and Dido's. This kind of thinking makes us realize that both boys are simply ignorant about the way race is produced. To disabuse the little English boy, Olivia takes charge of the situation in a way that Bhide doesn't with the Lynchburg boy. She *allows* him to "try" to "rub" her "clean"—to attempt to wash her white—with her handkerchief.

Srinivas Aravamudan begins *Tropicopolitans* considering the historicized racism imbedded in the trope of 'washing a black-moor white.'[4] In literal

---

3. For other literary depictions of eighteenth- and nineteenth-century heiresses of color, see Appendix C in *The Woman of Colour* (2007). As, at once, the first mulatto heroine ever to appear as a major character in a British long prose fiction, and the first black heroine in a novel set in Europe, predating Claire de Duras's *Ourika* by fifteen years, Olivia Fairfield is, arguably, the most significant black female character to appear in a British novel after Aphra Behn's Imoinda.

4. For another brief history of the term, see Virginia Mason Vaughan's *Performing Blackness on English Stages, 1500–1800* (Cambridge: Cambridge University Press, 2005), 6–7.

terms, he explains that "experimental observation has led to experiential truth" (2): a "tropological blackamoor [is a] sign of *failed whitening*," and, in turn, a "stereotype of *unchangeable uselessness*."[5] This understanding of the trope has literally worked in the self-interest of the eighteenth-century white men who codified it since it articulates the impossibility of transforming blacks into whites, thereby creating ample space to justify arguments that blacks are stubbornly inferior, and their enslavement, acceptable. But Robert Young's *Colonial Desire: Hybridity in Theory, Culture and Race* (1995) has explored how failed acts of whitening marked an important reevaluation of the British colonial enterprise when Anthony Trollope and others from the Victorian era advocated race-mixing, or what they called "amalgamation," as a "means of achieving an honourable withdrawal from an uneconomic colony."[6] "When sufficient of our blood shall have been infused into the veins of those children of the sun," Trollope writes, "then, I think, we may be ready, without stain to our patriotism, to take off our hats and bid farewell to the West Indies."[7] Young interprets Trollope's "argument for the breeding of a new strain of mixed-raced colonial" as "a proposal for a more efficient form of colonialism"[8] where the nation's ideals are carried out by individuals who may physically resemble the native colonials yet identify ideologically with British ideals. For these kinds of individuals, amalgamation was seen as a success. "The lighter the shade," Patricia Mohammed writes in her essay "The Emergence in Eighteenth and Nineteenth Century Jamaica of the Mulatto Woman as the Desired," "the higher was the person's rank on the social ladder."[9] So amalgamation or race-mixing gives birth to the idea of a superior race of mulattos who understand that their superiority is in the service of upholding a racial hierarchy that white British men have been actively involved in establishing.

However, when she encourages the boy's "experimental observation" with the hope that the "little fellow" might learn a lesson about blackness, Olivia refutes the terms to which amalgamation is being put to use. Her experiment involves a specific symbol of "*failed whitening*"—a free, literate, mulatto heiress—using her own body to do the work of not confirming the little boy's racial superiority but improving his attitude toward a formerly enslaved illiterate Negress—equalizing work that directly goes against the ambitions of the white men who support the idea of amalgamation. Olivia's

---

5. Ibid., 4.
6. Robert J. C. Young, *Colonial Desire* (London: Routledge, 1995), 142.
7. Ibid.
8. Ibid., 143.
9. "'But most of all mi love me Browning': The Emergence in Eighteenth and Nineteenth Century Jamaica of the Mulatto Woman as the Desired," *Feminist Review* 65 (2000): 25.

fervent advocacy for Dido is also quite a unique position for a woman of color in literature to take at this particular time. Alicia Seldon and Miranda Vanderparke are other contemporary examples of superior women of color from the Caribbean.[10] But they are not depicted as actively involved in using their bodies to advocate for Africans. I have come to read Olivia's use of this whitewashing trope as dangerous in a useful rather than malevolent sense because, in applying it to herself, Olivia takes on the threatening role of subtly critiquing, challenging, deconstructing, and influencing the ignorant yet impressionable mind of a potential Englishman in a way that also offers a radical rebuttal to the racist actions of self-interested white men at one of the most important times in British abolitionist history.

THIS CHAPTER places Olivia's relationship to the English boy in a larger context by exploring how the trope of 'washing a black-moor white' was used literally and metaphorically in a wide variety of eighteenth-century English texts and iconography. I am specifically concerned with one contradiction that these multivarious deployments of the trope unearth: the fact that it was employed as a way of articulating the liberation of white British men from the stigmas of the slave trade and slavery at the same time that it signified the inability to liberate blacks from these very same stigmas. British women writers such as Fanny Burney and Jane Austen complicate this contradiction with yet another. Although they employ the trope allegorically to signify the liberation of blackened women in *The Wanderer* and *Mansfield Park,* each author's use of a marriage plot prevents their allegory from articulating more than a very limited form of social liberation, and one that exclusively addresses white women's rights and ignores those of black people.

The Woman of Colour, however, exposes these gendered contradictions, first, by allowing Olivia to appropriate the trope as a way of exonerating Dido's blackness, and then in the author's use of symbolic names and characterizations which undermine the traditional ways white writers have used the trope. In other words, the pivotal whitewashing scene and others from *The Woman of Colour* that relate to her bigamous marriage to Augustus Merton must be read as a series of strategic deployments that forcefully resist, and hence radically attack, the trope's racist sentiments and racially biased supporters. *The Woman of Colour*'s greatest triumph of resistance, however, appears when we examine the ways it is actively involved in undermining the nefarious intentions behind a self-interested abolitionist marriage plot

---

10. Mulatto heiresses from the novels *Edmund and Eleonora* (1797) and *Memoirs of a Scots Heiress* (1791).

carefully orchestrated by the will of Olivia's father. The clauses in Mr. Fairfield's ironclad will seek not merely to continue his paternalist ascendancy over Olivia beyond the grave; his will also seeks to involve her in an arranged marriage that attempts to obliterate blackness from his hereditary line. By marrying white, Olivia ensures that her children (should she bear them) will be lightened. However, Olivia's reinvention of herself as a widow, and the novel's final conception of its heroine as a vibrant, living educator-activist, are both subject positions that undermine Mr. Fairfield's conception of his daughter as an object designed to whitewash his hereditary line.

In these ways, *The Woman of Colour* establishes a mulatto heiress as a resistant abolitionist figure—a "tropicopolitan" in the fullest sense of the word—that is, "the colonized subject who exists both as fictive construct of colonial tropology *and* actual resident of tropical space, object of representation *and* agent of resistance."[11] While the image of an English boy setting "to work" on Olivia—rubbing her black hand "with all his might"—gives the impression that abolition is a voracious process of racial obliteration,[12] a woman of color from the West Indies resists this work and reinstates abolition in a larger sense that involves gender as well as racial liberation. If working on Olivia can produce useful resistant work of this magnitude, she is being deceptively unthreatening when she remarks, "an unportioned girl of *my* complexion can never be a dangerous object" (I, 13). On the contrary, *The Woman of Colour* makes clear that the mulatto heiress in England is a real threat to the ascendancy of paternalism. For this reason, Olivia, like no other fictional heroine of African descent before her, represents the realization of the threat to paternalism that Imoinda first embodied as she brandished her bow and arrow against the Deputy Governor during the rebellion against slavery in Surinam. In short, *The Woman of Colour* marks the fictional African woman's boldest charge against the institution of slavery by her deft ability to attack paternalism not merely on its own terra firma as Cubba and Savanna have done, but within the paternalist's own bloodline.

THE 'WASHING A blackamoor white' trope has appeared in biblical texts, Greek literature, and anecdotes too numerous to mention.[13] However, it is, probably, the multitude of Latin, French, and English translations of Aesop's *Fables* that are largely responsible for the dispersal and reinforcement of the

---

11. *Tropicopolitans*, 4.

12. This idea of abolition as a total obliteration of blackness from English culture dates back to Queen Elizabeth's two proclamations abolishing blackamoors from England in 1596 and 1601. See Fryer's *Staying Power,* 8–12.

13. See Jean Michel Massing's "From Greek Proverb to Soap Advert: Washing the Ethiopian," *Journal of the Warburg and Courtauld Institutes* 58 (1995): 181–85 for this discussion.

morals that the trope has come to represent: "to labor in vain," "a fruitless undertaking," "a useless endeavor," and "to attempt the impossible."[14] As Aravamudan has pointed out, each of these morals relies on the reiteration of the black object's permanent complexion in order to illustrate the message of futility at the heart of the moral. Yet, with all the critical attention focused on the trope's racial dynamics, far less notice has been paid to the gender dynamics that the trope's deployments have also raised. The majority of the trope's deployments involve white men washing black men.[15] But since Toni Morrison has made a point of stressing "how avoided and unanalyzed is the effect of racist inflection on the subject,"[16] one must also ask if any difference appears when white women do the washing?

Published in 1805 under the pseudonym Edward Baldwin and written expressly for children, William Godwin's interpretation of the Aesop fable feminizes the white washer and identifies her with a surname: Miss Moggridge. Despite being washed for three hours by a fleet of the washerwomen whom Moggridge has hired, the black man, Nango, does not racially transform (figure 18). In fact, he disappears from the end of the text altogether in favor of this explicit critique of the white female washer:

> The washerwomen had agreed to do Miss Moggridge's work, because they wanted Miss Moggridge's money for themselves and their families. But secretly they laughed at her ignorance and folly. They told their neighbours what had happened. And when Miss Moggridge's one-horse chaise was brought to the door for the young lady to take an airing, people pointed and said, That chaise and horse belong to the young lady who undertook to wash a blackamoor white. What a pity that her uncle, who could leave her such a pretty fortune, and who was otherwise so good a man, never thought of sparing a farthing to send her to school! She would then certainly have learned that there were negroes as well as white people in the world; and would not have been silly enough to try at impossibilities.[17]

Godwin's decision to allow Nango to disappear suggests that his didacticism is less focused on teaching children about racial difference and more focused

---

14. See M. P. Tilley's *A Dictionary of the Proverbs in England in the Sixteenth and Seventeenth Centuries* (Ann Arbor: University of Michigan Press, 1950), 190, no. E186, for a discussion of the trope as it was used by the English.

15. For a typical example, see E. Stacy's verse "Fable CLIX: The Washing of a Blackmoor" in *Aesop. Sir Roger L'Estrange's Fables, with Morals and Reflections in English Verse* (London, 1717), 253–54.

16. *Playing in the Dark*, 11.

17. "Washing the Blackamoor White," *Fables Ancient and Modern* (London: Godwin, 1824), 147–48.

Figure 18.
"Washing the Blackamoor White," 1807, William Mulready (1786–1863)
(illustrated in William Godwin's *Fables, Ancient and Modern*)

on exposing Moggridge as provincial, uneducated, and "silly enough to try at impossibilities." Material wealth, at once, provides Moggridge with the means to distinguish herself from other white people in her society although not in the way that she or her rich uncle intended. Rather than consolidating her rank and reputation, the money that Moggridge expends on attempting to whiten Nango succeeds in exposing her "Dark Brains,"[18] the character trait that leads to financial exploitation by her social inferiors as well as the derision and ridicule of her entire neighborhood.

But the lack of reason displayed by this white female washer actually does some constructive work. Godwin's belief that "school" would have been the remedy for Moggridge's ignorance underscores that his particular deployment of the trope intervenes in a contemporary debate about the need for educating independent women of rank. Such a proposal would not have been made at the beginning of the eighteenth century, when women's fortunes were expected to be managed by their fathers and husbands, never themselves—Mary Astell being the unique exception to this rule since she had her own bank account. Yet it makes perfect sense at the end of the century, when Godwin's recently deceased wife, Mary Wollstonecraft, had made contemporary ideas about female education and independence causes célèbres for ordinary women. Godwin retains the moral behind the trope, but by changing the gender of the washer he also develops its social deployment.

Jean Michel Massing's extensive work on the sixteenth- and seventeenth-century European iconography about the trope raises two further assumptions about the effects the trope had on the white female washer, neither of which he pursues in his excellent essay. First, within the wide array of portraits and prints that he reproduces and analyzes, there is a noticeable emphasis on deployments of the trope that involve white women washing black men or boys. These visual depictions of beautiful white women seen applying water and rags to black boys and men show the power of the ideal white woman to objectify her white beauty and consolidate its permanence through contrast, just as ladies used to employ young black boys as foot servants not only to display their wealth but also to conspicuously draw attention to their whiteness. This gendered reading of the trope shows that it has the ability to underscore the superiority of white complexions within Nature even as it ridicules white women for their inability to reason correctly about race in accordance with Mother Nature and their own white peer-group. The trope's ability to oscillate in this manner demonstrates its

---

18. "Who against Nature, Reason, Wit and Sense, / T'impossible Attempts would make pretence; / Might try th'Experiment with as much Hope, / To wash his own Dark Brains, as Blanch the Ethiope." Joseph Jackson's "Moral" from his translation of Aesop's *Fables* (London: Tebb, 1708), 258.

ability to generate unstable, even contradictory, meanings when the gender dynamics involved in the trope's deployment are analyzed.

But what about black women? How are they involved with the whitewashing trope? Massing does not reproduce any iconographic representations of African women being whitewashed with soap, water, rags, and brushes in the manner of the black males, which suggests either that such portraits do not exist, or if they do, they are not anywhere near as popular and widely dispersed as those that involve black males. He does, however, present Isaac Cruikshank's satirical print "Washing the Blackamoor" (1795) (figure 19), which shows the Prince of Wales holding a basin of water while two female attendants attempt to scrub the noticeably blackened face of his mistress, Lady Jersey, as the Princess of Wales enters exclaiming "It vont do she must put on another face." Here, the whitewashing of the blackened white woman is clearly an attempt to show that the indelible stain of Lady Jersey's adulterous behavior will not be removed but known wherever she goes. Although the print clearly refers to a white British woman, its gendered illustration of a white man actively participating in whitewashing a blackened woman does present literal implications about the African woman in British literature and how her literal presence affects the trope's deployment and meaning.

Early modern portraiture may not allow us to glean the African woman's involvement with the trope, but literature from this period does. On the subject of white male–black female representations in literature, Lynda Boose has pointed out that there seems to be a deliberate attempt to police such unions in early modern and medieval texts.

> In terms of the ideological assumptions of a culture such as that of early modern England, the black male–white female union is not the narrative that requires suppression. What challenges the ideology substantially enough to require erasure is that of the black female–white male, for it is in the person of the black woman that the culture's pre-existing fears both about the female sex and about gender dominance are realized.[19]

Boose's suggestion that the black female–white male relationship challenges the ideology of early modern England substantially, and must be erased because of the power of the black woman's body, brings another, in this case new and somewhat shocking, dimension to the meaning and deployment of the 'washing a blackamoor white' trope. Boose believes that black women are essentially "unrepresentable" in works by white, male, British,

---

19. Lynda E. Boose, "'The Getting of a Lawful Race,'" 45–46.

Figure 19.
"Washing the Blackamoor," 1795, Isaac Cruikshank (1756–1811)

early modern writers because of "free-floating anxieties" about black women "contaminating the father's designs for perfect self-replication."[20] In other words, the black woman is a threatening influence to paternalist society because her reproductive body signifies an inability to reproduce a white child-heir for the white man, thereby ruining not the possibility but the purity of his hereditary line.[21] In this, she appears to resemble Henry Neville's Philippa from *The Isle of Pines* (1668), the "Negro Slave" whom Amy Boesky describes as "a female version of Cush"—Cush being the "black and loathsome" grandson of the biblical patriarch Noah, by his son, Ham. "Like Cush," Boesky continues, "[Philippa] is doomed to bequeath her 'loathsome' blackness to her progeny."[22] However, Neville does not allow Philippa to appear as an overwhelming threat to George Pine's genealogy since the first child she gives birth to by him is described as a "fine white childe." Boesky believes this is an indication that "Pine's whiteness has so overwhelmed [Philippa] that her children . . . take on his features and none of her own."[23] Thus, Philippa's reproductive ability to maintain the white male's whiteness intact provides an example of a successful act of whitening since it leaves the paternalist's hereditary bloodline at least phenotypically pure.

But it is the instances of black women lightening but not completely whitening the white male's line that are so destabilizing to the meaning and moral of the 'washing a blackamoor white' trope. Instead of merely putting the white washer's "Dark Brains" on display, the black woman's involvement in the trope shows that she has the ability to reproduce a far more permanent signifier of the white paternalist's failed whiteness: his dark offspring. This offspring is far more damaging to the reputation of the male whitewasher than the social stigma of ignorance leveled at Miss Moggridge, because he or she involves the black woman's body in the process of threatening to actively deconstruct the white male washer's power to reproduce himself. As Boose points out, the black female's "signifying capacity as a mother threatens nothing less than the wholesale negation of white patriarchal authority,"[24] and she confirms this negation by considering George Peel's *The Battle of Alcazar* and *The Legend of Morien, the Black Knight*—texts in which the black woman produces black sons from unions with white men—sons whose blackness confirms her dominance in her relationship with the white paternalist. But a daughter produced from such a union might offer the white

---

20. Ibid., 46.
21. Ibid.
22. Amy Boesky, "Nation, Miscegenation: Membering Utopia in Henry Neville's *The Isle of Pines*," *Texas Studies in Literature* 37 (1995): 166.
23. Ibid., 176.
24. Boose, "'The Getting of a Lawful Race,'" 46.

paternalist an opportunity to not merely assuage his anxiety about his bloodline but secure its future. If this white male washer could use his financial influence to rig the marriage market and ensure that his black daughter would marry another white male he might reset in motion the whitening of his hereditary line. This could be achieved if the white paternalist made this black daughter an heiress and arranged her marriage in a document that duty would compel her to uphold. When Mr. Fairfield dies leaving explicit clauses about marriage in his will for his daughter, Olivia, to follow, *The Woman of Colour* realizes the complex dynamics involved in this reproductive deployment of washing a blackamoor white.

ALTHOUGH WRITTEN in an epistolary style already outmoded in 1808,[25] *The Woman of Colour* still manages to radically transform a marriage plot that, according to Ann duCille, has been traditionally "coded white, female and European."[26] In letters composed by Olivia Fairfield to Mrs. Millbanke, her English governess who resides in Jamaica, the tale focuses on the problems that arise when this Jamaican mulatto heiress travels to England intending to marry her Caucasian first cousin, Augustus Merton, in a marriage arranged unilaterally in the will of her recently deceased father. Mr. Fairfield never met Augustus before his death; yet in choosing him as Olivia's spouse he wanted to "secure his child a proper protector in a husband" (I, 9). Only one fact suggests why Mr. Fairfield considers this unknown nephew a "proper protector": Augustus's mother's letters to Jamaica describe this son as the "image" (I, 22) of Mr. Fairfield. It is this strong physical affinity which drives Mr. Fairfield's hope that his nephew will be as predisposed to bestow on Olivia a spousal brand of the protection that he has already provided as a father. But the very act of enforcing an arranged marriage to one's double contains within it emotions other than protection—self-interest being one. In Jamaica, "the prejudices which [Mr. Fairfield] had imbibed in common with his countrymen, forbade his" (I, 7) marrying Olivia's enslaved African mother, Marcia, before her untimely death. In light of this failure, Mr. Fairfield's determination to reproduce, in England, the almost identical marriage that could not take place in Jamaica, resonates as a convenient posthumous attempt by the reformed rake to, proverbially, kill two birds with one act: absolve himself of his past "prejudices" as well as protect his daughter from the stigmas of her impure racial and sexual history. It is clear, however, that Mr. Fairfield's act will not achieve these outcomes with equal success if we compare him with his contemporary peers.

---

25. See Garside's *Bibliographical Survey*, 53–54.
26. *The Coupling Convention*, 3.

This idea that an English paternalist can absolve the ethical indiscretions of his own past with an act designed to protect a person of color from future stigma is historicized in one of the most important acts that eighteenth-century English paternalists undertook. "When a change of ministry took place," Samuel Taylor Coleridge writes in his 1808 review of the *History of Abolition,*

> Mr. Fox and Lord Grenville brought not only their own, but all their *official interest, to cleanse away this guilt from the national character;* and our author [Thomas Clarkson] and his virtuous coadjutors received the final reward of their labours in the legal abolition of the [slave] trade relatively to the British empire.[27]

Although one would expect the 1807 abolition act's primary concern to be the protection of free Africans from future enslavement, Coleridge's response to it reveals a motivation of even greater importance. His cleansing metaphor presupposes that Britain has been sullied or blackened by its involvement in the slave trade,[28] and that the paternalists' act of abolition washes both the stain of the trade, and the guilt of Britain's participation in it, away. We do not, however, get as concrete a depiction of the social protection that millions of vulnerable Africans were to receive as a result of abolition. As Peter Fryer has pointed out, "As late as 1822, Thomas Armstrong of Dalston, near Carlisle, bequeathed a slave in his will,"[29] leaving us with an impression that even on ostensibly free soil, abolitionist legislation was motivated less by a concern for the protection of blacks and more by a need to display the enlightened legal identity of an ethically cleansed British nation.

My reading of Coleridge is confirmed further by the opinions of other British paternalists expressed in the *Substance of the Debates on A Resolution for Abolishing the Slave Trade* (1806). In this, the most extensive record of speeches given in both Houses of Parliament on the pros and cons of abolition, it is clear that the focus on documenting and recording the inhumanity of the slave trade that had characterized previous efforts on behalf of the

---

27. Samuel Taylor Coleridge, "Review of The History of the Abolition of the Slave Trade By T. Clarkson," in *Edinburgh Review* 12 (1808), taken from Slavery, Abolition & Emancipation: The Abolition Debate, vol. 2, ed. Peter Kitson (London: Pickering and Chatto, 1999), 242 (my emphasis).

28. Deirdre Coleman's excellent article "Janet Schaw and the Complexions of Empire," *Eighteenth-Century Studies* 36 (2003): 169–93, confirms that Coleridge felt this way, and it also mentions the general "proliferation of metaphors of whitening and blackening during the last two decades of the eighteenth century, when metropolitan culture became increasingly agitated about its complicity in the cruelties of the slave trade" (170).

29. *Staying Power,* 203.

abolitionist movement are significantly toned down from this last, successful attempt to pass an abolition bill. Instead, friends of abolition, such as Fox and the Solicitor General, Sir Samuel Romilly, are more concerned with the cultural effect that a prolonged involvement with the slave trade will have on the British Parliament, the national character, and the economic reputation of the nation. Postponing abolition, they argued, showed that British MPs were, both, incapable of making good the 1792 resolution that had originally called for abolition within four years, and perversely content to continue involving the nation and its economy in a trade that was already perceived as an incontrovertible moral error against "justice, humanity and sound policy."[30]

The abolitionist historian Roger Anstey has observed that "abolitionists consistently used the argument of national interest in support of particular measures of abolition,"[31] and his statement acknowledges, once again, the nationally biased motives behind abolition that I have described in the *Debates* and Coleridge's review. Given this nationalist bias, I want to suggest that a narcissistic spirit lurks behind the 1807 abolition act. Even though it professed to, and of course did, aid Africans, "all [the] official interest" that successfully brought it into being spoke more of a paternal need to resolve Britain's ethical quandary over the slave trade than of Britons' desire to protect Africans. For this reason, the abolition act ethically misused the Africans that it professed to aid, (ab)using[32] them only as a pretext for what seems to be a vainglorious attempt to distinguish British paternalists as ethical legislators, and, by extension, a British nation ethically absolved—indeed whitewashed—of all association with "the vile trade." Some Britons appear to have recognized this narcissism. As Eric Williams recounts, "Coleridge had been awarded the Browne Gold Medal at Cambridge for an ode on slavery. . . . But in 1811 he sneered at the 'philanthropy-trade,' accused Wilberforce of caring only for his own soul, and criticized Clarkson as a man made vain by benevolence, 'the moral steam engine or the giant with one idea.'"[33]

WHEN IT PRESENTS Mr. Fairfield's will demanding that Olivia marry Augustus for her own protection while also entertaining the idea that Mr. Fairfield

---

30. (London: Dawson's, 1968). This phrase was a familiar refrain throughout a large majority of the speeches.

31. Roger Anstey, *The Atlantic Slave Trade and British Abolition, 1760–1810* (Atlantic Highlands, NJ: Humanities Press, 1975), 346.

32. '(ab)using,' should be read as 'using' but I include the suggestive prefix to remind us that, under hegemony, 'abuse' and 'use' are not mutually exclusive. Under hegemony, abuse is always a part of being used.

33. *Capitalism and Slavery* (Chapel Hill: University of North Carolina Press, 1994), 195.

has self-interested motives of his own for making this demand, *The Woman of Colour* links this English-Creole paternalist with his enlightened English contemporaries; they are all narcissistic abolitionists who use antiracial acts for their own benefit. But the novel also explores the interesting corollary that these antiracial acts are as useful in absolving the stigmas that surround Olivia as they are the sins of her father.

Mr. Fairfield's will attempts to whitewash his mulatto daughter's stigmas in one of two possible ways. The first involves her inheritance. "It is a Dowry, Methinks should make the Sun-burnt proverb false, And wash the Ethiop White" (V, i), remarks the Moorish woman, Zanche, in Nahum Tate's reworking of John Webster's *The White Devil* as *Injur'd Love, or The Cruel Husband* (1707). Her statement could not be truer of Mr. Fairfield's rationale. By sending to England a daughter with a dowry worth nearly sixty thousand pounds, Mr. Fairfield shares Zanche's hope that an awesome fortune can liberate a woman of color from the vagaries of racial prejudice, the dowry acting as a protective shield alleviating Olivia from the stigmas of blackness, illegitimacy, and slavery so that she may appear in a guise commonly associated with wealthy whiteness. Although we can use the same whitewashing trope to define Zanche and Olivia's social transformations into figures who are able to enjoy the privileges of wealthy whiteness, they are very different when it comes to the issue of consent. In her narrative, Zanche proposes to steal her dowry, and in doing so, consents to and controls the terms under which she is transformed.[34] But Mr. Fairfield's will apportions Olivia's dower with Augustus if she marries him and with Augustus's older brother, George, if she does not. This means that he conceives Olivia's transformation into a figure of wealthy whiteness without her consent and within a transferable purview of white male familial control.

Because of this, Mr. Fairfield's behavior must also be considered in the cruder, far more malevolent light captured in the *Adventures of Jonathan Corncob* (1787). In the chapter titled "The West-Indian way of white-washing, or rather the true way of washing the blackamoor white," this anonymous novel vividly illustrates the conditions under which an English-Creole paternalist nonconsensually controls a black woman's transformation into a figure of whiteness. While in Barbados, Jonathan and a West Indian friend visit the plantation of the aptly named Creole, Mr. Winter, who is not at home:

---

34. See the epigram at the beginning of Part Two for another example. Bissett's ridicule of dame Heureux cannot hide the fact that her artistic endeavors are a deliberate attempt to control her own transformation into a figure of wealthy whiteness.

We were, nevertheless, ushered into an apartment, at one end of which was sitting an old negress, smoking her pipe. Near her was an elderly mulatto woman; at a little distance was a female still less tawny of complexion, called in the country, as I believe, a mestee; and at the other end of the room I observed a yellow quadroon giving suck to a child, which, though a little sallow, was as white as children in Europe generally are. I could not help remarking to the West-Indian this regular gradation of light and shade.

"This," said he, "is the family of my friend, Mr. Winter; the three younger females and the child are the progeny of the old negress."

"And who are the fathers?"

"Mr. Winter himself is the father of them all," replied he: "when he was very young he had the mulatto woman by the negress: when the mulatto was twelve years old, he took her for his mistress, and had by her the mestee. At about the same age his intimacy with the mestee produced the quadroon, who had by him a few months ago the white child you see in her arms. *This is what is called in this country washing a man's self white*, and Mr. Winter has the credit of having washed himself white at a very early age, being at this time less than sixty years old."

This complicated incest, and the coolness with which my friend spoke of it, made me begin to think it no wonder that Barbadoes was subject to hurricanes.[35]

The shades of complexion resulting from Mr. Winter's blatantly incestuous rapes physically testify to his nonconsensual villainy. Most importantly, however, although Jonathan sees only the cumulative display of whitewashed black female bodies, the reproductive act itself ("*he had* the mulatto woman by the negress . . . and [*he*] *had* by her the mestee" etc.) "is called . . . washing a *man's* self white." This "West-Indian way of white-washing" involves black women continually reproducing lighter versions of themselves as a result of repeated, violent, nonconsensual paternalist acts that are only indicative of a Creole paternalist's interest—his brash, narcissistic desire to gratify himself without regulation, abusing even his own immediate bloodline. In the age of slavery, the epidermal transformations of West Indian women occur under perversions[36] of paternal authority.

---

35. (Boston: D. R. Godine, 1976), 72–73 (my emphasis). Another reference to this West Indian way of whitewashing appears in this note from Thomas Morris's "Quashy, or, The Coal Black Maid" (1796). In the American version (Philadelphia: Humphreys, 1797), the reference is whitewashed from the text.

36. Michael Ragussis states, "'Perversion' is a specialized term, especially prominent in the nineteenth century, for the wrong kind of conversion." *Figures of Conversion*, 132.

By forcing his daughter to marry his physical surrogate without her consent, then, Mr. Fairfield's behavior to Olivia can be read as a similarly perverse 'West-Indian way of white-washing' akin to Mr. Winter and as vainglorious as the British paternalists who abolished the slave trade. In this "complicated incest," Mr. Fairfield displaces his own incestuous desire for Olivia onto his physical surrogate, Augustus, not so much because he wants this marriage to protect his daughter or symbolically absolve him of his sexual depredation against Marcia, as I suggested earlier, but because he is interested more in *reveling* in that sexual depredation so that, like Mr. Winter, he too can commit a *heinous act of abolition* against his offspring—the abolition of her blackness. For Mr. Fairfield uses Olivia as Mr. Winter does his slaves: they are all responsible for whitening a Creole paternalist's familial line of descendants. Indeed, Mr. Fairfield insinuates that this benefit to his ancestral name interests him more than the protection of his daughter in another clause to his will which demands that Augustus adopt the "Fairfield" name if he marries Olivia. This clause ensures that not only will Olivia and Augustus's whitewashed offspring resemble Mr. Fairfield even more than Olivia does because of their parents' combined physical traits, they will also bear his revered name and reestablish its legitimate connection to whiteness.

Thus, *The Woman of Colour* explores how a forced interracial marriage of a wealthy mulatto woman to a white man in England enacts the violent history of abuse experienced by enslaved women of color in the West Indies but also how this abuse is also a narcissistic boon to white men, literally whitewashing their ancestral involvement with, and connection to, slavery and the slave trade. I want to bring a new perspective to this history of West Indian abuse, however, by considering it through a comparative racial lens. Since the issues of race, transformation, and consent are all important components in the discourse of Jewish Conversion, and Michael Ragussis has described this abusive movement as an "English madness"[37] during the era of slavery, I find it helpful to think of washing a black-moor white as an equally abusive example of the "English madness" to improve the situation of another of its racial others. Isaac Land's work on Jonas Hanway, the English philanthropist who directed the Committee for the Relief of the Black Poor, also proves helpful in establishing the connection between Jewishness and blackness in the construction of the English national identity. Hanway's organization was responsible for shipping large number of the black poor to Sierra Leone in West Africa to found a new colony, literally getting rid of the black poor that littered the streets of London. But as Land points out, "In the early 1750s—before he became famous as the friend of orphans, chimney sweeps,

---

37. Ibid., 17–25.

and unwed mothers—Hanway first became a public figure as the author of pamphlets opposing Jewish naturalization."[38] Hanway's efforts to resist the naturalization of Jews on the basis that they "would undermine the foundations of Britain's greatness . . . and his efforts to expel 'foreign' elements from Britain" through the Committee for the Relief of the Black Poor were "two sides of the same coin"[39] in Land's opinion. Yet Hanway's reputation for philanthropy made his work for the Committee seem progressive. As Land states, "humane actions could serve many purposes at once"[40] some of which are not commendatory. Manipulating Ragussis's terminology, I want to classify these women of color as West Indian 'figures of conversion' who are forced to endure epidermal 'acts of conversion' without their consent because of British writers' belief that such abusive acts are racially progressive.[41]

CONSENT IS essential in any act of conversion because one must agree to transform oneself. In this way, every act of conversion is also a consensual act of abolition: if he converts, the Jew consents to abolish his former religious identity for a completely new one. But, as I have shown, Creole paternalists force black women to commit acts of whitewashing during the era of slavery that are, in fact, perverse acts of abolition since they involve the convert in a nonconsensual process of racial improvement allegorically akin to ethnic cleansing. These perverse acts of abolition, however, are complicated in that they are also perceived as improving the social lives of people of color: British paternalists protect free Africans from future enslavement with their vainglorious abolition act, Mr. Fairfield liberates Olivia from the stigma of illegitimacy with his arranged marriage, and even Mr. Winter's successive rapes eventually create a child light enough to escape slavery by passing as white. These are all occasions where black figures who are whitewashed might consent to abide by perverse acts of abolition because they carry with them the benefits of freedom. Thus, washing a black-moor white—an act I will henceforth refer to as 'epidermal conversion' to reflect the potential for liberation enabled by an individual's *consensual* transformation from blackness to whiteness—might be a useful trope from which to build a progressive discourse about the abolition of slavery. But can British writers present acts

---

38. Isaac Land, "Bread and Arsenic," 97.
39. Ibid.
40. Ibid., 98.
41. Ragussis also acknowledges a connection between epidermal conversion and Jewish conversion in *Figures of Conversion:* "The impossibility of racial transformation—the black man becoming white—becomes an analogy for the impossibility of religious conversion—the Jew becoming Christian" (25–26).

of epidermal conversion in ways that do liberating work, and without the racial, national, or incestuous narcissism that I attributed to the 1807 act of abolition and the actions of Messirs Winter and Fairfield?

Samuel Jackson Pratt's unproduced two-act farce, *The New Cosmetic, or The Triumph of Beauty* (1790), implies that they can. It briefly touches on the possibility that a perverse yet unbiased act of epidermal conversion can liberate a black man.[42] Pratt's title refers to a caustic Caribbean elixir that whitens complexions, and a colonial Irishman, Greville, who wants to use it "to improve his pretty face" (I, iv). However, the pain associated with the process so scares him that he decides to test it first on a black slave named Quacou, "and if he endures it" (I, iv), Greville will then try it on himself. "Does it make a negroe man white, massah?" Quacou asks. "It does more," Greville replies:

> For it makes him so lovely, that the very white women will be glad to adopt him as a husband; but I will tell you it is kept a profound secret from all the blacks, least they should become as white as ourselves, and so no longer continue in subjection to us. (I, iv)

Underscoring the fact that slavery is an arbitrary condition predicated on epidermal difference rather than an innate sense of inferiority, Greville offers Quacou seductive and unbiased benefits for consenting to the perverse act of racial obliteration. It will allow the "lovely" slave to personally "triumph" over two liberties that his blackness continually withholds from him: interracial marriage and social equality.[43] Quacou's use of the 'new cosmetic' ultimately ends in complete failure, however, a fact which suggests that *The New Cosmetic* cosmeticizes its own racial biases by proposing the benefits and then withholding the triumph of Quacou's perverse act of epidermal conversion.

We can trace the idea that acts of epidermal conversion liberate black women with more success in two texts published in 1814. Jane Austen's *Mansfield Park* and Frances Burney's *The Wanderer* represent the theme of

---

42. For white male West Indians, the theme of conversion differs. Creole men, such as *Cecilia*'s (1782) Mr. Albany, transform into morally excessive bastions of virtue after successfully overcoming the profligate vices that were common in eighteenth-century characterizations of West Indians. A male Creole's inability to convert from profligacy to virtue ended in exile, as *Belinda*'s (1801) Mr. Vincent illustrates. But the notion of white male West Indian conversion, while extremely interesting and open for enquiry, does not enter the scope of this essay.

43. See Tassie Gwilliam's "Cosmetic Poetics: Coloring Faces in the Eighteenth Century," in *Body and Text in the Eighteenth Century*, ed. Veronica Kelly and Dorothea E. von Mücke (Stanford, CA: Stanford University Press, 1994), 144–62 for more discussion of the racial dynamics at work in this play.

abolition prominently, openly employ the trope of epidermal conversion, and furtively debate the issue of consent in the characterizations of Fanny Price and Juliet Granville.⁴⁴ In her edition of *The Wanderer*, Margaret Doody has already pointed out the abolitionist themes surrounding Juliet's introduction in the novel.⁴⁵ Having left France disguised as a black woman, Juliet sees the English shore and darts "forward with such eagerness, that she was the first to touch the land, where, with a fervour that seemed resistless, she rapturously ejaculated, 'Heaven, Heaven be praised!'" (I, i, 22, *Wand*). Burney's portrayal of this black woman's desperate need to touch British soil can be no less than an explicit invocation of the Mansfield myth of immediate freedom for any slave who set foot on this ostensibly hallowed land of liberty. Joseph Lew also evokes Lord Mansfield's memory in his very insightful reading of the abolitionist elements at play in the title and narrative of *Mansfield Park*.⁴⁶ In his and Doody's analyses, Austen and Burney are clearly harking back to a very specific abolitionist past involving black slaves, Lord Mansfield, and debates about freedom for all English residents irrespective of race. But neither critic has considered the way their respective text addresses abolition in terms of epidermal conversion, something I will now discuss using Fanny and Juliet's characterizations.

During her introduction to the text, Fanny is described as a child with "no glow of complexion" (I, ii, 12, *Mans*), a description that draws attention to her unchanging color. She is epidermally dull. This physical trait has an explicit connection to Negroes. Aravamudan's *Tropicopolitans* reveals that, to the English, black people—whose fixed, dark complexions could not display the gradations of color prized in blushing—were considered ugly and, by extension, useless because of their epidermal inabilities to "glow." While Fanny clearly isn't Negro in any literal sense, her unchanging complexion indicates that she is marred by the same stigmas that Negroes faced: ugliness and especially uselessness, something that reveals itself in the contradictory family "habit of employing" (I, xv, 116, *Mans*) her to run useful errands for their benefit while refusing to consider her an equal member of their

---

44. *Mansfield Park* (New York: Signet Classic, 1964), and *The Wanderer*, ed. Margaret Doody (Oxford: Oxford University Press, 1991).

45. In Doody's edition of *The Wanderer*, see Appendix II, "Burney and Race Relations," 884–87. Also, Burney's characterization of Juliet should be considered in relation to William Wordsworth's poem "The Banished Negroes" (1802), which also describes a Negro woman on her way to Britain from France.

46. Joseph Lew, "'That Abominable Traffic': Mansfield Park and the Dynamics of Slavery," in *History, Gender & Eighteenth-Century Literature*, ed. Beth Fowkes Tobin (Athens: University of Georgia Press, 1994), 271–300. See also Moira Ferguson's "Mansfield Park: Slavery, Colonialism, and Gender," *Oxford Literary Review* 13 (1991): 118–39.

society, just like a black slave.[47] The same problems plague the blackened Juliet. Once she reveals the "dusky hue" of her face, hands, and arms, Elinor, Juliet's rival for Harleigh's affections, gave a "look of triumph" (I, i, 19, *Wand*) aimed at deflating in his eyes the allure of a woman now exposed as nothing more than a "tawny Hottentot" (I, i, 12, *Wand*). Moreover, Mrs. Maple, "incessantly . . . surveying the stranger," emphasizes Juliet's uselessness in financial terms when she complains to Harleigh, "I don't think that we are much indebted to you for bringing us such company as this [Juliet] into our boat!" (I, i, 20, *Wand*). Unlike Negro women, however, these Caucasian females are not indefinitely consigned to the stigmas of "unchangeable uselessness." As Ben Jonson's masques of 1605 and 1608 remind us, when blackness is performed by virtuous white women it only precedes their epidermal conversions to beauty.

In both novels, female transformations from blackness to beauty are openly witnessed. Juliet enacts hers in front of Mrs. Ireton, the extremely wealthy proprietress who pays Juliet's fare to London from Dover. Over the course of four days Mrs. Ireton notices how Juliet's complexion changes "from a tint nearly black, to the brightest, whitest, and most dazzling fairness" (I, iv, 43, *Wand*). Fanny undergoes similar transformations in front of her own benefactor, Sir Thomas Bertram. "But where is Fanny? Why do I not see my little Fanny?" (II, i, 139, *Mans*), he asks as soon as he arrives back from Antigua, his diminutive adjective underscoring the visual image of his niece that he recalls from memory. When he actually sees her, "little Fanny" physically transforms before him; Sir Thomas observed "with decided pleasure how much she had grown." An epidermal transformation accompanies this physical one:

> He led her nearer the light and looked at her again—inquired particularly after her health, and then correcting himself, observed that he need not inquire, for her appearance spoke sufficiently on that point. A fine blush having succeeded the previous paleness of her face, he was justified in his belief of her equal improvement in health and beauty. (II, i, 139, *Mans*)

Sir Thomas's "little Fanny" transforms not simply into a woman in front

---

47. Indeed, if, as I am suggesting here, Fanny's employment early in the novel defines her black position within the Bertram household, we see even more evidence of her blackness as she contemplates visiting Portsmouth near the novel's end. Fanny proclaims, "She was of *use* to no one else" (*Mansfield Park*, ed. Claudia Johnson [New York: Norton, 1998], 251; my emphasis) but Aunt Bertram, and in this companionate relationship we know that she is largely employed to get through the "few difficulties" of some piece of "needle-work of *little use and no beauty*" (16; my emphasis), two direct phrases about the work Fanny does which, once again, connect her to Aravamudan's Negroes.

of him; the "fine blush" that "succeeded the previous paleness of her face" specifically illustrates Fanny's epidermal conversion from a useless black girl with "no glow of complexion" to a beautiful white woman only slightly less striking than Juliet's own transformation "from a tint nearly black, to the brightest, whitest and most dazzling fairness."

From associations with the ugly and "unchangeable uselessness" of blackness then, Fanny and Juliet achieve the impossible—epidermal conversions to attractive whiteness. But to what end? Since Aravamudan has pointed out that 'washing a black-moor white' is an English trope used to express the idea of a "fruitless undertaking" as witnessed on the bodies of an unchangeable and useless race of ugly black people,[48] I think Austen and Burney have appropriated this trope and they have transformed it into an expression of some advantage to white women whose ugly, useless, and unchangeable conception of themselves *is changing* because of contemporary debates about the rights of women.

These white women display successful acts of epidermal conversion that allegorize the issue of female consent in the face of hegemony. For Sir Thomas and Mrs. Ireton represent a collective notion of hegemony in the Gramscian sense of predominance obtained over individuals by consent rather than force. Although Fanny and Juliet silently consent to abide by hegemony when they accept acts of charity performed on their behalves, the actions of their hegemonic leaders are fraught with the same use and abuse of white women that I described between English-Creole paternalists and West Indian women of color. Mrs. Ireton uses Juliet in front of her opulent house in fashionable Grosvenor Square; the wealthy proprietress "turned exultingly" to the impoverished woman and "intently watched the impression which, when her servants appeared, would be made by their rich liveries" (I, v, 47, *Wand*). Here, Mrs. Ireton abuses Juliet's physical response to opulence in order to perversely gratify her own narcissism.

Sir Thomas's use of Fanny is even more narcissistically perverse than this because it has all the characteristics of Mr. Fairfield's abuse of Olivia. The Baronet abuses his niece's body in the marriage market, "sending her away" to bed at the end of the night "of her ball in order to recommend her as a wife [to Henry Crawford]" (II, x, 220, *Mans*) just as the Creole's will unilaterally orders Olivia to England to marry Augustus. With these ostentatious displays of "absolute power," Sir Thomas shares Mr. Fairfield's "pleasing anticipation of what would be" (II, x, 219, *Mans*) the gratifying result of using these women in this way: the stain of poverty that blemishes Fanny will be whitewashed with marriage to Mr. Crawford just as Mr. Fairfield

---

48. *Tropicopolitans*, 1–4.

hopes that his daughter's marriage to Augustus will obliterate her black heritage. Sir Thomas's use of Fanny even takes a self-interested turn immediately after his return from Antigua, when Edmund tells Fanny, "the truth is, your uncle never did admire you till now, and now he does. Your complexion is so improved! . . . and your figure" (II, iii, 154, *Mans*). Here, Edmund implicates his father's admiration of Fanny's "improved" body and complexion in a "complicated incest" reminiscent of *Jonathan Corncob*'s "West-Indian way of white-washing." In this instance, the Antiguan plantocrat, Sir Thomas, commits repeated, violent, nonconsensual acts against Fanny's body—sending her to bed, and later, to Portsmouth—not with the intention of raping her, but to force her to gratify his interest in her becoming Mrs. Henry Crawford just as the conditions in Mr. Fairfield's will force Olivia to become Mrs. Augustus Fairfield.

Thus, Sir Thomas and Mrs. Ireton only use women as opportunities on which to inscribe their own narcissistic fantasies. While Fanny and Juliet consent to be ruled by hegemony, they do not consent to being perversely abused by hegemonic authority. Their critique of these figures appears in the act of epidermal conversion itself. Fanny and Juliet convert *in the face* of hegemony rather than *because of it*. Where the epidermal transformations of Ben Jonson's Ethiopian Nymphs and Mr. Winter's slaves take place outside the purviews of those texts, Fanny and Juliet's epidermal conversions occur right before the eyes of Sir Thomas and Mrs. Ireton. In *The Masque of Beauty* (1608) and *Jonathan Corncob* we do not see any of the incestuous violence or transformative magic associated with epidermal transformation; we see only the completed acts—black women *already* re-produced as white through the violent nonconsensual act of a Creole slaveholder and the consensual will of a male monarch. When they commit their own self-controlled acts of epidermal conversion within the purview of hegemony, Fanny and Juliet show, allegorically, that they are *free* and able to *act by themselves*—to re-produce lighter, more attractive versions of themselves without the consent or influence of hegemony and despite its ostensibly benevolent yet undeniably self-interested and abusive gaze.

After these liberating acts of self-transformation, Fanny and Juliet are ultimately rewarded with marriage to the heroes, Edmund and Harleigh. But these marriages also integrate them back into the system of hegemony that formerly abused them, making the epidermal acts of conversion that Fanny and Juliet perform seem even more perverse than those of British paternalists and Creole slaveholders since, like Pratt's *New Cosmetic*, they give the illusion of a black person's liberation from hegemony only to ultimately revoke it.

Allegorically, then, Austen and Burney show that Fanny and Juliet's perverse acts of epidermal conversion cannot do the work of racial liberation on behalf of oppressed women of color because they exhibit a bias toward white proponents of the female cause. In their examples of epidermal conversion, Austen and Burney are not trying to draw attention to radically transformative acts such as the abolition of slavery or racism, and they make this clear by historicizing each text in an abolitionist past explicitly associated with black complexions and the question of liberty in England. Fanny and Juliet's representations only address the relationship British women have with the promise of freedom that the 1772 Mansfield Judgment appeared to ratify with its mythical claim of immediate freedom for black slaves. Austen and Burney appropriate the most potent example of Britain's ability to grant freedom to all—blackness—only to aesthetically transform it using a discourse of beauty and virtue of which the ultimate reward is marriage and not freedom. Thus, the figures of epidermal conversion in *Mansfield Park* and *The Wanderer* are only allegorical representations of the need for white women to consent to the way their bodies are to be (ab)used under hegemony, an undecidedly conservative and only moderately progressive approach to the rights of women even for its day.

IN *THE WOMAN OF COLOUR,* Olivia also consents to abide by Mr. Fairfield's will despite the fact that the marriage he arranges for her is racially abusive. Nevertheless, it takes place, and the newlyweds are happy; that is, until a combination of circumstances reveal a new fact: prior to Olivia's arrival in England, Augustus had made a clandestine marriage with Angelina Forrester, a white Englishwoman of low birth who he has been led to believe had perished while he was away on business. Augustus's conniving sister-in-law, Letitia Merton, had maliciously hidden Angelina away, however, only to reproduce her midway through the novel. Olivia's interracial marriage is abruptly annulled once Angelina reclaims her husband by prior contract. During the text's dramatic epilogue, a reader, identified as the "Friend" of the text's "Editor," complains about this ending: Olivia was "not rewarded . . . even with the usual meed of virtue—*a husband*" (II, 219). The Friend implies that denying marriage to a woman who deserves its protection is just as unfair as forcing her into an arranged one. The Editor, however, makes it clear that this choice is deliberate; marriage was never Olivia's ultimate objective. Her role in the novel is greater. She is designed to wrest the trope of epidermal conversion away from the English paternalists and champions of the female cause who, as I have shown, appropriated it for their own biased purposes.

To witness the occasions where Olivia resists the perverse acts of epidermal conversion imposed by paternalists and performed by English heroines, we must look closely at the author's deliberate use of names, the most significant being the English surname "Fairfield." It literally refers to the place where fairs and carnivals are held, and in doing so, recalls Stallybrass and White's *Politics and Poetics of Transgression* and its discussions of fairs as carnivalesque sites of transgression where binaries—high/low, rich/poor, local/foreign, clean/dirty, fair/grotesque—occur and collapse.[49] As an unportioned Jamaican mulatto heiress, Olivia is a 'fair field' in exactly this binary sense of the word; her racial, geographic, and financial hybridity situates her "at the intersection of economic and cultural forces" (29–30) that incorporate and collapse all of the binaries Stallybrass and White associate with the fair. However, Terry Eagleton and others have pointed out the limitation of fairs as sites of transgression since they are "*licensed* affair[s]" and are, therefore, "permissible rupture[s] of hegemony"(13) that only give the illusion of transgression. Stallybrass and White counter this suggestion, claiming that in "the presence of sharpened political antagonism, [a carnivalesque site] may often act as *catalyst* and *site of actual and symbolic struggle*" (14). I contend that during the era of abolition, *The Woman of Colour* is one such "catalyst and *site of actual and symbolic struggle*" against hegemony, a symbolic struggle that we come to understand by considering the author's use of carnivalesque names, naming, and characterization.

By calling this novel *The Woman of Colour*, the author seems well aware of the resistance that carnivalesque discourse offers to a mulatto heroine struggling against racially oppressive forces. The title functions in the same way that an advertisement for an attraction at an English fair would, inviting the reader/fairgoer to view up close a dark-skinned female body.[50] The epistolary genre, however, allows Olivia to control the way she represents her undeniably Negroid body in a manner not available to Saartjie Baartman, Olivia's contemporary with respect to being a black woman on display.[51] Conflating her position as an object on display with the fact that she is also a literate subject controlling how her body appears, the author makes Olivia into a bourgeois racial character in England with a perspective that Stallybrass and White did not account for and Saartjie Baartman could not possibly imagine: the subject who not only understands how carnivalesque rhetoric and imagery work but also uses these things in a narrative that deconstructs the terms under which she herself is considered a grotesque black female object in the first place.

---

49. Peter Stallybrass and Allon White, *The Politics and Poetics of Transgression* (Ithaca, NY: Cornell University Press, 1986). (All subsequent references are in parentheses.)

50. See Garside's *Bibliographical Survey*, 46–63, for the importance of a novel's title at this time.

51. See Richard Altick's "The Noble Savage Reconsidered," Chapter 20 (268–73) in *The Shows of London* (Cambridge, MA: Belknap Press, 1978), for discussions about Saartjie Baartman, the Venus Hottentot, and her appearances in Britain between 1810–12.

This deconstructive work begins with Olivia's descriptions of characters whose names are explicit signifiers of conversion's failure—figures such as the geriatric bachelor and spinster twins Colonel and Miss "Singleton," who both make futile attempts to transform themselves. The Colonel had "nearly reached his grand climacteric yet had taken wonderful pains in trying to put himself back at least thirty years by powdering and pomatuming his grey hairs" (I, 122). And "Miss Singleton's labours [were] as arduous as her brother" (I, 124), since her "feathers of the ostrich . . . mounted in several directions from her head . . . her bared ears, and elbows, and back, and bosom . . . [and] her volatility and frisky . . . airs" were the many tools of conversion by which she "threw herself back into the *girl*" (I, 124–25). Thoroughly amused by their absurd actions, Olivia concludes, "this brother and sister . . . must never marry, but grow *young* (for old they can never be) together" (I, 123–24).

The "Ingots" are a "*genteel vulgar*" (I, 192) family of Nabobs, and, as their family name indicates, they are awaiting conversion to a more refined state that, ironically, will never happen. Olivia observes that "lady [Ingot] is a masculine woman" (I, 194), her son Frederic "is very effeminate and diminutive in his person" (I, 196), and Sir Marmaduke is a Singleton clone of which "the powder on his head, seems to be laid on with no sparing hand, to cover the depredations of time" (I, 196). "The Pagoda, the newly raised edifice of Sir Marmaduke" (I, 193), is his biggest travesty of conversion, however, since it signifies an attempt to re-produce Eastern culture in an English setting and earns from Augustus a moniker that perfectly reflects its comical inhabitants: "*temple of folly*" (I, 194).

These characters—the young oldsters, the masculine woman, the effeminate young man, the English Nabob—are all walking oxymorons, rhetorical figures who clown conversion by juggling two identities in ways that blur the distinctions between those identities. In other words, these clowns of conversion become perversions of what they should be (old, female, masculine, English) because they are absurdly trying to convert themselves into things that they are not (young, masculine, etc.). Of course, under this definition, a mulatto woman with a complexion not far removed from that of a Negro slave and a dowry far exceeding that of many a wealthy white heiress could be considered a clown of conversion too; yet Olivia's letters take pains to distinguish her hybridized body from these other grotesque characters.

The Singletons' absurdly effusive dancing (I, 121–25); Frederic Ingot's "non-descript," "monkey"-like clothes (I, 196) and "recumbent" (I, 199), "serpentine" (I, 231) body; Sir Marmaduke's "dazzling" (I, 194) equipage; Lady Ingot's "nervously *strong*" (I, 194) voice: these grotesque acts contrast with Olivia's own black body in action. She is not, in any way, a colonial character who merely mimics European forms of culture and politeness to absurd effect, such as Stallybrass and White's "manteger" who "drinks with his lips 'like a man'" (41). "You have frequently remarked that I walk in a manner peculiar to myself," she tells her English governess, Mrs. Millbanke:

> *You* have termed it majestic and graceful; I have been fearful that it carried something of a proud expression; but I believe it very difficult to alter the natural gait and I am too much of the common size, with regard to height, to walk like the generality of my sex. There must surely, however, be something very particular in my air . . . many a gentleman follows to repass me, and to be mortified at his folly when he has caught a view of my mulatto countenance. I laugh at this. (I, 111–12)

Olivia's uncommon "height," "majestic and graceful" walk, and "natural gait" are different from the "generality of [her] sex" but clearly more attractive than the grotesque contortions that the clowns of conversion perform. Here, Olivia refutes Stallybrass and White's assumption that civilized behavior is "the essential and unchanging possession which distinguishes the European citizen from the West Indian" (41); she shows that civilized behavior comes as naturally to her black body as its obverse, savagery, comes to Europeans.

Additionally, Olivia's ability to "laugh" at the "folly" of the white male viewer who is attracted to her "air" but "mortified" by her "mulatto countenance" illustrates the ascendant position she takes over white men. Her laugh is an indication that she dismisses, as irrelevant, the white male viewer's blatant prejudice; instead, she enjoys the befuddled horror of his realization that he has found someone he considers grotesquely black undeniably attractive. Olivia's ascendancy over the white male viewer becomes even more pronounced once her blackness itself is on display. During her first appearance at a ball she tells Mrs. Millbanke: "the men also—believe me—they walked up in pairs, hanging one on another's arm, and, with a stare of effrontery, eyed your Olivia, as if they had been admitted purposely to see the *untamed savage* at a shilling a piece!" (I, 117). Here, Olivia responds to the white male viewers' blatant prejudice with a carnivalesque perspective of her own. She describes them as "*animals*" (I, 117) who "*slouched* (for it could not be called walking) up to [her]" (I, 118), a movement that confirms their savagery just as her "natural gait" confirms her civilization. Furthermore, their parrotlike snatches of Continental languages (*"Pauvre diable," "Allons," "ma bella"*) (I, 117) indicate that these men are animalistic hybrids of a particular sort—grotesque Macaronis, the eighteenth-century dilettante that an issue of the *Ladies Magazine* described as "A thing that has some resemblance to a man."[52] In these letters, the empire doesn't merely write back; Olivia, its grotesque offspring, enjoys her part in exposing the fact that whenever a black person becomes an object of derisive attention in England, it is the white male viewer's prejudice rather than the African's inferiority that one actually witnesses.

In the circus that *The Woman of Colour* presents England to be, white male viewers, Macaronic "animals," and clowns of conversion are freaks for the reader's amusement. Meanwhile, Olivia's poised and graceful performance of black femininity transcends the grotesque stereotypes of savagery and inferiority that usually plague people of color because of the stigma of slavery. Of course, Aphra Behn's *Oroonoko* (1688) contains another well-known example of an African who transcends such stereotypes and stigmas. But where Behn uses Oroonoko's class and Europeanized beauty to signal that he is unique and deserves to be distinguished from the ordinary Africans she considers physically inferior, *The Woman of Colour*'s author uses Olivia's class and European heritage to make the exact opposite point. "Though the jet has been faded to the olive in my own complexion," Olivia remarks, "I am not ashamed to acknowledge my affinity with the swarthiest negro that was ever brought from Guinea's coast" (I, 3). Within this assertion of racial allegiance, Olivia conflates her Christian name with her complexion when she uses the word "olive," and indicates that, despite her being a mulatto heiress, ordinary African blackness is inscribed in her skin as well as her identity. It is here that Olivia implicitly attacks the progressiveness of washing a black-moor white. Black people cannot and *need not* be turned white since she stands as a perfect example of the fact that blacks of all classes and colors can be just as civilized in their own skins and "equal with their masters, if they had the same advantages, and the same blessings of education" (I, 101). The idea of epidermal conversion is discredited even further by the oxymoronic clowns and Macaronic "animals" who remind us just how grotesque converted bodies are while Olivia illustrates how beautiful black ones, such as hers, can be.

Indeed, *The Woman of Colour*'s array of grotesque white bodies makes its black heroine seem fair or pleasing in appearance. But Olivia is not the fairest of them all; that distinction literally belongs to Augustus's real wife, Angelina Forrester, whose "transparent complexion" (II, 96) and Christian name suggest an ideal, seraphic whiteness. Angelina's full name (Angel-in-a-Forest) even spells out the enclosed place where Augustus discovers the wife he thought was dead, living quietly in the cottage where Letitia had hidden her. Angelina's name and complexion are the most significant parts to her

---

52. Fenja Gunn, *The Artificial Face*, 122.

extraordinarily silent character since they are the keys to understanding her purpose in this novel. By transforming from a woman presumed dead to one whose name and whiteness portray her as a living embodiment of eternal life and whose liberation from the forest is rewarded with marriage to Augustus—the man whose "regularly handsome" (I, 69) face bespeaks a more appealing, less abusive brand of hegemony than his colonial double, Mr. Fairfield—Angelina performs the same perverse act of epidermal conversion that we have already seen in the transformations of Fanny Price and Juliet Granville. Furthermore, Olivia notices that Angelina seemed "peculiarly to require the assistance and support of the lordly creature Man, and to be ill-calculated for braving the difficulties of life alone" (II, 96–97). Weakness and dependence do not merely characterize Angelina, they represent the classic, desirable attributes that a hegemonic figure such as Augustus (his name, itself, a neoclassical archetype) looks for in an ideal wife. Together, the names and physical descriptions of Augustus and Angelina epitomize not only ideal forms of whiteness but also the ideal type of marital union that readers are usually expected to admire in a novel.

Despite its literal appeal, however, this marriage does not embody the fairest ideal of liberation championed in *The Woman of Colour*. Olivia embodies this distinction. Once her marriage ends, Olivia decides to give Angelina the Merton family jewels that she had formerly received. On her way through the forest that leads to Angelina's cottage she happens upon a stunned Augustus, who is taken aback by Olivia's decision to seek out and essentially reward her nemesis. "Are you not a being of ethereal mould?" (II, 88) he asks Olivia. With this question, Augustus constructs his black ex-wife as another 'angel-in-a-forest,' not for the way she *looks* inside an ideal marriage but for how she *acts* without one. By bequeathing valuable property to Angelina, Olivia performs a symbolic act of benevolence that teaches hegemonic figures such as Augustus (and by virtue of physical similarity, Olivia's father) the spirit of performing selfless, unbiased acts of philanthropy that protect, aid, and truly liberate a vulnerable woman rather than use and abuse her. In this way, Olivia takes another dominant rather than submissive role in relation to white Englishmen—in practice, she demonstrates how a Fairfield will should liberate a woman through the autonomy gained from financial independence.

Such progressive behavior can *only* come from a woman of color. For although Augustus refers to Olivia in angelic terms similar to Angelina, the author clearly implies that, of the two, the black female's example of ideal womanhood is far more active. When we hear Olivia state: "I was going to say, that I almost envied the shade of Angelina!—But I will try to be more rational" (I, 224), the author ostensibly shows her considering, yet ultimately rejecting, the perverse act of epidermal conversion that could transform her into another transparent angel—another Angelina. What Olivia actually rejects, however, is the possibility of becoming another silenced, weak, colorless, and dependent representation of angelic white femininity that *is* Angelina in this novel. Thus, *The Woman of Colour* advocates that the most virtuous black woman should never try to transform herself to fill the space of an angelic white wife. For outside the marriage contract, the ideal black woman represents a more actively liberating challenge to hegemony than her bland white counterpart who depends on, and is content to be enslaved by, the usual reward of marriage to a benign hegemonic figure.

The author's deliberate refusal to reward Olivia "with the usual meed of virtue—*a husband*" is, then, a direct critique of a novel genre that continually reinforces the appeal of female dependence. With her marriage over, Olivia decides to become a widow for the remainder of her life; not even a sincere proposal of marriage from the benign white Creole, Charles Honeywood, can tempt her out of this decision. Olivia's steadfast adherence to widowhood is a resonant contrast to Fanny Price and Juliet Granville at the ends of their respective novels. She aggressively resists the final perversion that I have described Fanny and Juliet agreeably consenting to—marriage to benign figures of hegemony—and presents a radical alternative to British women. Instead of again venturing into the precarious arena of a marriage market always skewed toward the interests of white men, Olivia chooses to return to Jamaica to "zealously engage [her]self in ameliorating the situation, in instructing the minds . . . of our poor blacks" (II, 216). Olivia's behavior here explicitly contrasts with another "portionless . . . HEIRESS," Fanny Burney's Cecilia, who renounces her fortune at the end of her narrative and "with cheerfullest resignation,"[53] consents to change her surname to Delville. Instead of the dependent marriage that Cecilia cheerfully resigns herself to, Olivia chooses independent activism. Because it makes a deliberate point of privileging this choice, *The Woman of Colour* openly displays its difference from British novels that tend to present white women such as Fanny, Juliet, and Cecilia in plots that ostensibly support a woman's transformation into a figure of freedom and independence only to propose a benign hegemonic marriage as her ultimate reward. In 1808, *The Woman of Colour* presents Olivia as an independent black female activist dedicated to the ultimate reward of her own emancipation as a woman as well as that of Negroes from the precarious institutions of marriage and slavery that have traditionally favored the interests of white men.

Olivia's decision to remain a widow-for-life also rebuts her father's abusive use of the "Fairfield" surname. Where the arrangements made in her

---

53. *Cecilia* (London: Virago Press, 1986), 919.

father's will are designed to ensure that she begins reproducing whiter Fairfields, Olivia's deliberate refusal to marry and procreate puts an end to her father's dreams of racial obliteration, essentially resisting his "West-Indian way of white-washing" and blackening the Fairfield name for the remainder of Olivia's life. In this way, a black widow gains complete control of the Fairfield name; and as a black widow[54]—a human representation of the arachnid notorious for slaying its mate after mating—the author, once again, shows Olivia taking an ascendant rather than submissive position over Fairfield men. The author makes this black widow much more than a grotesque attraction for the amusement of Britons.[55] Olivia has been designed to "teach one *sceptical* [sic] *European* to look with compassionate eye towards the *despised native of Africa*" (II, 220)—certainly a reference to the English boy and Dido who opened this chapter and whose symbolic importance cannot be understated. Here, the author/Editor assures us that, rather than the figure of racial obliteration that Mr. Fairfield intended, the seemingly grotesque black widow Fairfield is responsible for reproducing at least one racially and religiously ethical European while she puts to rest the ethically abusive one represented in the composite image of her father and his physical double, Augustus.

And it is with this reproductive act that *The Woman of Colour* makes its most compelling case for resisting perverse acts of epidermal conversion. In the scene with the little English boy that begins this chapter, so much depends on the impression that Olivia has on him: not only the vindication of the Negress, Dido, but also the conversion of the adolescent into a racially tolerant Englishman of the future.[56] Once Olivia's experiment proves to the boy that it is impossible to wash her, or any other black person, white, she asks him, "So you still dislike my poor Dido?" "She is *very* dirty," said he . . . shaking his head; but colouring, he said, "I mean *very black*" (I, 98). Here, we witness the results of Olivia's experiment. The boy's conception of Negroes has improved; he now sees them as "very black" rather than "very dirty." Moreover, his "colouring" betrays his feelings of guilt; he is aware

---

54. Kathleen Wilson's *The Island Race* (New York: Routledge, 2003), 129–68, proves that the very concept of a black widow was not alien to Olivia's contemporaries. Teresia Constantia Neville, the subject of Wilson's chapter, was known by this moniker after burying two of her rich colonial husbands in mysterious circumstances.

55. Wilson notes that "The Black Widow . . . hinted at the dangers West Indian topography posed to civilized English people" (ibid., 132). But as I go on to show, Olivia's portrayal at the end of *The Woman of Colour* defuses this threatening perception of a black widow by stressing her independence and useful ability to produce a less prejudiced English child.

56. For another interesting example of the way adults can instill racial tolerance in their English children, see the fragment from Amelia Opie's aborted autobiography contained in Cecilia Brightwell's *Memorials of the Life of Amelia Opie* (Norwich: Fletcher and Alexander, 1854), 12–13.

of, and embarrassed about, his earlier narcissistic presumption that Negroes like Dido are "dirty" and whites like himself are clean. The experiment is so successful that "the little fellow" exclaims, "Miss Fairfield, if you are going to Dido, let me go with you" (I, 104). Presumably, his desire to seek out Dido indicates that he has been liberated from the prejudices he could have potentially "imbibed in common with his countrymen."

This instructive scene is given an overtly political valence when we consider the little fellow's name. He is called George, his father is called George, and there is every reason to believe that the eldest Mr. Merton is called George too since we're twice told that the elder of the Merton brothers was the favorite of the father and the most like him in disposition. Therefore, little George Merton must be none other than the anonymous author's invocation of the archetypal contemporary paternalist, George III,[57] the "one *sceptical European*" who most needs "to look with compassionate eye towards the *despised native of Africa*." Olivia's inflexible black complexion becomes a useful and progressive political tool, making the archetype of British paternalism perform an unbiased and consensual act of conversion that abolishes his potential for prejudice. Allegorically, *The Woman of Colour*'s author inverts the political structure here, allowing Olivia to adopt an ascendant position over the monarch to reeducate him about the continued need for liberation—not of the Negroes from their blackness, but of Britons from their racial biases. Despite the 1807 abolitionist act that the supreme British paternalist has already ratified, *The Woman of Colour*'s author still wants this symbolic figure to be recognized as one of the first to liberate himself from the racial prejudices of his countrymen, an act which, in 1808, also marks one of the first direct literary calls for leadership on the issue of abolishing slavery.

"WHENEVER A stranger has identified me as something I'm not," writes Monica Bhide,

> I have always felt a need to correct the misimpression.... Now, more and more often, I find myself resisting that temptation ... if I tell you what I am, I am going against my very essence. For some, their skin color defines them. For me, it sets me free—free of boundaries, free of geography. The color of my skin allows me to belong to many countries and yet be owned by none.[58]

---

57. The importance that I attach to the author's use of names is further enhanced by the fact that George III's sixth son was called Augustus.
58. *Washington Post*, October 30, 2005, B2.

Clearly, Bhide feels emancipated by, and revels in, her complexion's ambiguity. But ultimately, her ideas about racial emancipation seem as racially naïve as those of the little Lynchburg boy whom she babysits. By embracing her complexion's link to a host of possible Others and resisting the urge to advocate for the Other that she is, Bhide avoids directly addressing the political significance of her complexion at a time in which the politics of terrorism affects the ways society and its functionaries read people like her. Viewed under the aegis of rigorous security checks at airports, greater scrutiny of charitable donations and mosque activities, and the tragic death of the Brazilian, Jean Charles de Menezes, on the London underground, Bhide's anecdotes, ending in a desire for racial emancipation, read like tales told by an idiot, full of the sound and fury of racial injustice, but ultimately signifying nothing by their avoidance of the very real political, social, even deadly, consequences of race and racism.

Bhide's resistance to contemporary racial realities locates her somewhere between a "Diminisher" and a "Denier," two terms that the Nigerian novelist Chimamanda Ngozi Adichie creates from her own bodily confrontation with the racial naivety of an American child. She also documents this experience as a *Washington Post* op-ed titled "The Color of an Awkward Conversation":

> In college I babysat for a Jewish family, and once I went to pick up first-grader Stephen from his play date's home. The lovely house had an American flag hanging from a colonnade. The mother of Stephen's play date greeted me warmly. Stephen hugged me and went to look for his shoes. His play date ran down the stairs and stopped halfway. "She's black," he said to his mother and stared silently at me before going back upstairs. I laughed stupidly, perhaps to deflate the tension, but I was angry.
>
> I was angry that this child did not merely think that black was different but had been taught that black was not a good thing. I was angry that his behavior left Stephen bewildered. . . .
>
> "That kid's mother is so ignorant," one friend said. . . ." It was just a kid being a kid. It wasn't racist," another said . . . I called the first friend a Diminisher and the second a Denier and came to discover that both represented how mainstream America talks about blackness.[59]

Diminishers, Adichie states, "believe that black people still encounter unpleasantness related to blackness but in benign forms and from unhappy people or crazy people or people with good intentions that are bungled in execution. Diminishers think that people can be 'ignorant' but not 'racist.'"

---

59. *Washington Post*, June 8, 2008, B7.

Deniers, on the other hand, "believe that black people stopped encountering unpleasantness related to their blackness when Martin Luther King Jr. died. They are 'colorblind' and use expressions like 'white, black or purple, we're all the same'—as though race were a biological rather than a social identity." Adichie's anger is leveled at those who fail to recognize the seriousness and social significance underlying seemingly benign incidents of racism generated by her own and other black bodies. Her anger is a clear rejection of the racial emancipation that Bhide promotes in favor of another type of liberation:

> The word "racist" should be banned. It is like a sweater wrung completely out of shape; it has lost its usefulness. It makes honest debate impossible, whether about small realities such as little boys who won't say hello to black babysitters or large realities such as who is more likely to get the death penalty. In place of "racist," descriptive, albeit unwieldy, expressions might be used. . . .

By banning the word "racist," Adichie suggests that resisting the urge to appropriate it at every turn will prevent the conflation of all prejudiced acts under one all-inclusive rubric, thereby leaving room for the creation of a more precise language about racism in its many different and unique forms.

This racist emancipation is an aggressive, confrontational approach to the problems generated by the appearance of a woman of color's body since it seeks to establish not the liberation of the female subject from the racial significations that her body generates, as Bhide proposes, but a more precise understanding of the ways in which a woman of color's body is being signified in different contexts on a daily basis. But Adichie's resistance to the word "racist" also does some serious diminishing and denying of its own. In one fell swoop, her proposal threatens to discount not merely the valence of the word that best speaks to the systemic problems of being a minority of color in a majority white society, but also the complex part that centuries of linguistic turns such as 'washing a blackamoor white' have played in the formation of racist thought. Critics like myself are still engaged with, and struggling to understand, this history and its influence in past and present Western societies.

It falls, then, to a two-hundred-year-old woman of color to temper the extremes of these modern women of color by providing tangible ways of both acknowledging a female body of color and resisting the racism leveled at it, and, by extension, those whom she racially represents. My discussion of Olivia's English experience in *The Woman of Colour* has shown that this mulatto heiress can claim, as Adichie does, that "my skin color did not determine my identity, did not limit my dreams or my confidence,"[60] even while she was forced to exist under the spectral influence of her white father's ironclad will. By putting the political, social, and potentially disastrous consequences of race and racism at the forefront of a tale that refuses to involve her in the emancipation of blackness from her father's hereditary line as his will intended, but instead uses the transformation of little George Merton to illustrate the greater need for the emancipation of Britons from their ignorant prejudices, *The Woman of Colour* provides a context for Bhide's and Adichie's essays, proving to be far more politically and socially astute about discussing race than the former, and showing that the latter's advocacy for new ways of confronting prejudice may be premature or even unnecessary. Olivia Fairfield's characterization as the failed object of whiteness in *The Woman of Colour* is the "very essence" which makes us realize that the abolition of prejudice—true racial and racist emancipation—comes about, not by avoiding race as Bhide does, or avoiding the "racist" word as Adichie proposes, but by the privileged individual's active participation in confronting, resisting, and destabilizing the racial biases that collectively exist in the English bloodline, English society, the English language, and the English-speaking world at large.

OLIVIA'S PRESENCE in *The Woman of Colour* shows the extent to which this novel has extended the influence of "Imoinda's shade" from its original Restoration roots. The novel positions the biracial heiress clearly at the intersection of an inauspicious plot involving slavery and marriage with a unique, bigamous twist which is different from that Imoinda initially established in Behn's and Southerne's *Oroonoko*s. The novel's action works to make this location a site of Olivia's emancipation from the stigmas associated with her blackness as well as the ascendancy of paternalism.

Moreover, its heroine illustrates a host of other subject positions that neither Behn nor Southerne could ever have imagined for either of their heroines: a female author of African descent who (except for the interjection of two letters and two short narratives) completely controls the voice of an entire text in stark contrast to Imoinda's silence; a woman warrior of African descent who successfully attacks the ascendancy of paternalism from within its bloodline rather than on a battlefield as Imoinda did in Surinam; a widowed woman of African descent whose precarious experience in the marriage market challenges the sentimental genre's tradition of elevating ideal heroines by killing them, offering instead a living heroine who is able to establish

---

60. Ibid.

female independence as an attractive alternative for all women irrespective of race and that there is life after, and even without, marriage; a biracial heiress of African descent who, despite the privileges associated with her rank and biological connection to whiteness, is "not ashamed to acknowledge [her] affinity with the swarthiest negro that was ever brought from Guinea's coast" (I, 3) irrespective of their class, as Olivia's relationship with Dido shows; an educator-activist of African descent who decides to "again zealously engage [herself] in ameliorating the situation, in instructing the minds—in mending the morals of our poor blacks" (II, 216) in Jamaica only after she has reeducated the "morals," "minds," and "situation" of prejudice in England; a biracial woman of African descent who demonstrates that a female who considers herself "more than half an English woman" (I, 205), is just as, if not more than, capable of performing the social graces and behaviors the English are led to believe that their women alone are capable of performing.

In short, "though the jet has been faded to the olive in [her] own complexion" (I, 3), it is in the shade of this olive-skinned woman of African descent that we find the best illustration of how a fictionalized woman of African descent extends the seminal spirit of "Imoinda's shade" into the arena of British abolition through an amalgamation that goes beyond the simple union of Mr. Fairfield and Marcia, and instead embodies the spirit of female resistance that the black and white shades of Behn's and Southerne's heroines stood for throughout the eighteenth century.

AFTERWORD

Well! I am really haunted by black shadows . . . a black Lady, covered with finery, in the Pit at the Opera . . .

—Hester Thrale, "Letter to Mrs. Pennington," No. 5 George St., Manchester Square, Saturday, June 19, 1808, *The Letters of Mrs. Thrale* (1926), 143

The story of Imoinda as a story of a strong woman who went through immense tragedy through her life . . . really resonated with many of our young women in the school, not only in terms of their identity as young women and young women of colour, but . . . the last scene . . . where, as Imoinda is giving birth she's also debating her own suicide and struggling with these *big* questions, we actually had a couple of young women in the core class that had faced some of these difficult issues of teenage pregnancy and whether or not to keep their children; And . . . because of school policies, because of other things having to do with urban education, there are relatively few venues for those girls to explore that part of their life . . . with adults . . . in a safe environment. I tell you, when we set the conceptual framework for that last scene, several girls who during the rest of the project had been very antagonistic to the process and *very* difficult to deal with from a behavior standpoint, they took the lead on that scene and it was *so* powerful, and of course, they never had to open up to the group and tell them that this was their story because they could explore their own experience through Imoinda's voice and therefore step forward and make a *huge* artistic contribution to that final scene. . . .

—Glenn L. McClure[1]

---

1. Response during question-and-answer section of one-day conference "Critical Perspectives on Imoinda," http://www.gold.ac.uk/wow/shortvideo2/. Glen McClure is a composer who teaches at the State University of New York at Geneseo.

Afterword

> I'm teaching a class on Caribbean literature and its diasporas. I just wanted to make an observation . . . when I saw *Imoinda* on the stage there at the school it . . . came across to *me very* strongly then, of course it was a wonderful moment of detachment . . . it was a very *very* luxurious moment, believe me, being able to see this. But it came across . . . *so* obviously now . . . as a text of the Diaspora. Because what I saw inscribed in your performance . . . it came across very much as an American piece . . . whereas . . . in my head it was a Caribbean piece, and of course it was *meant* to function—it *is* a diasporic text, but what I was able to do seeing it in that context was to see it placed elsewhere, it should . . . [someone] asked earlier about when it's going to go to Brazil. . . .
>
> —Joan Anim-Addo[2]

ON NOVEMBER 7, 2009, Goldsmiths, University of London presented a one-day seminar titled "Words from Other Worlds: Critical Perspectives on Imoinda." A promotional poster for this seminar states that it was a student-led initiative seeking "to develop a range of critical perspectives on the silenced female Imoinda in Aphra Behn's *Oroonoko*,"[3] using, as a context, a rewriting of Behn's novella by Joan Anim-Addo entitled *Imoinda: or, She Who Will Lose Her Name. A Play for Twelve Voices in Three Acts* (2007). The very fact that this seminar bases itself in Behn's work and yet reconstructs Imoinda as a completely independent manifestation of Anim-Addo's imagination confirms that the eighteenth-century process of imoindaism that I have outlined in this book is currently ongoing. *Imoinda* is an explicit indication that contemporary writers such as Anim-Addo and Biyi Bandele (who produced *Aphra Behn's Oroonoko* [1999] for the Royal Shakespeare Company) continue to ground themselves in, yet distinguish themselves from, Behn, Southerne, and their texts.

For a number of reasons, Anim-Addo's textual engagement with *Oroonoko* offers, perhaps, the most explicit example of the type of creative detachment that this book has articulated as a facet of imoindaism. First, her prominent use of the "Imoinda" name in her title speaks deliberately to a contemporary need to detach this fictional African heroine from the "Oroonoko" name under which she originally appeared. Second, Anim-Addo's *Imoinda* is a libretto—opera being a curious choice for a revisionist slave narrative, but one that firmly distinguishes Anim-Addo's text from the novella and tragicomedic drama that initially established Imoinda as a literary presence. Third, Anim-Addo, a Grenadian native with an African name who resides and works as a writer and academic in Britain, explicitly identifies herself

---

2. Response during question-and-answer section of one-day conference "Critical Perspectives on Imoinda," http://www.gold.ac.uk/wow/shortvideo3/.

3. http://www.beyondtext.ac.uk/imoinda.shtml.

as a woman of the African Diaspora, an identity that is markedly different from the English origins of Behn and Southerne. As is her creative work, which Anim-Addo also identifies as equally detached from national borders. After being developed in English theater readings and workshops from 1996, *Imoinda* was published first as a bilingual English–Italian edition in 2003, and it received an American performance at School of the Arts (SOTA) in Rochester, New York, in 2007. Anim-Addo's comments in the third epigram indicate that she is even looking toward Brazil as another place for its future production.

Imoinda's international circulation continues to publicize this fictional African woman's story, and as Glen McClure's comments in the second epigram point out, *Imoinda* allows others to reflect on some aspect of love in contemporary society. For those young women who were a part of McClure's student production at SOTA, the play was an opportunity for them to scrutinize their own reproductive choices in a curriculum that does not let them speak about such concerns, and McClure suggests that they use that scrutiny to make a positive creative statement about themselves. This kind of imoindaism represents one way in which Behn's and Southerne's heroine continues to be reconstructed and employed to suit the current needs of a new generation. But its translation into other languages also means that this African woman's experience is also being reinterpreted to suit the needs of other cultures, providing them with the creative space to speak about, reflect on, and act out their own unique concerns in their own specific tongues. That such a concerted attempt is being made to understand, view, and popularize Imoinda in her own right implies that this fictional African woman's influence has, perhaps, reached a transformative moment of recognition at the beginning of the twenty-first century.

The current moment seems right, therefore, for a book that seeks to reclaim the African Imoinda by considering how evocations of this fictional African woman have been employed in eighteenth-century British literature. To this end, this book has established a deliberate trajectory. Part One of *Imoinda's Shade* demonstrates that writers from the mid-to-late eighteenth century use the *Oroonoko* marriage plots from Aphra Behn's novel and Thomas Southerne's drama as bases for their own fictions in which they develop representations of African heroines who are involved in making deliberate interventions into antislavery activism. Even though the 1760 anonymous *Oroonoko* and Edgeworth's *The Grateful Negro* market amelioration as a progressive, reasonable, and benevolent course of action in the colonies, I read the white African, Imoinda, and the black African, Clara, as fictional figures whose representations and marriages do not only call into question the adequacy of this policy, but expose its extreme inadequacy by laying bare the sexual and paternal tyranny against African women that an ameliorist regime enacts. Earle's Amri and Kotzebue's Ada resurrect the spirit of the black African Imoinda and privilege the African romance in order to present radical alternatives to amelioration in the forms of gynecological rebellion and immigration. Yet, despite the progressive ways in which these fictional African heroines are employed, their texts ultimately point to the ascendance of the *Oroonoko* legend and its insistence on the African heroine's death. In other words, *The Negro Slaves* and *Obi; or, the History of Three Fingered Jack* do not allow readers to observe their progressive black heroines achieving the freedom that Imoinda is an advocate for.

To address this need, Part Two of *Imoinda's Shade* focuses on narratives that eschew the *Oroonoko* text and legend but still make politicized interventions into the marriage plots of British dramas and novels in ways that show fictional African women continuing to advance antislavery as well as postslavery discourse. These fictional women present three different approaches to the idea of abolition in England. In Macready's *Irishman in London*, Cubba represents abolition as a humorous yet politicized expression of complete relief from the pain of slavery that she advocates for all people in the colonies and accesses for herself through her "happy" marriage to Delany. A coupling between two kinds of victimized activists also appears to be one of the focuses of Opie's *Adeline Mowbray*. But when Savanna's role as a member of the black poor is compared with Adeline's role as a radical white woman advocating for the abolition of marriage, Opie looks more triumphantly on the legal credibility of the mulatto woman's role in the novel's English society. For Savanna, abolition is about the legal freedom to be seen as a black British "street citizen" in a society in which the black poor were disparaged as socially transgressive and foreign, and shipped abroad accordingly. Being shipped abroad is also an experience familiar to Olivia Fairfield, who arrives in England from Jamaica under the terms of an arranged marriage orchestrated by her father's will. Although its stipulations initially involve this mulatto heiress in a biological process of whitening, the anonymous author involves her in an alternative marriage plot that shows this woman actively resisting her father's attempts to abolish her existence as a heroine of African descent. For Olivia, abolition is about confronting her father's bloodline—a confrontation in which she ultimately triumphs by her active resistance to the abolitionist terms that this paternalist's literal and figurative wills seek to enforce from beyond the grave.

In these ways, *Imoinda's Shade* uses marriage plots to establish a trajectory for reading the fictional African woman's involvement in advancing antislavery and abolitionist positions in British literature. It also develops our understanding of how women were responsible for the changing perception of African-ness in the eighteenth century. From its initial start as a concept fluid enough to accommodate whiteness in Southerne's *Oroonoko*, African-ness is disparaged for its primitivism in Edgeworth's *The Grateful Negro* and celebrated for its purity in Kotzebue's *The Negro Slaves*, in Earle's *Obi; or, The History of Three Fingered Jack,* and even in Macready's *The Irishman in London; or, The Happy African.* When people of African descent are depicted in the pages of dramas and novels that are set in England, African-ness appears to settle into an uneasy yet reconcilable association with Britishness in the characterizations of black Creole women such as Cubba and Savanna, implying that, for at least the working class, Africans can be silently integrated into British society as street citizens. But African-ness appears to be most threatening when it is embodied in a character like Olivia Fairfield, a woman who identifies equally with members of the white upper-middle class as well as the black people associated slavery. In her tale, this fictional woman of color demonstrates that she can perform all of the admirable characteristics associated with Englishness—propriety, temperance, humility, religious fervor—as well as, and sometimes better than, white English women. Like the "black Lady, covered with finery, in the Pit at the Opera" who so alarms Hester Thrale in the first epigram of this afterword, Olivia's presence in British literature creates the impression that the negative stigmas routinely ascribed to people of African descent are unreliable, and thus, the "wall of separation . . . *within England* that had safely divided black from white" is swiftly "crumbling,"[4] as Felicity Nussbaum puts it. Consequently, although Vincent Carretta asserts that Olaudah Equiano is "African by birth . . . British by acculturation and choice" but "can . . . never be *English*,"[5] Olivia's presence speaks to the possibility that a concept of African Englishness is a closer reality than most eighteenth-century Britons imagine.

In drama—a genre that has been noticeably underutilized in critical discussions of British antislavery literature when compared with poetry and prose fiction—the women of "Imoinda's shade" have also been employed to bring out the resonance of antislavery and abolitionist activism contained within the pages of published texts rather than staged performances. The fictional African women in the anonymous *Oroonoko* (1760), *The Negro Slaves*, and *The Irishman in London; or, The Happy African* differ widely with respect to race, class, genre, and function. Yet, together, these dramas account for the wide diversity of ways that the African woman was constructed on the published page as a speaking subject, not in the highly stylized language of poetry, but in dialogically politicized language that was written expressly to

---

4. Nussbaum, *Limits of the Human,* 239.
5. Vincent Carretta, The *Interesting Narrative and Other Writings* (Penguin, 1995), xvii.

connect with, and influence, British audiences as well as readers. Whether their African heroines speak in Standard or Jamaican English, British dramatists are as involved in making readers read for the antislavery meaning contained with their texts as they are responsible for allowing spectators to look at African bodies onstage for pleasure.

In privileging the words spoken by fictional African characters rather than the portrayals of their bodies as they were performed by whites in British theatres, *Imoinda's Shade* makes a case for the importance of understanding antislavery activism as a reading rather than an acting enterprise, an idea that is supported in the prose fictions of Earle, Edgeworth, Opie, and *The Woman of Colour*'s anonymous author. Perhaps to distinguish their efforts from the tawdry rubric "novels," and to claim some kind of moral legitimacy for their creations, it is noticeable that all of these writers consciously identify their works in total or in part as "tales" or histories. "The narrator in *Tristram Shandy*," Miriam Wallace observes, "argued that good reading is less for the pleasure of the plot and more for self education and reflection,"[6] and it appears that the writers of antislavery tales and historical dramas understood this distinction. They were able to produce two levels of discourse in their works that accommodate both kinds of reader, and the women of "Imoinda's shade" are associated with the level that corresponds to edification and reflection about the issues of slavery and freedom.

Reading Imoinda's literal and imaginative presences throughout a series of eighteenth-century texts also provides a working methodology that can account for a writer's views on antislavery and abolition at a time when extant information about their actual opinions on these issues is not available. This methodology provides a gauge for assessing how far British writers were willing to go in conveying the ideal of freedom. When focused on the colonies, the women of "Imoinda's shade" are employed to run the gamut of positions on antislavery and abolition, ranging from amelioration in the 1760 anonymous *Oroonoko* to the Jacobin notion of popular and violent revolt in Earle's *Obi*. However, this range is not always as progressive as it seems, or could be. As Edgeworth's depiction of Clara shows, not all British writers who evoke Imoinda are progressively in favor of giving Africans complete liberty, and in general, texts that are set in the West Indian colonies have a hard time imagining the black African woman experiencing freedom there. The fictional women of African descent who are depicted on English shores, however, offer more extensive examples of a lived kind of freedom by their access to interracial marriages and British rights, their recognition as British subjects, their involvement in plots that circumvent the Yorke–

---

6. Miriam Wallace, *Revolutionary Subjects in the English Jacobin Novel*, 32.

Talbot tradition and advocate for the African's humanity, as well as texts that align with the Mansfield myth of immediate freedom for slaves in England or undermine stigmas of race prejudice and social degeneration that plague the African body. In all, these diverse depictions of Africans being legally, racially, and emotionally liberated in England from the stigmas associated with slavery speak to one of the ways in which British writers used the African woman to propagandize the nation's love of, and commitment to, freedom. Events such as the Mansfield Judgment and the Sierra Leone scheme, however, confirm that this propaganda is not as ideal as its literature suggests. While Britain might have reveled in the self-righteousness of freedom for all within its borders, it did not actively work to provide legal safeguards for all its figures of empire who lived there, and as Olivia Fairfield's example shows, skin-color prejudice in England was still a reality even for the most idealized women of color. But this type of propaganda does work to morally distinguish Britons from white Creoles in the run-up to the abolitions of the slave trade and slavery, and it also promotes England as a haven for blacks—a haven that nineteenth-century black women such as Mary Seacole and Mary Prince would continue to market in their respective narratives.

These fictional women are also a testament to the concerted effort made within British culture to keep Behn's and Southerne's names and texts alive long after their authors' deaths. The women who fall under "Imoinda's shade" and the texts that embody them speak to the longevity and necessity of the "Oroonoko legend,"[7] as Wylie Sypher calls it, and they also create an understanding as to why the nineteenth-century poet Algernon Swinburne can speak so knowledgeably about Behn as the first literary abolitionist. Works such as *The Negro Slaves* and the many revisions of *Oroonoko* keep alive the themes and issues that Behn and Southerne originated. And, moreover, this book has also shown that texts such as *The Irishman in London*, *Adeline Mowbray*, and *The Woman of Colour* keep Imoinda's spirit alive through their literal and imaginative reinventions of African heroines who continue to raise concerns particular to enslaved women of African descent by scrutinizing Britain's involvement in slavery, as well as the nation's attitude toward the citizenship rights of, and prejudices against, African figures of empire.

Last, in the absence of an abundance of texts written by black women, the women of "Imoinda's shade" offer an opportunity to reflect on the concerns of the slave woman—but only as effectively or ineffectively as a white writer's imagination created them. These concerns are numerous: rape, rebellion, violence, citizenship, reproduction, interracial marriage, social trans-

---

7. Sypher, *Guinea's Captive Kings*, 108.

gression, sexual stigmatization, liberty, family, pain, pleasure, and equality. To evoke these concerns, the fictional African woman's body is used in a multitude of ways: she is a fighter, a saint-mother, a rebel-wife, a political comedian, a primitive African, a rich mulatto heiress, and a black British street citizen. In short, by focusing on the African women and the British marriage plots that incorporate their experiences, this book brings to light Britain's engagement with slavery and freedom from a particular fictional woman's perspective. The names Clara, Amri, Ada, Cloe, Quasheba, Cubba, Savanna, Dido, and Olivia are one manifestation of the women who fall under "Imoinda's shade," and together they form an important part of a historical trajectory that begins with Behn and Southerne, and ends (for now) with Anim-Addo's *Imoinda*.

BIBLIOGRAPHY

Primary Sources

Amory, Thomas. *The Life of John Buncle, Esq; containing Various Observations and Reflections, made in Several Parts of the World, and Many Extraordinary Relations*. London: J. Johnson and B. Davenport, 1766.

Anonymous. *The Adventures of Jonathan Corncob, loyal American refugee, written by himself*. Boston: D. R. Godine, 1976.

———. *Athenian Sport: or, Two Thousand Paradoxes Merrily Argued, To Amuse and Divert the Age: . . . By a Member of the Athenian Society*. London: B. Bragg, 1707.

———. *The Fair Cambrians: A Novel in Three Volumes*. London: William Lane, 1790.

———. *The Fortunate Transport, or The Secret History of the life and adventures of the celebrated Polly Haycock, the lady of the gold watch. By a Creole*. London: T. Taylor, 1748.

———. *Obi; or, Three Finger'd Jack. A Melodrama*. London: Thomas Hailes Lacy, 1830.

———. *Oroonoko A Tragedy altered from the Original Play of that name. Written by the late Thomas Southerne, Esq; To which the EDITOR has added near Six Hundred Lines in Place of the comic Scene. Together with an addition of Two New Characters. Intended for One of the THEATRES*. London: Printed for A & C. Corbett in Fleet Street, 1760.

———. *Reflections, Moral, Comical, Satyrical, &c. on the Vices and Folies of the Age*. London, 1707.

———. *Rewards for Attentive Studies; or Stories Moral and Entertaining*. London: Printed for J. Wallis by J. Cundee, 1800.

———. *Slavery no oppression: or, some new arguments and opinions against the idea of African liberty. Dedicated to the committee of the company that trade to Africa*. London: Lowndes and Christie, 1788?.

———. *Substance of the Debates on A Resolution for Abolishing the Slave Trade*. London: Dawson's, 1968.

———. *Substance of the Report of the Court of Directors of the Sierra Leone Company to the General court, Held at London on Wednesday the 19th of October, 1791. To Which is Added a Postscript*. London: James Philips, George Yard, 1792.

———. *West-India Trade and Islands. Commercial Reasons for the Non-Abolition of the Slave Trade, in the West-India Islands, by A Planter, and Merchant of many Years Residence in the West Indies*. London: W. Lane, 1789.

———. *The Woman of Colour: A Tale,* ed. Lyndon J. Dominique. Peterborough, Ontario: Broadview, 2007.

———. *The Woman of Colour. A Tale in Two Volumes.* London: Black, Parry and Kingsbury, 1808.

Arnold, Samuel. *The Creole, or The Haunted Island.* London: C. Whittingham, 1796.

Ashton, John. *The Fleet, Its River Prison and Marriages.* London: T. Fisher Unwin, 1889.

Astell, Mary. *Some Reflections Upon Marriage with Additions. The Fourth Edition, 1730.* New York: Source Book Press, 1970.

Austen, Jane. *Mansfield Park.* New York: Signet Classic, 1964.

———. *Mansfield Park,* ed. Claudia Johnson. New York: Norton, 1998.

Beckford, William. *Remarks upon the situation of negroes in Jamaica, impartially made from a local experience of nearly thirteen years in that island, by W. Beckford.* London: T. and J. Egerton, 1788.

Behn, Aphra. *All the histories and novels written by the late ingenious Mrs. Behn in one entire volume. The Fourth Edition with Large Editions.* London: R. Wellington, 1700.

———. *Oroonoko,* ed. Joanna Lipking. New York; London: Norton, 1997.

———. *Oroonoko,* ed. Janet Todd. London: Penguin Classics, 2003.

Bellamy, Thomas. *Benevolent Planters. A Dramatic Piece as performed at the Theatre Royal Haymarket.* London, Debrett, 1789.

Bickerstaff, Isaac. *Love in the City; A Comic Opera as it is Performed at the Theatre Royal in Covent-Garden. The Words Written and Music Composed by the Author of Love in a Village.* London: W. Griffin, 1767.

———. *The Padlock.* London: Griffin, 1768.

Bissett, Robert. *Douglas; or the Highlander.* London: Anti Jacobin Press, 1800.

Blackstone, Sir William. *Commentaries on the Law of England: In Four Books. The Thirteenth Edition.* London: A Strahan, 1800.

Boswell, James. *The Life of Samuel Johnson LLD.* London, 1791.

Brightwell, Cecilia. *Memorials of the Life of Amelia Opie.* Norwich: Fletcher and Alexander, 1854.

Brydges, Samuel Egerton. *Arthur Fitz-Albini.* London: J. White, 1799.

Burney, Frances. *Cecilia, or Memoirs of an Heiress.* London: Virago Press, 1986.

———. *The Wanderer,* ed. Margaret Doody. Oxford; New York: Oxford University Press, 1991.

Chapone, Sarah. *The Hardships of the Laws in Relation to Wives.* London, 1735.

Clarkson, Thomas. *The True State of the Case Respecting the Insurrection at St. Domingo.* Ipswich: J. Bush, 1792.

Colman, George, and David Garrick. *The Clandestine Marriage.* London: Becket and De Hondt, 1766.

Cumberland, Richard. *The West Indian: A Comedy As it is Performed at the Theatre Royal in Drury Lane By the Author of The Brothers.* London: W. Griffin, 1771.

Davies, Thomas. *Memoirs of the life of David Garrick.* London, 1780.

Day, Thomas. *The History of Sandford and Merton, a Work Intended for the Use of Children, in two volumes. Volume II.* Dublin: Printed by P. Byrne, 1787.

Defoe, Daniel. *The History and Remarkable Life of the Truly Honourable Col. Jacque, Commonly call'd Jack, who was born a Gentleman etc.* London: Printed and Sold by J. Brotherton et al., 1723.

Dibdin, Charles. *A Complete History of the Stage written by Mr. Dibdin. Vol. IV.* London: Printed for the Author, n.d.

Dibdin, Thomas. *Family Quarrels, A Comic Opera, in Three Acts. As performed at the Theatres Convent-Garden and New York.* New York: D. Longworth, 1806.

Dodsley. *The Annual Register, or a view of the History, Politics, and Literature for the year 1798.* London: Printed by T. Burton for the proprietors of Dodsley's Annual Register, etc., 1800.

Duras, Claire de. *Ourika, an English Translation by John Fowles.* New York: Modern Language Association, 1994.

Earle, William. *Natural Faults.* London: Earle and Hemet, 1799.

———. *Obi; or, The History of Three Fingered Jack,* ed. Srinivas Aravamudan. Peterborough, Ontario: Broadview, 2005.

Edgeworth, Maria. *Popular Tales by Maria Edgeworth illustrated by Miss Chris Hammond with an introduction by Anne Thackeray Ritchie.* London: Macmillan and Co., 1895.

———. *Practical Education.* London: J. Johnson, 1798.

———. *Tales and Novels.* Vol. 2, *Popular Tales.* New York: AMS Press, 1967.

Edwards, Bryan. *The History, Civil and Commercial, of the British Colonies in the West Indies.* Vol. 2. London: Stockdale, 1793.

Equiano, Olaudah. *The Interesting Narrative of the Life of Olaudah Equiano, or Gustavus Vassa, The African. Written By Himself. Eighth Edition Enlarged.* Norwich: Printed for, and Sold by the Author, 1794. First published in 1789.

Gent, T. M. *A Miscellaneous Collection of Poems, Songs and Epigrams. By Several Hands. Publish'd by T.M. Gent.* Dublin: A. Rhames, 1721.

Gentleman, Francis. *Oroonoko, or the Royal Slave, A tragedy altered from Southerne. As it was performed at the theatre in Edinburgh with universal applause.* Glasgow: Printed by Robert and Andrew Foulis, 1760.

Godwin, William. *Fables Ancient and Modern. Adapted for the Use of Children. Tenth edition.* London: M. J. Godwin & Co., 1824.

Goldsmith, Olivier. *The Bee: Being Essays on the Most Interesting Subjects.* London, 1759.

Grégoire, Henri. *On the Cultural Achievements of Negroes,* trans. Thomas Cassirer and Jean-François Brière. Amherst: University of Massachusetts Press, 1996.

Griffith, Mrs. *A collection of novels, selected and revised by Mrs. Griffith.* Vol. 1. London: Printed for G Kearsly, 1777.

———. *English Nights Entertainments. The History of Oroonoko; or, the Royal Slave. Written originally by Mrs. Behn, and revised by Mrs. Griffiths.* London: Printed by T. Maiden, for Ann Lemoine, 1800.

Hamilton, Elizabeth. *Letters of a Hindoo Rajah,* ed. P. Perkins and S. Russell. Peterborough, Ontario: Broadview, 1999.

Hawkesworth, John. *Oroonoko, A Tragedy as it is now performed at Drury Lane. By Thomas Southern with alterations.* London; Printed for C Bathhurst, at the Cross-key, in fleet-street; and the rest of the proprietors, 1759.

Hays, Mary. *The Victim of Prejudice,* ed. Eleanor Rose Ty. Peterborough, Ontario: Broadview, 1998.

Jackman, Isaac. *The Divorce. A Farce: As it is performed at the Theater-Royal, Drury Lane. Written by the Author of All the World's A Stage.* London: G. Kearsley, 1781.

Kotzebue, August Von (anonymously translated). *The Negro Slaves. A Dramatic Historical Piece in Three Acts.* London: Printed for T. Cadell, Junior and W. Davies (successors to Mr. Cadell) and J. Edwards, 1796.

———. *The Negro Slaves.* London: Printed for J. Boosey; J. Hurst; Bickerstaff; J. Hatchard; J. Gray, 1800.

L'Estrange, Roger. *Aesop, Fables . . . with Morals and Reflexions. By Sir Roger L'Estrange*. London, 1692.
Lavallée, Joseph. *The Negro Equalled by Few Europeans*. Translated from the French by J. Trapp. London, 1790.
Lee, Charles. *Memoirs of the Life of the Late Charles Lee, Esq*. Dublin: P Byrne, J Moore et al., 1792.
Long, Edward. *History of Jamaica*. 3 Vols. London: T. Lowndes, 1774.
Luckman, T., ed. *The Universal Museum; or the Entertaining Repository for Gentlemen and Ladies*. Coventry: Printed by and for T. Luckman, 1765.
Macaulay, Catherine. *The History of England from the Revolution to the Present Time*. Vol. 1. Bath: R Cruttwell, 1778.
Macready, William. *The Irishman in London; or, The Happy African: A Farce. In Two Acts*. London: Woodfall, 1793.
Mahew, Henry. *London Labour and the London Poor*. London, 1862.
Moseley, Benjamin. *Medical Tracts*. London: Nichols, 1800.
Nugent, Mary. *Lady Nugent's Journal of Her Residence in Jamaica from 1801–1805*, ed. Philip Wright. Mona, Jamaica: University of the West Indies Press, 2002.
Oldfield, Anne. *An Epistle from Mrs. Oldfield, in the Shades, to Mrs. Br—ceg—dle, upon Earth: containing, A dialogue between the Most Eminent Players in the Shades, upon The Late Stage Desertion*. London: Printed for Jacob Robinson, 1793.
Opie, Amelia. *Adeline Mowbray; or The Mother and Daughter*. New York: Woodstock Books, 1995.
———. *Poems, by Mrs. Opie*. London: Longman, Hurst, Rees, and Orme, 1806.
Paine, Thomas. *The Rights of Man*, ed. Hypatia Bradlaugh Bonner. London: Watts & Co., 1906.
Peacock, Lucy. *The Rambles of Fancy; or, Moral and Interesting Tales*. London: T. Bensley, 1786.
Plowden, Francis. *A Short History of the British Empire, from May 1792 to the Close of the year 1793*. Philadelphia: Mathew Carey, 1794.
Prince, Mary. *The History of Mary Prince*, ed. Sarah Salih. London: Penguin, 2000.
Prince, Nancy. *A Black Woman's Odyssey through Russia and Jamaica: The Narratives of Nancy Prince*, intro. by Ronald G. Walter. New York: M. Wiener, 1990.
Reeve, Clara. *Plans of Education with remarks on the system of other writers. In a series of Letters between Mrs. Darnford and her friend*. London: T. Hookham and J. Carpenter, 1792.
Roscoe, William. *The Wrongs of African, A Poem. Part, The First*. London: R. Faulder, 1787.
Sansay, Leonora Mary Hassal. *Secret History, or, The Horrors of St. Domingo*. Philadelphia: Bradford & Inskeep; R. Carr, Printer, 1808. Reprinted 1971.
Seacole, Mary. *Wonderful Adventures of Mrs. Seacole in Many Lands*, ed. Sara Salih. London: Penguin, 2005.
Sellier, W. *Kotzbue in England*. Leipzig, 1901.
Shadwell, Thomas. *Dedication to Charles Sedley* from *A True Widow, A Comedy Acted by the Duke's Servants*. London: Printed for Benjamin Tooke, 1679.
Southerne, Thomas. *Oroonoko*, ed. Maximillian E. Novak and David Stuart Rodes. Lincoln: University of Nebraska Press, 1976.
Stacy, E. *Aesop. Sir Roger L'Estrange's Fables, with Morals and Reflections in English Verse. By E. Stacy*. London, 1717.
Swinburne, Algernon. *Studies in Poetry and Prose*. London: Chatto & Windus, 1894.

Tate, Nahum. "A Preface concerning Farce." *A Duke and no Duke As it is Acted by their Majesties Servants*. London: Henry Bonwicke, 1693.
Taylor, John. *Elements of the Civil Law*. Cambridge, 1755.
Thrale, Hester. *The Letters of Mrs. Thrale*. London: Lane, 1926.
Townley, James. *High Life Below Stairs. A Farce of Two Acts As it is performed at the Theatre-Royal in Drury-Lane*. London: Printed for J. Newberry, at the Bible and Sun in St, Paul's Church-Yard; R. Bailye, at Litchfield; J. Drake and W. Frederick, at Bath; B. Collins and S. Stabler at York, 1759.
Tyler, Royall. *The Algerine Captive: or, The Life and Adventures of Doctor Updike Underhill: Six Years a Prisoner Among the Algerines*. Walpole, NH: David Carlisle Jr., 1797.
Wedderburn, Robert. *The Horrors of Slavery*, ed. and intro. Iain McCalman. New York and Princeton, NJ: Markus Wiener Publishing, 1991.
Wesley, John. *Thoughts Upon Slavery*. London: printed by R. Hawes, 1774.
Winer, Lise, et al. *Adolphus, A Tale & The Slave Son*. Mona, Kingston, Jamaica: University of the West Indies Press, 2003.
Winkfield, Unca Eliza (pseudonym). *The Female American*, ed. Michelle Burnham. Peterborough, Ontario: Broadview, 2001.

Secondary Sources

Alexander, Ziggi. "Let It Lie Upon the Table: The Status of Black Women's Biography in the UK." *Gender and History* 2 (1990): 22-33.
Altick, Richard. *The Shows of London*. Cambridge, MA: Belknap Press, 1978.
Anderson, Misty. *Female Playwrights and Eighteenth-Century Comedy: Negotiating Marriage on the London Stage*. New York: Palgrave, 2002.
Anstey, Roger. *The Atlantic Slave Trade and British Abolition, 1760–1810*. Atlantic Highlands, NJ: Humanities Press, 1975.
Aravamudan, Srinivas. "Introduction" to *Slavery, Abolition and Emancipation: Writings in the British Romantic Period*. Vol. 6, *Fiction*, ed. Peter J. Kitson and Debbie Lee. London; Brookfield, VT: Pickering & Chatto, 1999.
———. *Tropicopolitans: Colonialism and Agency, 1688–1804*. Durham, NC: Duke University Press, 2000.
Armstrong, Nancy. *Desire and Domestic Fiction: A Political History of the Novel*. Oxford: Oxford University Press, 1995.
Arrizón, Alicia. "Race-ing Performativity through Transculturation, Taste and the Mulata Body." *Theatre Research International* 27, no. 2 (2002): 136–52.
Bannet, Eve Tavor. "The Marriage Act of 1753: 'A Most Cruel Act for the Fair Sex.'" *Eighteenth Century Studies* 30, no. 3 (1997): 233–54.
Bartels, Emily. "*Othello* and Africa: Postcolonialism Reconsidered." *William and Mary Quarterly* 54 (1997): 45–64.
Barthelemy, Anthony. *Black Face, Maligned Race: The Representation of Blacks in English Drama from Shakespeare to Southerne*. Baton Rouge: Louisiana State University Press, 1987.
Bartlett, Lynn C. "High Life Below Stairs or Cribbage in the Kitchen." *English Language Notes* 23 (1985): 54–61.
Beckles, Hilary. *Centering Woman: Gender Discourses in Caribbean Slave Society*. Kingston, Jamaica: Ian Rand Publishers, 1999.

Berry, Ralph. *Shakespeare and the Awareness of Audience.* New York: St. Martin's Press, 1985.
Bhabha, Homi. "Of Mimicry and Man: The Ambivalence of Colonial Discourse" and "Signs Taken for Wonders: Questions of Ambivalence and Authority under a Tree outside Delhi, May 1817." In *The Location of Culture.* London and New York: Routledge, 1994.
Boesky, Amy. "Nation, Miscegenation: Membering Utopia in Henry Neville's *The Isle of Pines.*" *Texas Studies in Literature* 37 (1995): 165–84.
Boose, Lynda. "'The Getting of a Lawful Race': Racial Discourse in Early Modern England and the Unrepresentable Black Woman." In *Women, "Race," and Writing in the Early Modern Period,* ed. Margo Hendricks and Patricia Parker. London: Routledge, 1994. 35–54.
Bost, Suzanne. *Mulattas and Mestizas: Representing Mixed Identities in the Americas, 1850–2000.* Athens: University of Georgia Press, 2003.
Boulukos, George. "Maria Edgeworth's 'Grateful Negro and the Sentimental Argument for Slavery.'" *Eighteenth Century Life* 23 (1999): 12-29.
———. *The Grateful Slave.* Cambridge: Cambridge University Press, 2008.
Braithwaite, Kamau. *The Development of Creole Society in Jamaica, 1770–1820.* Oxford: Clarendon Press, 1971.
Brody, Jennifer DeVere. *Impossible Purities.* Durham, NC: Duke University Press, 1998.
Burnard, Trevor. *Mastery, Tyranny, and Desire: Thomas Thistlewood and His Slaves in the Anglo-Jamaican World.* Chapel Hill: University of North Carolina Press, 2004.
Burton, Richard D. E. *Afro-Creole: Power, Opposition, and Play in the Caribbean.* Ithaca, NY: Cornell University Press, 1997.
Bush, Jonathan A. "The First Slave (and Why He Matters)." *Cardozo Law Review* 18 (1996): 599–630.
Campbell, Mavis Christine. *The Dynamics of Change in a Slave Society: A Sociopolitical History of the Free Coloreds of Jamaica, 1800–1865.* Rutherford, NJ: Fairleigh Dickinson University Press, 1976.
Carey, Brycchan, Markman Ellis, and Sara Salih, eds. *Discourses of Slavery and Abolition: Britain and Its Colonies, 1760–1838.* Basingstoke, Hampshire; New York: Palgrave Macmillan, 2004.
Castle, Terry. *Masquerade and Civilization: The Carnivalesque in Eighteenth-Century Culture and Fiction.* Stanford, CA: Stanford University Press, 1986.
Charney, Maurice. *Comedy High and Low: An Introduction to the Experience of Comedy.* New York: Oxford University Press, 1978.
Coleman, Deirdre. "Janet Schaw and the Complexions of Empire." *Eighteenth-Century Studies* 36, no. 2 (2003): 169–93.
Colley, Linda. *Britons.* New Haven, CT: Yale University Press, 1992.
Craton, Michael, and James Walvin, eds. *A Jamaican Plantation: The History of Worthy Park, 1670–1970.* London and New York: W. H. Allen, 1970.
Craton, Michael, James Walvin and David Wright, eds. *Slavery, Abolition and Emancipation: Black Slaves and the British Empire.* London: Longman, 1976.
Dabydeen, David. *Hogarth's Blacks: Images of Blacks in Eighteenth Century English Art.* Athens: University of Georgia Press, 1987.
Davis, David Brion. *Inhuman Bondage: The Rise and Fall of Slavery in the New World.* Oxford: Oxford University Press, 2008.
———. *The Problem of Slavery in the Age of Revolution, 1770–1823.* New York; Oxford: Oxford University Press, 1999.

Davis, Leith. *Acts of Union: Scotland and the Literary Negotiation of the British Nation, 1707–1830*. Stanford, CA: Stanford University Press, 1998.
Davis, Jessica Milner. *Farce: The Critical Idiom*. London: Methuen & Co., 1978.
———. *Farce. With a new introduction by the author*. New Brunswick, NJ: Transaction Publishers, 2003.
Donoghue, Eddie. *Black Women / White Men: The Sexual Exploitation of Female Slaves in the Danish West Indies*. Trenton, NJ: Africa World Press, 2002.
DuCille, Ann. *The Coupling Convention: Sex, Text, and Tradition in Black Women's Fiction*. Oxford: Oxford University Press, 1993.
Earle, Ann Morse. *Two Centuries of Costume in America, MDCXX–MDCCCXX*. New York: Macmillan Company, 1903.
Eberle, Roxanne. "Amelia Opie's *Adeline Mowbray:* Diverting the Libertine Gaze; or The Vindication of Fallen Woman." *Studies in the Novel* 26, no. 2 (1994): 121–52.
———. "'Tales of Truth?': Amelia Opie's Antislavery Poetics." In *Romanticism and Women Poets: Opening the Doors of Reception*, ed. Harriet Kramer Linkin and Stephen C. Behrendt. Lexington: University Press of Kentucky, 1999. 71–98.
Ellis, Markman. *The Politics of Sensibility: Race Gender and Commerce in the Sentimental Novel*. Cambridge: Cambridge University Press, 1996.
Ferguson, Moira, ed. *The Hart Sisters: Early African Caribbean Writers, Evangelicals, and Radicals*. Lincoln and London: University of Nebraska Press, 1993.
———. "Mansfield Park: Slavery, Colonialism, and Gender." *Oxford Literary Review* 13 (1991): 118–39.
———. *Subject to Others: British Women Writers and Colonial Slavery, 1670–1834*. London; New York: Routledge, 1992.
Fiddes, Edward. "Lord Mansfield and the Sommersett Case." *Law Quarterly Review* 50 (1934): 499–511.
Flynn, Christopher. "Challenging Englishness from the Racial Margins: William Macready's *Irishman in London; or; The Happy African*." *Irish Studies Review* 16 (2008): 159–72.
Fryer, Peter. *Staying Power: The History of Black People in Britain*. Atlantic Highlands, NJ: Humanities Press, 1984.
Garside, Peter, James Raven, and Rainer Schowerling, eds. *The English Novel 1770–1829: A Bibliographical Survey of Prose Fiction Published in the British Isles*. Vol. 2, *1800–1829*. Oxford: Oxford University Press, 2000.
Garside, Peter, J. E. Belanger, and S. A. Ragaz. *British Fiction, 1800–1829: A Database of Production, Circulation, and Reception*, designer A. A. Mandal. http://www.britishfiction.cf.ac.uk.
Gaspar, David Barry. "Ameliorating Slavery. The Leeward Islands Slave Act of 1798." Chapter 13 in *The Lesser Antilles in the Age of European Expansion*, ed. Robert L. Paquette and Stanley L. Engerman. Gainesville: University Press of Florida, 1996.
Gaspar, David Barry, and Darlene Clark Hine, eds. *Beyond Bondage: Free Women of Color in the Americas*. Urbana: University of Illinois Press, 2004.
Gerzina, Gretchen. *Black London: Life before Emancipation*. New Brunswick, NJ: Rutgers University Press, 1995.
Gilman, Sander. "Black Bodies, White Bodies: Toward an Iconography of Female Sexuality in Late Nineteenth Century Art, Medicine and Literature." In *"Race," Writing, and Difference*, ed. Henry Louis Gates, Jr. Chicago: University of Chicago Press, 1986. 223–61.

Gordon, Shirley C. *God Almighty, Make Me Free: Christianity in Pre-Emancipation Jamaica*. Bloomington: Indiana University Press, 1996.
Green, Cecilia. "'A Civil Inconvenience'? The Vexed Question of Slave Marriage in the British West Indies." *Law and History Review* 25 (2007): 1–59.
Grenby, M. O. *The Anti-Jacobin Novel: British Conservatism and the French Revolution* Cambridge: Cambridge University Press, 2001.
Gunn, Fenja. *The Artificial Face: A History of Cosmetics*. Worcester and London: Trinity Press, 1973.
Gwilliam, Tassie. "Cosmetic Poetics: Coloring Faces in the Eighteenth Century." In *Body and Text in the Eighteenth Century*. Ed. Veronica Kelly and Dorothea E. von Mücke Stanford, CA: Stanford University Press, 1994. 144–62
Hall, Catherine. *Civilising Subjects: Colony and Metropole in the English Imagination*. Chicago: University of Chicago Press, 2002.
Hall, Douglas. *In Miserable Slavery: Thomas Thistlewood in Jamaica, 1750–86*. London: Macmillan, 1989.
Hall, Kim. "Reading What Isn't There: 'Black' Studies in Early Modern England." *Stanford Humanities Review* 3 (1993): 23–33.
———. *Things of Darkness: Economies of Race and Gender in Early Modern England*. Ithaca, NY: Cornell University Press, 1995.
Handler, Jerome S. *The Unappropriated People: Freedmen in the Slave Society of Barbados*. Baltimore: Johns Hopkins University Press, 1974.
Hart, Richard. *Slaves Who Abolished Slavery*. Kingston, Jamaica: Institute of Social and Economic Research, University of the West Indies, 1980.
Harth, Erica. "The Virtue of Love: Lord Hardwicke's Marriage Act." *Cultural Critique* 9 (1998): 123–54.
Hartman, Saidiya V. *Scenes of Subjection: Terror, Slavery, and Self-Making in Nineteenth-Century America*. Oxford and New York: Oxford University Press, 1997.
Harvey, Alison. "West Indian Obeah and English 'Obee': Race, Femininity, and Questions of Colonial Consolidation in Maria Edgeworth's *Belinda*." In *New Essays on Maria Edgeworth*, ed. Julie Nash. Burlington, VT: Ashgate, 2006. 1–30.
Hendricks, Margo, and Patricia Parker, eds. *Women, "Race," and Writing in the Early Modern Period*. London and New York: Routledge, 1994.
Henriques, Fernando. *Family and Colour in Jamaica*. Bristol, UK: Macgibbon and Kee, 1968.
Heuman, Gad. *Between Black and White: Race Politics and the Free Coloreds in Jamaica, 1792–1865*. Westport, CT: Greenwood Press, 1981.
Hill, Errol. *The Jamaican Stage 1655–1900: Profile of a Colonial Theatre*. Amherst: University of Massachusetts Press, 1992.
Holgersson-Shorter, Helena. "Illegible Bodies and Illegitimate Texts: Paradigms of Mulatta Literature." PhD diss., University of California, Berkeley, 2001.
Holland, Peter. *The Ornament of Action*. Cambridge: Cambridge University Press, 1979.
Hooper, W. Eden. *History of Newgate and the Old Bailey and a Survey of the Fleet and Other London Jails*. London: Underwood Press, 1935.
Howard, Carol. "'The Story of the Pineapple': Sentimental Abolitionism and Moral Motherhood in Amelia Opie's *Adeline Mowbray*." *Studies in the Novel* 30, no. 3 (1998): 355–76.
Howe, Elizabeth. *The First English Actresses*. Cambridge: Cambridge University Press, 1992.

Hughes, Leo. *A Century of English Farce.* Princeton, NJ: Princeton University Press, 1956.
Hume, Robert D. *The Rakish Stage: Studies in English Drama, 1660–1800.* Carbondale; Edwardsville: Southern Illinois University Press, 1983.
Imtiaz, Habib. "'Hel's Perfect Character'; or The Blackamoor Maid in Early Modern English Drama: The Postcolonial Cultural History of a Dramatic Type." *LIT: Literature Interpretation Theory* 11, no. 3 (2000): 277–304.
Iwanisziw, Susan B. "Behn's Novel Investment in Oroonoko: Kingship, Slavery and Tobacco in English Colonialism." *South Atlantic Review* 63, no. 2 (1998): 75–98.
Jagendorf, Zvi. *The Happy End of Comedy.* Newark: University of Delaware Press, 1984.
Jones, Vivien, ed. *Women and Literature in Britain, 1700–1800.* Cambridge: Cambridge University Press, 2000.
Jordan, Elaine. "Jane Austen Goes to the Seaside: *Sanditon,* English Identity and the 'West Indian' Schoolgirl." In *The Postcolonial Jane Austen,* ed. You-me Park and Rajeswari Sunder Rajan. London: Routledge, 2000. 29–55.
Kelly, Gary. "Discharging Debts: The Moral Economy of Amelia Opie's Fiction." *Wordsworth Circle* 11 (1980): 198–203.
Kim, Elizabeth S. "Maria Edgeworth's *The Grateful Negro*: A Site for Rewriting Rebellion." *Eighteenth Century Fiction* 16 (2003): 103–26.
Kirkpatrick, Kathryn. "'Gentlemen Have Horrors Upon This Subject': West Indian Suitors in Maria Edgeworth's *Belinda.*" *Eighteenth Century Fiction* 5 (1993): 331–48.
Kriz, Kay Dian. "Marketing Mulatresses in the Paintings and Prints of Agostino Brunias." In *The Global Eighteenth Century,* ed. Felicity Nussbaum. Baltimore: Johns Hopkins University Press, 2003. 195–210.
Land, Isaac. "Bread and Arsenic: Citizenship From the Bottom Up in Georgian London." *Journal of Social History* 39 (2005): 89–110.
Lemmings, David. "Marriage and the Law in the Eighteenth Century: Hardwicke's Marriage Act of 1753." *Historical Journal* 39 (1996): 339–60.
Leslie, Kent Anderson. *Woman of Color, Daughter of Privilege: Amanda America Dickson, 1849–1893.* Athens: University of Georgia Press, 1996.
Lew, Joseph. "'That Abominable Traffic': Mansfield Park and the Dynamics of Slavery." In *History, Gender & Eighteenth-Century Literature.* Athens: University of Georgia Press, 1994: 271–300.
Macdonald, Joyce Green. "The Disappearing African Woman: Imoinda in *Oroonoko* after Behn." *English Literary History* 66 (1999): 71–86.
———. "Race, Women and the Sentimental in Thomas Southerne's *Oroonoko.*" *Criticism* 40, no. 4 (1998): 555–70.
Macfarlane, Alan. *Marriage and Love in England: Modes of Reproduction, 1300–1840.* Oxford, UK; New York, USA: B. Blackwell, 1986.
Massing, Jean Michel. "From Greek Proverb to Soap Advert: Washing the Ethiopian." *Journal of the Warburg and Courtauld Institutes* 58 (1995): 180–201.
Matthews, Gelien. *Caribbean Slave Revolts and the British Abolitionist Movement.* Baton Rouge: Louisiana State University Press, 2006.
McBride, Dwight A. *Impossible Witnesses: Truth, Abolition and Slave Testimony.* New York: New York University Press, 2001.
McCann, Andrew. "Conjugal Love and the Enlightenment Subject: The Colonial Context of Non-Identity in Maria Edgeworth's *Belinda.*" *Novel: A Forum on Fiction* 30 (1996): 56–77.

Midgley, Clare. *Women Against Slavery: The British Campaigns, 1780–1870*. London and New York: Routledge, 1992.

Milhous, Judith, and Robert D. Hume. "Isaac Bickerstaff's Copyrights—And a Biographical Discovery." *Philological Quarterly* 83 (2004): 259–73.

Monteith, Kathleen E. A., and Glen Richards, eds. *Jamaica in Slavery and Freedom: History, Heritage and Culture*. Kingston, Jamaica: University of the West Indies Press, 2002.

Morrison, Toni. *Playing in the Dark: Whiteness and the Literary Imagination*. New York: Vintage, 1992.

Morrissey, Marietta. *Slave Women in the New World: Gender Stratification in the Caribbean*. Lawrence: University of Kansas Press, 1989.

Myers, Norma. *Reconstructing the Black Past: Blacks in Britain, 1780–1830*. London; Portland, OR: Frank Cass, 1996.

Nash, Julie. "Standing in Distress Between Tragedy and Comedy: Servants in Maria Edgeworth's Belinda." In *New Essays on Maria Edgeworth*, ed. Julie Nash. Burlington, VT: Ashgate, 2006. 161–74.

Nussbaum, Felicity. *Limits of the Human: Fictions of Anomaly, Race and Gender in the Long Eighteenth Century*. Cambridge: Cambridge University Press, 2003.

———. *Torrid Zones: Maternity, Sexuality, and Empire in 18th Century English Narratives*. Baltimore: Johns Hopkins University Press, 1995.

O'Gorman, Frank. *The Long Eighteenth Century: British Political and Social History 1688–1832*. London: Arnold Press, 1997.

O'Reilly, Andrea, and Silvia Caporale Bizzini, eds. *From the Personal to the Political: Toward a New Theory of Maternal Narrative*. Selinsgrove, PA: Susquehanna University Press, 2009.

Oldfield, J. R. *Popular Politics and British Anti-Slavery: The Mobilization of Public Opinion Against the Slave Trade, 1787–1807*. Manchester, UK; New York: St. Martin's Press, 1994.

———. "'The Ties Of soft Humanity': Slavery and Race in British Drama, 1760–1800." *Huntington Library Quarterly* 56 (1993): 1–14.

Oldham, James. *Mansfield Manuscripts and the Growth of English Law in the Eighteenth Century*. Chapel Hill: University of North Carolina Press, 1992.

———. "New Light on Mansfield and Slavery." *Journal of British Studies* 27 (1988): 45–68.

Ortiz, Joseph. "Arms and the Woman: Narrative, Imperialism and Virgilian *Memoria* in Aphra Behn's *Oroonoko*." *Studies in the Novel* 34 (2002): 121–40.

Outhwaite, R. B. *Clandestine Marriage in England, 1500–1800*. London and Rio Grande, OH: Hambledon Press, 1995.

Paton, Diana. *No Bond But the Law: Punishment, Race, and Gender in Jamaican State Formation, 1780–1870*. Durham, NC: Duke University Press, 2004.

Paton, Diana, and Pamela Scully, eds. *Gender and Slave Emancipation in the Atlantic World*. Durham, NC: Duke University Press, 2005.

Picker, John. "Shylock and the Struggle for Closure." *Judaism* 43, no. 2 (1994): 173–89.

Pratt, Mary Louise. *Imperial Eyes: Travel Writing and Transculturation*. London and New York: Routledge, 1992.

Ragussis, Michael. *Figures of Conversion: "The Jewish Question" & English National Identity*. Durham, NC, and London: Duke University Press, 1995.

Raimon, Eve Allegra. *The "Tragic Mulatta" Revisited: Race and Nationalism in Nineteenth-Century Antislavery Fiction*. Rutgers, NJ: Rutgers University Press, 2004.

Ramchand, Kenneth. *The West Indian Novel and Its Background*. 2nd ed. London; Kingston; Port of Spain, Jamaica: Heinemann, 1983.

Rich, Adrienne. *Of Woman Born*. New York: Norton, 1976.

Richardson, Alan. "Romantic Voodoo: Obeah and British Culture, 1797–1807." *Studies in Romanticism* 32 (1993): 3–28.

Roach, Joseph. *Cities of the Dead*. New York: Columbia University Press, 1996.

Russell, Gillian. "'Keeping Place': Servants, Theater and Sociability in Mid-Eighteenth-Century Britain." *Eighteenth Century Life* 22 (2001): 21–42.

Scarry, Elaine. *The Body in Pain*. New York: Oxford University Press, 1985.

Scott, Sarah. *The History of Sir George Ellison*. Lexington: University Press of Kentucky, 1996.

Seeber, Edward D. "*Oroonoko* in France in the Eighteenth Century." *PMLA* 51, no. 2 (1936): 953–59.

Sharpe, Jenny. *Allegories of Empire: The Figure of Woman in the Colonial Text*. Minneapolis and London: University of Minnesota Press, 1993.

———. *Ghosts of Slavery: A Literary Archaeology of Black Women's Lives*. Minneapolis and London: University of Minnesota Press, 2003.

Shepherd, T. B. *Methodism and the Literature of the Eighteenth Century*. New York: Haskell House, 1966.

Shepherd, Verene A., ed. *Women in Caribbean History*. Kingston, Jamaica: Ian Randle, 1999.

Shyllon, Folarin. *Black People in Britain, 1555–1833*. London; New York: Oxford University Press, 1977.

Sollors, Werner. *Neither Black Nor White Yet Both: Thematic Exploration of Interracial Literature*. Cambridge, MA: Harvard University Press, 1999.

Stallybrass, Peter, and Allon White. *The Politics and Poetics of Transgression*. Ithaca, NY: Cornell University Press, 1986.

Steinmetz, George. *The Devil's Handwriting: Precoloniality and the German Colonial State in Qingdao, Samoa, and Southwest Africa*. Chicago: University of Chicago Press, 2007.

Stone, Lawrence. *The Family, Sex and Marriage in England, 1500–1800*. New York; Hagerstown, MD; San Francisco and London: Harper & Row, 1977.

———. *Uncertain Unions: Marriage in England, 1600–1753*. Oxford: Oxford University Press, 1992.

Straub, Kristina. *Sexual Suspects*. Princeton, NJ: Princeton University Press, 1992.

Sussman, Charlotte. *Consuming Anxieties: Consumer Protest, Gender, and British Slavery, 1713–1833*. Stanford, CA: Stanford University Press, 2000.

Sutherland, Wendy-Lou Hilary. "Staging Blackness: Race, Aesthetics and the Black Female in Two Eighteenth-Century German Dramas: Ernst Lorenz Rathlef's 'Die Mohrinn zu Hamburg' (1775) and Karl Friedrich Wilhelm Ziegler's 'Die Mohrinn' (1801)." PhD diss., University of Pennsylvania, 2002.

Sypher, Wylie. *Guinea's Captive Kings: British Anti-Slavery Literature of the Eighteenth Century*. Chapel Hill: University of North Carolina Press, 1942.

———, ed. *Comedy*. Baltimore: Johns Hopkins University Press, 1956.

Thompson, L. F. *Kotzebue: A Survey of his Progress in France, & England, Preceded by a Consideration of the Critical Attitude to him in Germany*. Paris: Librarie Ancienne Honoré Champion, 1928.

Tilley, M. P. *A Dictionary of the Proverbs in England in the Sixteenth and Seventeenth Centuries*. Ann Arbor: University of Michigan Press, 1950.

Tobin, Beth Fowkes. *Picturing Imperial Power: Colonial Subjects in Eighteenth-Century British Painting*. Durham, NC, and London: Duke University Press, 1999.

Todd, Janet. *Sensibility: An Introduction*. London: Methuen, 1986.

Trumbach, Randolph, ed. *The Marriage Act of 1753: Four Tracts*. New York: Garland Publishing, 1984.

Ty, Eleanor. *Empowering The Feminine: The Narratives of Mary Robinson, Jane West, and Amelia Opie, 1796-1812*. Toronto: University of Toronto Press, 1998.

Vaughan, Virginia Mason. *Performing Blackness on English Stages, 1500–1800*. Cambridge: Cambridge University Press, 2005.

Ward, J. R. *British West Indian Slavery, 1750–1834: The Process of Amelioration*. Oxford: Clarendon Press, 1988.

Watson, Tim. *Caribbean Culture and British Fiction in the Atlantic World, 1780–1870*. Cambridge: Cambridge University Press, 2008.

Wheeler, Roxann. *The Complexion of Race: Categories of Difference in Eighteenth-Century British Culture*. Philadelphia: University of Pennsylvania Press, 2000.

Wiecek, William M. "*Somerset:* Lord Mansfield and the Legitimacy of Slavery in the Anglo-American World." *University of Chicago Law Review* 42 (1974): 86–146.

Wilson, Kathleen. *The Island Race: Englishness, Empire and Gender in the Eighteenth Century*. London and New York: Routledge, 2003.

Woodard, Helena. *African-British Writings in the Eighteenth Century: The Politics of Race and Reason*. Westport, CT: Greenwood Press, 1999.

Wright, Richardson. *Revels in Jamaica 1682–1838*. New York: Dodd, Mead, 1937.

Young, Robert J. C. *Colonial Desire: Hybridity in Theory, Culture, and Race*. London and New York: Routledge, 1995.

Zackodnik, Teresa C. *The Mulatta and the Politics of Race*. Jackson: University Press of Mississippi, 2004.

INDEX

abolition, 19, 24, 68, 125, 141, 143, 157, 182, 185, 186, 187, 193, 221, 223, 228, 240, 243, 248, 259, 263, 265; and Behn, 110; and paternalism, 231–37; bill (1807), 23, 73, 236–38, 241–42, 255; heinous act of, 240; in Denmark 112, 125; in England 263; of blackness 240, 258, 263 (*see also* epidermal conversion); of marriage 186, 189, 193, 205, 213, 221, 222, 263; of pain, 182–83, 184, 188 (*see also* relief); perverse act of, 241; of poverty, 193, 197, 204, 219; of prejudice 193, 197, 204, 219, 258; of slave trade, 22, 36, 76, 106, 113, 116, 266; of slavery, 214, 221, 241, 247, 266

abolitionist (*see also* antislavery), 22, 27, 30, 67, 71, 83, 106, 112, 125, 140, 147, 186, 202, 215, 221, 236–38, 243, 263, 264; Behn as first literary, 131, 266; discourse, 8, 188, 193, 205, 219; history 197, 227–28, 237, 247; marriage plot, 227; movement, 24, 237; paraphernalia, 116; politics, 187, 216, 220; positions, 22, 188, 263

Act of Union, 1, 4–6; and Imoinda, 5–6
Adichie, Chimamanda Ngozi, 256–58
Adventures of Jonathan Corncob, 238–39, 246
African: beauty, 1, 2, 3, 28, 52, 54, 88, 92, 108, 110, 121–22, 170, 190, 223, 244; bride, 126, 214; common, 71, 105–6, 113, 116, 120–26, 130–31, 138, 140, 146, 182, 196, 250; contrasted with black Creole, 62; contrasted with Europeans, 27–28, 64; couple, 64, 130; coupling, 71, 75, 94, 101; de-Africanized, 58, 59, 62, 86; descent, 17, 23, 136, 140, 186, 194, 201, 203, 219, 221, 228, 258, 259, 263, 264, 265, 266; fictional, 2, 3, 6, 7, 15–16, 17, 18, 19, 21, 22, 23, 24, 29–30, 31, 69, 71, 74, 103 106, 107, 111, 130, 137, 140, 147, 188, 189, 192, 228, 261, 262, 263, 264, 265, 267; freedom, 23, 74, 188; girl, 28, 70, 76; happy, 178–81, 183–84; hate, 132–35; hero, 15, 92; heroine, 1, 8, 18, 20, 23, 30, 56, 57, 88, 89, 91, 92, 99, 101, 104, 105, 106, 111, 120, 121, 124, 125, 126, 146, 188, 261, 262, 263, 265, 266; immigration, 106, 125, 126, 138, 146, 188, 214, 263; Imoinda, 14–16, 17, 19, 31, 47–54, 56, 57, 58, 68, 105, 106, 262, 263; in England, 159, 172, 188, 215; ladies 2, 28–29; man, 64, 111, 133, 188; marriage, 58, 67, 69, 109–11; marital virtue, 27–28, 94; men, 20, 40, 61, 130; mother, 132; pain in farce, 152–54, 168–69, 171, 172–73;

paternalist, 60; primitivism, 92, 264; princes, 40, 59; rebel-wife, 110, 111, 123, 124, 125, 138, 140, 188, 267; relief of pain, 173, 178–84; romance, 75, 92–96, 99 105, 125, 189, 263; saint-mother, 111, 138, 140, 188, 267; suicide, 37, 38, 90, 96, 103 108; tale, 130–35, 136; temperament, 65; in *The West Indian,* 158–59; and whiteness, 19, 56, 65; widow, 106, 126, 228, 253–54, 258; wives, 28; wife, 28, 103, 106, 125, 143; woman, 2, 6, 7, 8, 15, 16–17, 18, 19, 21, 22, 23, 24, 28, 29, 30, 31, 46, 52, 54, 56, 57, 61, 68, 69, 70, 74, 75, 76, 85, 97, 98, 99, 101, 102, 104, 105, 110, 111, 119, 120, 121, 122, 123, 124, 132, 147, 172, 173, 175, 184, 188, 194, 228, 232, 262, 263, 264, 265, 266, 267; women, 2, 7, 8, 15, 16, 17, 18, 19, 20, 22, 23, 28–29, 30, 36, 66, 69, 70, 71, 73, 75, 76, 77, 79, 81, 83, 84, 85, 86, 87, 89, 91, 93, 94, 95, 97, 99, 100, 101, 102, 103, 104, 106, 107–8, 120, 121, 122, 124, 132, 137, 140, 188, 189, 192, 194, 232, 263, 264, 267; women in British poetry, literature, and history, 19, 27–30

Africanism, 18, 19, 21
Africanist, 18, 29
African-ness, 19–20, 28, 47–48, 52, 55, 57–58, 65, 68, 92, 99, 101, 121 148, 155, 179, 181, 264
amelioration, 23, 68, 70, 74, 75, 83–85, 95, 97, 100, 102, 103, 105, 106, 111, 112, 122, 137, 140, 179, 253, 259, 262, 263, 265; Act (1798), 75, 83–84, 93–94, 95–96, 100, 101, 118; in anonymous *Oroonoko,* 67–68; in *The Grateful Negro,* 76, 83, 84–85, 92–96; proslavery reformism, 76, 83
Anderson, Misty, 33–34
Anim-Addo, Joan, 261–62, 267
Anstey, Roger, 237
antislavery, 19, 25, 30, 31, 46, 63, 67, 106, 113, 115, 126, 138–39, 140, 265; agenda, 31, 74, 107; British Antislavery Society, 18; discourse, 8, 124, 125, 263; drama 69, 113–19, 126; intervention, 31, 126; literature, 107, 112, 131, 146, 264, 265; messages, 18, 22, 59, 67, 69, 125; movement, 21, 22, 24, 106, 140; poetry, 19, 22; positions, 22, 77, 83, 188, 263, 265; propaganda, 112; stance, 22, 105, 119, 131; thought, 18, 112
Aravamudan, Srinivas, 10, 14–16, 57, 64, 76, 83, 100, 109, 118, 127, 128, 130, 225, 229, 243, 244, 245
Arbuckle, James, 11–12
Astell, Mary, 20, 193, 231
Austen, Jane, 227; *Mansfield Park,* 227, 242–47

Baartman, Saartjie, 248
Bannet, Eve Tavor, 33
Barbauld, Anna Letitia, 70–74, 102
Barker, Jane, 52; *Exilius,* 52, 54
Barry, Elizabeth, 3
Bartels, Emily, 21
Beckles, Hilary, 84, 103, 120, 124
Behn, Aphra, 69, 105, 107, 112, 130, 131–32, 258, 261–62, 266, 267; (works) *Adventure of the Black Lady, The,* 105, 189–92, 204, 205, 210, 238; *Oroonoko,* 1, 2, 4, 6–10, 14–17, 20–21, 22, 23, 30, 45, 56, 57, 76, 85–87, 89, 92, 104–5, 108–11, 123, 130, 132, 139, 189, 223, 251, 258, 261, 262, 266; (characters) Imoinda, 8, 10, 14–17, 20, 23, 46, 56, 86–87, 88–89, 92, 102–3, 104–6, 108–11, 121–23, 129, 130, 188–89, 225, 259, 261, 262; Oroonoko, 15, 86–87, 89, 102–3, 130, 251
Bellamy, Thomas, 52, 53, 120, 179
Bergson, Henri, 147
Bhide, Monica, 224–25, 255–58
Bickerstaff, Isaac, 22, 111, 143, 146, 150, 152, 159, 164–65, 168, 169, 172; (works) *Love in the City,* 22, 146, 148, 150, 155, 160, 164–67, 168, 171, 172, 174; *Padlock, The,* 143, 152, 159; (characters) Priscilla, 146, 164–69, 171, 172, 180; Quasheba, 168–69, 172–73, 180–81, 195 (Edward Long's), 267

Index

black: British, 20; cat, 190–91; complexion, 2, 186, 193, 198, 199, 217, 220–21, 247, 255; Creole, 20, 62, 89, 92, 133, 180, 264; heroine, 14, 56, 88, 105, 121, 225, 251, 263; Imoinda, 1–2, 3, 5, 9, 10, 17, 45, 69, 105; lady, 2, 189, 190–92, 204–5, 260, 264; magic, 192; market, 192; pain, 159–60, 168–69, 171, 178–79; poor, 71, 79–80, 196–97, 202–3, 216–21, 240–41, 263; power, 192; shade, 185; widow, 254; woman, 7, 9, 19, 23, 28, 46, 56, 89, 97, 98, 104, 112, 122, 124, 131, 132, 169, 173, 184, 190, 193, 204, 225, 232, 234, 238, 243, 248, 253; women's concerns, 17, 23, 102, 140

blackamoor, 141, 165, 168, 223, 225–27, 228–35; trope of washing the, 238, 240–41, 245, 251, 257

blackness (*also see* abolition), 28, 124, 170, 190, 193, 206, 221, 226, 228, 234, 241, 242, 247, 255–57; African, 19–20, 27; and white women, 190–92, 205–6, 210–11, 232–33, 243–47; as a trope, 192, 193; Cubba's, 183; Dido's, 227, 254–55; metaphorical, 194; Olivia's, 227–28, 238, 240, 250, 251, 254–55; Oroonoko's, 47, 56, 58; Philippa's, 234; reading 155; Savanna's, 194, 197, 205, 206, 216

Blackstone, William, 31, 185, 197, 213; *Commentaries*, 197–99, 201, 204, 213, 222

Boesky, Amy, 234
Boose, Lynda, 7, 17, 56, 232–34
Bouloukos, George, 76
Bracegirdle, Anne, 3
Burnard, Trevor, 84, 165
Burton, Richard, 133
Burney, Frances, 227; (works) *Cecilia*, 253; *Wanderer, The*, 227, 242–47

Carretta, Vincent, 264
Categories of Difference, 28, 55–56, 57, 58, 65, 68, 69, 120–21, 147–48, 152
Catholic emancipation, 176

Charney, Maurice, 148
Chatterton, Henry, 19
Clarkson Thomas, 135–37, 152, 236–37
Coleridge, Samuel Taylor, 236, 237
Colley, Linda, 5
Committee for the Relief of the Black Poor, 196, 197, 216, 240–41
complexion, 2, 3, 7, 59, 92, 185, 186, 197, 198, 199, 200, 204, 206–7, 209, 210, 211, 218, 220, 221, 223, 224, 229, 239, 243, 244, 245, 246; African, 52, 59, 87–88 (Eboe), 92; Angelina's, 251–52; black, 2, 52, 186, 193, 198, 199, 217, 220, 221, 247, 255; English rose, 208, 213, 218, 222; Imoinda's, 2, 7, 8, 58; in *Adeline Mowbray* (male), 206–7, 208–9, 210; in *Adeline Mowbray* (female), 207–8, 210–11; in *Oroonoko*, 59; Monica Bhide's, 256; mulatto, 193–94, 197, 206, 213, 225, 249–50; Olivia's, 223, 228, 249, 251, 259; rouged, 208, 210–13; Savanna's, 185, 186, 193, 194, 203, 205, 206, 213, 218, 222; sunburn, 3, 207–10; unchanging, 243; white, 2, 3, 29, 55, 57, 121, 231, 242

Congreve, William, 63–64
Coramantien (*see also* Koromantyn), 85, 86, 87, 88, 90, 92, 109, 130
Corbett, Mary Jean, 147
coupling, 21, 96; African, 94, 98, 100–101; interracial, 70–75, 81–83, 98, 99, 100, 101, 263; slave, 36–38; unnatural, 29
Cowper, William, 214
Cox, Jeffrey, 128
creative defamation, 75, 91–92, 101–2, 105, 115
creative reformation, 115, 116, 118, 119, 120, 122, 130; in *The Negro Slaves*, 115–19, 119–26; in *Obi; or, The History of Three Fingered Jack*, 130–38; of *Oroonoko*, 119
Creole (*see also* black, white), 62, 65, 66, 68, 91, 101, 119, 143, 144, 145, 159, 162, 164, 165, 167, 169, 171, 174, 175; and violence, 165–66; assimilated, 146, 158, 160; body in

pain, 146, 157–58, 161–63, 164–66; hatred of, 133–35; hero/heroism, 101, 144, 159; homecoming plot, 155–60, 162–63, 164, 171, 174; in England, 146, 155–60; (Belcour), 160–63; (Lovel), 164–67; (Priscilla), 169, 174, 181; intemperance, 62–64, 65, 166, 168–69; ladies, 167; marriage plot, 67; part in building British Empire, 144–45; paternalists, 68, 101, 132, 238–40, 241, 245; realism, 75–76, 101; stage, 145, 146, 155, 159, 167, 171 174, 182; template, 167, 174; tyrants/tyranny, 64, 68, 111, 119, 132, 139, 144, 145, 168, 180, 181 238–89; unchanged, 169, 171; woman, 167–68, 220
Cruikshank, Isaac, 232–33
Cumberland, Richard, 76, 143, 146, 155, 158–60; (works) *The West Indian*, 76, 143, 146, 155, 158–60, 162, 166, 167; *The Jew*, 159–60; (characters) Belcour, 143, 155, 157–60, 165, 166, 179, 180; black servants, 158–59; Louisa, 158; Stockwell, 157–58

Dabydeen, David, 155
Davis, Jessica Milner, 147
Davis, Leith, 6
Day, Thomas, 71, 203; (works) *Dying Negro, The*, 71, 72, 79, 152, 214; *Sandford and Merton*, 78–81, 84
Defoe, Daniel, 6
Doody, Margaret, 243
DuCille, Ann, 21, 235
Dunton, John, 2, 28, 29, 57
Duras, Claire de, 118
dynamic reciprocity, 80–84, 99

Earle, William, 22, 103, 106–68, 126–28, 129–39, 166, 263, 264, 265; (works) *Natural Faults*, 127–28, 130; *Obi; or, the History of Three Fingered Jack*, 100, 103, 106–7, 126–38, 139, 140, 188, 263, 264, 265; *Obi; or, the History of Three Fingered Jack* plot, 130–31; (characters) Amri, 106, 126, 129, 130–38, 188, 189, 263, 267; George Stanford, 133–39; Jack, 102, 127–39
Eberle, Roxanne, 187, 210, 214
Eboe (Igbo), 87–91, 92, 94, 100
Edgeworth, Maria, 22, 70–77, 81, 82, 87, 94, 96, 98, 100, 101, 102, 105, 115, 124, 168, 194, 203; (works) *Belinda*, 71–74, 75, 76, 79, 91, 102, 125, 128, 188, 194, 214, 242; *Grateful Negro, The*, 22, 70, 71, 74–77, 81–83, 84–91, 92, 94–96, 98–100; (footnotes) 101, 102, 105, 106, 110, 112, 113, 115, 118, 119, 126, 128, 135, 137, 168; *Harrington*, 91; letter to Barbauld, 70–74; (characters) Caesar, 75, 81–82, 83, 86, 87, 88, 92–95, 100–101, 102; Clara, 75, 81, 82, 84, 86–91, 92–95, 97, 99, 100, 101, 102; Durant, 81, 95; Esther, 75, 84, 95, 99–101, 102; Hector, 81, 82–83, 98, 99, 100; Hector's wife, 75, 84, 98–99, 101, 102; Mr. Edwards, 75, 81–82, 83, 92–96, 102–3; Mr. Jeffries, 81, 82, 95, 99, 203; Mrs. Jeffries, 75, 84, 98, 99, 100
Edwards, Bryan, 75, 76, 87, 88–89, 90, 94, 96–97, 98, 99, 100, (work) *History*, 75, 76, 87–91, 96–97, 98, 100, 112, 195
Elizabeth I, 4
Ellis, Markman, 68
epidermal conversion (*see also* abolition): definition of, 241; discrediting, 247–55; observing, 242–47; perverse acts of, 246, 249, 252
Equiano, Olaudah, 70, 71, 72, 74, 75, 76, 88, 89, 107, 264

farce, 144, 146; definitions of, 147–48; reading and seeing, 148, 152
father, 10, 39, 63, 167, 190, 231, 234, 239, 246, 255; Edgeworth's, 70, 72–74, 76, 79, 81, 188, 194; English, 34, 39, 136; Imoinda's, 55–56, 57–58, 61, 65, 87, 108–9; in *Adeline Mowbray*, 207, 216 (stepfather), 219;

Index

in *Irishman in London,* 174; in *The Negro Slaves,* 119; in *Obi; or, the History of Three Fingered Jack,* 130, 131, 139, 138; in *West Indian, The,* 157, 158; in *Woman of Colour, The,* 159, 228, 235, 237–38, 240–41, 245–46, 252, 253–54, 258, 263; Oroonoko's, 60, 63; Oroonoko as a, 110; Wedderburn's, 98
Fawcett, John, 99–100, 128–29
Ferguson, Margaret, 15, 189, 192
Ferriar, John, 113
Flynn, Christopher, 175, 176, 178, 179
Fothergill, John, 165, 167, 168
Fryer, Peter, 72, 145, 171–72, 214, 228, 236

Garrick, David, 143
Gaspar, David Barry, 84, 93
Gentleman, Francis, 22, 30; (work) *Oroonoko,* 30, 41, 43, 45, 57, 61–63; (seeing/reading), 64, 66, 68, 139; (characters) Deputy Governor, 62–63; Massingano, 41, 61–62; Zinzo, 41, 61
Gentleman's Magazine, 40, 59
Gerzina, Gretchen, 172, 198, 214, 217
Godwin, William, 187, 229–31
Grateful Negro, The (Anon.), 75, 77–78, 79–81; analysis of, 84, 203
Green, Cecilia, 21, 36–37, 137, 145, 146
Greenfield, Susan, 71, 187, 205
Grenby, M. O., 186–87, 207
gynecological rebellion, 15, 106, 138, 188, 263

Hall, Catherine, 29, 37, 144–45
Hall, Kim, 7, 17
Hardwicke, Lord (Philip Yorke), 38
Hardwicke Marriage Act, 30–31, 32–35, 37, 60–61, 66; Eighteenth Clause, 35–36, 38
Harth, Erica, 34, 35
Hartley, Elizabeth, 47, 51, 52–54
Harvey, Allison, 72
Hawkesworth, John, 22, 30, 41–42, 45, 57–61, 62, 63, 64, 66, 68, 139, 143, 144; (work) *Oroonoko,* 30, 41–42, 45, 57–59; (reading it), 59–61 (seeing it), 63, 64, 66, 68, 139 143, 144; (characters) Imoinda, 58–59, 61; the King, 60; Stanmore, 60
Hogarth, William, 155–56, 190–91
Holland, Peter, 41, 45, 148
homecoming, 143, 144, 145, 147, 158, 160, 163, 164, 167, 171, 174, 182; creole, 155–60; politics of, 145, 155–67, 182, 199
Howard, Carol, 187, 196, 201, 216, 218
Howe, Elizabeth, 3
Hugo Victor, 118

Imoinda: African, 14–16, 19, 68–69; and Ada, 120–24, 189; and Africanism, 21; and Amri, 137–38, 189; and Bellamora, 189, 192; and Charlotte Welldon, 57, 63–64; and Clara, 86–91, 189; and Cubba, 147, 184, 189; and her father, 54–56, 57–58, 61, 65, 108–9; and love, 9–17; and Maria, 65–67; and marriage, 21, 64, 109; and Olivia, 228, 250–59; and pregnancy, 60, 104, 108, 109–10, 124; and rebellion, 89, 108–9; and religion, 55, 57–58, 110; and Savanna, 189, 194; as Clemene, 88–89, 90, 91, 109; as rebel-wife, 108–9; as saint-mother, 109–11; black, 1, 2, 3, 5, 8, 16, 17, 105; complexion of, 59; confronting tyranny, 106, 108, 110, 189; considered dialogically, 5–6; difference from other fictional African women, 19–20; Dunton's use of, 1–2; English, 13, 54, 56; eyes of, 1–4, 16; Heroick, 103, 104, 108, 123; in English literature and society, 4, 7, 8, 13–14, 22; in paradox, 1–2, 3–4, 6, 16, 17, 19; in satire, 1, 3–4, 6, 16, 17, 19; Indian, 9–10; Irish, 10–12; Italian, 12; name, 6, 8, 14, 105; non-black non-African, 9–13, 14, 15, 16, 19; performing, 25, 47–54; politicized representations of,

5–7; reputation of, 105; sigh, 110; white, 3, 5, 8, 10, 16, 17, 19, 121; as white Christian, 58; and whiteness, 54–55, 57

Imoinda; or, She Who Will Lose Her Name, 260–62, 267

Imoinda's Shade, 7, 16, 17–18, 22, 23–24, 188, 189, 262, 263, 264, 265

Imoinda's shade, 8–9, 16–17, 18, 22–24, 25, 69, 105, 107, 111, 122, 124, 138, 140, 141, 147, 185, 188, 192, 194, 221, 258, 259, 265, 266, 267

Imoindaism, 14–16, 261–62

interracial (*see also* mulatto), 76, 88, 183, 188, 194, 195; couple, 59, 116, 194, 203, 204; coupling, 70–75, 80–82, 84, 98–101, 137, 184, 194–95, 196; desire, 15, 183; family, 203; love, 70; marriage, 70–74, 181–84, 188, 194, 197, 240, 247, 265, 266; play, 56, 59; relationship, 59, 71, 113, 147, 188, 196; sex, 173

Jamaica, 27, 29, 36, 37, 81–84, 86, 88, 90–92, 99–103, 106, 115–16, 118–20, 122, 124–27, 129–33, 135, 139, 140, 144, 145, 158, 159, 160, 165, 170, 171, 174, 180, 181, 195, 203, 214, 218, 219, 220, 224, 225, 226, 235, 248, 253, 259, 263, 265

James I/VI, 4

James II, 6, 131

Jew, 28, 34, 89, 91, 146, 159, 240–41, 256

John Buncle, 10–11

Johnson, Joseph, 182

Johnson, Samuel, 148, 165, 177

Jonson, Ben, 244; *Masque of Beauty, The*, 246

Kelly, Gary, 187

Kemble, Sarah, 47, 48, 52–53

Kirkpatrick, Kathryn, 71, 76

Kleist, Heinrich von, 118

Koromantyn (*see also* Coramantien), 82, 85, 86, 87, 90–91, 92, 100, 130

Kotzebue, August von, 22, 27–28, 29–30, 57, 69, 75, 85–86, 96–98, 99, 101, 106, 107, 108, 111–26, 138, 188, 214, 263, 264; (works) *East Indian, The*, 111; *Lover's Vows*, 111; *Negro Slaves, The*, 22, 27, 29, 69, 75, 85–86, 96, 97, 98, 101, 103, 106–7, 111–26, 138–39, 140, 146, 188, 214, 263, 264, 266; (characters) Ada, 27, 30, 92, 93, 97, 102, 106, 119, 120–25; (as a creatively reformed Imoinda), 138–39, 188, 189, 263, 267; Lilli, 97, 102, 119, 121; "Negro Woman," 97, 102; wild girl, 97, 102, 123; Zameo, 27, 119, 122, 123, 124–25, 138

Land, Isaac, 147, 182–83, 196, 216–17, 219, 240–41

Lemmings, David, 31, 33, 34, 39

Lew, Joseph, 243

Litchfield, Harriet, 47, 49, 52, 54

Lofft, Capel, 8–9, 69

Long, Edward, 29, 62, 86, 92, 122, 133, 144, 152, 166, 167, 195, 196, 202, 206

Lounger, The, 12

love: and Imoinda, 8–14, 15–17; and *Imoinda: or, She Who Will Lose Her Name*, 262; and property, 34; connubial, 8, 16, 21; of freedom, 16, 17, 23, 266; idealized, 14; in *Adeline Mowbray*, 187; in *Grateful Negro, The*, 94; in *High Life Below Stairs*, 161–62, 173; in *Irishman in London*, 174, 183; in *Love in the City*, 164, 166, 172; *Negro Slaves, The*, 115, 121–22; in *Obi; or, the History of Three Fingered Jack*, 133

MacClaren, Archibald: *The Negro Slaves*, 120, 126, 214

Macdonald, Joyce Green, 17, 46, 54, 56

Macready, William, 22, 146, 151, 173–74, 175, 176, 177, 178, 179, 181, 182, 183, 184, 263, 264; (work)

Irishman in London; or, The Happy African, 22, 146, 147, 148, 151, 155, 173, 177, 178, 184, 188, 215, 263, 264, 266; (characters) Cubba, 140, 143, 147, 174, 175, 178–84, 188–89, 215, 228, 263, 264, 267; Murtoch Delany, 174–84, 188–89, 263; Colloony, 174–80, 183–84
Mandeville, Bernard, 201
Manly, Susan, 91
Mansfield Judgment, 22, 39, 160, 181, 198–99, 200, 213–15, 217, 219–22, 243, 247, 266
marriage, 18, 19–22; acts in British West Indian colonies, 36; and the African, 29, 58, 67, 69, 109–11; and antislavery, 19, 20–21; and slavery, 30–31, 37–38, 39; and suicide, 37, 39; arranged, 235; bigamous, 219–20, 227, 258; clandestine, 31–33, 60; Christian, 36, 37, 95, 96, 99, 172; eighteenth clause of Hardwicke's Act, 31, 34–36, 38; forced, 240; formal, 36, 95, 99; Hardwicke Act (1753), 30–31, 32–36, 38–39, 60–61, 66, 69, 74, 96, 118; informal, 36; in *Grateful Negro, The*, 92–96; in *Love in the City*, 166–67, 171; in *West Indian, The*, 158, 159; plot, 8, 16, 17, 21, 22, 23, 29, 30, 31, 59, 67, 125, 126, 147, 172, 173, 188, 227, 235, 262, 263, 267
Mary of Modena, 6
Massing, Jean Michel, 231–32
Matthews, Gelien, 106
McClure, Glenn, 260, 262
Mirror, The, 14
Mohammed, Patricia, 226
Monimia, 14
Monmouth Rebellion (1685), 82
More, Hannah, 19
Moreton, J. B., 167–68, 195–96, 203, 206
Morrison, Toni, 17–18, 29–30, 229
Morrissey, Marrietta, 98
mulatto (*see also* complexion), 120, 186, 187, 195–96, 203, 223, 225–27, 238–40, 263; heiress, 223, 225–28, 235, 248–51, 257, 263, 267; heroine, 225, 248; metaphorical, 205–6, 210–15; Savanna, 186–89, 193, 194, 197, 203, 205–6, 215, 219–21, 222; women, 219–21
Murphy, Sharon, 75, 85
Myers, Norma, 172

Nabob, 207, 208, 209, 211, 216, 249
nanny, 101, 132
Nash, Julie, 91
Neville, Henry: *Isle of Pines, The*, 19, 234
Nussbaum, Felicity, 17, 31, 46–47, 52, 54, 73, 217, 264

Obeah, 72, 73, 82–83, 89, 94, 99–100, 128, 138
O'Gorman, Frank, 4
Oldfield, J. R., 45
Opie, Amelia, 18, 22, 185–86, 189, 192–94, 196–216, 218–19, 221–22, 254, 263, 265; (works) *Adeline Mowbray*, 22, 184, 185, 186–87, 189, 192–94, 196, 197, 200, 205, 206, 208, 210, 214, 219, 221, 222, 263, 266; "Negro Boy's Tale, The," 214–15; (characters) Adeline, 185–86, 193–94, 201, 203, 204–6, 210–13, 215, 216–19; Berrendale, 194, 212, 216, 219–21; Langley, 202, 207–8, 210–13, 220; Mary Warner, 208, 210–13, 216, 220–21; Savanna, 186, 187–88, 189, 192, 193–94, 196, 197, 200–206, 213, 215, 216–19, 219–21, 222; showy woman, 207–8, 210–11; William, 186, 188, 194, 196, 197, 199, 200, 201, 202, 203, 204, 217, 218; Zambo, 214–15
Oroonoko: adaptations of, 30–31, 39, 40–45, 111; Anonymous (1760), 30, 41, 44–45, 57, 63–67, 69; (reading it), 65, 67; (two kinds of white femininity), 65–66; (marriage in), 105, 106, 112, 113, 118, 119, 126, 139; as interracial play, 46, 54–57, 59; as intratribal play, 56, 59; bow

and arrow in, 47, 54, 55, 56, 58, 65, 89, 92, 104, 108–9, 111, 123, 228; Deputy Governor in, 54, 56, 59, 62 65–67, 89, 92, 108–11, 122, 132, 189, 228; frontispieces, 46–54; heathenism in, 61; legend, 20, 23, 69, 92, 113, 120–21, 263, 266; Mrs. Griffiths editions of, 85–86; reading, 41, 45–46, 54–56, 57, 63–69; seeing, 41, 45–54, 56, 57, 101–2

Othello, 71, 72, 190

Otway, Thomas, 14

Outhwaite, R. B., 32, 34

Paine Thomas, 107, 127, 135–37

paternal: bias, 34, 39, 60; power, 34, 38; tyranny, 31, 39, 40, 45, 57, 59, 63, 65, 66, 67, 68–69, 70, 74, 76, 98, 99, 102, 103, 106, 112, 122, 137, 180, 200, 201–4, 208–9, 215, 219, 263

paternalism, 23, 60, 74, 102, 111, 122; and abolition, 231–37; and *Adeline Mowbray*, 199–204, 219–21; and *Adventure of the Black Lady, The*, 189–92; and Imoinda, 20, 106, 108, 110, 189, 228; and *Oroonoko*, 60–61, 62–63, 65–67; and *Woman of Colour, The*, 228, 236–41, 255, 258; benevolent, 74–76, 101–2, 124; colonial, 31, 75, 140

Phibba, 101, 103, 121

Pratt, Samuel Jackson, 242, 243

prejudice, 59, 91, 194–97, 202, 202–6, 219, 225, 235, 238, 250–51, 254–59

Quaker, 18, 34, 116, 137, 187, 208, 221, 222

Ragussis, Michael, 239–41

rape, 15, 76, 102, 120, 207, 239, 241, 266; and *Adeline Mowbray*, 207, 212; and *Negro Slaves, The*, 97–101, 122–23; and *Oroonoko*, 62, 76, 102; on the plantation, 70, 76, 96–98

Reeve, Clara, 72–73

relief (see also Creole): abolitionist, 184; Catholic Relief Act (1793), 174, 178; comic, 175, 181–82; complete, 147, 178, 183, 263; from pain, 146–47, 158, 175, 178, 179, 263; of African pain, 146–47, 169, 171, 172–74, 178–84, 263; of Catholic poor, 176–77, 178; of Irish pain, 175, 177; of white Creole pain, 146, 158, 163, 166–67

reproduction, 166; and Adrienne Rich, 110; and African woman, 85, 95, 122, 132, 234–35, 239, 254, 262; and Amri, 131–36; and Imoinda, 110, 121–22; and Samuel Johnson, 177; by natural increase, 36, 84; in *Grateful Negro, The*, 85; in *Obi; or, Three Finger'd Jack* (pantomime), 129; in *Woman of Colour, The*, 232–35, 238–41, 246, 249, 254; interracial, 74, 81, 84, 94, 99; of hate in *Obi; or, the History of Three Fingered Jack*, 132–37; of prejudice, 91

Restoration, 3, 7, 16, 19, 41, 57, 104, 258

revolution: Glorious, 6, 20, 32, 82, 131; American, 22, 196; French, 22, 107, 135, 136, 216; Haitian, 22, 118, 135–36; working class, 137

Robinson, Mary, 19

Roscoe, William, 116–18

Scott, Sarah, 73, 168, 203; *Sir George Ellison*, 59

Shadwell, Thomas, 147

Shakespeare, William, 129, 160, 190

Sharp, Granville, 160

Sharpe, Jenny, 18, 101, 132

Shyllon, Folarin, 172, 214

Sierra Leone Colonial Experiment, 22, 71, 80–81, 196–97, 217, 240, 266

Smith, Adam, 164

Smith, Sarah, 47, 51, 52, 54

Somerset, James, 160, 199, 213–14, 217

Southerne, Thomas, 15, 20–21, 41, 45–46, 69, 107, 112, 117; (works) *Isabella, or The Fatal Marriage*, 144;

Oroonoko, 2, 4, 7–9, 11–12, 13, 15, 16, 20–22, 23, 30–31, 39–40 (in the 1740s and 50s), 45–57, 58, 59, 63, 64, 65, 68, 69, 70, 76, 102, 112, 113, 120–21, 123, 143, 223, 258, 262, 264, 266; (characters) Charlotte, 30, 57, 58, 64; Imoinda, 3, 8, 10, 16, 17, 20, 23, 31, 46, 55–8, 65, 67–69, 88, 111, 121–22, 259, 262; Lucy, 30, 58; Oroonoko, 40

Stallybrass, Peter and Allon White, 248, 250

Stedman, John Gabriel, 152–54

street citizenship, 147, 182–83, 218

Sussman, Charlotte, 202

Swinburne, Algernon, 131, 266

Sypher, Wylie, 63, 155, 157, 161, 266

Tacky's Rebellion, 22, 100, 118

Thistlewood, Thomas, 101, 103, 120–21

"To The Bee," 13

Todd, Janet, 88, 89, 155

Townley, James, 22, 144, 146, 149, 161, 162, 163, 169, 171, 173, 198; (work) *High Life Below Stairs,* 22, 144, 145, 146, 148, 149, 155, 160–63, 166, 167, 169, 171, 172, 173, 174, 180, 198; (characters) Cloe, 170–71, 173, 181, 198, 267; Kingston, 161, 170–71, 173, 181, 198; Lovel, 144–45, 146, 160–63, 166, 167, 170–71, 180

Ty, Eleanor, 215

United Irishmen, 176

Washington Post, 224, 256

Watson, Tim, 71, 74, 75

Webster, John, 238

Wedderburn, Robert, 97–98, 137

Wells, Helena, 167, 168

Wesley, John, 152

Wheeler, Roxann, 10, 28, 55, 57, 147, 190

white (*see also* African): actress, 2–3, 46–57, 63–64, 105, 111, 148, 155; African, 3, 20, 31, 56, 65, 68–69; Christian, 58; Creole, 62, 63, 67, 94, 139, 140, 144–46, 158, 159, 160, 167, 168, 169, 171, 179, 180, 181, 203, 253, 266; Imoinda, 2, 3, 5, 9, 10, 17, 19–20, 31, 46, 58; Imoindas, 46–57, 67; washing, 141, 211, 227–28, 232, 234, 237–41, 245; West Indians, 145, 146, 157; woman, 3, 7, 9, 52, 58, 59, 70, 74, 98, 120, 134, 179, 189, 197, 231–32, 245, 263; women, 2, 19, 20, 29, 39, 52, 54, 66, 67, 70–71, 98, 107, 118, 120, 164, 167, 172–73, 194, 227, 229–32, 242–47, 253

Wilberforce, William, 36, 112, 125, 237

Williams, Eric, 237

Wollstonecraft, Mary, 107, 187, 210, 231

Woman of Colour, The: (work) 18, 22, 73, 159, 221, 224, 225, 227, 228, 235, 238, 240, 247, 248, 251, 252, 253, 254, 255, 257, 258, 265, 266; (characters) Angelina, 247, 251–53; Augustus, 227, 235, 237–38, 240, 245–46, 247, 249, 251–52, 254, 255; Dido, 159, 224–25, 227, 254–45, 259, 267; Marcia, 235, 240, 259; Mr. Fairfield, 228, 235, 237–38, 240–41, 245–46, 247, 252, 254, 259; Olivia, 140, 159, 225–28, 235, 237–38, 240–41, 245–46, 247–55

Wood, Marcus, 12, 19, 22

wordplay, 146, 155, 162, 163, 165, 169, 171, 175, 177

Yorke–Talbot Decision, 38–39, 170–71, 197

Young, Robert, 226

Zong Case, 22

www.ingramcontent.com/pod-product-compliance
Lightning Source LLC
Chambersburg PA
CBHW030108010526
44116CB00005B/145